Fodor's 90 Montreal & Quebec City

Fodor's Travel Publications, Inc.
New York and London

**Copyright © 1990
by Fodor's Travel Publications, Inc.**

Fodor's is a trademark of Fodor's Travel Publications, Inc.

All rights reserved under International and Pan-American Copyright Conventions. Published in the United States by Fodor's Travel Publications, Inc., a subsidiary of Random House, Inc., New York, and simultaneously in Canada by Random House of Canada Limited, Toronto. Distributed by Random House, Inc., New York.

No maps, illustrations, or other portions of this book may be reproduced in any form without written permission from the publisher.

ISBN 0-679-01793-3

Grateful acknowledgment is made to Random House, Inc. and Harper & Collins Publishers Ltd. for permission to reprint excerpts from *The Maple Leaf Rag* by Stephen Brook. Copyright © 1987 by Stephen Brook.

Fodor's Montreal & Quebec City

Editors: David Low, Julia Lisella
Editorial Contributors: Josée Blanchette, Suzanne Brown, Andrew Coe, Mary Kelly, Patricia Lowe, Alice H. Oshins
Art Director: Fabrizio La Rocca
Cartographer: David Lindroth
Illustrator: Karl Tanner
Cover Photograph: J.A. Kraulis/Masterfile

Design: Vignelli Associates

Special Sales

Fodor's Travel Publications are available at special discounts for bulk purchases (100 copies or more) for sales promotions or premiums. Special editions, including personalized covers, excerpts of existing guides, and corporate imprints, can be created in large quantities for special needs. For more information, write to Special Marketing, Fodor's Travel Publications, 201 E. 50th St., New York, NY 10022. Inquiries from the United Kingdom should be sent to Fodor's Travel Publications, 30-32 Bedford Square, London WC1B 3SG.

MANUFACTURED IN THE UNITED STATES OF AMERICA
10 9 8 7 6 5 4 3 2

Contents

Foreword *vi*

Highlights '90 *ix*

Fodor's Choice *xiii*

Introduction *xx*

1 Essential Information *1*

Government Tourist Offices *2*
Tour Groups *2*
Package Deals for Independent Travelers *3*
When to Go *3*
Festivals and Seasonal Events *4*
What to Pack *7*
Taking Money Abroad *8*
Getting Money from Home *9*
Canadian Currency *10*
What It Will Cost *10*
Passports and Visas *10*
Customs and Duties *11*
Tips for British Travelers *12*
Traveling with Film *13*
Language *13*
French-Canadian Cuisine *14*
Staying Healthy *15*
Insurance *15*
Air Travel *17*
Renting Cars *18*
Rail Passes *18*
Student and Youth Travel *19*
Traveling with Children *20*
Hints for Disabled Travelers *21*
Hints for Older Travelers *22*
Telephones *23*
Mail *23*
Tipping *23*
Further Reading *23*
Credit Cards *24*

2 Portrait of Montreal and Quebec City *25*

"Maple Leaf Rag: Two Excerpts," by Stephen Brook *26*

3 Montreal *36*

Introduction *37*

Arriving and Departing *42*

From the U.S. by Plane *42*
From the U.S. by Train, Bus, and Car *43*

Staying in Montreal *44*

Getting Around *44*
Important Addresses and Numbers *45*
Opening and Closing Times *46*
Guided Tours *47*

Exploring Montreal *47*

Orientation *47*
Tour 1: Vieux-Montréal (Old Montreal) *51*
Tour 2: Downtown *57*
Tour 3: St-Denis, Prince Arthur, and North *64*
Parks and Gardens *69*
Churches, Temples, Mosques *72*
Montreal for Free *73*
What to See and Do with Children *73*
Off the Beaten Track *74*

Shopping *75*

Sports and Fitness *86*

Dining *89*

Lodging *106*

The Arts and Nightlife *116*

4 Excursions from Montreal *121*

Les Laurentides (the Laurentians) *122*
L'Estrie *138*

5 Quebec City *148*

Introduction *149*

Arriving and Departing *153*

By Plane *153*
By Car, Train, and Bus *153*

Staying in Quebec City *154*

Getting Around *154*
Important Addresses and Numbers *155*
Opening and Closing Times *156*
Guided Tours *156*

Exploring Quebec City *157*

Tour 1: Upper Town *157*
Tour 2: Lower Town *165*
Tour 3: Outside the City Walls *169*
Quebec City for Free *175*
What to See and Do with Children *175*

Contents v

Shopping *176*

Sports and Fitness *179*

Dining *182*

Lodging *188*

The Arts and Nightlife *193*

6 Excursions from Quebec City *197*

Côte de Beaupré *198*
Île d'Orléans *200*

French Vocabulary *208*

Index *212*

Maps

Montreal and Quebec City *xvi–xvii*
World Time Zones *xviii–xix*
Montreal Metro *45*
Montreal *48–49*
Tour 1: Vieux-Montréal *53*
Tour 2: Downtown Montreal *59*
Tour 3: St-Denis, Prince Arthur, and North *66*
Olympic Park and Botanical Garden *71*
Montreal Shopping *76–77*
Montreal Dining *92–93*
Montreal Lodging *108–109*
The Laurentians *127*
L'Estrie *141*
Metropolitan Quebec City *150–151*
Tours 1 and 2: Upper and Lower Towns *158–159*
Tour 3: Outside the City Walls *170*
Quebec City Dining and Lodging *184–185*
Île d'Orléans *203*

Foreword

This is an exciting time for Fodor's, as we continue our ambitious program to rewrite, reformat, and redesign all 140 of our guides. Here are just a few of the new features:

★ Brand-new computer-generated maps locating all the top attractions, hotels, restaurants, and shops

★ A unique system of numbers and legends to help readers move effortlessly between text and maps

★ A new star rating system for hotels and restaurants

★ Stamped, self-addressed postcards, bound into every guide, give readers an opportunity to help evaluate hotels and restaurants

★ Complete page redesign for instant retrieval of information

★ FODOR'S CHOICE—Our favorite museums, beaches, cafés, romantic hideaways, festivals, and more

★ HIGHLIGHTS—An insider's look at the most important developments in tourism during the past year

★ TIME OUT—The best and most convenient lunch stops along the shopping and exploring routes

★ Exclusive background essays create a powerful portrait of each destination

★ A minijournal for travelers to keep track of their own itineraries and addresses

We wish to express our gratitude to the Montreal Convention and Tourism Bureau, particularly Mary Baker and Willow Brown in New York, and Marilyne Benson and Gilles Gosselin in Montreal; the Quebec Government House in New York, particularly Pierre Valiquette, Jovette Lieou, Christine Landry, and Brian LeCompte; and the Quebec City Region Tourism and Convention Bureau in Quebec City; particularly Michel Gagnon and Patricia Germain; for their assistance in preparation of this guide.

While every care has been taken to ensure the accuracy of the information in this guide, the passage of time will always bring change, and consequently, the publisher cannot accept responsibility for errors that may occur.

All prices and opening times quoted here are based on information available to us at press time. Hours and admission fees may change, however, and the prudent traveler will avoid inconvenience by calling ahead.

Fodor's wants to hear about your travel experiences, both pleasant and unpleasant. When a hotel or restaurant fails to live up to its billing, let us know and we will investigate the complaint and revise our entries where the facts warrant it.

Send your letters to the editors of Fodor's Travel Publications, 201 E. 50th Street, New York, NY 10022.

Highlights '90 and Fodor's Choice

Highlights '90

Montreal

One of Montreal's primary east–west thoroughfares and a central square were given new appellations—but not without controversy. Dorchester Boulevard was renamed **boulevard René Lévesque** in honor of the popular Quebec premier who died in October 1987. (Street signs now show both names.) That done, there was a hue and cry that no site honored Lord Dorchester, the British governor-general who allowed French schools, churches, seminaries, and convents to continue in the new British territory following the Seven Years' War, essentially preserving the French language. Thus Dominion Square, in the heart of downtown, is now **Dorchester Square.**

It has taken 12 years to raise the money and construct the **retractable roof** over the Olympic Stadium, which was built for the track and field events of the 1976 Olympic Games as an open stadium and is now home to the Montreal Expos. The 26-ton roof, which now makes it a year-round facility, is made of Kevlar, the same material used in bulletproof vests. It folds into a niche in the Tilted Tower by a series of winches and cables in a 45-minute process. Designed by French architect Roger Taillibert, the Tilted Tower is the tallest of its kind in the world. The observatory atop the tower—reached by an exterior cable car which can carry up to 90 people—affords, on clear days, a 50-mile panorama of the city.

Montreal's era of megaprojects—thought to have ended with the Olympic Stadium and Place des Arts—is not over. Currently on the architect's drafting table are plans for what will be the tallest building in Montreal. To be known as the **IBM-Marathon building**, it has been designed by New York architect William Pedersen. The $120 million, 45-story office tower will feature an adjoining eight-story winter garden and a street-level plaza. Scheduled to open in 1991, it will occupy the entire city block bordered by Drummond, Stanley, la Gauchetière and boulevard René Lévesque.

Balancing all of this commercial development is the large-scale renovation and expansion of some of Montreal's major arts and cultural institutions.

The first three phases of the **Saidye Bronfman Centre** are already completed and open to the public. Designed by Montreal architect and Canadian Centre for Architecture founding director Phyllis Lambert, this Mies van der Rohe

–inspired arts and cultural center has undergone a $5 million transformation in the past four years.

The headquarters of **Le Centre Canadien d'Architecture** (Canadian Centre for Architecture), which officially opened to the public in May 1989, is the new "jewel" of boulevard René Lévesque Ouest, located not far from the downtown commercial megaprojects now under way. The premier museum in the world solely dedicated to architecture, this $45.4 million showcase is the brainchild of architect Lambert. The center houses one of the world's most important and most extensive collections of architectural material, including 20,000 master drawings and prints, a library of 130,000 volumes, and 45,000 photographs available to architectural scholars-in-residence. The new museum also houses exhibition halls, a bookstore, and auditorium open to the public.

Ready for public unveiling in the fall of 1991 is the $83 million expansion project of the **Musée des beaux-arts de Montréal (Montreal Museum of Fine Arts)**. The development and design of its new building has had Montrealers in an uproar for months. Facing the original museum designed in 1912 by Edward Maxwell, the new building's ultramodern design with its skylit galleries brazenly interrupts Golden Square Mile, the historic section of Montreal. The new building was designed by maverick architect Moishe Safdie and will take up most of the city block extending from Sherbrooke to de Maisonneuve, and from Crescent to Mackay.

While its new home is being readied across from the Place des Arts performing arts complex, the **Musée d'art contemporain** (Museum of Contemporary Art) will open its doors at Cité du Havre, part of the Expo '67 site. Its $28.5-million face-lift is expected to be completed in the spring of 1991.

Of more immediate interest is the unusual **Place de la Cathédrale** complex. Some might say it symbolizes the marriage between secular and religious interests. Place de la Cathédrale provoked mixed emotions among Montrealers when it first opened in the fall of 1989. Its office tower looms above the venerable Christ Church Cathedral and its 150-store retail mall rumbles beneath it. However, the controversy served to pique Montrealers' penchant for the new and unusual. Place de la Cathédrale has become a favorite shopping spot, and a "retreat" from the bustle of rue Ste-Catherine commerce. The complex will also be connected to the Eaton and La Baie department stores via the Underground City. You may wonder whether the cathedral was moved during construction. No; the building was placed on enormous steel stilts while workers dug under and around it.

The Botanical Garden grounds will soon be home to the **Montreal Insectarium.** The bug-shaped building will house more than 130,000 insect specimens collected from 88 countries by Georges Brossard, Montreal's barnstorming entomologist.

La Ronde Amusement Park, the city's great summertime attraction, has added activities that focus on children and the elderly. The erstwhile Québécois settlers' village has been redesigned into a children's village with exhibits, a petting zoo, etc. And a new viewing platform has been built for the ever-popular **Benson & Hedges International Fireworks Competition.**

Lachine Rapids Tours, which has been introducing people to the thrill of white-water rafting since 1983, has added a third aluminum jet boat to its fleet. Peak summertime capacity is now 500 rapids-runners a day.

Quebec City

The push is on for Quebec City to become an all-season tourist destination. Formerly the city's tourism efforts focused on the summer season and the Winter Carnival (the first two weeks in February). But new winter packages will allow Quebec City to attract visitors during the heart of winter as well. After all, there are four ski areas within a 30-minute drive from downtown, including Mont Sainte-Anne, the largest ski area in Eastern Canada, along with 11 cross-country ski areas (more than 1,000 miles of trails).

Last winter, the Quebec City Region Tourism and Convention Bureau's "White Sale" premiered. Hotels offer discount packages and transportation to ski areas, and restaurants and boutiques provide discounts as well.

It is welcome news that Quebec City's four largest hotels are being renovated. Courting more business travelers and tourists, the hotels are moving out of the beiges and browns of the '70s and into the modern elegance of subdued pastels and opaque marble fixtures of the 1990s. Most hotels have estimated completion of renovation by 1991.

By far, the largest renovation is at the national landmark, the **Château Frontenac.** Canadian Pacific Hotels, Canada's largest hotel chain, is spending $50 million to redecorate the Frontenac's 525 rooms and to install a health club. Although the exterior will not be altered, the hotel's clientele can expect the kind of services they are greeted with at other luxury hotels.

Likewise, the **Hilton International Québec** is spending $6 million to upgrade its rooms and lounges, as is the provincial hotel chain **Hôtel des Gouverneurs,** formerly Auberge des Gouverneurs. **Loews Le Concorde** is spending $9 million and adding more amenities for the business traveler, such as a floor exclusively for women executives.

There is also much *de nouveau* at Quebec City museums. Making the biggest splash is the new civilization museum, the **Musée de la Civilisation,** which officially opened its doors in October 1988. Located on Dalhousie Street near the Old Port, the museum, designed by architect Moshe Safdie, incorporates three historic sites: the former first Bank of Quebec, La Maison Estèbe, and Maison Pagé-Quercy. The large modern structure has already won a Canadian award for excellence in architecture for its success in being creatively integrated into the urban architecture of old Quebec. With a dozen permanent and traveling exhibits, the museum presents thematic exhibitions on the main currents of past and present Quebec civilization.

There's also a lot going on across town at the **Musée de Québec.** This stunning Beaux-Arts museum in Battlefields Park, which features traditional and contemporary Quebec art, is undergoing an expansion. By 1991, an extension will nearly double the museum's exhibition space. A building dating back to 1867 that once served as one of Canada's earliest prisons, along with an underground gallery of shops and cafés, will be joined to the museum.

This year a new **skating rink** at **Place d'Youville,** just outside St-Jean Gate, will make its debut. The city spent $400,000 over five years to upgrade facilities for skating behind the backdrop of a historic setting. Artificial ice will permit skating from October 15 through April, until it's warm enough to set up the outdoor stage and switch gears for the summer season.

Fodor's Choice

No two people will agree on what makes a perfect vacation, but it's fun and helpful to know what others think. Here, then, is a very personal list of Fodor's Choices. We hope you'll have a chance to experience some of them yourself while visiting Montreal and Quebec City. For detailed information about each entry, refer to the appropriate chapters in this guidebook.

Montreal

Special Moments The 50-mile (80-kilometer) view from the belvedere atop Mont Royal on a sunny day

A leisurely *calèche* ride along the cobblestone streets of Vieux-Montréal

Brunch in Eaton department store's ninth-floor Art Deco eatery

The aerial pyrotechnics of the Fireworks Festival as viewed from Île Ste-Hélène

People-watching at a sidewalk café on Prince Arthur Street on a warm summer night

A wet and wild jet-boat ride on the Lachine Rapids

A ride on the world's highest double-track roller coaster, Le Monster, at La Ronde

Tea in the Ritz's garden courtyard with a view of the famous ducklings (mid-May to mid-September)

The daredevil exploits of top Formula 1 drivers as they maneuver the hairpin turns of Gilles Villeneuve Race Track in the Canadian Grand Prix

A concert at the acoustically perfect Notre-Dame Basilica in Vieux-Montréal

Taste Treats A bologna, salami, and mustard-on-a-pretzel-roll sandwich with a strawberry soda at Moe Willensky's

Nibbling on smoked salmon, cheese, and pâtés at the Atwater Market

Poppy- and sesame-seed bagels—some say the best in the world—at Fairmount Bagels

A seven-course *menu de dégustation* at one of the top French restaurants

Dim sum in Chinatown

Off the Beaten Track A film buff's visit to the Cinémathèque Québécoise's movie museum and nightly screenings

The miniaturized furnishings of the Midget Palace

Fodor's Choice

The new Insectarium, a temple to this bizarre and beautiful kingdom at Montreal's Botanical Gardens

St. Joseph's Oratory, one of the largest and most important Catholic pilgrimage sites in the world

A day's outing at the Hot Air Balloon Festival and North American Championships at Montgolfière-Haut Richelieu

After Hours The elegant wood panel-and-leather surroundings of the Grand Prix bar at the Ritz-Carlton

Jazz riffs at the small, smoky L'Air du Temps

Avant-garde rock and wild styles at Foufounes Électriques

Thursday's, Montreal's liveliest singles bar

Rock, jazz, comedy—always a scene at Club Soda

Restaurants Les Mignardise *(Very Expensive)*

Milos *(Expensive)*

Cathay Restaurant *(Moderate)*

Les Filles du Roy *(Moderate)*

Hotels Hôtel de la Montagne *(Very Expensive)*

Le Quatre Saisons *(Very Expensive)*

Ritz-Carlton *(Very Expensive)*

Le Grand Hôtel *(Expensive)*

Château Versailles *(Moderate)*

Quebec City

Special Moments Walking the wall of the Old City

"Memoires" exhibit at the Musée de la Civilisation

The view of the Old City from the Québec-Lévis Ferry

The Plains of Abraham on an early morning

Winter Carnival

Taste Treats Fresh croissants and coffee at Chez Temporel

Homemade *tarte au sucre* (maple sugar pie)

Strawberries freshly picked on Île d'Orléans

Sampling at the food mall on avenue Cartier

A piece of three-chocolate chocolate cake at Le Saint Amour

French Québec The tiny street ruelle des Ursulines

People-watching along Grande Allée

Bonet's *La Liberté* sculpture at Grand Théâtre de Québec

Coffee and chess at Café Kreighoff

After Hours Jazz in the Art Deco splendor at Bar L'Emprise

Wine and blues at the romantic Le Pape George

A *spectacle* under the stars at an outdoor café

Dancing the night away at Le Tube Hi-Fi

Restaurants À La Table de Serge Bruyère *(Very Expensive)*

Gambrinus *(Very Expensive)*

Le Saint-Amour *(Very Expensive)*

Aux Anciens Canadiens *(Expensive)*

L'Échaudée *(Moderate)*

Chez Temporel *(Inexpensive)*

Hotels Château Frontenac *(Very Expensive)*

Hilton International Québec *(Very Expensive)*

Hôtel Loews Le Concorde *(Very Expensive)*

Manoir d'Auteuil *(Expensive)*

L'Auberge du Quartier *(Moderate)*

Manoir Victoria *(Moderate)*

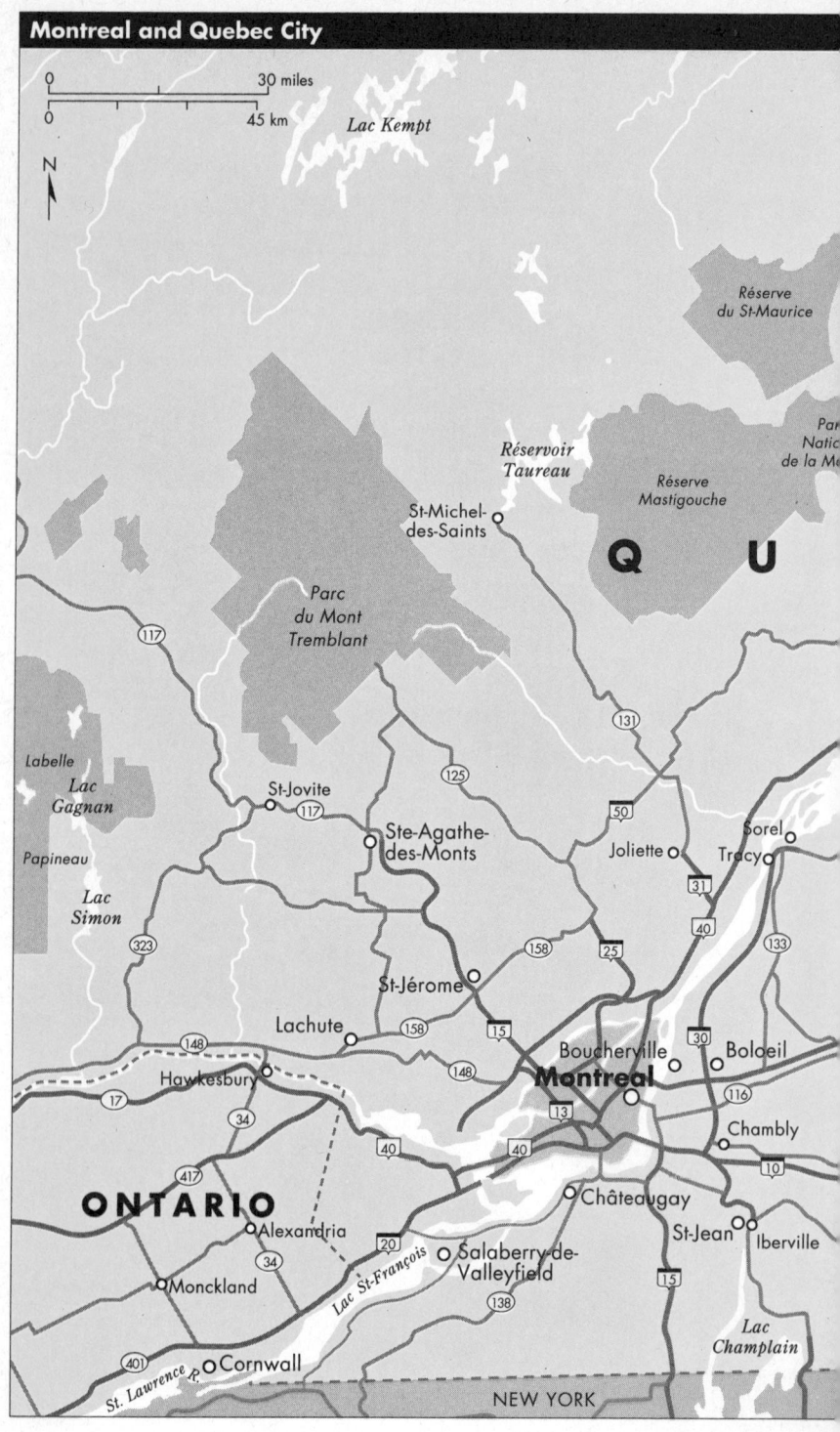

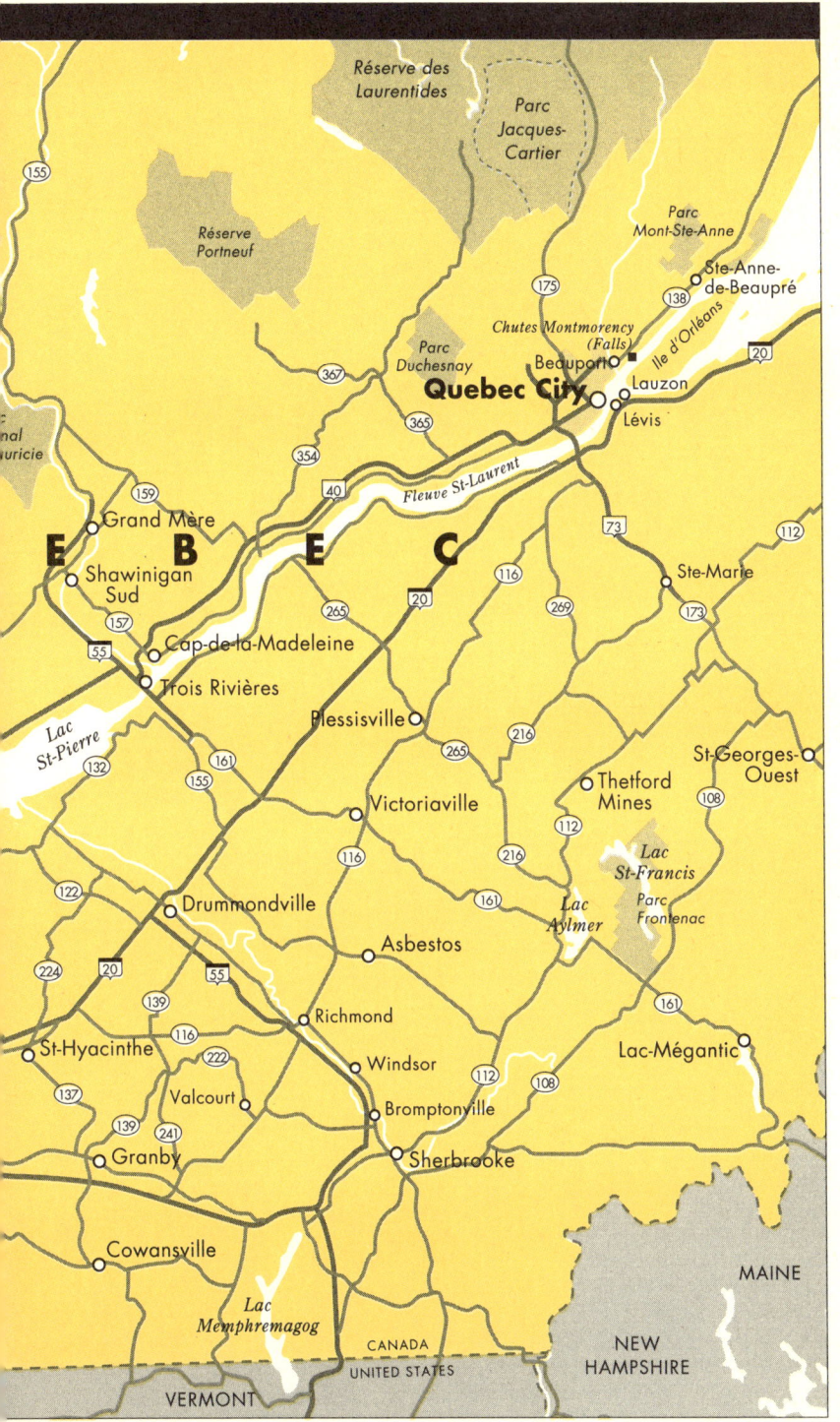

World Time Zones

Numbers below vertical bands relate each zone to Greenwich Mean Time (0 hrs.).
Local times may differ, as indicated by lightface numbers on the map.

Algiers, **29**
Anchorage, **3**
Athens, **41**
Auckland, **1**
Baghdad, **46**
Bangkok, **50**
Beijing, **54**

Berlin, **34**
Bogotá, **19**
Budapest, **37**
Buenos Aires, **24**
Caracas, **22**
Chicago, **9**
Copenhagen, **33**
Dallas, **10**

Delhi, **48**
Denver, **8**
Djakarta, **53**
Dublin, **26**
Edmonton, **7**
Hong Kong, **56**
Honolulu, **2**

Istanbul, **40**
Jerusalem, **42**
Johannesburg, **44**
Lima, **20**
Lisbon, **28**
London (Greenwich), **27**
Los Angeles, **6**
Madrid, **38**
Manila, **57**

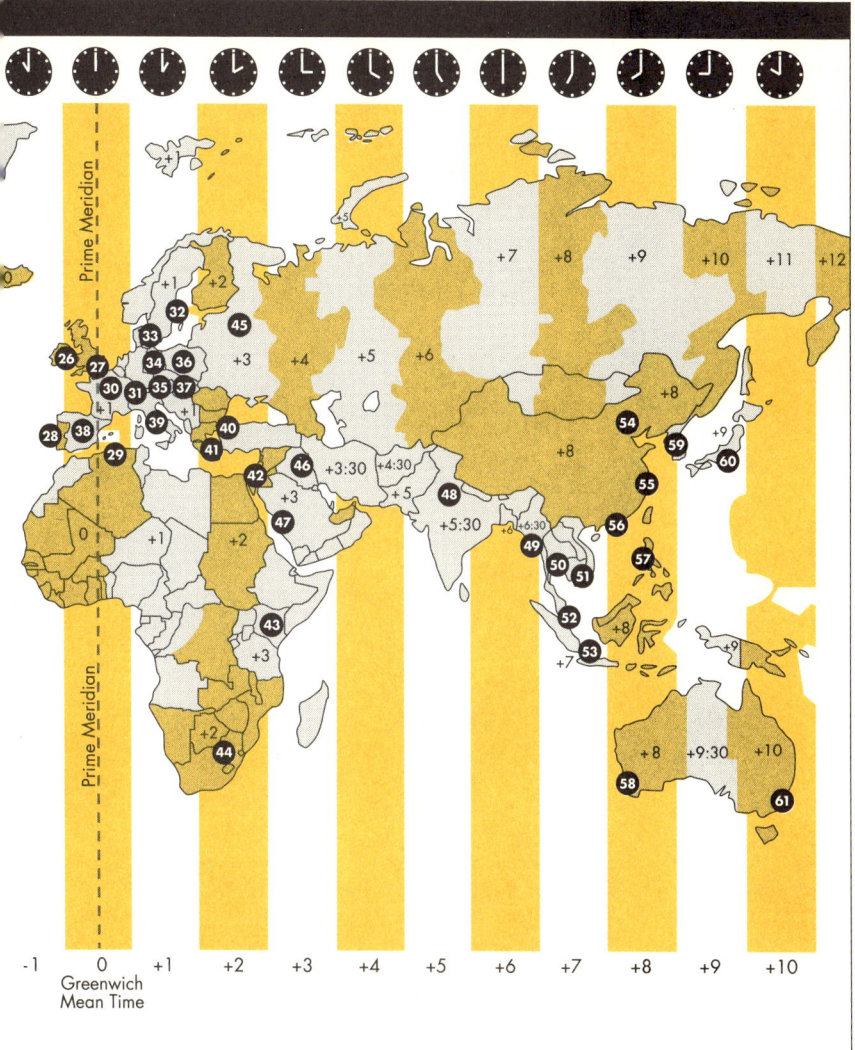

Mecca, **47**	Ottawa, **14**	San Francisco, **5**	Toronto, **13**
Mexico City, **12**	Paris, **30**	Santiago, **21**	Vancouver, **4**
Miami, **18**	Perth, **58**	Seoul, **59**	Vienna, **35**
Montreal, **15**	Reykjavík, **25**	Shanghai, **55**	Warsaw, **36**
Moscow, **45**	Rio de Janeiro, **23**	Singapore, **52**	Washington, DC, **17**
Nairobi, **43**	Rome, **39**	Stockholm, **32**	Yangon, **49**
New Orleans, **11**	Saigon, **51**	Sydney, **61**	Zürich, **31**
New York City, **16**		Tokyo, **60**	

Introduction

Quebec is the largest and oldest of Canada's provinces, covering 600,000 square miles of land and waterways, one sixth of Canada's land. Of Quebec's 6,627,000 inhabitants, 5,300,000 are French-speaking, 81.3 percent of the French-speaking population of Canada. Although Montreal and Quebec City are linked by their history and culture, no two cities could be more different.

History buffs and romantics will want to roam the winding cobblestone streets of Quebec City, the capital of the province. Its French colonial history is evident in its architecture, silver-spired churches, and grand cathedrals. In Montreal the Old World meets the New with French bistros and postmodern skyscrapers vying for the limelight. Quebec may be the center of the province's government, but Montreal is the business center. Much like New York City, Montreal has attracted a large immigrant population. Its ethnic diversity can be seen in its wide range of restaurants and enclaves. It is not only considered the Canadian center for book publishing, the film industry, and architecture and design; it is also considered the unrivaled bagel capital of Canada.

Quebec History

Montreal's and Quebec City's histories are inextricably linked. Montreal sits on the site that was called Hochelaga by the Indians who lived there. Quebec City was known as Stadacona. In 1534, Jacques Cartier, a young sea captain setting out to find a passage to China, instead came upon Canada and changed the course of events in that region forever. He returned in the following year seeking gold. But this time he found a wide river, sailed down it, and arrived at Stadacona, an Indian village. He admired the location of the village perched on the cliffs overlooking a *kebec*, the Algonquin word for a narrowing of the waters. He continued along to Hochelaga, which eventually became Montreal.

More than 1,000 surprised Iroquois greeted the Frenchman. It would take two centuries of fierce battles before the French made peace with the Iroquois people. Perhaps the violent meeting of the French explorers and the Canadian natives discouraged the French, because no more exploring was done until 1608, when Samuel de Champlain established a French settlement at Stadacona.

Throughout the 17th century, the French opened up Canada and some of what became the United States, using both Montreal and Quebec City as convenient trading posts and strategic military locations. They discovered and mapped a vast area stretching from Hudson Bay to the Gulf of Mexico. *Coureurs de bois* (fur traders), missionaries, and explorers staked out this immense new territory.

During this time France tamed and populated its new colonies across the ocean with the firm hand of *seigneurs*, aristocrats to whom the king distributed land. In turn, the seigneurs swore loyalty to the king, served in the military, maintained manor houses, ceded land to tenant farmers, and established courts to settle local grievances. Seigneuries were close knit, with sons and fathers able to establish farms within the same territory. In addition, the Roman Catholic Church's influence was strong in these communities. Priests and nuns acted as doctors, educators, and overseers of business arrangements among the farmers and between French-speaking traders and English-speaking merchants. An important doctrine of the church in Quebec was *survivance*, the survival of the French people and their culture. Couples were told to have large families, and they did. Ten to 12 children in a family was the norm, not the exception.

The Seven Years' War between England and France marked the second half of the 18th century. In 1756, France sent the commander Louis-Joseph, Marquis de Montcalm, to secure the frontier of New France and consolidate the new territory of Louisiana. Although Montcalm, leading a French and Indian expedition, was able to secure the Ohio Valley, turn Lake Ontario into a French waterway, and secure Fort Carillon (now Ticonderoga) on Lake Champlain, the tides began to turn in 1759 with the arrival of a large British fleet to the shores of Quebec City, commanded by James Wolfe.

After bombarding the city for several weeks, Wolfe and his 4,000 men decided the fate of Canada in a vicious battle that lasted 20 minutes. The British won, but both leaders were mortally wounded. Today, in Quebec City's Governors Park, there is a unique memorial to these two army men—the only statue in the world commemorating both victor and vanquished of the same battle. A year later the French regained the city of Quebec, but they were soon forced to withdraw when English ships arrived with supplies and reinforcements. The French were driven back to Montreal, where a large British army defeated them in 1760. In 1763, the Treaty of Paris ceded Canada to Britain. France preferred to give up the new country to preserve its sugar islands, which it believed were of greater value. At that time, all the French civil administrators, as well as the principal landowners and businessmen, returned to France. Of the leaders of New France, only the Roman Catholic clergy remained, and they became more important to the peasant farmers than ever before.

Quebec's trouble was in no way over with the Treaty of Paris. In 1774 the British Parliament passed the Quebec Act. It extended Quebec's borders, hemming in the northernmost of the independence-minded British colonies to the south. The Roman Catholic Church's authority and the seigneurial landlord system were maintained under the act, leaving traditional Québécois life fairly intact. But the American colonists were furious with the passing of the Quebec Act and hoped to incite a revolt in Quebec against British rule. After the American War of Independence broke out in 1775, Generals Richard Montgomery and Benedict Arnold led American troops that took over Montreal and set up headquarters in the Château de Ramezay, home of the British governor (and now a museum). The Americans then attempted to capture Quebec City, but they had misunderstood the Catholic Royalist heritage of the Canadians. Québécois did not share the Americans' love of independence and republicanism. Rather than incite a revolt, the Americans managed to draw the Canadians and British together. The Canadians stood with the British in Quebec City to fight off the invasions. Montgomery died in the attack and Arnold fled. The following year, British forces arrived and recaptured Montreal.

The Creation of Upper and Lower Canada

A number of British and American settlers left Albany in New York and settled in Montreal. They began to press the authorities, as did other British colonists west of the Ottawa River, to introduce representative government.

The British responded with the Constitutional Act of 1791, which divided Quebec into two provinces, Upper and Lower Canada, west and east of the Ottawa. The act provided for nominated legislative councils and elected assemblies, like those that had existed in the English colonies. The first election was held the following year.

Elected government was a novelty to the French Canadians, who had never known democracy and who had been shielded from the French Revolution of 1789. But democracy suited them well, and before long there was a rising demand for more rights. Heading the movement for greater rights was Louis Joseph Papineau, who was also leader of the French-speaking majority in the legislative assembly. He demanded that the English *château clique*, which made up the governor's council, should be subject to elections as the assembly was. In 1834 he and his associates issued a long list of grievances, "The 92 Resolutions." Papineau lost the support of many of his own associates, and that of the leaders of the church. The British responded with their own "10 resolutions" and refused elections to the council. That same year crops failed and unemployment spread. General unrest led to clashes between the English and young French *Patriotes* in Montreal. Soon a general insurrection broke out. Patriote irregulars fought British troops at St. Charles and St. Eustache near Montreal.

In spite of bad feelings, the upheavals led to major legislative changes in 1841. England passed the Act of Union, which produced a united Canada. Quebec was now known as Canada East, while Upper Canada became Canada West. Each sent an equal number of representatives to the elected assembly; the governor was not responsible to the assembly, but rather to the Colonial Office in London. This continued to bridle both English and French members of the assembly.

The Growth of Montreal

Toward the end of the 1700s, the fur trade declined so much that Montreal almost faced economic disaster. But in Europe the demand for lumber increased, and Quebec had lots of it. As a result, Montreal became the major trading center in British North America, helped by the fact that New York and New England had seceded from Britain.

Then the flood of immigration from Britain started, so much so that by the mid-1800s, Montreal was transformed into a predominantly English city. About 100,000 Irish immigrants came to work in Montreal's flour mills, breweries, and shipyards, which had sprung up on the shores of the river and the Lachine Canal, begun in 1821. By 1861 working-class Irish made up a third of Montreal's population. In the next 80 years, Polish, Hungarian, Italian, Chinese, Ukrainian, Greek, Armenian, Spanish, Czech, Japanese, German, and Portuguese immigrants, escaping from poverty and political hardships, arrived by the thousands, seeking freedom in the New World. By 1867 more than a half million immigrants had arrived from Europe, pushing Canada's population to more than 2 million. The demand for union came from all the provinces of British North America to increase trade and economic prosperity, to increase their strength militarily in case of attack from the United States, to create a government capable of securing and developing the Northwest (the vast lands west of Canada West), and to make possible the building of a railway that would contribute to the realization of all these ambitions.

The Dominion of Canada was created on July 1, 1867, by an act of the British Parliament, known as the British North America (BNA) Act. It divided the province of Canada into Quebec and Ontario and brought in Nova Scotia and New Brunswick. Manitoba joined in 1870, British Columbia in 1871, Prince Edward Island in 1873, Alberta and Saskatchewan in 1905, and Newfoundland in 1949. The BNA Act also enshrined French as an official language. The province of Quebec, like the other provinces, was given far-reaching responsibilities in social and civil affairs.

The Conscription Crisis

The entente between the French and English in Canada was viable until World War I strained it. At the outbreak of the war, the two groups felt equally supportive of the two European motherlands. Many volunteered, and a totally French regiment was created, the Royal 22nd. But two things ended the camaraderie.

On the battlefields in Europe, Canadians, along with the Australians, formed the shock troops of the British Empire and died horribly, by the thousands. More than 60,000 Canadians died in the war, a huge loss for a country of 7½ million. In 1915, Ontario passed Regulation 17, severely restricting the use of French in its schools. It translated into an anti-French stand and created open hostility. The flow of French Canadians into the army became a trickle. Then Prime Minister Robert Borden ordered the conscription of childless males to reinforce the ailing Canadian corps. A wider conscription law loomed in Ottawa, which resulted in an outcry in Quebec, led by nationalist journalist and politician Henri Bourassa (grandson of patriote Louis Joseph Papineau). The nationalists claimed that conscription was a device to diminish the French-speaking population. When, in 1917, conscription did become law, Quebec was ideologically isolated from the rest of Canada.

The crisis led to the formation of the Union Nationale provincial party in 1936, initially a reformist party. Under its leader Maurice Duplessis, it held control till 1960 and was characterized by lavish patronage, strong-arm methods, fights with Ottawa, and nationalistic sloganeering. Duplessis believed that to survive, Québécois should remain true to their traditions. Duplessis deterred industrial expansion in Quebec, which went to Ontario, and slowed the growth of reformist ideas until his death and the flowering of the Quiet Revolution.

The Quiet Revolution

The population of Quebec had grown to 6 million, but the province had fallen economically and politically behind Canada's English majority. Under Duplessis and the Union Nationale party, French-language schools and universities were supervised by the church and offered courses in humanities rather than in science and economics. Francophones (French-speaking Québécers) were denied any chance of real business education unless they attended English institutions. As a result, few of them held top positions in industry or finance. On a general cultural basis, the country overwhelmingly reflected Anglo-Saxon attitudes rather than an Anglo-French mixture.

In 1960 the Liberal Party under Jean Lesage swept to power. Though initially occupied with social reform, it soon turned to economic matters. In 1962, Lesage's minister of natural resources, René Lévesque, called for the nationalization of most of the electricity industry, which up to then had been in private hands. This was the first step toward economic independence for Quebec. The financiers of Montreal's St. James Street, the heart of the business district, opposed it, but ordinary Québécois were enthusiastic. In 1965, Lévesque's ministry established a provincial mining company to explore and develop the province's mineral resources.

Meanwhile U.S. capital poured into Quebec, as it did everywhere else in Canada. With it came American cultural influence, which increased Québécois' expectations of a high standard of living. English-speaking citizens remained in firm control of the large national corporations headquartered in Montreal. Indeed it became clear that they had no intention of handing power over to the French. Few Francophones were promoted to executive status. Successive provincial governments became increasingly irritated by the lack of progress.

The discontent led to a dramatic radicalization of Quebec politics. A new separatist movement arose that hoped to make Quebec a distinct state by breaking away from the rest of the country. The most extreme faction of the movement was the Front de Libération du Québec (FLQ). It backed its demands with bombs and arson, culminating in the kidnapping and murder of Quebec Cabinet Minister Pierre Laporte in October 1970.

The federal government in Ottawa, under Prime Minister Pierre Elliott Trudeau, himself a French-speaking Québécois, imposed the War Measures Act. This permitted the police to break up civil disorders and arrest hundreds of suspects and led to the arrest of the murderers of Laporte.

The political crisis calmed down but it left behind vibrations that affected all of the country. The federal government redoubled its efforts to correct the worst grievances of the French Canadians. Federal funds flowed into French schools outside Quebec to support French-Canadian culture in the other provinces. French Canadians were appointed to senior positions in the government and crown corporations. The federal government dramatically increased its bilingual services to the population.

In Quebec from the mid-1970s, the Liberal government and then the Parti Québécois, elected in 1976 and headed by René Lévesque, replaced the English language with the French language in Quebec's economic life. In 1974, French was adopted as the official language of Quebec. This promoted French language instruction in the schools and made French the language of business and government. The Parti Québécois followed up in 1977 with the Charter of the French Language, which established deadlines and fines to help enforce the program to make French the chief language in all areas of Quebec life. The charter brought French into the workplace; it also accelerated a trend for English companies to relocate their headquarters outside Quebec, particularly in and near Toronto. The provincial government is working to attract new investment to Quebec to replace those lost jobs and revenues.

The Parti Québécois proposed to go further by taking Quebec out of the confederation, provided that economic ties with the rest of Canada could be maintained. Leaders in the other provinces announced that such a scheme would not be acceptable. A referendum was held in 1980 for the authority to negotiate a sovereignty association with the rest of Canada. Quebec voters rejected the proposal by a wide margin. In the last provincial elections, held in fall 1985, the Parti Québécois government was itself defeated at the polls by the Liberal Party, headed by Robert Bourassa.

The People of Quebec

Although French is the official language of Quebec, Quebec also has a large English-speaking population (580,000), particularly in Montreal, the Ottawa Valley, and l'Estrie. They are descendants of those English, Irish, and Scots who landed here after the conquest of New France, and of immigrants from other nations whose main language is English. English-speaking Montrealers founded and financed a variety of great institutions such as universities, museums, hospitals, orchestras, and social agencies, as well as a number of national and multinational corporations in the worlds of banking and finance, transportation, natural resources, and distilled spirits.

Half a million immigrants from Europe, Asia, Latin America, and the Caribbean also live in Quebec. People from 80 different countries have made their new homes in the province. In proportion to its population, this land, along with the rest of Canada, has welcomed the greatest number of fugitives from political and economic unrest over the past 20 years. Between 1968 and 1982, for example, there arrived 60,000 immigrants from Czechoslovakia, Haiti, Uganda, Lebanon, Chile, and Southeast Asia. A much larger wave of immigrants, from Italy, Greece, and Eastern Europe, had arrived following World War II.

The native people of Quebec number more than 40,000. Nearly 30,000 of Quebec's Amerindians live in villages within reserved territories in various parts of Quebec, where they have exclusive fishing and hunting rights. The Inuit people (Eskimo) number over 5,000 and live in villages scattered along the shores of James Bay, Hudson Bay, Hudson Strait, and Ungava Bay. They have abandoned their igloos for prefabricated houses, but they still make their living by trapping and hunting.

Introduction

The French Canadians of Quebec, often called Latins of the North, have an ever-sparkling joie de vivre, especially at the more than 400 festivals and carnivals they celebrate each year. Even the long winter does not dampen their good spirits. The largest festival splash is on June 24, which was originally the Feast of Saint John the Baptist. Now it is called La Fête Nationale (National Day). Everyone celebrates the long weekend by building roaring bonfires and dancing in the streets.

February brings Quebec City's Winter Carnival, a two-week-long noisy and exciting party. Chicoutimi also has a winter carnival in which residents of the city celebrate and dress up in period costumes. In September international canoe races are held in Mauricie, and in August an international swim gets under way across Lac-Saint-Jean. Trois-Rivières celebrates the summer with automobile races through its streets, and Valleyfield is the scene of international regattas.

1 Essential Information

Government Tourist Offices

An excellent source of free information on Montreal and Quebec City and all aspects of travel in Canada is the **Canadian Consulate General** offices. Ask for the tourism department.

In the U.S. 1CNN Center, Suite 400, South Tower, Atlanta, GA 30303, tel. 404/577–6810; 3 Copley St., Suite 400, Boston, MA 02116, tel. 617/262–3760; 310 S. Michigan Ave., 12th floor, Chicago, IL 60604, tel. 312/427–1031; St. Paul Tower, 17th floor, 750 N. St. Paul St., Dallas, TX 75201, tel. 214/922–9806; 300 S. Grand Ave., 10th floor, Los Angeles, CA 90071, tel. 213/687–7432; 701 4th Ave. S, Minneapolis, MN 55415, tel. 612/333–4641; Exxon Bldg., 16th floor, 1251 Ave. of the Americas, New York, NY 10020, tel. 212/768–2400; 50 Fremont St., Suite 2100, San Francisco, CA 94105, tel. 415/495–6021; 501 Pennsylvania Ave., Washington, DC 20001, tel. 202/682–1740.

For your convenience, the province of Quebec also maintains information offices in the following American cities: Peachtree Center Tower, 230 Peachtree St. NW, Suite 1501, Atlanta, GA 30303, tel. 404/581–0488; Exchange Place, 53 State St., 19th floor, Boston, MA 02109, tel. 617/723–3366; 122 S. Michigan Ave., Suite 1910, Chicago, IL 60603, tel. 312/427–0240; 700 S. Flower St., Suite 1520, Los Angeles, CA 90017, tel. 213/689–4861; 17 W. 50th St., Rockefeller Center, New York, NY 10020, tel. 212/397–0200; 1300 19th St. NW, Suite 220, Washington, DC 20036, tel. 202/659–8990, 8991.

In Canada A Gouvernement du Québec tourism office is located at Toronto's Eaton Center (20 Queen St. W, Suite 1004, Box 13, Toronto, Ont. M5H 3S3, tel. 416/977–6060 or 416/977–1367).

Tour Groups

When considering a tour, be sure to find out: exactly what expenses are included (particularly tips, taxes, side trips, additional meals, and entertainment); ratings and the facilities of all hotels on the itinerary; cancellation policies for both you and for the tour operator; and the cost of a single supplement should you be traveling alone. Most tour operators request that bookings be made through a travel agent—in most cases there is no additional charge.

General-Interest Tours "Eastern Highlights" from **American Express Vacations** (Box 5014, Atlanta, GA 30302, tel. 800/241–1700; 800/282–0800 in GA) visits Montreal, Toronto, Quebec City, Boston, New York, and Washington, DC.

Cosmos/Globus Gateway (150 S. Los Robles Ave., Suite 860, Pasadena, CA 91101, tel. 818/449–0919 or 800/556–5454) offers a 13-day tour of the northeastern United States and Toronto, Ottawa, Montreal, and Quebec City.

Four Winds Travel (175 5th Ave., New York, NY 10010, tel. 212/777–0260) tours Montreal, Toronto, Ottawa, and Quebec City.

Maupintour (1515 St. Andrews Dr., Lawrence, KS 66046, tel. 913/843–1211 or 800/255–4266) offers an eight-day Montreal–Toronto tour.

Talmadge Tours (1223 Walnut St., Philadelphia, PA 19107, tel. 215/923–7100) has an escorted Montreal city package.

When to Go 3

Package Deals for Independent Travelers

Air Canada, through its tour booking agent, Bonanza Holidays (tel. 800/363-9603), has a two-night package with a choice of hotels—the cost depends on the hotel rating; other tour options are available. **American Express** includes a half-day sightseeing tour in its city package.

When to Go

The province of Quebec is a year-round destination. There is never an off-season, although between Christmas and New Year's Day it may seem as if half the city dwellers have headed for warmer climates. Autumn often arrives in mid-September, and the weather can be cold and rainy until the freezing temperatures set in in early December. Winter is long, cold, and snowy, but Quebecois in no way remain inactive or indoors. For the hearty there is skiing, skating, snowmobiling, and snowshoeing around the province. But for the thin-blooded there are plenty of indoor activities. Cultural life buzzes around Winter Carnival time in Quebec City, and concerts and performances reign at Montreal's Place des Arts complex.

With the spring thaw comes Quebec's maple-syrup season. City slickers and tourists alike migrate to the Laurentians' *cabanes à sucre* to down a traditional feast of maple-soaked beans, bacon, potatoes, bread, omelets, pancakes, and deep-fried dumplings, or maple taffy rolled in snow. Sidewalk cafés, street musicians, parades, and festivals enliven the two cities' streets in summertime. Peak season for the province begins with a literal bang in late May at the International Fireworks competition on Île Ste-Hélène. Many countries compete and the fireworks can be seen from points all over Montreal. For those who revel in the crisp air of autumn and in lazy excursions outside the city to small country inns, September and October are perfect months for a visit.

Deciding when to come to Quebec depends on your interests and inclinations rather than on the weather. Whenever you come you'll have to prepare for wide temperature variations. In July temperatures can crest at more than 90°F, while during the depths of winter—from late December to March—you may encounter 15°F and below.

Climate The following are the average daily maximum and minimum temperatures for Montreal and Quebec City.

Montreal

Jan.	23F	− 5C	**May**	65F	18C	**Sept.**	68F	20C
	9	−13		48	9		53	12
Feb.	25F	− 4C	**June**	74F	23C	**Oct.**	57F	14C
	12	−11		58	14		43	6
Mar.	36F	2C	**July**	79F	26C	**Nov.**	42F	6C
	23	− 5		63	17		32	0
Apr.	52F	11C	**Aug.**	76F	24C	**Dec.**	27F	−3C
	36	2		61	16		16	−9

Essential Information 4

Quebec City	Jan.	20F	− 7C	May	62F	17C	Sept.	66F	19C
		6	−14		43	6		49	9
	Feb.	23F	− 5C	June	72F	22C	Oct.	53F	12C
		8	−13		53	12		39	4
	Mar.	33F	1C	July	78F	26C	Nov.	39F	4C
		19	− 7		58	14		28	− 2
	Apr.	47F	8C	Aug.	75F	24C	Dec.	24F	− 4C
		32	0		56	13		12	−11

Current weather information for more than 500 cities around the world may be obtained by calling the WeatherTrak information service at 900/370–8728 or in TX, 900/575–8728. A taped message will tell you to dial a three-digit access code for the destination you're interested in. The code is either the area code (in the United States) or the first three letters of the foreign city. For a list of all access codes, send a stamped, addressed envelope to Cities, Box 7000, Dallas, TX 75209. For further information, phone 214/869–3035 or 800/247–3282.

Festivals and Seasonal Events

Montreal Montreal is festival city, especially from May to September, when celebrations of music, film, art, theater, and various sports abound. Major venues are Place des Arts, Île Ste-Hélène, and the Vieux-Port area. These festivals attract performers, entertainers, athletes, and visitors from around the world. Since many events coincide with the height of the tourist season, you are well-advised to make hotel reservations as early as possible. (Precise festival dates vary from year to year; for up-to-date information, contact the Quebec or City of Montreal tourist bureaus.)

Jan. 25–Feb. 5: La Fête des Neiges is a snow festival featuring ice sculptures and snowshoe, skating, and cross-country-skiing races. Notre Dame Island, Old Port, Old Montreal, Maisonneuve Park. Tel. 514/872–6093.

Mar.: International Festival of Young Cinema showcases the best in 16mm and video by young film- and video-makers. Venues include: National Film Board cinema in Complexe Guy-Favreau, tel. 514/283–8229; Cinéma Parallèle, tel. 514/843–6001; Institut Goethe, tel. 514/499–0159.

Mar.: International Festival of Films on Art features documentaries, biographies, and films about the visual and performing arts at the Montreal Museum of Fine Arts, tel. 514/285–1600; Cinémathèque Québécoise, tel. 514/842–9763; and the National Film Board cinema, tel. 514/283–8229, among other venues. Tel. 514/845–5233.

May: SuperMotocross Laurentide features the national motocross championship as well as all-terrain-vehicle, four-wheel-van, and buggy races. Olympic Stadium, tel. 514/252–4679, or 514/252–4646.

June: Montreal International Festival of Films and Videos by Women takes place at the Cinémathèque Québécoise and other theaters. Tel. 514/845–0243.

May 22–June 4: Theatre Festival of the Americas is a showcase of new plays and productions from all over the Western Hemisphere, performed at various theaters around the city. Tel. 514/842–0704.

June: Montreal International Music Competitions features top young musicians from around the world. Place des Arts, tel. 514/285-4380.

Late May–June: Benson & Hedges International Fireworks Competition pits pyrotechnicians from Canada, the United States, and Europe against one another in dazzling displays on consecutive Saturday evenings in the skies over La Ronde Amusement Park. Tel. 514/872-6222.

Early June–late Sept.: Images du Futur, a four-month annual exhibition, is an international showcase of the latest technological advances in the visual arts: laser and video displays, computer graphics, holography, sound-and-light-wave sculptures, computer-synthesized soundscapes, and multisensory, multimedia installations. It features works by a guest country each year—in 1990, Great Britain. Held at the former Louis Jolliet Maritime Museum in the Vieux-Port. Tel. 514/849-1612.

Early June: La Classique Cycliste de Montréal is a professional cycling competition through Lafontaine, Mont Royal, and Olympic parks. Tel. 514/251-6946.

June: Le Tour de L'Île de Montréal is when some 30,000 amateur cyclists of all ages circumnavigate the island of Montreal. Tel. 514/251-6955.

Mid-June: Molson Grand Prix is a competition of the world's top Formula 1 drivers held at the Gilles Villeneuve Race Track on Île Notre-Dame. Tickets, tel. 514/251-6955; info, tel. 514/392-9022.

Mid-June: Montreal International Rock Festival happens at the Spectrum and other arenas. Tel. 514/287-1847.

Mid-June–mid-Oct.: Expotec annual exhibition showcases the latest advances in scientific research and medical technologies, with a different theme each year. Held at the Vieux-Port, next door to Images du Futur. Tel. 514/283-8207.

Late June: Lanaudiere Summer Festival is a mix of classical music and 20th-century compositions that attracts 110,000 music lovers to Joliette, a city 45 minutes from Montreal. Tel. 514/875-6986 or 514/759-7636.

Late June–early July: Montreal International Jazz Festival hosts some 500,000 fans and 1,000 musicians from 15 countries at indoor and outdoor sites scattered all over the city. Tel. 514/289-9472.

June 24: La Fête Nationale des Québécois. Quebec's national festival, formerly St-Jean Baptiste Day, is the official provincial holiday when neighborhoods get together to celebrate publicly with parades, street dancing, performances by Québécois musicians, bonfires, and fireworks. Tel. 514/871-1595 or 514/873-2015.

Mid-July: Drummondville World Folklore Festival takes place at this site 62 miles (100 kilometers) from Montreal. Tel. 819/472-1184 or 800/567-1444.

Mid-July: Just For Laughs Festival is a multilingual, multinational celebration of comedy at various theaters. Tel. 514/845-3155.

Early Aug.: Le Grand Prix Cyclistes is a 124-mile (200-kilometer) cycling competition through the streets of Montreal. Tel. 514/879-1027.

Early–mid-Aug.: Player's Challenge Tennis Championships. The world's best players compete at Jarry Tennis Stadium. Odd years (1991 and 1993) the men play; even years (1990 and 1992) the women take over. Tel. 514/273-1515.

Mid-Aug.: Festival de Montgolfière du Haut-Richelieu Hot Air Balloon Festival and North American Championships takes place 25 miles (40 kilometers) from Montreal. Tel. 514/658-9675 or 514/346-6000.

Late Aug.: Montreal World Film Festival draws top films and international stars. Sites: Cinéma Le Parisien, Complexe Desjardins, and Place des Arts. Tel. 514/933-9699 or 514/848-3883.

Aug.–Nov.: 100 Days of Contemporary Art is an annual international invitational art festival. Tel. 514/288-0811.

Sept.: Montreal International Marathon attracts more than 12,000 professional and amateur competitors to a fund-raising event in honor of the late Canadian Terry Fox and cancer research. Registration is $15. Tel. 514/879-1027.

Sept.: Montreal International Music Festival features top classical performances at Place des Arts and other venues throughout Montreal. Tel. 514/866-2662.

Mid-Sept.: Festival Internationale de Nouvelle Danse. This international biennial of new dance introduces the latest in Japanese, European, American, and Canadian dance and features some 200 international dancers. Tel. 514/287-1423.

Oct.: Montreal International Festival of New Cinema and Video takes place at the Cinémathèque Quebecoise, Cinéma Parallèle, and other theaters. Tel. 514/843-4725 or 514/843-4711.

Quebec City Top seasonal events in Quebec City include the Winter Carnival in February, the International Jazz Festival in June, the International Summer Festival in July, the Expo-Québec in August, and the Festival of Colours in October. (For further details, contact the Québec City Region Tourism and Convention Bureau.)

Early Feb.: Québec Winter Carnival celebrates the season with cultural, social, and sports activities. Includes snow-sculpture contest, canoe races on the St. Lawrence River, costume balls, and a fireworks display. Tel. 418/626-3716.

Mid-Feb.: Pee-Wee Hockey Tournament features youths from Canada, the United States, and Europe. Colisée de Québec, Parc de l'Exposition. Tel. 418/623-0947.

Mid-Apr.: Québec International Book Fair exhibits the latest publications. Centre municipal des Congrès, Place Québec. Tel. 418/658-1974.

Late June: International Jazz Festival showcases many musicians in halls, bars, restaurants, and the streets of Old Quebec. Tel. 418/523-1296.

Late June: International Children's Folklore Festival gives children the opportunity to enjoy dancing, music, exhibitions, and guided activities of various ethnic origins and languages. Tel. 418/666-2153.

Late June: Saint-Jean-Baptiste Day is a celebration throughout the Quebec City region. Tel. 418/681-7011.

Early July: City of Québec Day commemorates the founding of the city in 1608 with entertainment and guided activities in Old Quebec and various parks throughout the city. Tel. 418/691-6284.

Early July: Quebec International Summer Festival is the largest French-language cultural event in North America. Tel. 418/692-4540.

Late July: Saint Anne's Day Celebrations honor Saint Anne and includes a torchlight parade. Saint-Anne-de-Beaupré Basilica. Tel. 418/827-3781.

Late Aug.: Expo-Québec is the province's largest agricultural exhibition. It includes a trade and industrial show, fun fair, rides, and entertainment. Parc de l'Exposition. Tel. 418/691-7110.

Late Aug.: Air Show features exhibits of military and civilian aircraft and in-flight demonstrations. Québec Airport. Tel. 418/872-9532.

Sept.: Fall Fest is organized by the English-language community of the city and features family activities. Tel. 418/683-2366.

Early Sept.: Québec International Film Festival emphasizes films from French-speaking countries. Tel. 514/848-3883.

Early Oct.: Festival of Colours marks the beginning of fall with two weekends of outdoor activities and cultural events. Parc du Mont-Sainte-Anne. Tel. 418/827-4561.

What to Pack

Clothing Your choice of dress will depend as much on the kind of touring and entertainment you'll indulge in as on what the weather dictates. Though you'll want to be prepared for both cities' nighttime activities (strolling, dancing, eating out) with some casual-chic or formal wear, you should also prepare for the varying temperatures of Quebec. During the winter (and winter often lingers into April), pack a warm hat (preferably one that covers the ears), gloves, and waterproof boots. Interiors are well heated so it is advisable to dress in layers: It traps heat better and allows you to shed a few "skins" when meandering through stores. Furs are popular outdoor wear. No matter what the season, bring a bathing suit. Many hotels have indoor or well heated outdoor pools that are open all year. From June through August, pack light, loose clothing that will keep you cool, but apply the layering theory in reverse. Most interiors are well air-conditioned in the summer, and you'll need a sweater or a light jacket. Bring a collapsible umbrella and a light raincoat for the occasional summer showers.

Miscellaneous Quebec operates on a U.S.-style 110-volt electrical system using flat, two-pronged plugs, so an adapter is not necessary.

Luggage
Carry-on Luggage Passengers on U.S. airlines are limited to two carry-on bags. For a bag you wish to store under the seat, the maximum dimensions are 9″ × 14″ × 22″. For bags that can be hung in a

Essential Information 8

closet or on a luggage rack, the maximum dimensions are 4" × 23" × 45". For bags you wish to store in an overhead bin, the maximum dimensions are 10" × 14" × 36". Any item that exceeds the specified dimensions may be rejected as a carryon and taken as checked baggage. Keep in mind that an airline can adapt the rules to circumstances, so on an especially crowded flight don't be surprised if you are allowed only one carryon.

In addition to the two carryons, you may bring aboard a handbag (pocketbook or purse), an overcoat or wrap, an umbrella, a camera, a reasonable amount of reading material, an infant bag, crutches, cane, braces, or other prosthetic device, and an infant/child safety seat.

Foreign airlines have slightly different policies. They generally allow only one piece of carry-on luggage in tourist class, in addition to handbags and bags filled with duty-free goods. Passengers in first and business class are also allowed to carry on one garment bag. It is best to call your airline to find out its current policy.

Checked Luggage Luggage allowances vary slightly from airline to airline. Many carriers allow three checked pieces; some allow only two. It is best to check before you go. In all cases, check-in luggage cannot weigh more than 70 pounds per piece or be larger than 62 inches (length + width + height).

Taking Money Abroad

Traveler's checks and major U.S. credit cards are accepted in Montreal and Quebec City. You'll need cash for some of the small restaurants and shops. Many establishments accept U.S. dollars. Although you pay more for Canadian dollars in the United States, it's wise to buy some before you leave home to avoid long lines at airport currency-exchange booths. If your local bank can't exchange your money into Canadian dollars, contact Deak International. To find the office nearest you, contact them at 29 Broadway, New York, NY 10006, tel. 212/635–0515.

The most recognized traveler's checks are American Express, Barclay's, Thomas Cook, and those issued through major commercial banks such as Citibank and Bank of America. Some banks will issue the checks free to established customers, but most charge a 1% commission fee. Buy part of the traveler's checks in small denominations to cash toward the end of your trip. This will save you from having to cash a large check and ending up with more foreign money than you need. You can also buy traveler's checks in Canadian dollars, a good idea if the U.S. dollar is falling and you want to lock in the current rate. Remember to take the addresses of offices where you can get refunds for lost or stolen traveler's checks.

Banks and bank-operated currency-exchange kiosks in airports, railway stations, and bus terminals are the best places to change money. Hotels and privately run exchange firms will give you a significantly lower rate of exchange.

Like the American dollar, the Canadian one floats (and often sinks) on the world's money markets, but it will probably remain in the U.S. 81¢–84¢ range for the foreseeable future. As of 1989, the $1 bill is being phased out in Canada and replaced with a funny-looking coin that has already been nicknamed

"The Loonie," due to the drawing of the Canadian loon on one side. But these bills (as well as the far more useful $5, $10, and $20 bills—and yes, the always welcome $2 Canadian denomination) should remain in circulation into the 1990s.

U.S. currency is eagerly accepted at most good-size stores and restaurants, and with good reason. Owners are always happy to give far less exchange than the daily rate—even as little as 10¢ or 15¢ less on the dollar. So it is financially wise for all visitors to go to a Canadian bank or exchange firm within a few hours of arrival. The sooner you exchange your money for the worth-less (if not yet worthless) Canadian dollar, the more money you'll save. When you use your credit cards, you can be assured that your expenditures will automatically go through as Canadian funds, and you will get the proper exchange rate.

Getting Money from Home

There are at least three ways to get money from home: (1) Have it sent through a large commercial bank with a branch in the city you're staying in. The only drawback is that you must have an account with the bank; if not, you'll have to go through your own bank and the process will be slower and more expensive. (2) Have it sent through American Express. If you are a cardholder, you can cash a personal check or a counter check at an American Express office for up to $1,000; $200 will be in cash and $800 in traveler's checks. There is a 1% commission on the traveler's checks. You can also receive money through American Express MoneyGram. With this service, you can receive up to $5,000 cash. It works this way: You call home and ask someone to go to an American Express office or an American Express MoneyGram agent located in a retail outlet, and fill out an American Express MoneyGram. It can be paid for with cash or any major credit card (except at American Express's own offices, where you must pay with an Amex card or cash). The person making the payment is given a reference number and telephones you with that number. The American Express MoneyGram agent calls an 800 number and authorizes the transfer of funds to an American Express office or participating agency in the city where you're staying. In most cases, the money is available immediately. You pick it up by showing identification and giving the reference number. Fees vary according to the amount of money sent. For sending $300, the fee is $24; for $5,000, $160. For the American Express MoneyGram location nearest your home, call 800/543-4080. You do not have to be a cardholder to use this service. (3) Have it sent through Western Union (tel. 800/325-6000). If you have MasterCard or Visa, you can have money sent for any amount up to your credit limit. If not, have someone take cash or a certified cashier's check to a Western Union office. The money will be delivered to a bank in Montreal or Quebec City within 24 hours. Fees vary with the amount of money sent. For sending $500, the fee is $40; for $1,000, $55. Note that you *cannot* use your credit card to place an order for receiving U.S. funds from your bank back home. To use a credit card, you must call the 800 number listed above.

Cash Machines Virtually all U.S. banks now belong to a network of automatic teller machines (ATMs) that dispense cash 24 hours a day. The largest of the major networks, Cirrus, owned by MasterCard, has now begun providing access to ATMs in Quebec. You can call Cirrus's toll-free number to find out where the nearest cash machine is in the city you are calling from. The Cirrus number is 800/424–7787. Note that cash cards for these machines are not issued automatically; they must be requested at your specific branch.

Cards issued by Visa, American Express, and MasterCard can also be used in the ATMs, but the fees are usually higher than the fees on bank cards (and there is a daily interest charge on the "loan"). All three companies issue directories that list the national and international outlets that accept their cards. You can pick up a Visa or MasterCard directory at your local bank. For an American Express directory, call 800/CASH–NOW (this number can also be used for general inquiries). Contact your bank for information on fees and on the amount of cash you can withdraw on any given day. Although each bank individually charges for taking money with the card, using your American Express, Visa, or MasterCard at an ATM can be cheaper than exchanging money in a bank, because of variations in exchange rates.

Canadian Currency

At press time, the U.S. dollar is worth about 16% more than its Canadian counterpart. Spending $50 (Canadian) for two on dinner comes out to about $42 (U.S.).

Currency is based on the same decimal system as in the United States and with the same denominations. An added bonus is the $2 bill, which is alive and well in Canada.

Credit cards are accepted just about everywhere a tourist might visit. The best known are American Express, Visa, MasterCard, and Diner's Club. Major credit cards use the exchange rate in effect on the date of the transaction. For safety and convenience, carry traveler's checks. You can buy them in Canadian dollars at most commercial banks—a good idea if the U.S. dollar is falling and you want to lock in the current exchange rate.

What It Will Cost

Note: All prices quoted in this guide are given in Canadian dollars.

Sample Prices in U.S. $ (1989)

Cup of coffee or soda	$1
Glass of wine	$3.50
Croque-monsieur (ham-and-cheese sandwich)	$4
Hamburger	$2.50–$5

Taxes A 9% sales tax applies to all goods and services except hotel rooms, books, home furnishings, shoes costing less than $125, and clothes costing less than $500. There is a 10% meal tax on all orders costing more than $3.25.

Passports and Visas

American Because there is so much border traffic between Canada and the United States—many people live in Windsor, Ontario, and work in Detroit, for example—entry requirements are fairly simple. Citizens and legal residents of the United States do not require a passport or a visa to enter Canada, though valid identification (passport or birth certificate) may be requested. Resident aliens should be in possession of their U.S. Alien Registration or green card.

British Citizens of the United Kingdom are also exempt from possessing a passport or visa, though proof of citizenship is required.

As of January 1989, entry requirements to Canada have become more stringent. Visitors from some countries now require visas, while others don't. Before traveling, check with the Canadian Embassy or Consulate nearest you. Once you are authorized to enter Canada, the customs official at your point of entry will issue a visitor's permit, indicating the length of time you are entitled to stay in Canada. Although this is mostly a routine rubber-stamping procedure, be aware that custom officials do have the right to change the length of this period arbitrarily. If this occurs, you can apply for an extension to lengthen your stay in Canada, which is usually granted.

Customs and Duties

On Arrival Clothing, personal items, and any professional tools or equipment (if you work in Canada) can be brought in without charge or restriction. American and British visitors can bring in the following items duty-free: 200 cigarettes, 50 cigars, and two pounds of tobacco; personal cars (for less than six months); boats or canoes; rifles and shotguns (but no handguns or automatic weapons); 200 rounds of ammunition; cameras, radios, sports equipment, and typewriters. A deposit is sometimes required for trailers and household equipment (refunded upon return), and if you are driving a rental car, be sure and keep the contract with you. Cats may enter freely, but dogs must have proof of a veterinary inspection to ensure that they are free of communicable diseases, such as rabies. Plant material must be declared and inspected.

On Departure Passengers flying from Montreal or Quebec City to the United States will clear U.S. Customs in Montreal, so allow extra time before your flight. If you have brought any foreign-made equipment from home, such as cameras, it's wise to carry the original receipt with you or register it with U.S. Customs before you leave (Form 4457). Otherwise you may end up paying duty on your return. **U.S. residents** visiting Canada for at least 48 hours may bring home up to $400 in foreign goods duty-free. Each member of the family is entitled to the same exemption, regardless of age, and exemptions can be pooled. For the next $1,000 worth of goods, a flat 9% rate is assessed on Canadian-made goods and 10% on imported goods purchased in Canada; above $1,400, duties vary with the merchandise. Included for travelers 21 or older are one liter of alcohol, 100 cigars (non-Cuban), and 200 cigarettes. Only one bottle of perfume trademarked in the United States may be brought in. However, there is no duty on antiques or art more than 100 years old. Anything exceeding these limits will be taxed at the port of entry, and may be taxed additionally in the traveler's home state. Gifts valued at less than $50 may be mailed duty-free to friends or relatives at home, but not more than one package per day to any one addressee and not to include perfumes costing more than $5 or tobacco or liquor.

Essential Information 12

Tips for British Travelers

Government Tourist Offices **Tourism Canada** (Canada House, Trafalgar Sq., London SW1Y 5BJ, tel. 01/629–9492) will send you brochures and information on Montreal and Quebec City, and advise you on your trip.

Tourisme Québec (Quebec General Delegation, 59 Pall Mall, London SW1Y 5JH, tel. 01/930–8314) is also a good source of information.

Passports and Visas You will need a valid passport (cost, £15). Visas and health certificates are not required.

Customs Returning to Britain you may bring home: (1) 200 cigarettes or 100 cigarillos or 50 cigars or 250 grams of tobacco; (2) two liters of table wine and, in addition, (a) one liter of alcohol over 22% by volume (most spirits), (b) two liters of alcohol under 22% by volume (fortified or sparkling wine), or (c) two more liters of table wine; (3) 50 grams of perfume and ¼ liter of toilet water; and (4) other goods up to a value of £32.

Insurance To cover health and motoring mishaps, insure yourself with **Europ Assistance** (252 High St., Croydon, Surrey CR0 1NF, tel. 01/680–1234).

It is also wise to take out insurance to cover loss of luggage (though make sure this isn't already covered in your existing homeowner's policy). Trip cancellation insurance is another wise buy. The **Association of British Insurers** (Aldermary House, Queen St., London EC4N 1TT, tel. 01/248–4477) will give comprehensive advice on all aspects of vacation insurance.

Tour Operators Here is a sampling of travel companies that offer packages to Canada. Also contact your travel agent for the latest information:

Albany Travel (Manchester) Ltd. (190 Deansgate, Manchester M3 3WD, tel. 061/833–0202).
Caravan Abroad Ltd. (56 Middle St., Brockham, Surrey RH3 7HW, tel. 073784/2735).
Poundstretcher (Airlink House, Hazelwick Ave., Three Bridges, Sussex RH10 1YS, tel. 0293/548241).
Thomas Cook Faraway Holidays (Thorpe Wood, Box 36, Peterborough, Cambs PE3 6SB, tel. 0733/503202).
Trek America Ltd. (Trek House, the Bullring, Deddington, Oxford, Oxon OX5 4TT, tel. 0869/38777.

In addition, many packages include car rentals at reasonable rates. **National Holidays Ltd.** (George House, George St., Wakefield, West Yorkshire WF1 1LY, tel. 0924/383–888) will put together a complete package to Canada, with flights, from £298, or a week's car rental alone, from £108. Similar schemes are offered by **Hickie Borman Holidays** (56 High St., Ewell, Surrey KT17 1RX, tel. 01/393–0127) and **American Airplan** (Marlborough House, Churchfield Rd., Walton-on-Thames, Surrey KT12 2TJ, tel. 0932/246347).

Airlines/Airfares Budget flights to the province of Quebec operate from London to Mirabel International Airport, north of Montreal. Check APEX and other money-saving fares before making your reservations and consult your travel agent about package tours. At press time (July 1989), a round-trip APEX fare from London to Montreal costs about £298. Major airlines serving Montreal are **Air Canada**, tel. 01/759–2636; **British Airways**, tel. 01/897–4000;

Northwest Airlines, tel. 01/629-5353; and Wardair, tel. 0345/222333. Travel agents can book charter flights through Regent Tours; the carrier is Worldways. **Thomas Cook Ltd.** can often book you on very inexpensive flights. Call the Cook branch nearest you at least 21 days before you want to travel and ask for the Airfare Warehouse. If you can afford to be flexible about when you travel, look for last-minute flight bargains advertised in the Sunday newspapers. Round-trip fares at press time cost about £185.

Electricity The current in Quebec is 110 volts. You should take along an adapter, since Canadian outlets usually require flat two-pronged plugs.

Traveling with Film

If your camera is new, shoot and develop a few rolls of film before leaving home. Pack some lens tissue, and don't forget an extra battery for your built-in light meter. Invest about $10 in a skylight filter and screw it onto the front of your lens. It will protect the lens and also reduce haze.

Film doesn't like hot weather. In summer, don't store film in a car glove compartment or on the shelf under the rear window; put it behind the front seat on the floor, away from the exhaust pipe.

On a plane trip, never pack unprocessed film in check-in luggage; if your bags get X-rayed, say good-bye to your pictures. Always carry undeveloped film with you through security checks and ask to have it inspected by hand. (It helps to isolate your film in a plastic bag, so it's ready for quick inspection.) Inspectors at U.S. airports are required by law to honor requests for hand inspection; abroad, you'll have to depend on the kindness of strangers.

The old airport scanning machines—still in use in some Third World countries—use heavy doses of radiation that can turn a family portrait into an early morning fog. The newer models—used in all U.S. airports—are safe for anything from five to 500 scans, depending on the speed of your film. The effects are cumulative; you can put the same roll of film through several scans without worry. After five scans, though, you're asking for trouble.

If your film gets fogged and you want an explanation, send it to the **National Association of Photographic Manufacturers** (600 Mamaroneck Ave., Harrison, NY 10528). NAPM representatives will try to determine what went wrong. The service is free.

Language

Montreal French is the official language of the province of Quebec. In Montreal, many people also speak English, however, and, in certain neighborhoods like Westmount, primarily English is spoken. Downtown, the majority of the people are bilingual. Neighborhoods like St-Denis, Outremont, and Plâteau Mont Royal are primarily French-speaking, and some shopkeepers here don't speak English. In the past, tourists have encountered instances of Francophone snobbery in hotels and restaurants, but this happens ever more rarely. The Quebec government, realizing how much tourism means to the economy, has enacted laws stating that menus, hotel brochures, and other tourist literature must be printed in both languages. The tension between Quebec and the rest of Canada and between French and English speakers has lessened in recent years, thus making it easier for English-speaking tourists.

Quebec City Unlike Montreal's English-speaking Westmount, there is no English-speaking community in Quebec City; about 95% of the population is French-speaking. However, because the city is so accustomed to tourists, English is not a problem; the Québécois are usually accommodating in either language.

However, you will probably notice that all signs are in French. In 1988, the provincial government passed legislation requiring all outdoor signs to be in French only. Indoor signs can be bilingual except for those of franchises and large corporations, which are in French only.

This new legislation should affect the English-speaking visitor only slightly: most tourist information, such as menus and brochures, is available in both languages. Yet there may be French-only signs inside museums and galleries if they are provincial institutions. Bilingual guides who can provide English translations are usually on hand.

French-Canadian Cuisine

Many tourists are not aware that French-Canadian cuisine, or *Quebec cooking*, is distinctly different from classical French cuisine. Its ingredients recall the province's rural, pioneer past. The people of Quebec are thrilled to rediscover its secrets and pleasures in the restaurants of traditional sugar huts or on dining room tables covered with holiday fare.

Since the first colonists made their way to New France in the 17th century, Quebec cooking has continued to integrate many local resources into its repertoire, such as maple syrup, beans, fiddleheads, and blueberries. In addition, the traditional Quebec cooks learned how to battle the harsh winters. The gifts of spring are still conserved with lard, salt, sugar, and vinegar to enjoy all winter. Quebec cooking makes use of many different kinds of condiments to spice up the dismal winter days.

The national dishes of Quebec have been influenced first by French, then English, cultural imperialism. However, the specialties of the indigenous peoples (Algonquins, Iroquois) have had very little influence on the cuisine of these first Quebec cooks, except perhaps for the contribution of corn and corn on the cob. Certainly, the natural resources of Canada have contributed amply to the typical Quebec meal. Québécois have inherited *les crêpes de sarrasin* (buckwheat pancakes) from their Breton cousins, and over the years other contributions have cropped up: *les fèves aux lards* (pork and beans), *les tourtières* (meat pies), *le ragoût de pattes de cochon* (pigs' feet stew), *le cipaille* (six pie, named for the six layers of pie-crust dough), maple-cured baked ham, *la graisse de roti* (a spread made from the drippings of roasted meats), *la dinde farcie aux atacas* (roast turkey stuffed with fruit and nuts), suet puddings, blueberry custards and *la tarte au sucre du pays* (sweet country tarts). Pork is prepared in a multitude of sauces and is the favorite meat among the people of Quebec because of its great versatility. This old adage attests to it: Anything from the pig is good!

Because this cuisine traces its roots from the first settlers and lumber camps, and because it has always been based on what could be hunted or fished, traditional Quebec cooking is often referred to as hearty fare. The vast Quebec region was teeming with caribou, deer, elk, bear, beaver, hare, partridge, trout, and salmon, and the small yet invincible Gallic population depended on the land for its survival. Game (now commercially raised) is still an important ingredient of Quebec cooking, and it is prepared with great patience and loving care. With the passage of time and the circumstances and demands of modern living, traditional Quebec cooking is no longer a part of daily life. However, it still holds an important place in the lives of the Québécois every winter, especially at Christmas dinners when grandmothers nostalgically recall what makes this cuisine so special.

Staying Healthy

Shots and Medications
There are no health risks associated with travel to Canada, and inoculations are not needed. If you have a health problem that might require your purchasing prescription drugs while in the country, have your doctor write a prescription using the drug's generic name. Brand names vary widely from country to country. Also note that if you are carrying prescription drugs into Canada, keep them in their original containers, showing the prescription information. Otherwise, they might be confiscated at your point of entry.

The **International Association for Medical Assistance to Travelers** (IAMAT) is a worldwide association offering a list of approved, English-speaking doctors whose training meets U.S. standards. For a list of Canadian physicians and clinics that are part of this network, contact IAMAT, 417 Center St., Lewiston, NY 14092. In Canada: 40 Regal Rd., Guelph, Ont. N1K 1B5. In Europe: 57 Voirets, 1212 Grand, Lancy, Geneva, Switzerland. Membership is free.

Insurance

Travelers may seek insurance coverage in three areas: health and accident, loss of luggage, and trip cancellation. Your first step is to review your existing health and homeowner policies; some health insurance plans cover health expenses incurred while traveling, some major medical plans cover emergency transportation, and some homeowner policies cover the theft of luggage.

Health and Accident
Several companies offer coverage designed to supplement existing health insurance for travelers:

Carefree Travel Insurance (Box 310, 120 Mineola Blvd., Mineola, NY 11501, tel. 516/294-0220 or 800/645-2424) provides coverage for medical evacuation. It also offers 24-hour medical advice by phone. For emergencies, call collect, tel. 214/699-0200.

Health Care Abroad, Wallach & Company (243 Church St. NW, Vienna, VA 22180; tel. 703/281-9500 or 800/237-6615), offers comprehensive medical coverage, including emergency evacuation, for trips of 10 to 90 days.

International SOS Insurance (Box 11568, Philadelphia, PA 19116, tel. 215/244–1500 or 800/523–8930) does not provide medical insurance but arranges medical evacuations for its clients, which are often international corporations.

Travel Guard International (1100 Centerpoint Dr., Stevens Point, WI 54481, tel. 715/345–0505 or 800/782–5151), underwritten by Cygna, offers medical insurance, with coverage for emergency evacuation when Travel Guard's representatives in the United States say it is necessary.

Loss of Luggage Luggage loss coverage is usually part of a comprehensive travel insurance package that includes personal accident, trip cancellation, and sometimes default and bankruptcy. Several companies offer broad policies:

Access America Inc., a subsidiary of Blue Cross-Blue Shield, Box 807, New York, NY 10163, tel. 212/490–5345 or 800/851–2800.

Near Services Inc., 1900 N. MacArthur Blvd., Suite 210, Oklahoma City, OK 73127, tel. 405/949–2500 or 800/654–6700.

Travel Guard International (*see* Health and Accident Insurance).

Luggage Insurance Airlines are responsible for lost or damaged property only up to $1,250 per passenger on domestic flights, up to $9.07 per pound ($20 per kilogram) for checked baggage on international flights, and up to $400 per passenger for unchecked baggage on international flights. If you're carrying valuables, either take them with you on the airplane or purchase additional insurance for lost luggage. Some airlines will issue additional luggage insurance when you check in, but many do not. One that does is American Airlines. Its additional insurance is only for domestic flights or flights to Canada. Rates are $1 for every $100 valuation, with a maximum of $400 valuation per passenger. Hand luggage is not included.

Insurance for lost, damaged, or stolen luggage is available through travel agents or directly through various insurance companies. Two that issue luggage insurance are **Tele-Trip** (tel. 800/228–9792), a subsidiary of Mutual of Omaha, and the **Travelers Insurance Co.** (tel. 800/243–0191). Tele-Trip operates sales booths at airports, and also issues insurance through travel agents. Tele-Trip will insure checked luggage for up to 180 days and for $500 to $1,000 valuation. For one to four days, the rate for a $500 valuation is $9; for 180 days, $69 for $500 valuation; $137 for $1,000 valuation. Rates and coverage available also vary depending upon whether the policy is issued in Canada, the United States, or Britain. The Travelers Insurance Co. will insure checked or hand luggage for $500–$2,000 valuation per person, and also for a maximum of 180 days. Rate for one to five days for $500 valuation is $10; for 180 days, $85. For more information, write the Travelers Insurance Co. (Ticket and Travel Dept., 1 Tower Sq., Hartford, CT 06183). Check the travel pages of your Sunday newspaper for the names of other companies that insure luggage. Before you go, itemize the contents of each bag in case you need to file an insurance claim. Be certain to put your address on each piece of luggage, including carry-on bags. (A business address is recommended, so thieves

Trip Cancellation — Flight insurance is often included in the price of a ticket when purchased with American Express, Visa, or another major credit card. It is usually included in travel insurance packages available from many tour operators, travel agents, and insurance agents.

Air Travel

Discount Flights — The major airlines offer a range of tickets that can increase the price of any given seat by more than 300%, depending on the day of purchase. As a rule, the further in advance you buy the ticket, the less expensive it is and the greater the penalty (up to 100%) for canceling. Check with airlines for details.

It's important to distinguish between companies that sell seats on charter flights and companies that sell one of a block of tickets on scheduled airlines. Charter flights are the least expensive and the least reliable—with chronically late departures and not-infrequent cancellations. They also tend to depart less frequently (usually once a week) than regularly scheduled flights. A wise alternative to a charter is a ticket on a scheduled flight purchased from a wholesaler or ticket broker. It's an unbeatable deal: a scheduled flight at up to 50% off the APEX fare. Tickets can usually be purchased up to three days before departure (but in high season expect to wait in line an hour or so).

The following brokers specialize in discount sales; all charge an annual fee of about $35–$50. **Discount Travel International** (114 Forrest Ave., Narberth, PA 19072, tel. 215/668–2182 or 800/458–0503), **Moment's Notice** (40 E. 49th St., New York, NY 10017, tel. 212/486–0503), **Stand-Buys Ltd.** (311 W. Superior, Suite 414, Chicago, IL 60610, tel. 312/951–7589 or 800/255–0200), **Worldwide Discount Travel Club** (1674 Meridian Ave., Miami Beach, FL 33139, tel. 305/534–2082).

Three international airlines: **Aerolineas Argentinas** (tel. 800/327–0276), **Lan Chile** (tel. 800/225–5526), and **Royal Air Maroc** (tel. 800/223–5858), have weekly or biweekly flights from New York to Montreal. As of April 1989 the round-trip airfare from New York is $100–$130; though tickets usually must be purchased seven days in advance. **Air Canada** also offers a number of reduced rate fares subject to special conditions.

Enjoying the Flight — If you're lucky to be able to sleep on a plane, it makes sense to fly at night. Unless you are flying from Europe or Great Britain, jet lag won't be a problem. There is little or no time difference between Montreal and Quebec City and most points in the United States and Canada. Sleepers usually prefer window seats to curl up against; those who like to move about the cabin should request an aisle seat. Bulkhead seats (adjacent to the "Exit" signs) have more legroom, but seat trays are attached rather awkwardly to the arms of your seat rather than to the back of the seat ahead.

Smoking — If smoking bothers you, ask for a seat far away from the smoking section. If the airline tells you there are no nonsmoking seats, insist on one: DOT regulations require airlines to find seats for all nonsmokers.

Due to popular demand, as well as for increased safety, some airlines, including Air Canada have now introduced exclusively nonsmoking flights to many of their North American destinations.

Renting Cars

If you're flying to Montreal or Quebec City and plan to spend some time there before exploring the rest of Quebec, save money by arranging to pick up your car in the city and then head off into the province. You'll have to weigh the added expense of renting a car from a major company with an airport location against the savings on a car from a budget firm with offices in town. You could waste precious hours trying to locate the budget company in return for only small financial savings. If you're arriving and departing from different airports, look for a one-way car rental with no drop-off charge. Rental rates vary widely, depending on car size and model, number of days you use the car, insurance coverage, and whether or not drop-off fees are imposed. In most cases, rates quoted include unlimited free mileage and standard liability protection. Not included are Collision Damage Waiver (CDW), which eliminates your deductible payment should you have an accident; personal accident insurance; gasoline; and 9% sales tax.

Drivers' licenses issued in the United States are valid in Canada. And though the driving age in Canada is 16, you must be 21 to rent a car. It's best to arrange a car rental before you leave home. You won't save money by waiting until you arrive in Canada, and the type of car you prefer may not be available at the last minute. Rental companies usually charge according to the exchange rate of the U.S. dollar at the time the car is returned or when the credit card payment is processed.

New York State residents driving anywhere within Quebec should be aware that their state and this province now have a reciprocal agreement on traffic violations. Traffic offenses committed in Quebec by New York drivers will be penalized, both by fines and demerit points, applied at the same rate as exists at home.

Montreal Rental-car companies that serve Montreal include **Avis** (1225 Metcalfe St., Metro Peel, tel. 514/866–7906 or 800/268–0303), **Budget** (1460 Guy St., Metro Guy-Concordia, tel. 514/937–9121 or 800/268–8900), **Hertz** (1475 Aylmer St., Metro McGill, tel. 514/842–8537 or 800/263–0600), and **Tilden** (1200 Stanley St., Metro Peel, tel. 514/878–2771 or 800/361–5334).

Quebec City Rental-car companies that serve Quebec City include **Avis** (airport, tel. 418/872–2861; 3 Place Québec, tel. 418/523–0041); **Hertz** (airport, tel. 418/871–1571; 44 côte de Palais, tel. 418/694–1224); **Budget** (29 côte du Palais, tel. 418/692–3660). **Tilden,** affiliated with National, is located at the airport (tel. 418/871–1224).

Rail Passes

Via Rail (tel. 418/692–3940) features the Canrailpass, which provides unlimited trips throughout Quebec, Ontario, and other areas within a given time period. It can be purchased for eight or 11 days ($189 and $252; lower rates for students).

Student and Youth Travel

The **International Student Identity Card (ISIC)** entitles students to youth rail passes, special fares on local transportation, and discounts at museums, theaters, sports events, and many other attractions. If purchased in the United States, the $10 cost of the ISIC also includes $2,000 in emergency medical insurance, plus $100 a day for up to 60 days of hospital coverage. A new service is the confidential-to-cardholders-only 24-hour, toll-free Travel Assistance Hotline for help regarding medical, financial, or legal emergencies. Apply to the Council on International Educational Exchange (CIEE, 205 E. 42nd St., New York, NY 10017, tel. 212/661–1414). In Canada, the ISIC is available from the Canadian Federation of Students-Services Travel Cuts (187 College St., Toronto, Ont. M5T 1P7) for CN$10.

Council Travel, a CIEE subsidiary, is the foremost U.S. student travel agency, specializing in low-cost charters and serving as the exclusive U.S. agent for many student airfare bargains and student tours. CIEE's 80-page *Student Travel Catalog* and "Council Charter" brochure are available free from any Council Travel office in the United States (enclose $1 postage if ordering by mail). In addition to the CIEE headquarters at 205 East 42nd Street and a branch office at 35 West 8th Street in New York City, there are Council Travel offices in Amherst, Atlanta, Austin, Berkeley, Boston, Cambridge, Chicago, Dallas, Evanston, La Jolla, Long Beach, Los Angeles, Milwaukee, Minneapolis, New Haven, New Orleans, Portland, Providence, San Diego, San Francisco, Seattle, Sherman Oaks, and Washington, DC.

The **Educational Travel Center** (438 N. Frances St., Madison, WI 55703, tel. 608/256–5551), another student travel specialist, is worth contacting for information on student tours, bargain fares, and booking.

Students who would like to work abroad should contact CIEE's **Work Abroad Department** (205 E. 42nd St., New York, NY 10017). The council arranges various types of paid and voluntary work experiences overseas for up to six months. CIEE also sponsors study programs in Latin America and Asia, and publishes many books of interest to the student traveler: These include *Work, Study, Travel Abroad: The Whole World Handbook* ($8.95 plus $1 postage); *Work Your Way Around the World* ($10.95 plus $1 postage); and *Volunteer! The Comprehensive Guide to Voluntary Service in the U.S. and Abroad* ($4.95 plus $1 postage).

The Information Center at the **Institute of International Education,** IIE (809 UN Plaza, New York, NY 10017, tel. 212/984–5413), has reference books, foreign university catalogues, study-abroad brochures, and other materials, which may be consulted by students and nonstudents alike, free of charge. The Information Center is open from 10 to 4, Monday through Friday, and until 7 Wednesday.

IIE administers a variety of grant and study programs offered by U.S. and foreign organizations, and it publishes a well-known annual series of study-abroad guides, including *Academic Year Abroad, Vacation Study Abroad,* and *Study in the United Kingdom and Ireland.* The institute also publishes

Essential Information 20

Teaching Abroad, a book of employment and study opportunities overseas for U.S. teachers. For a current list of IIE publications, prices, and ordering information, write to IIE Books, Institute of International Education, 809 UN Plaza, New York, NY 10017. Books must be purchased by mail or in person; telephone orders are not accepted.

General information on IIE programs and services is available from its regional offices in Atlanta, Chicago, Denver, Houston, San Francisco, and Washington, DC.

Traveling with Children

Publications *Family Travel Times,* an eight or 12-page newsletter, is published 10 times a year by TWYCH (Travel with Your Children, 80 8th Ave., New York, NY 10011, tel. 212/206-0688). Subscription includes access to back issues and twice-weekly opportunities to call in for specific information.

Villa Rentals **At Home Abroad, Inc.** (405 E. 56th St., Suite 6H, New York, NY 10022, tel. 212/421-9165), **Villas International** (71 W. 23rd St., New York, NY 10010, tel. 212/929-7585 or 800/221-2260), **Hideaways, Inc.** (Box 1464, Littleton, MA 01460, tel. 508/486-8955), **Villas and Apartments Abroad** (444 Madison Ave., Suite 211, New York, NY 10022, tel. 212/759-1025).

Home Exchange See *Home Exchanging: A Complete Sourcebook for Travelers at Home or Abroad* by James Dearing (Globe Pequot Press, Box Q, Chester, CT 06412, tel. 203/526-9571 or tel. 800/243-0495; in CT 800/962-0973).

Getting There Though exact details may vary depending upon the airline, on international flights, one infant under two years old (per accompanying adult) not occupying a seat pays 10% of adult fare. Various discounts apply to children 2-12, or in some cases 2-11. Airline policies for flights within North America (continental U.S. and Canada) may differ, so check around beforehand to get the best deal. Likewise, while some airlines allow you to reserve a seat behind the bulkhead of the plane, which offers more legroom and can usually fit a bassinet (supplied by the airline), others don't. Airline officials also point out that only a limited number of bassinets (known as Skycots at Air Canada) are available on most flights and some types of planes may not carry them. The bassinets are generally intended for sleeping infants of up to 35 pounds in weight. Air Canada's policy is no advance reservation, although it advises passengers to request a Skycot at the time a ticket is booked; this is then noted on the file. When the passenger arrives at the airport, he or she should advise officials that this service has been requested. It's available on a first-come, first-serve basis, so travelers are advised to check in early. At the same time, inquire about special children's meals or snacks, offered by most airlines. Most airlines request advance notice and reservation of these meals at least 24 hours in advance of travel. (See "TWYCH's Airline Guide," in the February 1990 issue of *Family Travel Times,* for a rundown on children's services furnished by 46 airlines.) Ask your airline in advance if you can bring aboard your child's car seat. (For the booklet *Child/Infant Safety Seats Acceptable for Use In Aircraft,* write Community and Consumer Liaison Division, APA 200 Federal Aviation Administration, Washington, DC 20591, tel. 202/267-3479.)

Baby-sitting Services	Child-care arrangements are easily made through your hotel concierge.

Hints for Disabled Travelers

The **Information Center for Individuals with Disabilities** (20 Park Plaza, Room 330, Boston, MA 02116, tel. 617/727-5540) offers useful problem-solving assistance, including lists of travel agents who specialize in tours for the disabled.

Moss Rehabilitation Hospital Travel Information Service (12th St. and Tabor Rd., Philadelphia, PA 19141, tel. 215/456-9603) provides information on tourist sights, transportation, and accommodations in destinations around the world. The fee is $5 for each destination. Allow one month for delivery.

Mobility International (Box 3551, Eugene, OR 97403, tel. 503/343-1284) has information on accommodations, organized study, and so forth, around the world.

The **Society for the Advancement of Travel for the Handicapped** (26 Court St., Penthouse Suite, Brooklyn, NY 11242, tel. 718/858-5483) offers access information. Annual membership is $40, or $25 for senior travelers and students. Send $1 and a stamped, self-addressed envelope.

Twin Peaks Press (Box 129, Vancouver, WA 98666, tel. 206/694-2462 or 800/637-2256 for orders only) specializes in books for the disabled. *Travel for the Disabled* offers helpful hints as well as a comprehensive list of guidebooks and facilities geared to the disabled. *Directory of Travel Agencies for the Disabled* lists more than 350 agencies throughout the world. They also offer a Traveling Nurse's Network, which provides registered nurses trained in all medical areas to accompany and assist disabled travelers.

The Itinerary (Box 1084, Bayonne, NJ 07002, tel. 201/858-3400) is a bimonthly travel magazine for the disabled.

Access to the World: A Travel Guide for the Handicapped by Louise Weiss is useful but out of date. Available from the publisher, Henry Holt & Co., tel. 212/886-9200. *Frommer's Guide for Disabled Travelers* is also useful but dated.

Montreal	Write to the Greater Montreal Convention and Tourism Bureau (*see* Chapter 3) for the folder, "Tourist Guide–4th edition," which also includes the Lodging Guide. Many streets have wheelchair ramps.

Shopping centers and main tourist and entertainment centers allot primary parking areas to disabled persons' vehicles bearing special stickers.

You can get wheelchair help from **Kéroul** (4545 ave. Pierre de Coubertin, Montreal, Quebec H1V 3R2, tel. 514/252-3104), Monday–Thursday 9–5 and Friday 9–noon.

You can reach the **Canadian National Institute for the Blind** (CNIB—1010 rue Ste-Catherine, Montreal, Quebec H2L 2G3, tel. 514/284-2040), weekdays 8:30–noon and 1–4:30.

Reserve at least 24 hours ahead for transportation for people in wheelchairs from **Voyageur Bus Service** (505 blvd. de Maisonneuve E, Montreal, Quebec H2L 1Y4, tel. 514/842-2281).

Essential Information 22

Quebec City Physically disabled motorists who display a special identification sticker or license plate indicating that the vehicle is owned by a disabled person can park in special spaces reserved for them.

"Access to Québec City" is a free booklet available from the Quebec City Region Tourism and Convention Bureau (*see* Chapter 5).

Kéroul (*see* above) has general information and also offers a comprehensive publication listing hotels, restaurants, and transportation services serving handicapped persons.

Transport adapté du Québec métro inc. (418/687-2641) will provide transportation for individuals in wheelchairs on a residual basis (residents of Quebec City are served before visitors). The standard bus fee is charged, and an eight-hour advance notice is required.

Canadian National Institute for the Blind (269 rue de la Couronne, Quebec G1K 6C9, tel. 418/529-9224) is open weekdays 8:30–4:30.

Hints for Older Travelers

The **American Association of Retired Persons** (AARP, 1909 K St. NW, Washington, DC 20049, tel. 202/662-4850) has two programs for independent travelers: (1) the Purchase Privilege Program, which offers discounts on hotels, airfare, car rentals, and sightseeing; and (2) the AARP Motoring Plan, provided by Amoco, which furnishes emergency aid and trip routing information for an annual fee of $33.95 per couple. AARP Travel Service also arranges group tours in conjunction with two companies: **Olson-Travelworld** (100 N. Sepulveda Blvd., El Segundo, CA 90245, tel. 800/227-7737) and **RFD, Inc.** (4801 W. 110th St., Overland Park, KS 66211, tel. 800/365-5358). AARP members must be 50 or older. Annual dues are $5 per person or per couple.

To use an AARP or other identification card, ask for a reduced hotel rate at the time you make your reservation rather than when you check out. At restaurants, show your card to the maître d' before you're seated, because discounts may be limited to certain set menus, days, or hours. When renting a car, remember that economy cars, priced at promotional rates, may cost less than cars that are available with your ID card.

Travel Industry and Disabled Exchange (TIDE, 5435 Donna Ave., Tarzana, CA 91356, tel. 818/343-6339) is an industry-based organization with a $15-per-person annual membership fee. Members receive a quarterly newsletter and information on travel agencies and tours.

National Council of Senior Citizens (925 15th St. NW, Washington, DC 20005, tel. 202/347-8800) is a nonprofit advocacy group with some 4,000 local clubs across the country. Annual membership is $12 per person or $16 per couple. Members receive a monthly newspaper with travel information and an ID card for reduced-rate hotels and car rentals.

Mature Outlook (Box 1205, Glenview, IL 60025, tel. 800/336-6330), a subsidiary of Sears, Roebuck & Co., is a travel club for people over 50, with hotel and motel discounts and a bimonthly newsletter. Annual membership is $7.50 per couple. Instant membership is available at participating Holiday Inns.

Travel Tips for Senior Citizens (U.S. Dept. of State Publication 8970, revised September 1987) is available for $1 from the Superintendent of Documents, U.S. Government Printing Office, Washington, DC 20402.

Telephones

Local Calls — **Directory assistance** is 411 and **operator** is 0. To use a pay phone for local calls, pick up the receiver, insert 25¢, and dial the number. A quarter is good for one call of unlimited time.

International Calls — To call the United States, simply dial 1, the area code, and the number. For calls to other countries, you must use the international calling system. If you want to call Britain, for example, dial 011, the country code (44), the routing code, and the number (remember the five-hour time difference).

Mail

International letters up to 20 grams sent outside North America need 76¢ worth of stamps, and $1.14 for letters from 20 to 50 grams. (On average, letters weigh 30 grams and postcards 15 to 20 grams.) Letters up to 30 grams to the United States cost 44¢ and 64¢ for 30 to 50 grams. Mail destined within Canada costs 38¢ for up to 30 grams and 59¢ for 30 to 50 grams.

Tipping

Restaurants: 10%–15%
Taxis: 10%–15%
Porters: 50¢–75¢ a bag
Doormen: $1 for hailing a cab or for carrying bags to check-in
Checkrooms: fixed fee
Ushers: no tipping expected in theaters and cinemas

Further Reading

Montreal — Mordecai Richler's *Son of a Smaller Hero* and *St. Urbain's Horseman* provide excellent descriptions of life in Montreal. One of Canada's best-known novelists and essayists, Hugh MacLennan wrote two novels, *Two Solitudes* and *Return of the Sphinx*, that delineate the relationship between French and English in contemporary Quebec. More recently, playwrights David Fennario (*On The Job, Balconville*) and Michel Tremblay (*St. Carmen of the Main, Albertine in Five Times, L'Impromptu d'Outremont*) have written about English and French working-class Montreal to great acclaim. Gail Scott's novel *Heroine* provides an amusing portrait of pseudo-anarchist intellectuals of both cultures during Quebec's "Quiet Revolution." Brian Moore's *The Luck of Ginger Coffey* is the story of an Irish family in Montreal. *The Main*, by Trevanian, is a suspense novel set in the underside of Montreal. *The Last Collection*, by Seymour Blicker, is a comedy about cons in the area. Roy Gabrielle's *The Tin Flute*, translated from the French, describes a poor section of Montreal called St. Henri. Other titles include Yves Beauchemin's *Le Metou*.

Quebec City For a good introduction to the rural life of Quebec City's backwoods, start with *Maria Chapedelaine* by Hemon Lewis. Works of contemporary fiction set in Quebec City include *A Season in the Life of Emmanuel*, a romantic novel of Quebec gentry by Marie Claire Blais, and Anne Herbert's romance, *Kamouraska*, a novel about social conditions in Quebec City before World War II. Good discussion of Quebec City's separatist movement can be found in Malcolm Reid's novel *The Shouting Signpainters*.

Credit Cards

The following credit card abbreviations are used throughout this book: AE, American Express; CB, Carte Blanche; DC, Diner's Club; MC, MasterCard; and V, Visa.

2 Portrait of Montreal and Quebec City

Maple Leaf Rag: Two Excerpts

Naked City

by Stephen Brook

In Maple Leaf Rag, *author Stephen Brook describes his travels through Canada. Mr. Brook's other works include* New York Days and New York Nights *and* Honkytonk Gelato.

In my short-trouser years my best friend came from Montreal. His father exchanged cash for erudition on a British television quiz show, but the entire family was Canadian. So was his nanny, previously his mother's nanny, who affected to be severe in the best Scottish-Canadian manner, but was in truth kindly and humorous beneath it. Christopher, whose disposable pocket-money income eclipsed mine and whose upbringing had been less orderly than my own, helped push me into swaggering adolescence. At the age of 13 he was a heavy smoker, swore skillfully, took me to amusement arcades to burn a couple of shillings, used a Leica when I was still twirling a Brownie, and talked knowingly about girls at a time when I knew none. He was handsome and confident, and I moved rather in his shadow. He was a boy of strong opinions, all of which he voiced regularly. Although most of his closest friends were Jewish, he was not above the occasional anti-Semitic jibe, unthinkingly based on received opinion more than personal experience. He was virulently anti-Catholic, a prejudice fueled and bolstered by the redoubtable nanny, who riveted me with terrible tales of how Catholic mothers perish in childbirth in order that their newborn infants shall live. And so forth.

When Christopher was 14, he returned to Canada and four years went by before we met again, this time in his native city. The Montreal he showed me was an English Montreal. At no time was I aware that he or anyone in his family had more than a rudimentary knowledge of the French language. Christopher had matured with all his prejudices intact. He took me to St. Joseph's Oratory not to pray or admire but to pour scorn on Catholic credulousness. At the time I thought little of it, but revisiting the city after a gap of 20 years, it was not difficult to appreciate why French-Canadian nationalism had triumphed so decisively a decade ago. I don't think it ever occurred to Christopher, or to tens of thousands of other British-Canadian Montrealers, that their attitude was arrogant; they took it as given that they belonged to an educated elite, and that French Canadians, whatever their numerical status, didn't count for much and were somehow ineligible for full human consideration by virtue of their barbaric religion, incomprehensible dialect and insular culture.

The Montreal of his youth has certainly been modified, but it was essentially French even then and language laws and other recent developments have only altered the city in its degree of Frenchness. The English-speaking citizens may have controlled the economic life of the province, but they had never been able to dominate the tone of the city. Yet I was surprised, having heard so many tales of executive flight, to find how intact the English quarters of Montreal still are. Twenty years ago the inner suburb of Westmount was exclusively English-speaking; now French is heard on its steep streets and from behind the high fences of its grand houses. You'll still find here some of the few remaining road signs in Quebec that say STOP instead of ARRÊT, and on Greene Street you can have tea at the Café Oxford, buy your clothes at Carriage Trade, order a catered meal from By George, and stop at the Avenue Bookshop to tickle the chin of Orwell the marmalade cat. On the same street I watched a dignified old lady parking a Jaguar which sported the following bumper sticker: LET ME TELL YOU ABOUT MY GRANDCHILDREN. I ran after her, imploring her to satisfy my curiosity, but the old tease wouldn't tell me a thing, not even whether they were legitimate.

A few blocks away, on Lansdowne, a condominium development is dangled before the moneyed public in a manner that suggested the matter-of-fact Canadians, when pushed, can exhibit as much vulgarity as any coven of copywriters in the United States: "In search of excellence? Finally. A luxury condominium that delivers your personal statement. Success. Unmatched anywhere in the city. Le 200 Lansdowne in Westmount. Beyond elite." The British style still gasps along at some of the old clubs in downtown Montreal on and near Sherbrooke Street; here all the rituals of London clubland have been embalmed in their North American setting. Perhaps there are French-Canadian members, but I heard no French spoken during the enjoyable claret-drenched evening I spent at the University Club, and I imagine that any Francophone Québécois would with some justification fail to see what purpose could possibly be served by joining such an institution.

Even though the walls between French and English have crumbled in recent years, Montreal is still a city of enclaves. Mordecai Richler's novels portray the Jewish quarters of the city that existed in his childhood. Of that thickly populated district little remains, for many Jews prospered sufficiently to allow them to move to more sedate suburbs, but their place has been taken by other, more recent arrivals. One Saturday morning I drove up the avenue du Parc, with its string of Greek restaurants, and then east along Laurier; these blocks along Laurier used to be unprepossessing, but now they are being smartened up, and bright shopfronts dazzle among less colorful facades. I turned up boulevard St-Laurent, which everyone in the city calls the Main, through what's left of the Jewish quarter, and soon found myself in the Italian quarter.

From rue Mozart, where I parked, it was just a few paces to the Marché du Nord, which resembles a display of prize fruits and vegetables suddenly invaded by the general public. There were huge sooty black plums the size of tennis balls, green and yellow watermelons stacked beneath the stalls, bulbs of garlic plaited on their stalks, a smell of ripe cantaloupes mugging occasional whiffs of greeny mint, peppers enthusiastically marked DOLCI DOLCI DOLCI!, bunches of basil hanging from chains suspended between the concrete pillars of the market square, a battalion of honeys, baby Italian aubergines erupting from green stalks with the texture of aged skin, green and yellow haricot beans, buckets of lumpish broad beans going cheap, scrubbed potatoes, fresh corn skinned back to reveal pale yellow grains (*"très sucré!"*), riotous spinach curling in on itself (*"Bueno, bueno,"* murmured a woman approvingly as she fingered the leaves), white radishes like mandrake roots, pale green "white" zucchini, lizardy sage, 2-foot-long wispy dill, orange zucchini blossoms destined to frolic with glistening wet cos lettuces in salads. And weaving their way between the crowded stalls were West Indians in straining shorts and hair curlers, determined Italians with shopping baskets that bulged as capaciously as their paunches, thoughtful chin-stroking invaders from Westmount, burly French-Canadians with packs of Craven A tucked beneath the shoulder straps of their white T-shirts. Officialdom's attempt to force a metric system on Canada was in disarray here for, though some stalls had signs scrawled in kilos as well, almost all gave equal prominence to the old system. The Mulroney government had given the nod to relaxations of enforced metrication, and in large cities and conservative rural townships alike, kilos and meters began to be displaced by the archaic yet familiar mysteries of pounds and yards.

The European profusion of the Marché du Nord was in vibrant contrast to the decorum of the Atwater Market, situated closer to the English-speaking districts on the other side of the city. Earlier that morning produce had been stacked onto the stalls with a bricklayer's precision, as though the goods were too lovely and precious to be sold or even fingered by jowly matrons feeling their way towards a ratatouille. Fruit and vegetables were scrubbed so as to extinguish any associations with such lowly elements as earth and compost. If the northern Montreal market was a marvelous mélange of Paris, Naples, and Lisbon, Atwater was more American in style; its teeth had been capped and there were no gray hairs . . .

The pleasures of stuffing yourself with food were first elevated to the art of gastronomy in 19th-century Paris. The Canadian equivalent of bourgeois prosperity founded on the pursuit of trade and commerce had its roots in Vieux-Montréal. When Christopher had taken me there two decades ago at the midnight hour, it had been dark and sinister; bulky massive warehouses and commercial buildings glowered over deserted streets. Here and there dim yellow lights indicated that a restaurant or bar was still open, but for the most part the old town was still and forbidding. It's somber still, for the heavy gray stone buildings continue to overshadow the narrow lanes, but there are places among the network of austere commercial streets that reveal now, as they must have done a century ago, the grandeur of Vieux-Montréal. Where the Lower Town of Quebec City is archly quaint in its re-creation of bustling 17th century small businesses and maritime trading offices, Vieux-Montréal affirms the solidity and ambition of 19th century commercialism. True, there are older churches and seminaries from the 17th century, together with 18th century houses such as the Château Ramezay, but the mighty commercial buildings mostly date from a period of Victorian prosperity. As the city moved to preserve its most ancient quarter, new uses had to be found for these imposing buildings, and inevitably restaurants and studios and loft flats were carved out of spaces once taken up by winches and ledgers and bales.

Many sneer at such prosperous middle-class invasions of once dilapidated downtown areas, but I applaud adaptations that allow old districts to be preserved without being fossilized. Vieux-Montréal still feels alive, and its character has not been violated by the injection of new blood along the long handsome streets such as St. Paul. Vieux-Montréal succeeds where the Lower Town of Quebec City fails because there has been no programmatic zeal to remove "unhistorical" later accretions. The essentially 19th-century character of the old town, with its mighty church and massive municipal buildings—even the City Hall of 1926 resembles a French Renaissance extravaganza more typical of the previous century—is intact. While the Lower Town of Quebec City has been re-created essentially as a tourist attraction—admittedly a successful one—Vieux-Montréal remains integral to the city that has grown around it.

Quebec City is irretrievably provincial, which is in large part its charm. Vieux-Montréal, on the evidence of its architecture, always aspired to greater things. The scale is altogether more grandiose, reflecting Montreal's standing in the mid-19th century as a colonial capital and a major center of communications and finance. Take the neo-Gothic church of Notre Dame that dominates the spacious Place d'Armes. Here the fervour of institutional Catholicism blends happily with civic pride. Lavishly ornamented with wood carvings and gold leaf and polychrome decoration, there is little echo here of the Jansenism and cloistered piety of the Quebec City churches (a severity that can, however, be conveniently recaptured at the austere seminary of 1685 adjoining the church); the spirit here is closer to the proud splendor of Italian Baroque, where the worldly is used, with varying degrees of success, as a vehicle for the spiritual. The nave and the double-decker galleries overlooking it were built to seat 3,000, a remarkable number when one recalls that when the church was built in the 1820s the population of Montreal was no more than 15,000.

The Place d'Armes is not the only spot where the urban pride of old Montreal lives on. A few hundred yards to the east are two more squares, named after Cartier and Vauquelin; both are spacious and invigorating, since even on hot days a breeze often wafts up from the St. Lawrence. (It was Cartier who first came to what was then the Indian village of Hochelaga in 1535, though the Europeans didn't settle here until a century later, when Montreal proved a well-situated base for the French fur trade.) Shoppers and visitors congregate here, and there's always somebody around who has unpacked a guitar at the base of Canada's version of Nelson's Column and is strumming tunelessly to the accompaniment of cigarette or marijuana smoke, while tourists enjoy an overpriced ice cream or beer at a café before ambling down to the rue Bonsecours and its famous sailors' church. Fewer tourists stroll as far west as the loveliest spot in Vieux-Montréal, and indeed one of the most enchanting groups of buildings in Canada: the Youville Stables. A gate leads into a beautiful courtyard overlooked by dignified early 19th-century buildings, their walls awash with ivy; stately gravel paths flow across the lawns and tubs packed with flowers provide a welcome burst of color amid the restraint of gray stone and clipped green lawn.

Unconsummated Divorce

When, 15 years ago, I lived in Boston, I would occasionally drive up through Maine to Quebec City for a long weekend. Boston was a congenial city but an American one, and I missed Europe. I missed the texture of old stone and the scrawled *plat du jour* on a menu, and I could find both of those in Quebec. On returning to the city after a long absence my former affection welled up once again. Not that Quebec is an especially attractive city, despite its splendid site high over the St. Lawrence River. With its gray stone and raucous climate, it reminds me of Old Aberdeen—only physically, I hasten to add, for the atmosphere of Quebec City is almost hedonistic, and no one could say that about Aberdeen. Within its partially reconstructed walls, the old city covers a small area, and the bulk of the municipality spreads out through a string of modern suburbs such as Ste-Foy.

Quebec City is no Paris, and that is its very charm. It is unequivocally provincial. With its ancient university, its churches and convents, its hotels and restaurants, it is urban, but not cosmopolitan. It is, however, European, with that density of habitation that packs together public buildings and churches, boutiques and convents, into a thickly jumbled profusion of squares and streets, alleys and terraces. To me the appeal of Quebec City lies less in its superficial picturesque quality than in its austerity, and I dislike many of the attempts now being made to prettify the old town: the quaint signs, the colourful windowboxes, the heightening of antique architectural features. Streets such as Ste-Anne that cater to the tourists—and admittedly do it well—are not half as expressive as, say, rue Ste-Famille. This lane descends a hill and is flanked on the right by a harsh authoritarian building that is part of Laval University. The structure is relatively recent—it dates from 1920—but its uncompromising, unlovely bulk is closer to the grim Jansenist spirit of the town than the ardent but obsequious crowd-pleasing of many of the main streets. At the foot of rue Ste-Famille stands a row of cottages dating from the 1750s that bring some modest charm to the austere street. More characteristic of Quebec as a whole are the tall stone town houses, entered through raised doorways so that the ground-floor windows are often just above snooping level. On rue St-Louis most tourists walk straight past the fine Maison Maillou, for with its navy blue shutters set against rough gray stone walls, the house does not call attention to itself, but it is very French and very handsome. The townhouse interiors are guarded not only by stern doorways, but by shutters that fold over double glazing that shields a layer of starched lace curtains. Block-faced old women still lift a corner of those curtains to peer out at the weather. This is a city of exteriors; the houses are not welcoming but excluding.

An ecclesiastical atmosphere permeates the city like incense, for although the Catholic Church has lost its former stranglehold, the old town still seems packed with nuns. The ancient seminary is as severe as the houses, though the bright white-washed walls around the courtyard modify an austerity that would be oppressive were it not for the wealth of details that have accrued over the centuries. Most visitors rightly admire the great panoramas from the terraces overlooking the river and from the ancient citadel, but they are not what makes the town unique. Quebec, unlike a modern city, exalts the idiosyncratic. A chimney stack or a doorway or a previously unnoticed alley keeps one's interest alive, and though the city is small, it never seems to pall. There are still quiet spots frequented only by cats and tourists who have put the guidebooks away and allowed themselves to stray. At the end of rue Mont Carmel, for instance, is a small park, scarcely more than a garden, but the view is fine and the mood somber but tranquil, in contrast to its aura three centuries ago when a windmill supported a three-gun battery. The old fortifications of the city, which date from the late 17th century, have been more or less rebuilt, and it's possible to walk their length for about 3 miles.

The churches in this very ecclesiastical city are resplendent. The Anglican cathedral of 1804 has a magnificent interior, complete with box pews and wood gallery; its broad but shallow apse is, like any English church of the same vintage, lined with memorial tablets. A few streets away stands, in complete contrast, Notre Dame de Québec. There has been a church on this site since the 1640s, though the present structure dates from 1925. The conservative citizens didn't adopt a modern idiom when the church was rebuilt, and the interior is resolutely Baroque, with voluptuous gilt furnishings. Another rebuilt church is the equally sumptuous chapel of the Ursuline convent, adorned with a pulpit and reredos in luxurious black, white and gold. An elaborate screen divides the nuns' choir from the public area of the chapel. More grilles—how rigidly the laity was kept at bay!—fence off the founder's burial chapel. This is a historical spot, for Montcalm is buried here, and a notice sternly informs visitors, RESPECTUOUS CLOTHES REQUIRED. Another contrast to Catholic elaboration is provided at St. Andrew's Church of 1810, the oldest Presbyterian church in Canada, though the country has certainly made up for lost time since. Here, in contrast with the more stratified disposition of the Anglican Cathedral, an appropriately nonconformist note is sounded by having the pews curved so that the entire congregation can face the elevated pulpit behind the altar.

The provincial motto is *Je me souviens* (I remember), though a translation of "I haven't forgotten" catches the hint of aggrieved menace I always detect in the words. Ironically, the motto was taken from a Loyalist poem. History was not kind to the people of Quebec. The Frenchman Champlain was astute enough to nail this site as a future colonial center in 1608, and the settlement grew rapidly. Bishop Laval, after whom the university is named, arrived in 1659 and initiated the unremitting ecclesiastical control that strangled Quebec for three centuries. When, during the 18th century, Britain and France began to battle it out for control of the strategically crucial river, it was inevitable that Quebec City would be much fought over. The decisive encounter took place in 1759. The British general James Wolfe began to besiege the city in July. Late on September 12 the British forces crept up on to the Plains of Abraham, the broady grassy plateau adjoining the present-day citadel. The following day the French commander Montcalm led his troops into battle against the encroaching besiegers. For Wolfe as well as Montcalm it was a fatal encounter, and the outcome was a rout of the French forces. This was the end of New France, and the beginning of the French-Canadian mentality enshrined in the motto *Je me souviens*.

Although the battle heralded the beginning of the end of French rule, it certainly wasn't the end of French influence. To this day Quebec City remains resolutely French in language and culture. Its half million inhabitants are, unlike the population of Montreal, overwhelmingly of French descent. As Montreal became increasingly important as a cultural and commercial center within Canada, the influence of Quebec City began to diminish. Montreal had to participate, at least commercially, in the life of the rest of North America, leaving Quebec free to retreat into the certainties of French-Canadian culture, an ethos dominated by the church. As recently as 30 years ago the province was, notoriously, a society ruled by demagogues in league with the power of the church; the *curé* and the *notaire*, as the only educated citizens of innumerable small towns and villages, exercised a powerful, and usually reactionary, influence. Education rarely proved intellectually liberating, since it reiterated the largely authoritarian values current when the province was originally colonized. In the 1960s, with what became known as the Quiet Revolution, these traditional cultural arbiters rapidly lost influence, and within a decade or so Quebec had become more outward-looking, more sophisticated, more liberal. The schools and universities no longer supplied a constant stream of small-town priests, doctors and lawyers, but began to educate scientists and engineers as well. Churchgoing is no longer ubiquitous, and, most astonishing of all, the birthrate is decreasing for the first time. The Quiet Revolution also brought political changes. The province gained the confidence to assert its identity within the larger Canadian confederation, even though it chose to do so by insisting on the irreconcilable differences between its culture and that of the predominantly English culture that enveloped it. Political separatism gathered force and in 1968 the Parti Québécois was founded. Just eight years later, to the astonishment not only of the rest of Canada but of the Parti's own leaders, it was elected into office, and for nine years the province was ruled by a party that officially espoused separatism . . .

Québécois worry about their identity almost as much as other Canadians do, though with less justification. French Canada is instantly identifiable as a place apart. Glancing through the visitors' book at Louisburg, I easily identified the French-Canadian signatories, because their handwriting differs from that of their British-Canadian compatriots. It would surely be impossible to distinguish between the handwriting of Americans or Germans from different parts of their respective countries, but here in Canada this minor cultural indicator signified the almost total cultural separation of French Canadians. There are other such indicators. French Canadians seem, and I say this on the basis of observations in crowded cafés rather than on statistical evidence, to be far heavier smokers than their compatriots outside the province . . .

The events that brought about the downfall of French Quebec are most easily recalled at the citadel, positioned on a formidably fortified hill on the edge of the old town. The ramparts that surround it include outer walls spacious enough to enclose a tennis court. Before touring the citadel, which was built in the 1820s and is still in use, visitors are compelled to attend the Changing of the Guard. The soldiers' uniforms are essentially British in design: red coats and bearskin hats. But all commands are issued in French, which I found culturally dislocating. An excellent band wandered about the parade ground, and the pounding of the drums and the growl of the brass reverberated thunderously off the barrack walls. One soldier gripped a leash attached to a goat with gilded horns, and at various times during the long ceremony, the goat was tugged around the parade ground and, despite the splendor of its outfit, did not seem to be enjoying itself. How unsoldierly these French Canadians were! While at ease, they grinned and smirked, mostly in the direction of teenage girls in tight shorts. The drills were of a high standard, but there was no sense of military preparedness, and without any doubt a platoon of halberdiers could have taken the citadel that morning with a minimum of casualties. Myself, I'd have had that guard changed and back at work in half the time. Almost without exception, the soldiers were mustachioed. Mustaches are common in Quebec but here they seemed almost part of the uniform. When I questioned a soldier about this urgent matter, he confirmed my observation but couldn't explain it. During the tedious moments on the parade ground, I could at least admire the views: of the Château Frontenac, which like most buildings named Château in Canada turns out to be a luxurious Canadian Pacific hotel, and, in another direction, of the typically undistinguished Hilton tower. The best view of all unfurls itself from the Prince of Wales bastion, which overlooks the St. Lawrence and the Plains of Abraham, now a park.

Back in the city, the most popular panorama is enjoyed from the Terrasse Dufferin, a boardwalk that carpets the clifftop in front of the Château Frontenac. The spot is overlooked by a statue of Champlain, who is depicted as stamping his foot with impatience ("Merde! Vaincu encore"), though more probably he was just feeling the cold. While the bulky Frontenac looks splendid from a distance, a closer view reveals it as pastiche, and brings into focus the dull caramel brick of which it is built. Steep flights of steps lead down from the Terrasse to the lower town, for old Quebec thrived at two levels, the lower of which huddles around the port. During the 19th century the Lower Town, which architecturally must have equaled the Upper, became a slum. In recent years it has been renovated at a cost of over $30 million. Without the efforts of the restorers, there's little doubt that the entire area would have been razed and replaced by container warehouses and car parks, so it seems churlish to carp at what has been done here. But I'll carp anyway, for the restoration struck me as extreme, and lacking in the sensitivity displayed at Louisburg. In the Lower Town features not deemed "authentic"—post 17th and 18th century, in other words—were simply removed. Extra stories built on to older houses in later decades were dismantled, and new "authentic" roofs have taken their place. Brand-new dormer windows and rearranged fenestration contort the ramshackle old structures into pattern-book shape. Old buildings and their accretions eventually become stylistically coherent, with occasional exceptions. By ignoring this principle, the restorers of the Lower Town have preserved the letter and throttled the spirit. As a tourist attraction it works well, for some of the old mansions have been converted into excellent small museums; and the Place Royale, the ancient square surrounded by former merchants' houses in the heart of the Lower Town and the very spot where in 1608 Champlain founded French North America, is always crowded. Notre-Dame des Victoires, founded here in 1688 and rebuilt in the same style in 1759, is the most charming of Quebec's churches, with its cream and gold interior and the castlelike construction of the High Altar. By wandering down some of less tampered-with streets, such as rue St-Pierre and rue St-Paul, towards the Vieux-Port, I filtered through my mind a better sense of what the old Lower Town must have been like, say, a century ago. The old houses along these streets have been less fanatically restored than those around the Place Royale. Small restaurants, chic and high-priced, as well as design and crafts boutiques, keep the lights burning, more, I suspect, in anticipation of a steady influx of lucre than in response to a present demand. Even more off the tourist beat are the streets beyond the fortifications that slope down to the Lower Town. Here, along Olivier, Richelieu, and D'Aiguillon are tucked-in houses and artisans' cottages, vestiges of old Quebec that lie midway between the walled city and the sprawling suburbs.

Quebec reserves its greatest charm for nighttime. The terraces of cafés and bars are crowded with people sipping an aperitif or a brandy. The vigorous rooflines of Château Frontenac and some of the large public buildings are floodlit. Down in the Lower Town a string quartet had found a vacant corner and was sending a divertimento by Mozart spinning into the night. In the Upper Town, near the central Place d'Armes, musicians—playing a mouth organ, a variety of banjo, and a clackety castanet tapped against the thigh—sang out fast and lively Québécois songs, and passersby joined in the choruses. In front of the musicians an old man, his white hair spilling out from beneath a well-chewed panama, danced a stately jig. From the Terrasse Dufferin, the lights of the town of Lévis, on the opposite bank of the St. Lawrence, twinkled brightly, and I could see the fat little ferry chugging its way across the river.

3 Montreal

Introduction

by Patricia Lowe

A former reporter and editor for the defunct Montreal Star, *Patricia Lowe is a native Montrealer.*

Plus ça change, plus c'est la même chose," like other travel clichés, no longer applies to Montreal. For years, as Quebec's largest city and the world's second largest French-speaking metropolis, Montreal clung to an international reputation attained in the heyday of former Mayor Jean Drapeau, who brought his beloved hometown the 1967 World's Fair (Expo '67), the Metro subway, its underground city, and the 1976 Summer Olympics. During his nearly three decades in power, Drapeau's entrepreneurial spirit added pizzazz to this transportation and financial capital at the gateway to the St. Lawrence Seaway.

But with the arrival of a nationalist provincial government in 1976, the mayor and Montreal were forced to rest on their laurels as the province agonized over its place in Canada. Separation from the rest of the country was seriously considered. The provincial government passed Bill 101, a controversial language act (still in force) making French the official language of business and public communication. For the city it was a wrenching ideological change; the only differences visitors saw were English or bilingual billboards and public signs replaced by French ones.

The ensuing unstable political climate produced sluggish investment and construction, which in turn affected the travel business. Tourist offices could only promote the standbys: the former Expo site (transformed into a permanent international exhibition center), fine French restaurants, and the historic attractions of Vieux-Montréal (Old Montreal)—all worth seeing, but the city lacked novelty.

Montreal is again on the move. The provincial government elected in 1985 has for the most part promoted a more upbeat environment. The more confident atmosphere has attracted corporate investment, transforming the downtown area with 12 new or soon-to-be completed complexes. Federal money is revamping the once-derelict old port into a vibrant harborfront, and has shored up smaller projects, such as Parks Canada's restoration of the gracious home of Quebec's Father of Confederation, Sir George-Étienne Cartier.

Mayor Jean Doré and his Montreal Citizen's Movement party are changing the face of the municipal government. They have been busy enacting laws to protect green spaces—like Montreal's most famous landmark, Mont Royal—adding more parks to congested downtown areas, and promoting development.

Without losing any of its French flavor, the city has added what some feel are much-needed '80s-style North American accessories. With its juxtaposition of old France and the new Quebec, Montreal is one of North America's more intriguing destinations.

The melding of old and new is no more apparent than in the flamboyant office tower of Les Cooperants. Even though the design of this 35-story pink glass structure imitates the Gothic-style Christ Church Cathedral it overshadows, it was not what the earnest French missionaries who founded Montreal envisioned. What today is a metropolis of 2.8 million—some 20% of other ethnic origin—began as 54 dedicated souls from France who landed on Montreal island in 1642. Led by career military man Paul de Chomedey, Sieur de Maisonneuve, they had come to this 32-mile-long island in the middle of the St. Lawrence to convert the Indians to Christianity.

They first set foot on a spot they called Ville Marie, now Place Royale in Vieux Montréal. Although they were pioneer settlers, Place Royale had been named by French explorer Samuel de Champlain, who established a temporary trading post here in 1611.

The first white man to see Montreal was Jacques Cartier, discoverer of the St. Lawrence, who stopped off on the island in 1535, interrupting his search for a shortcut to the Orient to claim this piece of the New World for France. Montreal owes its name to the navigator from St. Malo, although there are conflicting anecdotes on its origin. One has Cartier accompanying a welcoming committee of friendly Indians to their village, Hochelaga, supposedly on Mont Royal's southern slope at the site today marked by a cairn on McGill University campus. Scaling this mountain, and greeted with a splendid panorama of the river and hills beyond, he is said to have exclaimed "quel mont royal!" (what a royal mount). (Visitors can enjoy this same view from the chalet lookout atop Parc Mont Royal.) It is more likely he named it later, at the French king's request, in memory of Cardinal Medici of Montreale (Sicily), who had obtained papal favors for the king.

A truer tale has de Maisonneuve, more than a century later, in 1643, planting a cross somewhere on the same Mont Royal, in gratitude for the fledgling colony's escape from a flood that Christmas. The present 100-foot (30-meter) lighted cross—the glare from its 158 bulbs can be seen for 40 miles (64 kilometers)—at the mountain's summit has commemorated the first wooden symbol since 1924.

For nearly 200 years, city life was confined to a 95-acre (385,000-square-meter) walled community, today's Vieux-Montréal and a protected historic site. Ville Marie became a fur-trading center, the chief embarkation point for the *voyageurs* setting off on discovery and trapping expeditions. This business quickly usurped religion as the settlement's *raison d'être*, along with its role as a major port at the confluence of the St. Lawrence and Ottawa rivers. However, the original Christian intent is still felt in the hundreds of church spires reflected in many a glass office tower and in street names like St-Denis, St-Gabriel, St-Pierre, and St-Sulpice.

Regardless of Montreal's enduring Roman Catholic nature, ever since the 18th century, warehouses have been elbowing religious institutions for room. Entrepreneurs like John Jacob Astor, whose fortune was based on his early fur-trading ventures, put up sheds to store pelts; convents built stables and granaries, and later, grain silos rose up along the port. Former storehouses used for all kinds of commodities are today luxurious condominiums, shopping complexes, and offices like Les Cours Le Royer, off boulevard St-Laurent in Vieux-Montréal, or the Youville Stables, now home to Gibby's, a popular steak house.

The old Montreal of the French regime lasted until 1759, when during one of the battles of the Seven Years' War, British troops easily forced the poorly fortified and demoralized city to surrender. The Treaty of Paris ended the war in 1763, and Quebec became one of Britain's most valuable colonies. British and Scottish settlers poured in to take advantage of Montreal's geography and economic potential. When it was incorporated as a city in 1832, it was a leading colonial capital of business, finance, and transportation.

Montreal is still Canada's transport hub: It is home to the national railway and airline, the largest private rail company (Canadian Pacific), as well as the International Air Transport Association (IATA) and the United Nations' International Civil Aviation Organization (ICAO) on Sherbrooke. But in the early 1980s, Toronto—already Canada's financial center—beat out Montreal as the business center and most populous metropolitan area.

When Montreal was Canada's financial core, rue St-Jacques (St. James Street) was lined with the head offices of 15 banks and financial institutions. Most have moved, though some retain branch offices in imposing limestone and griffin-capped structures, reminders of their powerful past. Today the Bank of Montreal, Canada's first, maintains its headquarters in a handsome domed building facing Place d'Armes (a free museum off the lobby is open during banking hours).

Although financiers and lawyers preferred St-Jacques, retailers moved uptown in the early and mid-19th century to follow their clientele who had begun to settle west, in the case of the English, and east, in the case of the French. These east-west distinctions are blurring but are still noticeable. In both directions, farming communities yielded to residential enclaves as Montrealers gradually moved out to places like côte-à-Baron (now the trendy St-Denis quarter) or Notre-Dame de Grâce to the west. The wealthy families of men who had made their mark in the brewing, fur, lumber, rail, and shipping industries—the Molsons, Allans, Shaughnessies, and Van Hornes—had already built staid Victorian piles up Mont Royal, along Dorchester Boulevard, and, later, up and down Sherbrooke and its side streets, in an area which came to be known as The Golden Square Mile.

Solidly established by the late 19th-century, downtown today still reminds visitors of its grand old days, particularly along Sherbrooke, the lifeline of chic Montreal. The busy flower-lined stretch between Guy and University takes in the de la Montagne-Crescent-Bishop-Mackay sector, where sophisticated restaurants, cafés, and bars share canopied facades with haute-couture salons, antiques shops, and art galleries.

This neighborhood earned its trendy reputation during Expo '67, the six-month international exposition that drew 50 million visitors from all over the world and marked Canada's Centennial. After touring the pavilions of 70 governments on the 1,000-acre site spread over Notre-Dame and Ste-Hélène's islands, vacationers would converge on Crescent's café *terrasses* and discos or de la Montagne's intimate little restaurants. Like the former fairgrounds and their popular amusement park, La Ronde, this stretch flourishes today as a major entertainment and cultural center.

Sherbrooke has preserved a number of its 19th- and early 20th-century limestone and gray-stone buildings—the castle towers

of the Château Apartments, for example—and is the address of
the Ritz-Carlton and Quatre Saisons (Four Seasons) hotels, as
well as McGill University and the prize-winning architectural
complex La Maison Alcan. International headquarters for Alcan Aluminium, the structure incorporates an old hotel and
several Victorian homes into a modern office building. Free
noontime concerts and art exhibitions are often staged in its
lobby.

Peel between Sherbrooke and Place du Canada, rolls through
the Montreal most tourists visit. Its Dorchester Square, formerly Dominion Square, was renamed in a controversial and
complicated changeover, a move that also saw Dorchester Boulevard on its south side rechristened boulevard René Lévesque.

Whatever the name, it has been the major tourist rallying point
for more than 35 years. The recently renovated Dominion
Square Building is the Art Deco home of municipal tourism offices and information bureaus. Bus tours, taxi guides, and
horse-drawn carriages *(calèches)* all depart from some point
around this public park. The square's monuments and buildings
are insightful commentaries on Montreal's multicultural history. Statues commemorate such varied personalities as heroes
of the Boer War, poet Robert Burns, and Sir Wilfrid Laurier, a
Québécois and Canada's Liberal prime minister from 1896 to
1911.

During the 1920s, the pillared Sun Life Building overlooking
the square was the tallest skyscraper in the Commonwealth,
and the classically elegant Windsor Hotel once hosted royalty.
The Windsor now houses offices and an atrium shopping mall.
On the south side of boulevard Réne Lévesque stands the Roman Catholic Mary Queen of the World Cathedral topped by a
row of solemn saints representing city parishes. Seen behind
and to the west of this magnificent minireplica of St. Peter's Basilica in Rome is the "Cheesegrater" tower of the Hôtel
Château Champlain and Place du Canada complex. Just one
block east is the cruciform structure of Montreal's first
modern-day high rise and the anchor of the underground city,
Place Ville Marie.

Some visitors never make it beyond this area, which is a shame,
because although the shopping, sightseeing, and dining don't
disappoint, attractions farther south and east reveal more unusual aspects of Montreal.

To the east, St-Denis and the surrounding Latin Quarter attract Francophiles, while a more ethnic flavor characterizes
the Chinese, Greek, Jewish, Portuguese, and other districts
around Prince Arthur's pedestrian mall, boulevard St-
Laurent, and avenue du Parc.

A bohemian atmosphere pervades Prince Arthur Street,
blocked off to traffic between-St-Laurent and Carré St.-Louis.
What the mall's many restaurants sometimes lack in quality,
they make up for in ethnic diversity—Chinese, Greek, Italian,
Polish, Québécois, and Vietnamese—and price, especially at
establishments where you supply the liquor (BYO). Some
12,000 Portuguese residents live in the area's St. Louis district, and their bright pastel houses and lush front gardens
have contributed to the neighborhood's renaissance.

Introduction

The Prince Arthur promenade ends at the once-grand Carré St.-Louis. Although its ornate Victorian fountain is spouting again, it is still a dusty public square surrounded by 19th-century houses, some nicely restored. A stroll across the Carré brings you to St-Denis.

Early in this century, St-Denis cut through a bourgeois neighborhood of large, comfortable residences. After a period of decline, it revived in the early 1970s, and then boomed, due largely to the opening in 1979 of Université du Québec's Montreal campus and the International Jazz Festival launched in the summer of 1980. Rows of French and ethnic restaurants, charming bistros, even hangouts for chess masters, cater to Franco- and Anglo-academics, while stylish intellectuals prowl the Quebec designer boutiques, antiques shops, and art galleries.

Activity reaches its peak during the 10 days in late June and early July when some 500,000 jazz buffs descend upon the city to hear the likes of Dizzy Gillespie, Montreal-born Oscar Peterson, and Pat Metheny. Theaters hosting the 1,000 or so performers range from sidewalk stages to Place des Arts, the main performing arts center in downtown Montreal, Théâtre St-Denis, and the Spectrum.

The popularity of the jazz festival is rivaled only by August's World Film Festival, also featured near this area at Place des Arts and Cinéma Le Parisien on Ste-Catherine, among other venues.

Place des Arts and the adjacent Complexe Desjardins constitute another intriguing hive of activity. Soon to be joined by the new home of the Musée d'art contemporain (now located at Cité du Havre), Place des Arts is really three separate halls built around a sweeping plaza overlooking Ste-Catherine.

The main concert hall, Salle Wilfrid Pelletier, is home to the Orchestre Symphonique de Montréal (Montreal Symphony Orchestra), which first came to prominence in the 1960s under a youthful Zubin Mehta. It has won acclaim for its "French" sound and classical recordings with its present conductor, Charles Dutoit. The Orchestre Métropolitain de Montréal and Les Grands Ballets Canadiens also perform here, as does the Opéra de Montréal, traveling companies of Broadway musicals, chamber orchestras, and guest artists. Place des Arts is linked to the "Underground City" via its Metro station, and via tunnels to Complexe Desjardins, aswirl with noontime shoppers and hordes of picnickers relaxing by its fountains and exotic greenery. When touring around, remember that city districts are spread out and, although parts of Montreal are within an easy stroll of one another, it is often a hike from east to west. The Metro, or subway, is an efficient means of whizzing from point A to B between 5:30 AM and 12:30 AM daily. The new Blue Line stops at 11 PM daily. (Have $1.05 in exact change ready, or buy eight tickets, also good on buses, for $7.50.)

One often-overlooked sector of the city requires a Metro ride but is worth the fare for a varied tour of Olympic and de Maisonneuve parks, the Château Dufresne Decorative Arts Museum, and the Botanical Gardens—all located at or near the corner of blvd. Pie-IX (Metro station of the same name) and Sherbrooke East.

This triangle in the east end is distinguished by the flying saucer design of the Olympic Stadium, completed by the world's "tallest inclined tower." The stadium's latest attraction is the funicular cable car that speeds sightseers to its observation deck for a spectacular view of Montreal Island. A decade in being built, the tower is finally in place, 12 years after the Olympics it was supposed to crown. The highly touted retractable roof to protect the world's finest athletes was first tested as late as the spring of 1988. There may be critics of French architect Roger Taillibert's stunning tower, but it has turned into a big draw. If visitors time it right, they may even be able to fit in an Expos baseball game in the "Big O" (for its doughnut shape), their home turf.

Arriving and Departing

From the U.S. by Plane

Airports Montreal is served by two airports: **Dorval International,** 14 miles (22½ kilometers) west of the city, handles domestic and most U.S. flights; **Mirabel International,** 34 miles (54½ kilometers) northwest of the city, is a hub for the rest of the international trade. A direct flight makes one or more stops before its final destination; a nonstop is just that; and a connecting flight means you will have to change planes at least once en route.

Airlines From the United States: **Air Canada** (tel. 800/422-6232) has nonstop service from New York, Miami, and Tampa; nonstop from Boston via Air Canada's connector airline, Air Alliance; direct service is available from Chicago, Los Angeles, and San Francisco. **American Airlines** (tel. 800/433-7300) has nonstop service from Chicago with connections to the rest of the United States. **British Airways** (tel. 800/247-9297) has nonstop service from Detroit to Montreal. **Canadian Airlines International,** formerly CP Air (tel. 800/426-7000) has a nonstop charter from Miami and direct or connecting service from Hawaii, Los Angeles, and Pittsburgh. **Delta Air Lines** (tel. 800/323-2323) has nonstops from Boston, Hartford, Connecticut, and Miami and connecting service from most major U.S. cities. **Piedmont Airlines** (tel. 800/251-5720) has nonstops to Montreal via Syracuse, NY. **US Air** (tel. 800/428-4322) has nonstop service from Buffalo, NY, and Pittsburgh.

Flying Time From New York, 1½ hours; from Chicago, 2 hours; from Los Angeles, 6½ hours (with a connection).

From the Airports to Center City The Dorval Airport is 20 to 30 minutes from downtown Montreal, while Mirabel is about 45 minutes away.

By Taxi A taxi from Dorval to downtown will cost about $20. The taxi rates from Mirabel to the center of Montreal average about $50, and you can count on about the same cost for a taxi between the two airports. All taxi companies in Montreal must charge the same rates by law. It is best to have Canadian money with you, because the exchange rate for U.S. dollars is at the driver's discretion.

By Bus **Aerocar** (tel. 514/397-9999) provides a much cheaper alternative into town from both airports. For $7 from Dorval or $9 from Mirabel, an Aerocar van will take you into the city with stops at the Sheraton Center, the Château Champlain Hotel, the Queen

Arriving and Departing 43

Elizabeth Hotel (next to Gare Centrale), and the Voyageur bus station. Service between the two airports is $9. Aerocar buses leave Dorval every 20 minutes on weekdays and every half hour on weekends. From Mirabel buses leave hourly or every half hour between 2 PM and 8 PM.

From the U.S. by Train, Bus, and Car

By Train The Gare Centrale (Central Station) on la Gauchetière between University and Mansfield (behind La Reine Elizabeth—Queen Elizabeth Hotel—on René Lévesque Ouest) is the rail terminus for all trains from the United States and other Canadian provinces. It is connected by underground passageway to the Metro's Bonaventure stop (schedule information, tel. 514/871-1331).

Amtrak (tel. 800/USA-RAIL) reinstated the all-reserved overnight Montrealer in July 1989, giving travelers in the Northeast the option of day or night transportation. The Montrealer begins in Washington, DC and stops in Baltimore, Philadelphia, Newark, New York (Pennsylvania Station), Stamford, New Haven, Amherst, and Montpelier, VT. It has a dining car with snacks, full dinners, and evening's entertainment. Sleepers are available and advised because the reclining seat-footrest combination is not conductive to a good night's sleep. Make sleeper reservations well in advance since they book early. The unreserved Adirondack departs New York's Grand Central Terminal every morning and takes 9½ hours to reach Montreal. It has a snack car but no dinner service or sleepers. A round-trip ticket on either train is cheaper than two one-way fares, except during major holidays.

VIA Rail (tel. 800/361-3677 or 514/871-1331) connects Montreal by train with all the major cities of Canada, including Quebec City, Halifax, Ottawa, Toronto, Winnipeg, Calgary, and Vancouver.

By Bus **Greyhound** has coast-to-coast service and serves Montreal with buses arriving from and departing for various cities in North America. **Voyageur** and **Voyageur-Colonial** primarily service destinations within Quebec and Ontario. **Vermont Transit** (tel. 800/451-3292) also serves Montreal, by way of Boston, New York, and other points in New England. Both lines use the city's downtown bus terminal, Terminus Voyageur (tel. 514/-842-2281), which connects with the Berri-UQAM Metro station in downtown.

By Car Travelers can reach Montreal by a number of highways. It is accessible from the rest of Canada via the Trans Canada Highway 401, which connects from the east and west via Highways 20 and 40. The New York State Thruway (I-87) becomes Highway 15 at the Canadian border, and then it's 30 miles (47 kilometers) to the outskirts of Montreal. U.S. I-89 becomes two-lane Route 133 at the boarder, which is Highway 10 at Iberville. From I-91 from Boston, you must take Highways 55 and 10 to reach Montreal. At the border you clear Canadian Customs, so be prepared with proof of citizenship and your vehicle's ownership papers. On holidays and during the peak summer season, expect waits of a half hour or more at the major crossings.

Once you're in Quebec the road signs will be in French but they're designed so you shouldn't have much trouble understanding them. The speed limit is posted in kilometers; on highways the limit is 100 kph (about 62 mph). There are extremely heavy penalties for driving while intoxicated, and drivers and front seat passengers must wear over-the-shoulder seat belts. Gasoline is sold in Imperial gallons (equal to 1.2 U.S. gallons), and lead-free is called *sans plomb*. If you're traveling in the depths of winter, remember that your car may not start on extra-cold mornings unless it has been kept in a heated garage. All Montreal parking signs are in French, so brush up on your *gauche* and *droit*. And you might see more of the city if you leave your car in a garage and hop aboard Montreal's extensive, excellent rapid transit system, the Metro.

You should be aware that, as of spring 1989, Montreal police have instituted a diligent tow-away and fine system for cars double-parked or stopped in no-stopping zones in downtown Montreal during rush hours and business hours. Penalties include a $35 ticket. If your car is towed away while illegally parked, it will cost an additional $35 to retrieve it. New York State residents should drive with extra care in Quebec. Traffic violations in the province are now entered on their New York State driving record (and vice versa) since the passage of a traffic accord in July 1988. Especially with the downtown construction boom causing the temporary closure of many streets or the rerouting of traffic onto side streets, police are being extremely vigilant about ticketing Montrealers and visitors alike for parking infractions.

Staying in Montreal

Getting Around

By Metro and Bus Armed with a few maps, you don't need a car to see Montreal; public transit will do quite well, thank you. The Metro is clean, quiet (it runs on rubber wheels), and relatively safe, and it's heated in winter and cooled in summer. Metro hours are from 5:30 AM to 12:30 AM (11 PM on the new Blue Line), and the trains run as often as every three minutes on the most crowded lines. It's also connected to the 6 miles (9½ kilometers) of the Underground City, so you may not need to go outside during bad weather. Each of the 65 Metro stops has been individually designed and decorated; Berri-UQAM has stained glass, and at Place d'Armes are exhibited a small collection of archaeological artifacts. The recently opened stations between Snowdon and Jean-Talon on the Blue Line are worth a visit, particularly Outremont with its glass-block design. Each station connects with one or more bus routes, which cover the rest of the island. The STCUM (Société de transport de la Communauté urbaine de Montréal) administers both the Metro and the buses, so the same tickets and transfers are valid on either service. You should be able to go within a few blocks of anywhere in the city on one fare. Here are the 1989 rates:

One fare: $1.05
Eight tickets: $7.50
Monthly pass: $31
Children: 50¢

The Metro

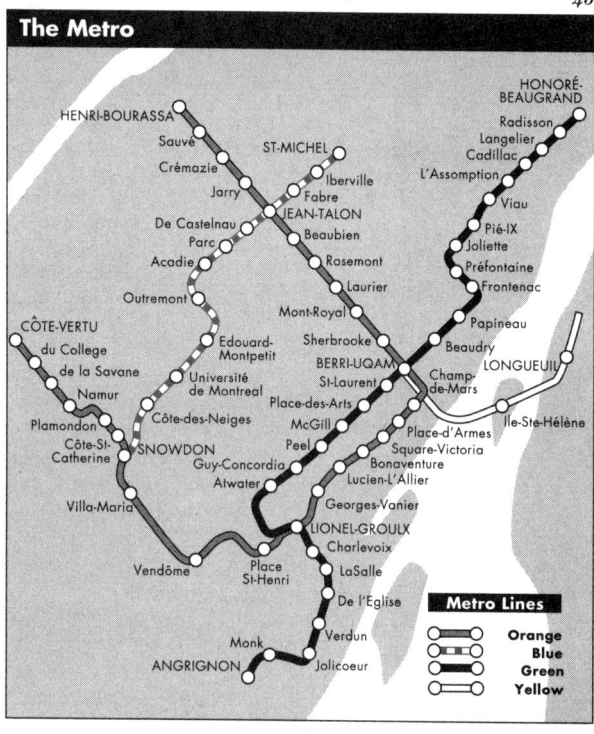

Metro map showing Orange, Blue, Green, and Yellow lines with stations including Honoré-Beaugrand, Henri-Bourassa, St-Michel, Côte-Vertu, Angrignon, and Longueuil terminals.

(Conventioneers may receive a free pass called La Carte Congrés good for the length of their stay. Call 514/280-5344 to arrange for this pass.)

Free maps may be obtained at Metro ticket booths. Try to get the *Carte Réseau* (system map); it's the most complete. Transfers from Metro to bus are available from the dispenser just beyond the ticket booth inside the station. Bus-to-bus and bus-to-Metro transfers may be obtained from the bus driver.

By Taxi Taxis in Montreal all run on the same rate: $2 minimum and 70¢ a kilometer (at press time). They're usually prompt and reliable, although they may be hard to find on rainy nights after the Metro has closed. Each carries on its roof a white or orange plastic sign that is lit when available and off when occupied.

Important Addresses and Numbers

Tourist Information The **Greater Montreal Convention and Tourism Bureau,** 1010 rue Ste-Catherine Ouest, Suite 410, Montreal, Quebec H3B 1G2 (514/871–1595 or 871–1129) or **Tourism-Québec,** Maison de Tourisme, 2 Place Ville Marie, room 70, Montreal, Quebec H3B 2C9 (514/873–2015).

Stop by the new downtown headquarters for Info-Touriste on the north side of Dorchester Square. Run by the Greater Montreal Convention and Tourism Bureau, it is open June 12–September 4, Monday–Saturday 8:30–7:30, Sunday 9–5; September 5–June 11, daily 9–5. Tel. 800/443-7000, eastern United States; 514/873-2015 Montreal; 800/361-5405 Quebec province. Info-Touriste also operates two smaller tourist information centers: at 174 rue Notre Dame Est in Vieux-Montréal (corner of Place Jacques Cartier), September–May weekdays 9–1 and 2:15–5, weekends 9–5; June–August, daily 9–6; and at Dorval Airport, September–May, 1–8; June–August, 10–8; tel. 514/871–595 for both locations. Maison du Tourisme Québec also has a year-round information kiosk, which is entered from the plaza level of 2 Place Ville Marie (around University and Cathcart sts.). Open daily summer, 8:30–7:30, rest of the year, 9–5.

Consulates **United States** (Complexe Desjardins South Tower, ground floor, Metro Place des Arts, tel. 514/281–1886).

United Kingdom (635 blvd. René Lévesque O, Metro Bonaventure, tel. 514/866–5863).

Emergencies Dialing 911 will put you through to the **police, fire,** and **ambulance.**

Doctors and Dentists The U.S. Consulate cannot recommend specific doctors and dentists but does provide a list of various specialists in the Montreal area. Call in advance (tel. 514/281–1886) to make sure the consulate is open.

Dental clinic (tel. 514/523–2151) open Mon.–Sat., 8–11, Sun. emergency appointments only; Montreal General Hospital (514/937–6011); the Quebec Poison Control Centre (800/463–5060); Touring Club de Montreal-AAA, CAA, RAC (514/861–7111).

Pharmacies There are pharmacies throughout the city—you might check the nearest shopping mall—and all of them carry American brand names. The Jean Coutu chain of pharmacies has a 24-hour store at 1370 Mont Royal Avenue E (tel. 514/527–8827), nearest Metro is Mont Royal.

English Bookstores Not all bookstores in this bilingual city sell books in English; if the name of the store begins with *libraire*, it's a good bet that it sells French books only. The **Coles** (1171 Ste-Catherine O and 4 other locations) and **W. H. Smith** (Central Station and 3 others) chains have stores throughout downtown. The **Paragraph Bookstore** (tel. 514/845–5811) at 2065 Mansfield, next to McGill, sells a wide selection of English books, tending toward the literary and academic. The **Double Hook** (1235A Greene, next to Westmount Square and Metro Atwater, tel. 514/932–5093) specializes in books from mostly English-Canadian authors and is a good source for books about Montreal and Quebec.

Travel Agencies **American Express** (1141 de Maisonneuve O, tel. 514/284–3300). **Thomas Cook** (2020 University St., Suite 434, tel. 514/842–2541).

Opening and Closing Times

Banks are open weekdays from 10 AM to 3 PM with some banks open until 5 PM on weekdays and on Saturday morning. Many Montreal banks also have 24-hour banking-machine services.

Museums are usually open during regular business hours, from 9 AM to 5 PM. Check individual listings.

Shops are open generally from 9 AM to 6 PM Monday to Wednesday, 9 AM to 9 PM Thursday and Friday, and 9 AM to 5 PM on

Saturday. You'll find most retail stores closed on Sunday and many specialty service shops closed on Monday, particularly in predominantly French neighborhoods.

Guided Tours

Orientation Tours Gray Line/STCUM (tel. 514/280–5327) offer six different tours of Montreal and its environs, including Île Ste-Hélène, the Laurentians, and the Underground City. They offer pickup service at the major hotels, or you may board the buses at their office at 1241 Peel Street (Metro Peel).

Murray Hill (tel. 514/937–5311) offers many different tours on buses departing from Dorchester Square (Metro Peel). You may buy tickets at major hotels or from Murray Hill personnel.

Boat Tours **Montreal Harbour Cruises** (tel. 514/842–3871) offers 1½-hour tours of the harbor on the M V *Concordia*, an 88-foot (27-meter) ship with a restaurant, two decks, and room for 290 passengers. Boats leave as often as six times a day from Victoria Pier at the foot of rue Berri in the Vieux-Port next to Vieux-Montréal (Metro Champs de Mars). Also available are sunset cruises, "Moonlight" cruises, the three-hour "Love Boat" cruise with music and dancing, and Sunday breakfast cruises. The season is early May through mid-October. The cruises are popular, so make reservations early (major charge cards accepted).

Amphi Tour Ltd. (tel. 514/386–1298) offers short tours of the harbor that leave every 45 minutes from the Vieux-Port.

Lachine Rapids Tours (tel. 514/284–9607) offers a jet boat trip through the Lachine rapids. In rainwear and a life jacket you roar down the river and crash through the serious rapids that stopped the first settlers' boats in the 16th century. The trip lasts 90 minutes. The specially designed jet boats leave from the same pier as the more staid cruises above.

Walking Tours The Greater Montreal Convention and Tourist Bureau Information Office at 1001 Dorchester Square and Place Jacques Cartier in Vieux-Montréal (Metro Champs de Mars) distributes a free 31-page booklet, "A Walking Tour of Old Montreal." It is an excellent guide to Montreal's oldest and most historic quarter.

Les Montrealistes, tel. 514/744–3009, organizes bus and walking tours daily during the summer.

Calèche Rides Open horse-drawn carriages—fleece-lined in winter—leave from Notre-Dame between rue Bonsecours and Gosford, Square Dorchester, Place des Armes and rue de la Commune. An hour-long ride is about $30 (tel. 514/844–1313 or 845–7995).

Exploring Montreal

by Andrew Coe

Andrew Coe has written for the San Francisco Examiner, *and other publications.*

Orientation

When exploring Montreal, there's very little to remind you that it's an island. It lies in the St. Lawrence River roughly equidistant (160 miles, 256 kilometers) from Lake Ontario and the point where the river widens into a bay. For its entire length, the St. Lawrence is flanked by flat, rich bottomland for 30

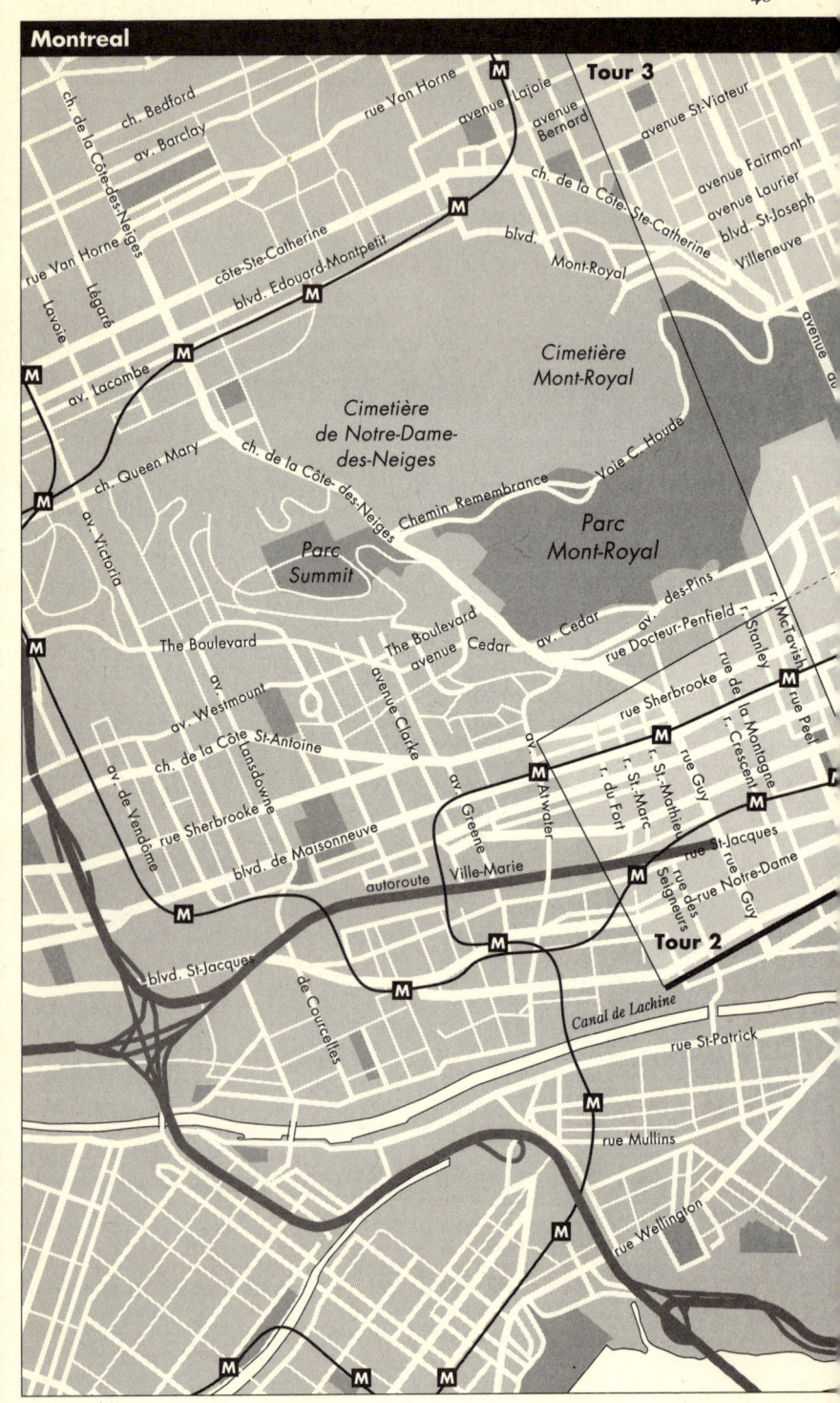

Montreal

48

49

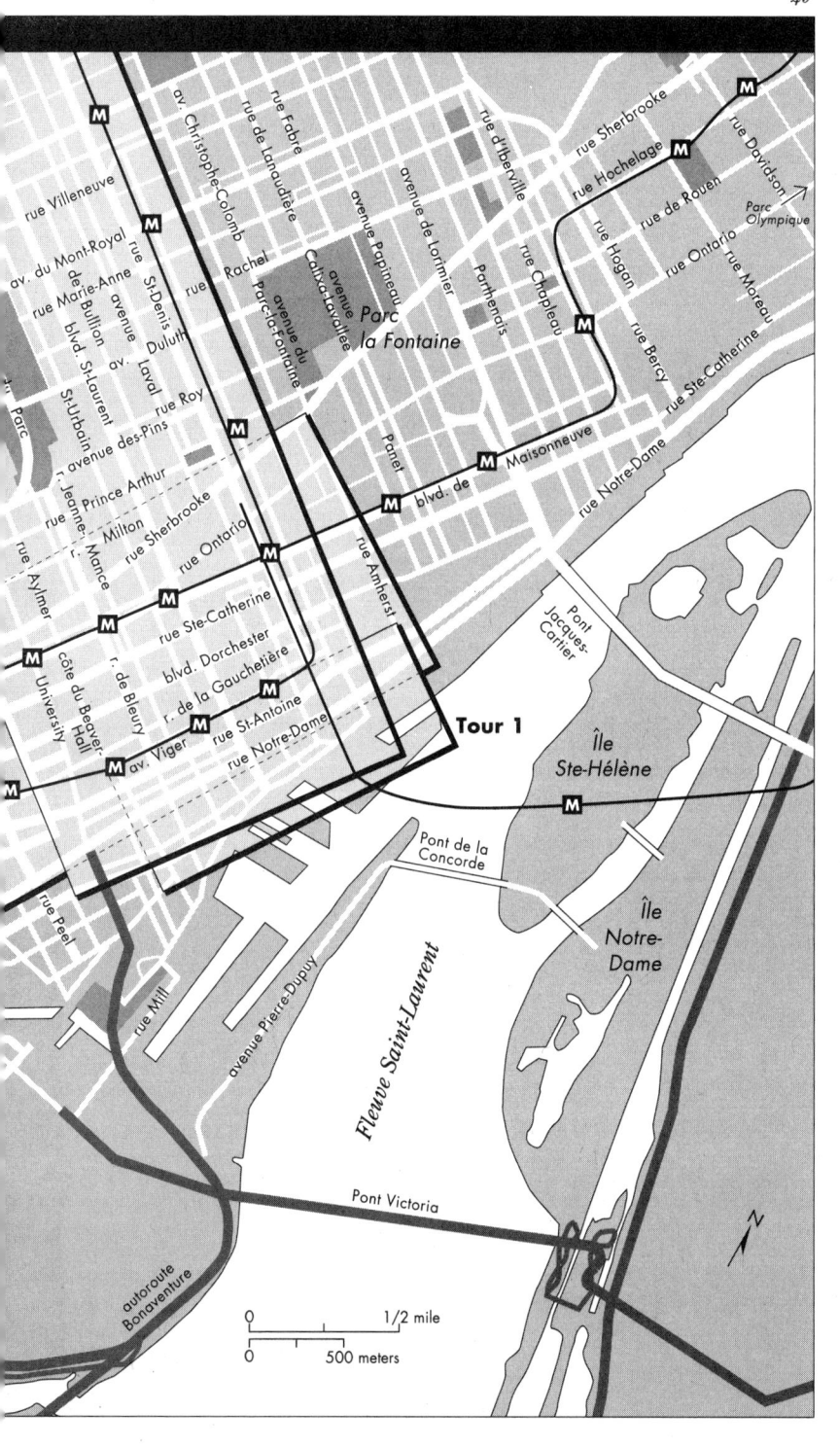

miles (48 kilometers) or more on either side. The only rise in the landscape is the 764-foot (233-meter) Mont Royal, which gave Montreal its name. The island itself is 32 miles (51 kilometers) long and 9 miles (14 kilometers) wide and is bounded on the north by the narrow des Prairies River and on the south by the St. Lawrence. Aside from Mont Royal, the island is relatively flat, and because the majority of attractions are clustered around this hill, most tourists don't visit the rest of the island.

Head to the Mont Royal Belvedere (lookout) for a panoramic view of the city. You can drive most of the way, park, and walk ¼ mile (½ kilometer) or hike all the way up from avenues Côte des Neiges or des Pins. If you look directly out—southeast—from the belvedere, at the foot of the hill will be the McGill University campus and, surrounding it, the skyscrapers of downtown Montreal. Just beyond, along the banks of the St. Lawrence, are the stone houses of Vieux-Montréal. Hugging the opposite banks are the Îles Ste-Hélène and Notre-Dame (St. Helen and Notre-Dame islands), sites of La Ronde amusement park and Man and His World exhibition center (former Expo '67 site), respectively. On a clear day you can see 40 miles (64 kilometers) or more past the river to the hills of l'Estrie (Eastern Townships) and even to Vermont's White Mountains across the U.S. border. If you look a few degrees to the right, or due south, you may be able to make out the foothills of the Adirondacks in New York State. Closest to the mount in this direction lies the predominantly Anglophone neighborhood of Westmount with its tree-lined avenues and large, elegant houses. To the left of the belvedere are St. Louis, Plateau Mont Royal, and Terrasse Ontario, three French-flavored quarters filled with row houses, restaurants, and shops. Beyond them rises the tilted white tower of the Olympic Stadium. On the back side of Mont Royal lies Outremont, another French district, traditionally the upscale French counterpart to English Westmount, as well as home to Quebec's premier, Robert Bourassa. It is also the site of much of the huge Université de Montréal (begun in 1928), designed by Art Deco architect Ernest Cormier.

The three areas of prime interest to tourists are Vieux-Montréal, downtown, and the French neighborhoods of St-Louis and Mont Royal. Naturally, Vieux-Montréal is of historic importance. It also possesses some fine French restaurants alongside tourist traps, and expensive shops next to souvenir stores. Downtown caters to those on the haute route who enjoy shopping in the most exclusive stores and dining in expensive restaurants. It harbors some of the city's best museums, as well as a few visit-worthy churches. St-Louis and Mont Royal exude a low-key charm and they are more residential than downtown or Vieux-Montréal. Many of the shops and restaurants may be expensive, but you can enjoy yourself even on a moderate budget. The street and nightlife attract a younger and more artistic crowd. There are some notable churches here, as everywhere in this city, but there are fewer edifices of historic interest. It's a place to soak in the ambience, people-watch, and relax.

There are a host of attractions that you can see on all-day and half-day trips. The most popular are the zoo, aquarium, and amusement park complex on Île Ste-Hélène and the Olympic Stadium and its neighbor, the Botanical Gardens. Often over-

Exploring Montreal 51

looked are the 500 forested acres (2 square kilometers) of Parc Mont Royal. Beyond the city limits are l'Estrie and the Laurentians for day trips or weekends in the country (*see* Chapter 4).

Montreal is easy to explore. Street signs, subways, and bus lines are clearly marked and the instructions usually given in both French and English. The city is divided by a grid of streets roughly aligned east-west and north-south. (This grid is tilted about 40 degrees off—to the left of—true north, so west is actually southwest and so on.) North-south street numbers begin at the St. Lawrence River and increase as you head north. East-west street numbers begin at boulevard St-Laurent, which divides Montreal into east and west halves. The city is not so large that seasoned walkers can't see all the districts around the base of Mont Royal on foot.

Tour 1: Vieux-Montréal (Old Montreal)

The St. Lawrence River was the highway on which the first settlers arrived in 1642. Just past the island of Montreal are the Lachine Rapids, a series of violent falls over which the French colonists' boats could not safely travel. It was natural for them to build their houses just above the rapids, at the site of an old Iroquois settlement on the bank of the river nearest Mont Royal. In the mid-17th century Montreal consisted of a handful of wooden houses clustered around a pair of stone buildings, the whole flimsily fortified by a wooden stockade. For the next three centuries this district—bounded by McGill and Berri streets on the east and west, rue St-Antoine on the north, and the river to the south—was the financial and political heart of the city. Government buildings, the largest church, the stock exchange, the main market, and the port were there. The narrow but relatively straight streets were cobblestoned and lined with solid, occasionally elegant houses, office buildings, and warehouses, also made of stone. Exiting the city meant using one of four gates through the thick stone wall that protected against Indians and marauding European powers. Montreal quickly grew past the bounds of its fortifications, however, and by World War II the center of the city had moved toward Mont Royal. The new heart of Montreal became Dominion Square (now Dorchester Square). For the next two decades Vieux-Montréal, as it became known, was gradually abandoned, the warehouses and offices emptied. In 1962 the city began studying ways to revitalize Vieux-Montréal, and a decade of renovations and restorations began.

Today Vieux-Montréal is a center of cultural life, if not of commerce and politics. Most of the summer activities revolve around Place Jacques Cartier, which becomes a pedestrian mall with street performers and outdoor cafés spilling out of restaurants. This lovely square is a good place to view the fireworks festival, and it's adjacent to the Vieux-Port exhibition grounds and the docks for the harbor cruises. Classical music concerts are staged all year long at the Notre-Dame Basilica, which possesses one of the finest organs in North America, and plays are staged in English by the Centaur Theatre in the old stock-exchange building. This district has six museums devoted to history, religion, decorative and fine arts, and its cobbled streets contain dozens of fine restaurants, most of them French or Québécois. Rue St-Paul has a load of fine shops, with an emphasis on furniture, antiques, and high quality crafts, as well as tacky souvenirs. In short, Vieux-Montréal has everything a visitor requires, except a place to rest your head (unless you count bed-and-breakfasts). The nearest hotel is Le Grand at 777 University, to the north.

Numbers in the margin correspond with points of interest on the Tour 1: Vieux-Montréal map.

To begin your tour of Vieux-Montréal, take the Metro to the Place d'Armes station, beneath the Palais des Congrès convention center, and walk 1½ blocks south on rue St-Urbain to **Place d'Armes.** En route you will pass **La Presse** building, the former headquarters of North America's largest French-language newspaper. In the 1600s, Place d'Armes was the site of battles with the Iroquois and later became the center of Montreal's "Upper Town." In the middle of the square is a statue of Paul de Chomedey, who was among the first settlers to Montreal. In 1644 he was wounded here in a battle with 200 Indians. Historians recently uncovered a network of tunnels beneath the square; they connected the various buildings, and one tunnel ran down to the river. These precursors of the Underground City protected the colonists from the extremes of winter weather and provided an escape route should the city be overrun. Unfortunately, the tunnels are too small and dangerous to visit. *Calèches* (horse-drawn carriages) are available at the south end of the square.

The north side of the square is dominated by the **Bank of Montreal,** an impressive building with Corinthian columns (remodeled by renowned architects McKim, Mead & White in 1905) that houses a small, interesting numismatics museum. *129 St-Jacques. Free. Open weekdays 10–4.*

The office building to the west of the square is the site of the old Café Dillon, a famous gourmet restaurant frequented by members of the fur traders' Beaver Club (*see* Dining, below). Two extremely important edifices form the south end of Place d'Armes: the Sulpician Seminary, the oldest building in Montreal, and the imposing Notre-Dame Basilica.

The first church called Notre-Dame was a bark-covered structure built within the fort in 1642, the year the first settlers arrived. Three times it was torn down and rebuilt, each time in a different spot, each time larger and more ornate. The enormous (3,800-seat) neo-Gothic **Notre-Dame Basilica,** which opened in 1829, is the most recent. The twin towers, named Temperance and Perseverance, are 227 feet (69 meters) high, and the western one holds one of North America's largest bells, the 12-ton Gros Bourdon. The interior of the church was designed in medieval style by Victor Bourgeau, with stained-glass windows, a stunning blue vaulted ceiling with gold stars, and pine and walnut wood carving in traditional Quebec style. The church has many unique features: It is rectangular rather than cruciform in shape; it faces south rather than east; the floor slopes down 4 feet (1¼ meters) from back to front; and it has twin rows of balconies on either side. The Casavants, a Quebec family, built the 5,722-pipe organ, one of the largest in the continent. Notre-Dame has particularly excellent acoustics and is often the site of Montreal Symphony concerts. Behind the main altar is the Sacre-Coeur Chapel, which was destroyed by fire in 1978 and rebuilt in five different styles. Also in the back of the church is a small museum of religious paintings and historical

Tour 1: Vieux Montreal

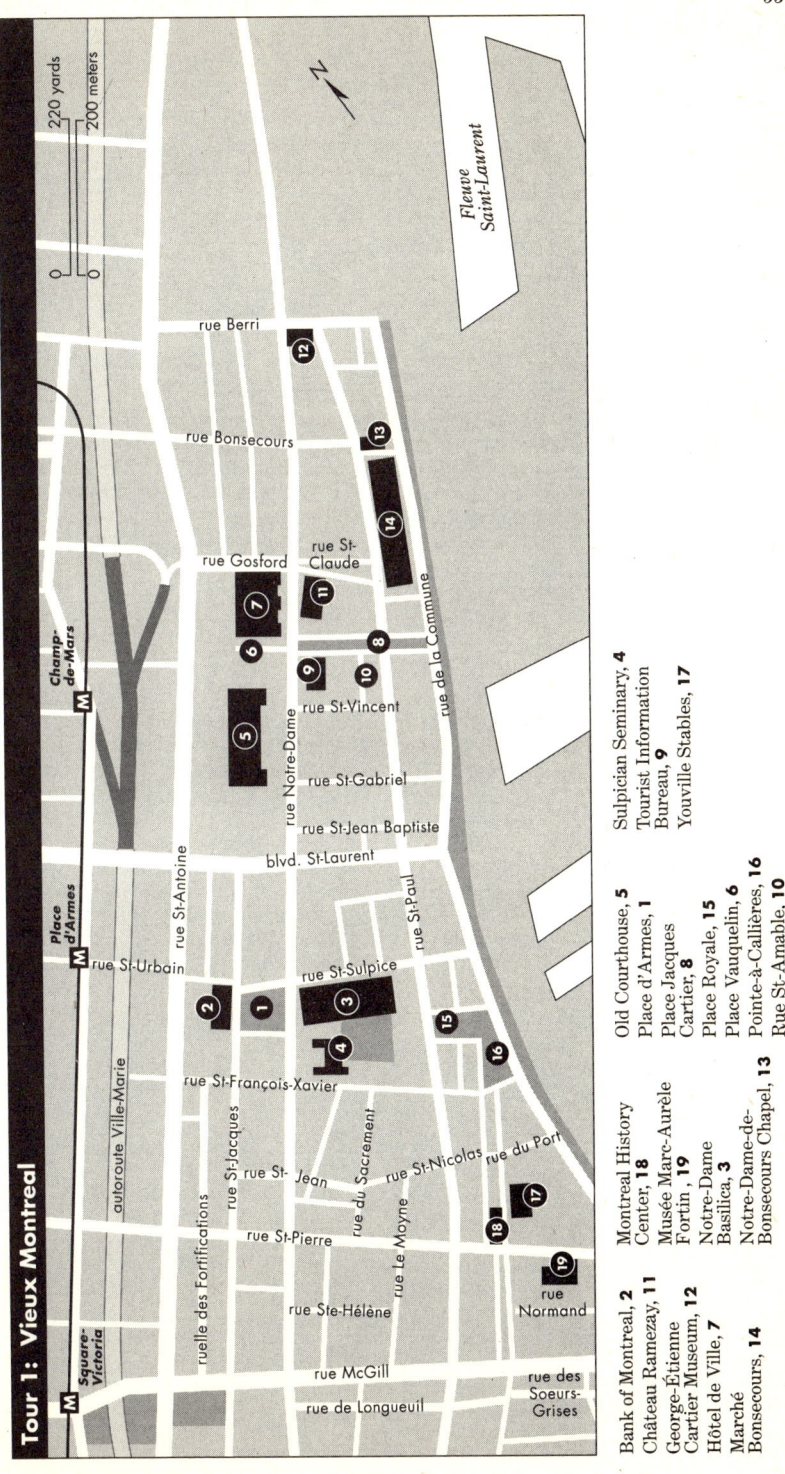

Bank of Montreal, **2**
Château Ramezay, **11**
George-Etienne Cartier Museum, **12**
Hôtel de Ville, **7**
Marché Bonsecours, **14**
Montreal History Center, **18**
Musée Marc-Aurèle Fortin, **19**
Notre-Dame Basilica, **3**
Notre-Dame-de-Bonsecours Chapel, **13**
Old Courthouse, **5**
Place d'Armes, **1**
Place Jacques Cartier, **8**
Place Royale, **15**
Place Vauquelin, **6**
Pointe-à-Callières, **16**
Rue St-Amable, **10**
Sulpician Seminary, **4**
Tourist Information Bureau, **9**
Youville Stables, **17**

objects. *116 Notre-Dame O. Basilica: tel. 514/849–1070. Open 9–5. Museum: tel. 514/842–2925. Admission: $1 adults, 50¢ children. Open 9:30–4 weekends.*

❹ The low, more retiring stone building behind a wall to the west of the basilica is the **Sulpician Seminary.** This is Montreal's oldest building, built in 1685, and is still a residence for Sulpician monks (unfortunately closed to the public). For almost two centuries until 1854, the Sulpicians were *the* political power in the city, because they owned the property rights to the island of Montreal. They were also instrumental in recruiting and equipping colonists for New France. The building itself is the finest, most elegant example of rustic 17th-century Quebec architecture. The clock on the roof over the main doorway is the oldest (pre-1701) public timepiece in North America. Behind the seminary building is a small garden, another Montreal first.

The street that runs alongside the basilica, **rue St-Sulpice,** was the first street in Montreal. On the eastern side of the street there's a plaque marking where the Hôtel-Dieu, the city's first hospital, was built in 1644. Now cross St-Sulpice—the Art Deco **Aldred Building** sits on the far left corner—and take Notre-Dame Est. One block farther, just past boulevard St-Laurent, on the left rises the black-glass-sheathed **Palais de Justice** (1971), which houses the higher courts for both the city and the province. (Quebec's legal system is based on the Napoleonic Code for civil cases and on British common law for criminal cases.)

❺ The large domed building at 155 Notre-Dame Est is the classic revival-style **Old Courthouse** (1857), now municipal offices. Across the street at 160 Notre-Dame Est is the **Maison de la Sauvegarde** (1811), one of the oldest houses in the city. The Old
❻ Courthouse abuts the small **Place Vauquelin,** named after the 18th-century naval hero who is memorialized by a statue in its center. North of this square is **Champs de Mars,** the former site of a colonial military parade ground but now a parking lot. The ornate building on the east side of Place Vauquelin is the Sec-
❼ ond Empire–style **Hôtel de Ville** (city hall, 1878). On July 24, 1967, French President Charles de Gaulle stood on the central balcony of the hotel and made his famous *"Vive le Québec libre"* speech.

❽ You are in a perfect spot to explore **Place Jacques Cartier,** the heart of Vieux-Montréal. This 2-block-long square opened in 1804 as a municipal market, and every summer it is transformed into a flower and crafts market. The 1809 monument at the top of the place celebrates Lord Nelson's victory at Trafalgar. At the western corner of Notre-Dame is a small building (1811), site of the old Silver Dollar Saloon, so named because there were 350 silver dollars nailed to the floor. Today it's the
❾ home of the **Montreal Tourist Information Bureau.** *(see* Important Addresses and Numbers, above). Both sides of the place are lined with two- and three-story stone buildings that were originally homes or hotels but live on today as restaurants.

Time Out Le St-Amable (188 rue St-Amable, tel. 514/866–3471) features a Businessmen's Lunch weekdays from noon to 3 PM, but you don't have to be an executive or even be dressed like one to sample such classics as fresh poached salmon or grilled New Zealand lamb chops.

Exploring Montreal 55

⑩ In the summer, the one block of **rue St-Amable** becomes a marketplace for local jewelers, artists, and craftspeople. From the bottom of Place Jacques Cartier you can stroll out into the **Port of Montreal Exhibition Ground,** where from Winter Carnival through summer there is always something going on. At the foot of boulevard St-Laurent and rue de la Commune are the port's major summertime exhibitions: **Images du Futur** and **Expotec.** Here you'll also find Montreal's new year-round **IMAX Super Cinema.**

Retrace your steps to the north end of Place Jacques Cartier, then continue east on Notre-Dame. At the corner of rue St-
⑪ Claude on the right is **Château Ramezay** (1705), built as the residence of the 11th governor of Montreal, Claude de Ramezay. In 1775–76 it was the headquarters for American troops seeking to conquer Canada. One of the most elegant colonial buildings still standing in Montreal, the château is now a museum, and it has been restored to the style of Governor de Ramezay's day. The ground floor is furnished like a gentleman's residence of New France, with dining room, bedroom, and office. The collection includes many period artifacts, furnishings, paintings, and costumes. The basement is devoted to displays on Indian and colonial rural life. *280 Notre-Dame E, tel. 514/861–3708. Admission: $2 adults, $1 senior citizens, 50¢ students and children under 16. Wheelchair visitors are advised to reserve 1 day in advance. Open Tues.–Sun. 10–4:30.*

At the end of Notre-Dame are two houses built by Sir George-Étienne Cartier, a 19th-century Canadian statesman. They re-
⑫ cently have been opened as the **George-Étienne Cartier Museum,** a showcase of decorative arts from colonial Quebec. Displays depict the daily life of Montreal's elite in that era. *458 Notre-Dame E, tel. 514/283–2282. Admission free. Open in summer, daily 9–5; rest of the year, Wed.–Sun. 10–5.*

One block back on Notre-Dame is rue Bonsecours, one of the oldest in the city. Turn left here, and on the left side near the end of the block you will come upon **Les Filles du Roy** (*see* Dining, below), an excellent Québécois eatery in an 18th-century house. The neighboring building, at the corner of Bonsecours and St-Paul, is the **Maison du Calvet** (1725). This fine colonial structure was the home of Pierre du Calvet, a printer and persecuted sympathizer with the American Revolution. It is now a gourmet food store. At the end of Bonsecours is the small but
⑬ beautiful **Notre-Dame-de-Bonsecours Chapel.** Marguerite de Bourgeoys, who was canonized in 1983, helped found Montreal and dedicated this chapel to the Virgin Mary in 1657. It became known as a sailor's church, and small wooden models of sailing ships are suspended from the ceiling just above the congregation. The chapel also contains a crude wooden statue of the Virgin that is said to hold a relic of St. Blaise. De Bourgeoys brought the statue from France to intensify the faith. The chapel was twice destroyed by fire and has been renovated a number of times, but the stained-glass windows, traditional wood carvings and murals give the chapel a special charm. In the basement there is a small, strange museum honoring the saint that includes a story of her life modeled by little dolls in a series of dioramas. A gift shop sells Marguerite de Bourgeoys souvenirs. From the museum you can climb to the rather precarious bell tower (beware of the metal steps in winter) for a fine view of Vieux-Montréal and the port. *400 St-Paul E, tel.*

514/845-9991. *Admission: $1 adults, 25¢ children. Chapel and museum open Tues.-Fri. 9-11:30 AM and 1-5 PM, weekends 9 AM-11:30 PM.*

Double back and head west on St-Paul. The long, large, domed building to the left is the **Marché Bonsecours** (1845), for many years Montreal's main produce, meat, and fish market. During part of the 19th century the upper floors of this neoclassic building were occupied by the city government—and even for a short time by the Canadian Parliament—while the basement was used as a market. Today the interior is not open to the public, because, like so many other fine buildings in Vieux-Montréal, it has been taken over by municipal offices.

Rue St-Paul is the most fashionable street in Vieux-Montréal. For almost 20 blocks it is lined with fine restaurants, shops, and even a few nightclubs. Québécois handicrafts are a specialty here, with shops at 88, 136, and 272 St-Paul Est. In the basement of the **Brasserie des Fortifications,** a French restaurant at 262 St-Paul Est, you can see remnants of the stone wall that once encircled Montreal. **L'Air du Temps,** at 191 St-Paul Ouest, is one of the city's top jazz clubs. Nightly shows usually feature local talent, with occasional international name bands. Take rue St-Paul eight short blocks west of Place Jacques Cartier, and you will come to **Place Royale,** the site of the first permanent settlement in Montreal. De Maisonneuve, the city's founder, shot and killed an Iroquois chief here and later built his house across the street where 151 St-Paul Ouest now stands. Place Royale was first used as a military parade ground and then became a public marketplace where, among other activities, criminals were pilloried, whipped, and hanged. Several famous duels were also fought here. The obelisk in the center of the square bears the names of the 53 founding colonists on its base. At the south end of the square stands the neoclassic **Old Customs House** (1837), currently government offices. If you turn right on the next street west on St-Paul, which is St-François-Xavier, you will see the **Old Stock Exchange** building (1903) at no. 453. The stock exchange occupied this fancy Beaux-Arts structure until 1965, when it moved to the new building on rue St-Antoine. It now houses the Centaur Theatre, Montreal's oldest English-language playhouse.

Return to Place Royale, and behind the Old Customs House you will find **Pointe-à-Callières,** a small park which commemorates the settlers' first landing. A small stream used to flow into the St. Lawrence here, and it was on the point of land between the two waters that the colonists landed their four boats at its mouth on May 17, 1642. After they built the stockade and the first buildings at this site, it was almost washed away the next Christmas by a flood. When it was spared, de Maisonneuve placed a cross on top of Mont Royal as thanks to God. A 1½-block walk down rue William takes you to the **Youville Stables** on the left. These low stone buildings enclosing a garden were originally built as warehouses in 1825 (they never were stables). A group of businessmen renovated them in 1968, and the buildings now house offices, shops, and restaurants. **Gibbys** is a French-style steak and seafood restaurant in the Youville Stables. For $7-$11 a person (dinners are $20 and up) you can get a hearty lunch in its comfortable, old-French dining rooms. The stable gardens are a pleasant place for relaxation after a hard day of sightseeing. The old fire station (1906), a mix of Dutch

Exploring Montreal 57

and English styles across rue William from the stables, has become the **Montreal History Center.** Visitors to this high-tech museum are led through a series of audiovisual environments depicting the life and history of Montreal. Small children and easily bored adults tend to fidget while enduring the rather cheesy displays. *335 Place d'Youville, tel. 514/845-4236. Admission: $2 adults, $1 senior citizens and children. Open daily 10-4:30, last show begins 3:30. Closed Mon.*

Half a block to the left on rue St-Pierre is the **Musée Marc-Aurèle Fortin.** This 19th-century impressionist Québécois painter produced intense, almost visionary, landscapes of the Quebec countryside reminiscent of Van Gogh. *118 St-Pierre, tel. 514/845-6108. Admission: $2 adults, 75¢ senior citizens and children. Open 11-5 Tues.-Sun. Closed Mon.*

We now are at the end of our tour of Vieux-Montréal. You can find the nearest Metro stop eight blocks north on McGill Street (a block west of the fire station). Or you can retrace your steps into Vieux-Montréal and visit one of the dozen shops, restaurants, and nightclubs.

Tour 2: Downtown

Downtown is a sprawling 30-by-8-block area bounded by Atwater Avenue and boulevard St-Laurent on the west and east, respectively, avenue des Pins on the north, and St-Antoine on the south. Three of the best museums are here, as well as fancy and cheap hotels, and hundreds of restaurants, bars, and shops catering to all tastes. It is also the financial center and the heart of the retail, fur, and fashion trades.

After 1700, Vieux-Montréal wasn't big enough for the rapidly expanding city. In 1701 the French administration signed a peace treaty with the Iroquois, and the colonists began to feel safe about building outside Montreal's fortifications. The city inched northward, toward Mont Royal, particularly after the English conquest in 1760. By the end of the 19th century, Ste-Catherine was the main commercial thoroughfare, and the city's elite built mansions on the slope of the mountain. The area west of downtown, settled primarily by the English, became known as Westmount. (The French equivalent, Outremont, is on the far side of Mont Royal.) At that time the intersection of Ste-Catherine and Peel was considered the absolute center of the city. Since 1960 city planners have made a concerted effort to move the focus eastward. With the opening of Place des Arts (1963) and the Complexe Desjardins (1976), the city center shifted in that direction. It hasn't landed on any one corner yet, although some Montrealers will tell you it's at the intersection of de Maisonneuve and University.

Another major development of the last 30 years is the inauguration of the **Underground City,** an enormous network of passages linking various shopping and office complexes. These have served to keep the retail trade in the downtown area, as well as to make shoppers and workers immune to the hardships of the Canadian winter. However, if you're not a fan of malls, which is, after all, what they are, the Underground City may hold no interest for you.

Numbers in the margin correspond with points of interest on the Tour 2: Downtown Montreal map.

Our tour of downtown—unless you are hale of limb you may not be able to do all of it in a day—begins at the McGill Metro station. The corner of University and de Maisonneuve has recently been the center of intensive development. Two huge office buildings, **2020 University** and **Galleries 2001,** with malls at street and basement levels, rise from the north side of the intersection. The southwest corner, indeed the entire block, is taken up by **Eaton,** one of the Big Three department stores in the city. Aside from many floors of mid-priced clothing and other merchandise, the real attraction of Eaton is the ninth-floor art deco dining room.

Time Out **Eaton le 9e** was modeled after the dining room of the luxury liner *Ile-de-France*, Mrs. Eaton's favorite cruise ship. Thirty-five-foot (11-meter) pink-and-gray marble columns hold up the ceiling, and the walls are decorated with two pre-Raphaelite murals on culinary themes. The patrons are usually shoppers, of course, dining on pasta, fish, and meat dishes. The service is practical and fast; the decor's the thing. *677 Ste-Catherine O, tel. 514/284-8421. AE, MC, V. Open Mon.–Wed. 11:30 AM–3 PM, Thurs. and Fri. 11:30 AM–3 PM and 5–7 PM, Sat. 11:30 AM–3 PM. Closed Sun.*

Eaton is connected to **Les Terrasses** shopping complex behind it via passageways; it is connected as well to the McGill Metro and La Baie store.

Across University from Eaton stands **Christ Church Cathedral** (1859), the main church of the Anglican Diocese of Montreal. In early 1988 this building was a sight. Plagued by years of high maintenance costs and declining membership, the church fathers leased their land and air rights to a consortium of developers for 99 years. All the land beneath and surrounding the cathedral was removed, and the structure was supported solely by a number of huge steel stilts. The glass 34-story office tower behind the cathedral, **La Maison des Cooperants,** and the Place de la Cathédrale retail complex beneath it, are the products of that agreement. During the entire excavation, the stone Gothic-style structure—built in the cruciform of a 14th-century English church—has not moved an inch, and services continue uninterrupted. Beside the cathedral, at Ste-Catherine Ouest and Philips Square, is **La Baie,** a branch of the nationwide chain founded in 1670 under the name Hudson Bay Company.

Below Ste-Catherine at the corner of University and Cathcart streets is the **Tourisme Québec Information Center,** which supplies brochures, maps, and advice on what to do throughout the province as well as in Montreal. *2 Place Ville Marie, Suite 70 (plaza level), tel. 514/873-2015. Open summer 8:30–7:30, 9–5 rest of the year.*

This entire block is **Place Ville Marie,** an office, retail, and mall complex that signaled a new era for Montreal when it opened in 1959. It was the first link in the huge chain of the Underground City, which meant that people could have access to all the services of the city without setting foot outside. It was also the first step Montreal took to claiming its place as an international city. The labyrinth that is the Underground City now includes six hotels, thousands of offices, 25 movie theaters, more than 1,000 boutiques, hundreds of restaurants, and almost 8 miles

Tour 2: Downtown Montreal

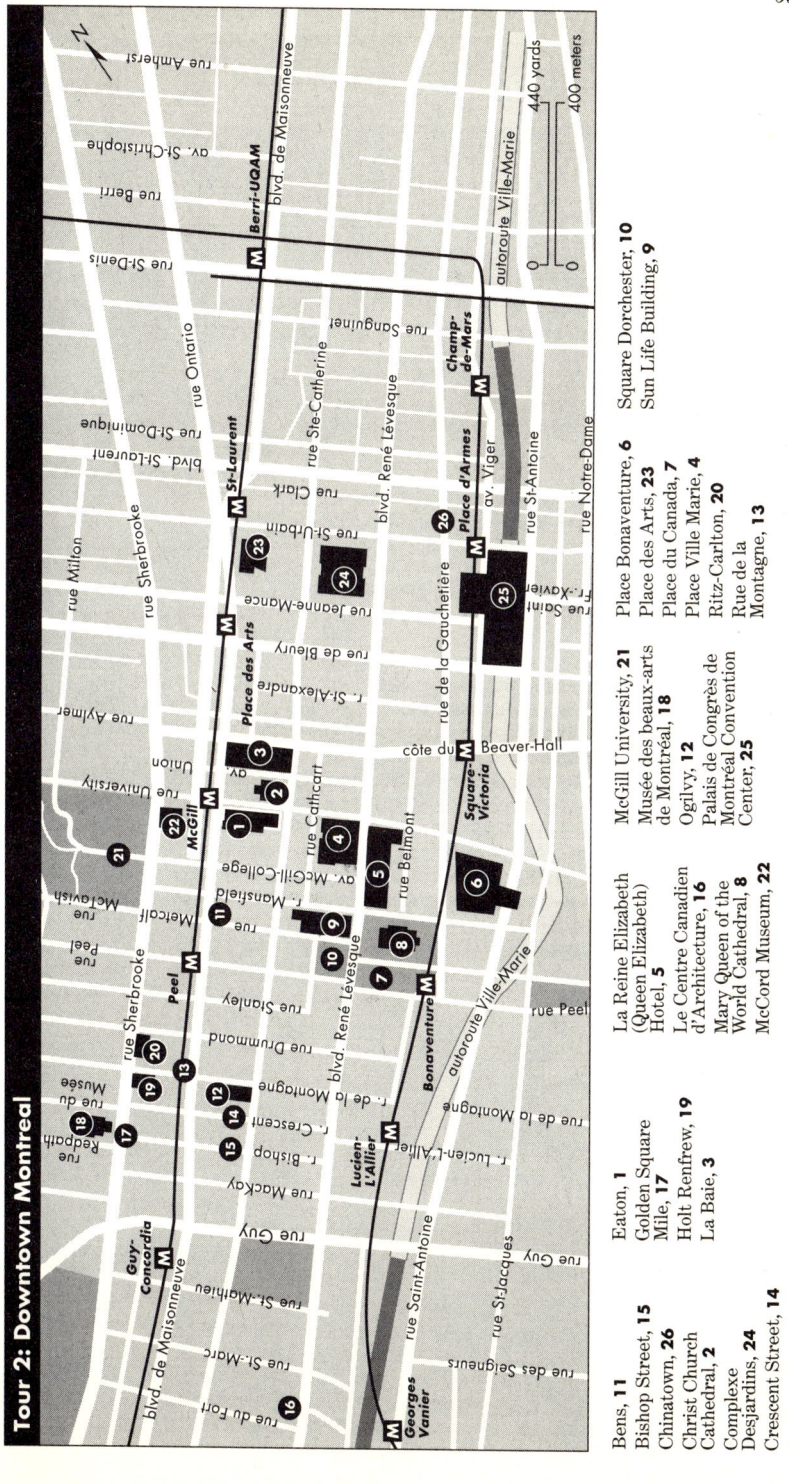

Bens, **11**
Bishop Street, **15**
Chinatown, **26**
Christ Church Cathedral, **2**
Complexe Desjardins, **24**
Crescent Street, **14**

Eaton, **1**
Golden Square Mile, **17**
Holt Renfrew, **19**
La Baie, **3**

La Reine Elizabeth (Queen Elizabeth) Hotel, **5**
Le Centre Canadien d'Architecture, **16**
Mary Queen of the World Cathedral, **8**
McCord Museum, **22**

McGill University, **21**
Musée des beaux-arts de Montréal, **18**
Ogilvy, **12**
Palais de Congrès de Montréal Convention Center, **25**

Place Bonaventure, **6**
Place des Arts, **23**
Place du Canada, **7**
Place Ville Marie, **4**
Ritz-Carlton, **20**
Rue de la Montagne, **13**

Square Dorchester, **10**
Sun Life Building, **9**

(13 kilometers) of passageways in its network. It should be noted that not everyone feels this has changed Montreal for the better. Some feel that an urban mall takes people out of the hustle and bustle of the street environment and places them in a sterile, essentially lifeless enclosure that lacks any sense of community. Nevertheless, 15,000 people work in the offices at Place Ville Marie, and an estimated 75,000 people pass through its subterranean corridors every working day. The public areas are popular for brown baggers and window-shoppers.

From Place Ville Marie head south via the passageways toward
❺ **La Reine Elizabeth (Queen Elizabeth) Hotel.** It's easy to lose your bearings and become "lost," since directions to the next malls are not always clearly marked. (Is its intent to keep you in its own shopping area?) The Queen Elizabeth, with more than 1,000 rooms, is by far the city's largest hotel (*see* Lodging, below). The Beaver Club (*see* Dining, below), named after the society of wealthy fur traders who used to meet at various gourmet restaurants, has a small museum devoted to it just off the lobby. Via the underground you can reach the **Gare Centrale (Central Railway Station)** just behind the hotel. Trains from the United States and the rest of Canada arrive here. Then follow the signs marked "Metro/Place Bonaventure" to **Place Bonaventure,** the largest commercial building in
❻ Canada. On the lower floors there are shops and restaurants, then come exposition halls and offices, and finally the whole thing is topped by the Bonaventure Hilton International (*see* Lodging, below) and 2½ acres (10,100 square meters) of gardens. From here take the route marked "Place du Canada," which will bring you to the mall in the base of the **Hôtel Château Champlain.** This building is known as the Cheesegrater because of its rows and rows of half-moon-shape windows (*see* Lodging, below). Our exploration of this leg of the Underground City will end at **Windsor Station** (follow the signs). This was the second railway station built in Montreal by the Canadian Pacific Railway Company. Windsor Station was designed in 1889 by George Price, a New York architect, with a massive rustic stone exterior holding up an amazing steel-and-glass roof over an arcade. Soldiers departed for both world wars here, and here, also, immigrants saw the city for the first time. The CPR planned to raze the station in the early '70s, but a citizens' protest saved it. Offices and snack bars now occupy the arcade.

It's time for a bit of fresh air now, so exit at the north end of Windsor Station and cross the street to the park known as
❼ **Place du Canada.** In the center of the park there is a statue to Sir John A. MacDonald, Canada's first Prime Minister. Then
❽ cross the park and rue de la Cathédrale to the **Mary Queen of the World Cathedral** (1894), which you enter on boulevard René Lévesque. This church is an exact, scale model of St. Peter's Basilica in Rome. Victor Bourgeau, the same architect who did the interior of Notre-Dame in Vieux-Montréal, thought the idea of the cathedral's design terrible but completed it after the original architect proved incompetent. Inside there is even a canopy over the altar that is a miniature copy of Bernini's *baldacchino* in St. Peter's. The massive gray granite edifice across
❾ boulevard René Lévesque from the cathedral is the **Sun Life Building** (1914), at one time the largest building in Canada. During World War II much of England's financial reserves and national treasures were stored in Sun Life's vaults. The park

Exploring Montreal 61

that faces the Sun Life building just north of René Lévesque is
⑩ **Dorchester Square,** for many years the heart of Montreal. Until 1870 a Catholic burial ground occupied this block (and there are still bodies buried beneath the grass), but with the rapid development of the area, the city fathers decided to turn it into a park. The statuary of Dorchester Square includes a monument to the Boer War in the center and a statue of the Scottish poet Robert Burns near Peel Street.

If you walk two blocks north on Metcalf Street, the eastern boundary of Dorchester Square, you will come to the world-
⑪ famous **Bens** (*see* Dining, below).

Facing Ben's on Metcalfe, the former Sheraton Mont Royal Hotel, now transformed into **Les Cours Mont-Royal,** has been beautifully restored and renovated. Dominating the block bordered by de Maisonneuve, Metcalf, Ste-Catherine, and Peel, this new luxury development features boutiques, restaurants, an atrium with live entertainment and mini exhibitions, an Egyptian-style cinema, and a thriving marketplace.

Just one block east of Ben's on Mansfield, **Place Montreal Trust** shopping complex has become an instant hit with Montrealers since it opened in May, 1988. It has 120 trendy boutiques and a glass-enclosed plaza on street level along the McGill College promenade that's an ideal lookout for people-watching.

A block north of Dorchester Square is Ste-Catherine, the main retail shopping street of Montreal. Three blocks west, at 1307
⑫ Ste-Catherine Ouest and rue de la Montagne, is **Ogilvy,** the last of the Big Three department stores. The store has been divided into individual name boutiques that sell generally pricier lines than La Baie or Eaton. Most days at noon a bagpiper plays
⑬ Scottish airs as he circumnavigates the ground floor. **Rue de la**
⑭ ⑮ **Montagne (Mountain),** and **Crescent** and **Bishop** streets, the two streets just west of it, form the heart of Montreal's downtown nightlife and restaurant scene. This area once formed the playing fields of the Montreal Lacrosse and Cricket Grounds, and later it became an exclusive suburb lined with millionaires' row houses. Since then these three streets between Sherbrooke and Ste-Catherine have become fertile ground for trendy bars, restaurants, and shops ensconced in those old row houses. The **Hôtel de la Montagne** at 1430 de la Montagne has a rather plain exterior, but inside it is lovingly overdecorated to something like a baroque disco. Its restaurant, La Lutetia, is known as one of the best nouvelle cuisine eateries in the city (*see* Dining, below). Crescent Street offers literally dozens of restaurants. Thursday's and the Winston Churchill Pub, at 1449 and 1459, respectively, are the mainstays of the Montreal bar scene.

While you're in the vicinity, take in one of downtown's newest
⑯ attractions, **Le Centre Canadien d'Architecture (Canadian Centre for Architecture),** just four blocks west at St-Marc on Baile. The lifelong dream of its founding director, Phyllis Lambert (of the Bronfman fortune), the CCA opened in May 1989 to great fanfare and is a source of civic pride. The premier museum in the world dedicated to architecture, it houses one of the world's most important and most extensive collections, available to architects and scholars for research. Its centerpiece is the magnificently restored Shaughnessy House mansion, saved from the wrecker's ball by Lambert's philanthropy in 1974.

Flanking it are the CCA's austerely modern, if classically influenced, new buildings designed by project architect Peter Rose under Lambert's direction. The new museum has exhibition halls, a bookstore, and auditorium open to the public. There are also regular tours of the museum and its grounds, which occupy the city block from Baile to boulevard Réne Lévesque Ouest and St-Marc to du Fort. *1920 Baile, tel. 514/939-7000. Admission: free to CCA members, ICOM-cardholders, children under 12, and general public Thurs. PM only; otherwise, $3 adults, $2 senior citizens and students. Group rates available. Advance reservation required.*

Now that you're in the mood for historic pursuits, backtrack to Ste-Catherine and Bishop. By walking two blocks north on Bishop Street to Sherbrooke Street, you enter a very different environment: the exclusive neighborhood known as the **Golden Square Mile.** In the 19th century this was the name of the area bounded by Guy and University streets on the east and west, on the north and south by avenue des Pins and what is now boulevard René Lévesque. The first wealthy inhabitants of this neighborhood were fur traders, who were followed by rail barons and other industrialists. At one time it was estimated that 70% of Canada's wealth was held by residents of the Golden Square Mile. As the commercial center edged northward after 1900, the rich moved away—either west or farther up the mountain—but the area still retains its glow of opulence.

Directly across the street from the end of Bishop Street is the **Musée des beaux-arts de Montréal (Montreal Museum of Fine Arts),** the oldest established museum in Canada. The present building was completed in 1912 and holds a large collection of European and North American fine and decorative art; ancient treasures from Europe, the Near East, Asia, Africa, and America; art from Quebec and Canada; and Indian and Eskimo artifacts. From June through October there is usually one world-class exhibition, such as the inventions of Leonardo da Vinci, or the works of Marc Chagall. In 1990, "Dutch Painters in the Italian Tradition" is showing. The Museum of Fine Arts is undergoing a massive expansion, which explains the construction on the south side of Sherbrooke between Crescent and Mackay, facing the original building. The museum has a gift shop, an art-book store, a boutique selling Inuit art, and a gallery in which you can buy or rent original paintings by local artists. *3400 ave. du Musée, tel. 514/285-1600. Admission: $6 adults, $2.50 students and senior citizens, $1 children under 12. Open Tues.–Sun. 10–7.*

Time Out The **Café du Musée** on the second floor sells a simple and inexpensive selection of soups ($1.35), quiches ($2.15), and sandwiches ($2.25–$2.95). Coffee, pastries, and the like are also available. *Dress: casual. No reservations or credit cards. Inexpensive. Open during museum hours.*

To the left of the museum is the **Church of St. Andrew and St. Paul** with Arts and Crafts Movement–style stained glass by Sir Edward Burne-Jones and William Morris. The **Erskine and American United Church** (1893), to the museum's right, is decorated with Tiffany stained-glass windows. Walking eastward on Sherbrooke brings you to the small and exclusive **Holt Renfrew** department store, perhaps the city's fanciest, at the corner of de la Montagne (*see* Shopping, below). One block far-

Exploring Montreal 63

(20) ther on, at Drummond Street, stands the **Ritz-Carlton,** the grande dame of Montreal hotels. It was built in 1912 so the local millionaires' European friends would have a suitable place to stay. Take a peek in the elegant Café de Paris restaurant. It's Montreal's biggest power dining spot, and you just might see the prime minister dining there. (For more on the Ritz-Carlton and its restaurants, see Lodging and Dining sections, below.) The Ritz-Carlton's only real competition in town is the modern and elegant **Hôtel Quatre Saisons (Four Seasons),** two blocks west at Sherbrooke and Peel. Just beyond this hotel on the other side of the street begins the grassy **McGill University** **(21)** campus. A wealthy Scottish fur trader, James McGill, bequeathed the money and the land for this institution, which opened in 1828, and is perhaps the finest English-language school of higher education in the nation. The student body numbers 15,000, and the university is best known for its medical and engineering schools. The campus is a fine place for a stroll, and during the school year you will see students and professorial types going about their rounds. The neighborhood east of the campus, the **McGill Ghetto,** was for years a haven for students living in rooming houses there, but lately professionals have been buying up the old buildings and renovating them.

The last stop on our tour of the Golden Square Mile is the **(22) McCord Museum,** on Sherbrooke between Victoria and University streets. Situated in the old granite McGill Union building (1907), the McCord houses Canada's finest ethnographic collection. David Ross McCord, the museum's founder, was an early collector of Canadian Indian and Eskimo artifacts, and his collection became the core of the museum. It includes an enormous totem pole from the Pacific Northwest, which towers in the main stairwell. The costume collection is one of the largest in Canada. Every year the museum presents 10 temporary exhibitions on subjects from old toys to primitive religious art. *The McCord is closed to the public until 1992, due to a major renovation and expansion. However, the museum will continue to present exhibitions at other sites in Montreal. Check with the tourist bureau or in the* Saturday Gazette *for whereabouts. 690 Sherbrooke O, tel. 514/398–7100.*

Turn right on University Street and walk a block to the McGill Metro station. Take the train one stop in the direction of Honoré-Beaugrand to the Place des Arts station.

Montreal's Metro opened in 1966 with well-designed stations—many decorated with works of art—and modern trains running on quiet pneumatic wheels. Today there are 65 stations on four lines with 40 miles (65 kilometers) of track. The 759 train cars carry more than 700,000 passengers a day. When you exit at **(23) Place des Arts,** follow the signs to the theater complex of the same name. From here you can walk the five blocks to Vieux-Montréal totally underground. Place de Arts, which opened in 1963, is reminiscent of New York's Lincoln Center in that it is a government-subsidized complex of three very modern theaters. The largest, Salle Wilfrid Pelletier, is the home of the Orchestre Symphonique de Montréal (Montreal Symphony Orchestra), which has won international raves under the baton of Charles Dutoit. The Orchestre Métropolitain de Montréal, Grands Ballets Canadiens and the Opéra du Québec also stage productions here. At the smaller Théâtre Maisonneuve you can see less grandiose dance and theater pieces, while the smallest theater, the Théâtre Port-Royal, is devoted exclusively to drama. Large pieces of '60s-style public art are scattered throughout the theaters and lobbies. If you want to attend a performance, there's a ticket booth near the Metro entrance on the underground level. A monthly guide to upcoming events is also available here.

㉔ While still in Place des Arts, follow the signs to the **Complexe Desjardins**. Built in 1976, this is another office building, hotel, and mall development along the lines of Place Ville Marie. The luxurious Meridien Hotel (*see* Lodging, below) rises from its northwest corner. The large galleria space is the scene of all types of performances, from lectures on Japanese massage techniques to pop music, as well as avid shopping in the dozens of stores. The next development south is the **Complexe Guy-Favreau**, a huge federal office building named after a Quebec politician. If you continue in a straight line, you will hit the ㉕ **Palais de Congrès de Montréal Convention Center** above the Place d'Armes Metro stop. But if you take a left out of Guy ㉖ Favreau onto rue de la Gauchetière, you will be in **Chinatown**, a relief after all that artificially enclosed retail space.

The Chinese first came to Montreal in large numbers after 1880 following the construction of the transcontinental railroad. They settled in an 18-block area between boulevard René Lévesque and avenue Viger to the north and south, and by Hôtel de Ville and Bleury streets on the east and west, an area that became known as Chinatown. At its peak around 1900, there were more than 6,000 Chinese here, but a series of racist anti-immigration laws soon led to a dwindling of the population. After World War II many Chinese moved to other parts of the city and became assimilated. The last blow to Chinatown was the 1978 construction of the Complexe Guy-Favreau, which demolished 20% of the buildings and cut the neighborhood in half. In the last three years, however, there has been a revitalization of Chinatown due to the money being pumped into the community by Hong Kong investors worried about their own city's fate. If few Chinese live here, they still come to the old neighborhood on the weekend, particularly on Sunday, to shop and eat in the restaurants. De la Gauchetière between St-Urbain and boulevard St-Laurent is Chinatown's main drag, and along it you will find many restaurants and food and gift shops. The shopping continues if you turn north on St-Laurent.

Tour 3: St-Denis, Prince Arthur, and North

After a long day of fulfilling your touristic obligations at the historical sites and museums of downtown and Vieux-Montréal, it's good to relax and indulge in some primal pleasures, such as eating, shopping, and nightlife. For these and other diversions, head to the neighborhoods east and north of downtown. Our tour begins in the Latin Quarter, the main student district, then wends its way north past some excellent restaurants, through a square that attracts many artists, over a pedestrian mall that is a center of night life, along a street of incredible ethnic diversity, then crosses one of the ritziest shopping streets and stops at what some consider the best bagel bakery in the world. Along the way you'll see how regular Montrealers of all ethnic backgrounds—French, English, Jewish, Portuguese—live in blocks of row houses decorated with two-story outdoor spiral staircases.

Exploring Montreal

The southern section of this area, around the base of rue St-Denis, was one of the city's first residential neighborhoods, built in the 19th century as the city burst the bounds of Vieux-Montréal. Then known as Faubourg St-Laurent, it was the home of many wealthy families. The lands to the north of present-day Sherbrooke Street were mostly farms and limestone quarries. In 1852 much of rue St-Denis was destroyed by a devastating fire. As the upper-class families moved north, the old mansions were subdivided and rented to the many students drawn to the area by the schools built there after 1900. The St-Louis and Plâteau Mont Royal neighborhoods attracted many middle-class families in the late 19th century. After World War II many of those same families moved out to the recently opened suburbs. All these neighborhoods emptied and the housing stock deteriorated. In the mid-'60s young people began to move back to the city and buy and renovate the old houses. Since then the area has been revitalized, and a decidedly youthful air prevails.

Numbers in the margin correspond with points of interest on the Tour 3: St-Denis, Prince Arthur, and North map.

Our tour begins at the **Berri-UQAM** Metro stop, perhaps the most important in the whole city, as three lines intersect here. This area, particularly along **rue St-Denis** on either side of boulevard de Maisonneuve, is known as the **Latin Quarter** and is the site of the **Université du Québec à Montréal** and a number of other educational institutions. St-Denis is lined with cafés, bistros, and restaurants that attract the academic crowd. On Ste-Catherine there are a number of low-rent nightclubs popular with avant-garde rock-and-roll types. Just west of St. Denis

❶ you find the **Cinémathèque Québécoise,** a museum and repertory movie house. For the price of one admission you can visit the permanent exhibition on the history of filmmaking equipment and see two movies. The museum also houses one of the largest cinematic reference libraries in the world. *335 de Maisonneuve O, tel. 514/842-9763. Admission free; movies $2. Library open weekdays 12:30–5; Museum and theater open Tues.–Sat. 6–9 PM, Sun. 2:30–4:30.*

Around the corner and half a block north on St-Denis stands the
❷ 2,500-seat **Théâtre St-Denis,** the second-largest auditorium in Montreal (after Salle Wilfrid Pelletier in Place des Arts). Sarah Bernhardt and numerous other famous actors have graced its stage. It currently is the main site for the summertime concerts of the Montreal International Jazz Festival. On the next block north you see the Beaux Arts **Bibliothèque nationale du Québec** (1915), a library that houses Quebec's official archives (1700 St-Denis; open Tues.–Sat. 9–5). If you have a lot of money and some hours set aside for dining, try **Les Mignardises** at 2035–37 St-Denis just south of Sherbrooke *(see* Dining, below*).*

Continue north on St-Denis past Sherbrooke. On the right, above the Sherbrooke Metro station, is the **Hôtel and Restaurant de l'Institut,** the hands-on training academy of the government *hôtelier* school *(see* Lodging, below*).* To the left is
❸ the small **Square St-Louis,** considered one of the most beautiful in Montreal, which gives its name to the neighborhood. Originally a reservoir, these blocks became a park in 1879 and attracted upper-middle-class families and artists to the area. French-Canadian poets were among the most famous creative people to occupy the houses back then, and the neighborhood is

Tour 3: St-Denis, Prince Arthur, and North

Cinémathèque Québecoise, **1**
Duluth, **6**
Fairmount Avenue, **8**
Moe Willensky's Light Lunch, **9**
Parc Jeanne-Mance, **7**
Prince Arthur, **4**
Schwartz's Delicatessen, **5**
Square St-Louis, **3**
Théâtre St-Denis, **2**

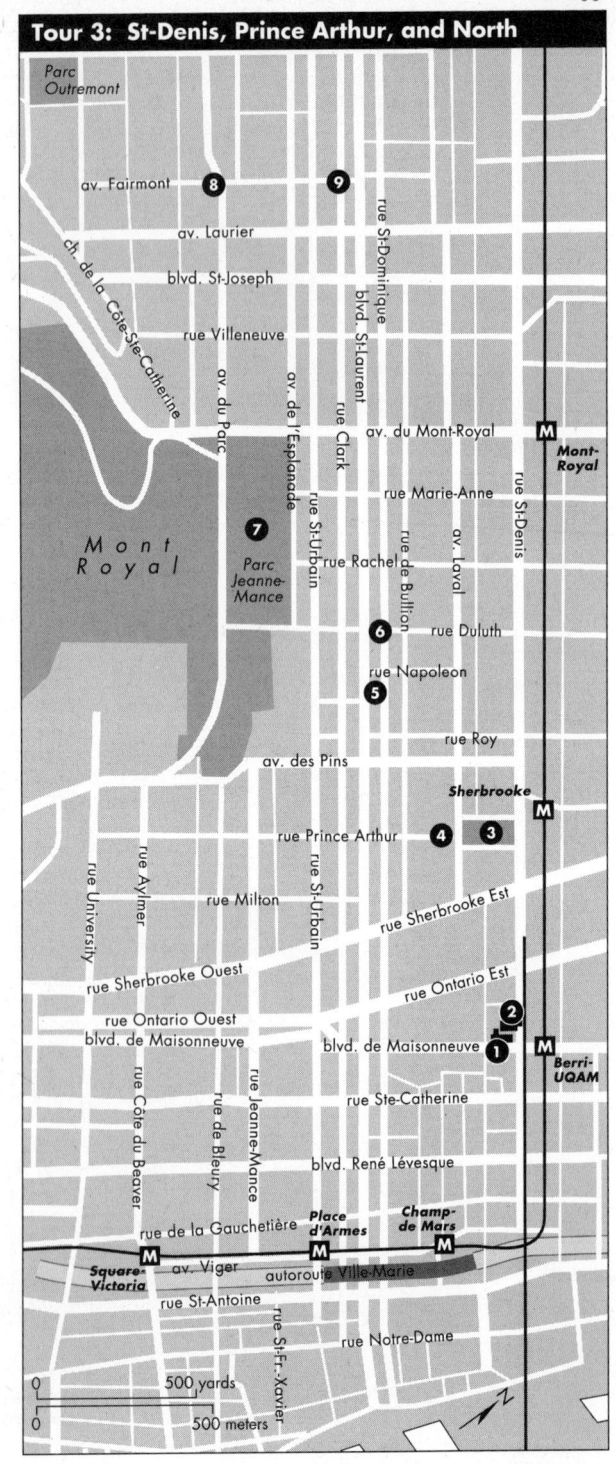

the home today for Montreal painters, filmmakers, musicians, and writers. On the wall of 336 Square St-Louis you can see—and read, if your French is good—a long poem by Michel Bujold. Many of the houses around the park are works of art themselves; take a look at the castle roof of 357 Square St-Louis. During the winter the paths are flooded to make a skating rink, and during the summer it forms the eastern extremity of the Prince Arthur street show.

❹ **Prince Arthur** begins at the western end of Square St-Louis. In the '60s the young people moving to the neighborhood transformed the next few blocks into a small hippie bazaar of clothing, leather, and smoke shops. It remains a center of youth culture, although it's much tamer and more commercial. In 1981 the city turned the blocks between avenue Laval and St-Laurent into a pedestrian mall. Hippie shops live on today as inexpensive Greek, Vietnamese, Italian, Polish, and Chinese restaurants and *boîtes* of the singles-bar variety. Every summer dozens of performers—jugglers, escape artists, musicians, mimes—take to the streets, and the restaurants' open terraces overlook the show. On warm weekend nights the action can go on until daybreak. Most of the eateries are BYOB, but there are grocery stores as well as state liquor stores selling alcohol in the area. If you gaze up the cross streets, particularly avenue Coloniale, you should see brightly painted houses; this is a tradition of the many recent Portuguese immigrants who live in St-Louis.

When you reach **boulevard St-Laurent,** take a right and stroll north on the street that cuts through Montreal life in a number of ways. First, this is the east–west dividing street; like the Greenwich meridian, St-Laurent is where all the numbers begin. The street is also lined with shops and restaurants that represent the incredible ethnic diversity of Montreal. Until the late 19th century this was a neighborhood first of farms and then of middle-class Anglophone residences. It was on St-Laurent in 1892 that the first electric tramway was installed that could climb the slope to Plâteau Mont Royal. Working-class families, who couldn't afford a horse and buggy to pull them up the hill, began to move in. In the 1880s the first of many waves of Russian-Jewish immigrants escaping the pogroms arrived and settled here. St-Laurent became known as The Main, as in "main street," and Yiddish was the primary language spoken along some stretches. The Russian Jews were followed by Greeks, Eastern Europeans, Portuguese, and, most recently, Latin Americans. The next seven blocks or so are filled with delis, junk stores, restaurants, luncheonettes, and clothing stores as well as fashionable boutiques, bistros, cafés, bars, nightclubs, bookstores, and galleries exhibiting the work of the latest wave of "immigrants" to the area—gentrifiers and artists. The block between Roy and Napoleon is particularly rich in delights. Just east at 74 Roy is **Waldman's Fish Market,** reputed to be the largest wholesale/retail fish market in North America. **Warshaw's Supermarket** at 3863 St-Laurent is a huge Eastern European–style emporium that sells all sorts of delicacies.

❺ A few doors up the street from Warshaw's is **Schwartz's Delicatessen.** Among the many contenders for the smoked-meat king title in Montreal, Schwartz's is most frequently at the top. Smoked meat is just about all it serves, but the meat comes in lean, medium, or fatty cuts and only costs $3 a sandwich. The waiters give you your food and take your money, and that's that (*see* Dining, below).

A block north is **Moishe's Steakhouse** (*see* Dining, below), home of the best, but priciest, steaks in Montreal as well as the noisiest atmosphere. The next corner is **Duluth**, where merchants are seeking to re-create Prince Arthur Street. If you take a walk to the right all the way to St-Denis, you will find Greek and Vietnamese restaurants and boutiques and art galleries on either side of the street. A left turn on Duluth and a three-block walk brings you to **Parc Jeanne-Mance**, a flat, open field that's a perfect spot for a picnic of delicacies purchased on The Main. The park segues into the 494 wooded, hilly acres (2 square kilometers) of **Parc Mont Royal**.

Avenue du Parc forms the western border of Parc Jeanne-Mance. To get there either cut through the park or take a left on avenue du Mont Royal at the north end. No. 93 Mont Royal Ouest is the home of **Beauty's**, a kosher restaurant specializing in bagels, lox, and omelets, i.e., breakfast. Expect a line weekend mornings. Turn right and head north on avenue du Parc to see houses with two- or three-story outdoor staircases, sometimes elaborate spirals. Developers built these houses with the staircases outdoors to save interior space during the building boom time earlier in the century. During the winter it's cold and dangerous climbing up and down those stairs, as you can imagine, and today it's a violation of the building code to construct such vertigo-inducing steps. It's a five-block walk to **avenue Laurier**. All along Laurier, from Côte Ste-Catherine to St-Laurent, are some of the fanciest fur stores, boutiques, pastry shops, and jewelers in the city. For a quick chocolate eclair bracer or two, go to **Lenôtre Paris**, at 1050 Laurier, a branch of the Parisian shop of the same name.

Time Out **La Petite Ardoise** is a casual, slightly arty café that serves soups, quiches, sandwiches, and more-expensive daily specials. The onion soup is lovingly overdosed with cheese, bread, and onions. Whether it's breakfast, lunch, or dinner, the best accompaniment for your meal is a big, steamy bowl of creamy café au lait. This café is a perfect place to take a breather from shopping. *222 Laurier O, tel. 514/495-4961. AE, DC, MC, V. Open 8 AM-midnight, later on weekends.*

The next three blocks of avenue du Parc form the heart of the Greek district. Try **Symposium** at No. 5334 or the neighboring **Milos** at 5357 Parc (*see* Dining, below) for some of the best Greek appetizers, grilled seafood, and atmosphere you'll find in this hemisphere.

Fairmount Avenue, a block north of Laurier, is the site of two small but internationally known culinary landmarks. The **Fairmount Bagel Factory** at 74 Fairmount Avenue West claims to make the best bagels in the world. This is no small boast, and some people, particularly New Yorkers, are quick to dispute it. The Shlafman family has been making bagels in this storefront since 1950 (and in Montreal since 1929). They boil the uncooked bagels in honey-sweetened water and then place them on long wooden planks and slide them into the roaring wood-fired oven. The result is a smaller, slightly cakier bagel than a classic New York bagel. The Shlafmans make all varieties of bagel, but the

Exploring Montreal 69

most popular are those smothered in sesame or poppy seeds. The Fairmount Bagel Factory is always open.

Half a block east, on the corner of Fairmount and Clark streets, stands the famous **Moe Willensky's Light Lunch** (*see* Dining, below). Moviegoers will recognize this Montreal institution from *The Apprenticeship of Duddy Kravitz*, based on the Mordecai Richler novel of the same name. Lunch is all that's served here, and it certainly is light on the wallet. A couple of dollars will get you a hot dog or a bologna, salami, and mustard pretzel roll sandwich and a strawberry soda. Books are available for entertainment. The atmosphere is free.

From here you're on your own. You have a lot of possibilities. You can walk to rue St-Viateur, the next street north, which is the center of the Hasidic Jewish neighborhood. The **Bagel Shop** at No. 263 also claims to make the best bagels in the world. Or you can walk one block east to St-Laurent. Young fashion designers and artists have cleaned up these blocks, which used to be the kosher meat district, and turned them into a chic and arty neighborhood. In both directions you can find avant-garde boutiques, hairdressers, and some excellent bars, cafés, and restaurants, like **Prego** (*see* Dining, below) or the 24-hour "Parisian drugstore" **Lux**, at 5229 St-Laurent. This extraordinary bar-restaurant-tobacconist-newsstand attracts Montrealers of all ages and all classes (from the jet set to the working class) at all times of the day or night. It's a perfect people-watching place for visitors intent on sampling *le vrai Montréal*. Or you can return to the Metro by walking eight blocks east on avenue Laurier (a block south) to the Laurier station.

Parks and Gardens

Of Montreal's three major parks, **Lafontaine** is the smallest (the other two are Parc Mont Royal and Île Ste-Hélène). Parc Lafontaine, founded in 1867, is divided into eastern and western halves. The eastern half is French style; the paths, gardens, and lawns are laid out in rigid geometric shapes. There are two public swimming pools on the north end along rue Rachel. In the winter the park is open for ice-skating. The western half is designed on the English system, in which the meandering paths and irregularly shaped ponds follow the natural contours of the topography. Rowboats can be rented for a paddle around one of two man-made lakes. Its bandshell is the site of many free outdoor summertime concerts and performances by dance and theater groups. The park also possesses the world's only statue of Tintin, the immensely popular French comic-book character. Take the Metro to the Sherbrooke station and walk five blocks east along rue Cherrier. *4000 Calixa-Lavallée, tel. 514/872-6211. Open mid-May–end of Sept., 10 AM–sunset.*

Numbers in the margin correspond with points of interest on the Olympic Park and Botanical Garden map.

The giant, mollusk-shape **Olympic Stadium** and the tilted tower that supports the roof are probably the preeminent symbols of modern Montreal. Planning for the Olympic Stadium complex began in 1972, and construction in the old Parc Maisonneuve started soon afterward. The Olympics took place in 1976, but the construction still isn't finished. Montreal authorities are nevertheless proud of what they have so far. The Olympic Park

① ② includes the 70,000-seat **Olympic Stadium,** the **Tilted Tower,** six
③ swimming pools, the **Maurice Richard Arena,** and the Olympic Village. You can tour the entire complex twice a day (at 12:30 and 3:30 PM) during the off-season, more often from June to August (tel. 514/252–4737). Anyone who delights in superlatives will not be disappointed. The guides will astound you with all the facts and figures that have been collected about the complex. During baseball season, you can see the Expos (baseball) or Alouettes (Canadian Football League). Perhaps the most popular visitor activity is a ride up to the Tilted Tower's observatory on the Funicular, the exterior cable car. The two-level cable car holds 90 people and takes two minutes to climb the 890 feet (270 meters) up to the observatory, from which you can see up to 50 miles (80 ki-
④ lometers) on clear days. The **Velodrome** will not be in operation again until 1991. If you've brought your swimsuit and towels,
⑤ take a dip at the **Aquatic Center** (tel. 514/252–4737 for hours). There is also a cafeteria and a souvenir shop on the grounds. You can reach the **Olympic Park** via the Pie IX or Viau Metro stations (the latter is nearer the stadium entrance).

For a back-to-nature experience after all this technology, cross Sherbrooke to the north of the Olympic Park to reach the
⑥ **Botanical Garden** (closest Metro stop is Pie IX). Founded in 1931, this garden is said to be one of the largest in the world. During the summer you can visit the 200 acres (809,000 square meters) of outdoor gardens—a favorite is the poisonous plants garden; the 10 greenhouses are open year-round. There are more than 26,000 species of plants here, including bonsai in the
⑦ **Japanese Garden,** as well as notable collections of orchids, begonias, and African violets. Montrealers are houseplant mad, as you can imagine with all those months of cold, so the Botanical Garden occupies a special place in the city dwellers' psyches.
⑧ The **Insectarium,** a bug-shape building, will house more than 130,000 insect specimens collected by Montreal entomologist Georges Brossard. *4101 Sherbrooke E., tel. 514/872–1400. Greenhouse admission: $3 adults, $1.50 senior citizens, handicapped, and children 5–7. Gardens open sunrise–sunset, greenhouses 9–6.*

Île Ste-Hélène, opposite Vieux-Montréal in the middle of the St. Lawrence River, draws big crowds, particularly during the warm months. You can reach it via either the Victoria or Jacques Cartier bridges, via the Metro to the Île Ste-Hélène station, or by city bus (summer only) from downtown. It's a wooded, rolling park perfect for picnicking in the summer and cross-country skiing and ice-skating during the snow season. Originally this park was only one small island, but in the early '60s all the soil excavated during the construction of the Metro was dumped here, and it doubled in size and gained a neighbor, Île Notre-Dame. Next to the Metro stop there is a large free public pool, open in summer only (tel. 514/872–6211).

A walk along the south side of the island leads to **Château Hélène de Champlain,** a large brick mansion, now a restaurant, named after the wife of the French explorer. During Expo '67, Mayor Jean Drapeau received visiting royalty here. If you continue under the Jacques Cartier Bridge—a long, cold walk in winter—you will reach **La Ronde Amusement Park,** built on the landfill from the Metro dig. La Ronde was created as part of the Expo '67 celebration. This world-class amusement park boasts a huge new roller coaster (the second highest in the world), wa-

Aquatic Center, **5**
Botanical Garden, **6**
Insectarium, **8**
Japanese Garden, **7**
Maurice Richard Arena, **3**
Olympic Stadium, **1**
Tilted Tower, **2**
Velodrome, **4**

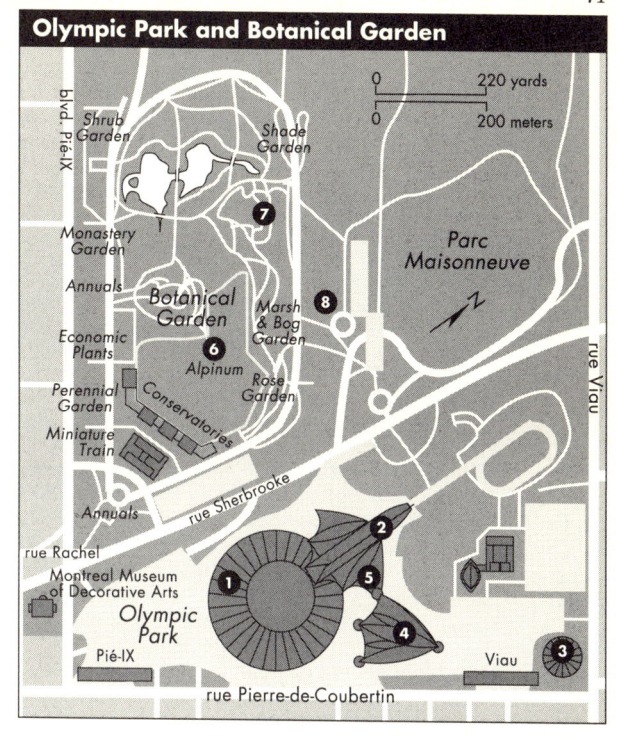

Olympic Park and Botanical Garden

ter slides with incredible drops, an international circus, Ferris wheels, boat rides, and rides, rides, rides. To mix a little education with your sightseeing, visit the reconstructed Quebec village and Fort Edmonton on the grounds. There are also haunted houses, musical cabarets, Wild West shows, restaurants, snack bars, and the obligatory monorail and cable-car rides. *Île Ste-Hélène, tel. 514/872-6222 or 800/361-7178. Admission: $15 adults, $9 children (includes all rides and entertainment), family and special Wed. rates available. Open weekends in May and early June and daily mid-June–Labor Day, Sun.–Thurs. 11 AM–midnight, Fri.–Sat. 11 AM–1 AM.*

Admission to La Ronde allows access to the neighboring **Aquarium de Montréal.** Anyone who enjoys seeing marine life should stop in. The penguin tank is billed as the highlight, but there are also fascinating exhibits of tropical fish and local freshwater environments (see what you're having for dinner). Children (and adults who like a few chills) will enjoy looking at the poisonous lionfish, the sharks, the enormous and grotesque South American red-tailed catfish, and the 10-foot-long (3 meters) armored sturgeon. The seals perform a circus show in the summer. During the summer a bus ferries visitors from the La Ronde entrance to downtown. *Tel. 514/872-4656. Admission: $2.50 adults, $1.25 children 5–17. Open daily 10–8 in summer, to 5 PM off-season.*

A stroll back along the north side of the island brings you to the **Old Fort** just under the Jacques Cartier Bridge. This former British arsenal has been turned into the **David M. Stewart Museum** (a museum of military history named after a historian)

Montreal

and a dinner theater called **Le Festin du Gouverneur.** The latter is a re-creation of an 18th-century banquet complete with balladeers and comedy skits. In the military museum are displays of old firearms, maps, scientific instruments, uniforms, and documents of colonial times. During the summer the parade ground is the scene of mock battles—cannons and all—by the Compagnie Franche de la Marine and bagpipe concerts by the 78th Fraser Highlanders. *Tel. 514/861-6701. Admission: $3 adults, $2 senior citizens, students, and children. Open daily 10–5, off-season closed Mon.*

From the fort you can climb the small hill at the center of the island to the **Watchtower,** from which you get a good view of the city and the St. Lawrence Seaway in the other direction. Just past the Metro station where this tour began are two small bridges to **Île Notre-Dame.** This was the site of the Olympic rowing races and most of Expo '67. The Expo pavilions still stand and are collectively called **Man and His World.** Each summer they are the site of major exhibitions. The French pavilion is now the Palais de la Civilisation, where the largest shows, like past years' Chinese and Egyptian exhibits, have been held. The enormous geodesic dome designed by Buckminster Fuller, which was the U.S. pavilion, is slated to become a science and technology museum (open during summer, daily 10–10). In mid-June, Île Notre-Dame is the site of the Molson Grand Prix du Canada, a top Formula I international circuit auto race at the Gilles Villeneuve Race Track that inspires all quiet-loving residents within earshot to take their vacations.

The **Parc Mont Royal,** the finest in the city, is easy to overlook. These 494 acres (2 square kilometers) of forest and paths at the heart of the city were designed by Frederick Law Olmstead, the celebrated architect of New York's Central Park. He believed that communion with nature could cure body and soul. The park is designed following the natural topography and accentuating its features, as in the English mode. You can go skating on Beaver Lake in the winter, visit one of the three lookouts and scan the horizon, or study the park interpretation center in the chalet at the Mont Royal belvedere. Horse-drawn transport is popular year-round: sleigh rides in winter, and calèche rides in summer. On the eastern side of the hill stands the 100-foot (30-meter) steel cross that is the symbol of the city. It stands on the site where de Maisonneuve placed his famous wooden cross following the settlers' first winter. Just beyond the park on the far slopes lie two huge cemeteries in which many famous Montrealers are buried. Pedestrians can climb the hill on paths beginning at the top of Peel Street and at the corner of avenue du Parc and rue Rachel. Cars can climb most of the way up on roads off either Chemin de la Côte-desNeige or avenue du Mont Royal, but then you must park and finish the journey on foot.

Churches, Temples, Mosques

St. Joseph's Oratory, on the northwest side of Mont Royal, is a Catholic shrine on a par with Lourdes or Fatima. Take the blue Metro line to the Côte des Neiges station, then walk three blocks uphill on the Chemin de la Côte-des-Neiges. You can't miss the enormous church up on the hillside. Brother André, a monk in the Society of the Brothers of the Holy Cross, constructed a small chapel to St. Joseph, Canada's patron saint, in

1904. Brother André was credited with a number of miracles and was beatified in 1982. His chapel became a pilgrimage site, the only one to St. Joseph in the world (St. Joseph is the patron saint of healing). Inspired by the miracles and Brother André's simple, devout life, believers began sending in offerings for a shrine. The construction of the enormous basilica began in 1924 and took 31 years. The dome is among the world's largest, and while the interior is of little aesthetic interest—it resembles a blimp hangar—there is a small museum dedicated to Brother André's life, and many displays, including thousands of crutches discarded by the formerly crippled faithful. Carillon, choral, and organ concerts are held weekly at the oratory during the summer, and you can still visit Brother André's original chapel and tomb at the side of the massive basilica. *3800 Queen Mary Rd., tel. 514/733-8211. Open daily summer, 7 AM; fall and spring, 8 AM-8:30 PM; winter, 8-5.*

Montreal for Free

The Saidye Bronfman Centre "hands-on" fine arts school's open-house activities, gallery exhibitions, and public affairs lectures (*see* Off the Beaten Track, below).

Musée d'art contemporain (*see* Off the Beaten Track, below).

Classical and pop concerts, dance performances, and theater at **Parc de la Fontaine,** rue Rachel.

Picnic in **Parc Mont Royal,** swim in its Beaver Lake during the summer, and skate on it during the winter (*see* Parks and Gardens, above).

Bicycle along Montreal's waterfront to the Lachine Canal, atop its mountain, or through the Vieux-Port (*see* Participant Sports, below).

Le Centre Canadien d'Architecture, Thursday evenings (*see* Tour 2, above).

What to See and Do with Children

La Ronde's Amusement Park (*see* Parks and Gardens, above).

Images du Futur offers futuristic, interactive exhibitions. *Vieux-Port at blvd. St. Laurent and rue de la Commune, tel. 514/849-1612. May 31-Sept. 24 daily, noon-11 PM.*

Imax Super Cinema offers films on a seven-story-tall screen. *Vieux-Port, Shed no. 7, tel. 514/496-IMAX for information, 514/522-1245 for tickets.*

Expotec. Zoom up the Olympic Stadium's "tallest-inclined-tower-in-the-world," Tilted Tower, by its Funicular cable car for a stunning view of Montreal island and beyond. *June 8-Oct. 1, 10-10.*

The Botanical Garden's **Insectarium** (*see* Parks and Gardens, above).

Montreal's **Aquarium** on Île Ste-Hélène and its **Dow Planetarium** just west of Vieux-Montréal (*see* Parks and Gardens, above).

At the Old Fort on Île Ste-Hélène, now the site of the David M. Stewart Museum, mock battles, military-history exhibitions and bagpipe concerts take place all summer long (*see* Parks and Gardens, above).

The **Midget Palace** (*see* Off the Beaten Track, below).

Off the Beaten Track

Just two blocks west of Victoria and the Metro Côte Ste-Catherine station is the **Saidye Bronfman Centre.** This multi-disciplinary institution has long been recognized as a focus of cultural activity with the Jewish community in particular and with Montreal as a whole. The center was a gift from the children of Saidye Bronfman in honor of their mother's lifelong commitment to the arts. In fact, the Mies van der Rohe-inspired building was originally designed by Mrs. Bronfman's daughter, Montreal architect Phyllis Lambert. Accessible by car, just one block east of the Decarie Expressway and about four blocks north of Queen Mary Road, the center is well worth the trip.

Open year-round, many of its activities, such as gallery exhibits, lectures on public and Jewish affairs, performances, and concerts, are offered free to the public. The center is home to the Yiddish Theatre Group, the only Yiddish company performing today in North America. Many an artist has passed through the doors of the center's School of Fine Arts. *5170 Côte Ste-Catherine, tel. 514/739-2301; box office 514/739-7944. Closed Sat. and Jewish holidays. Call for information and program schedule.*

Far from the Saidye Bronfman Centre, but equally accessible by car, Metro, and bus, is the original **Musée d'art contemporain de Montréal,** located at Cité du Havre on part of the former Expo '67 site. The museum's large permanent collection represents works by Quebec, Canadian, and international artists in every medium. The museum often features weekend programs, with many child-oriented activities, and almost all are free. There are guided tours, though hours vary and groups of more than 15 are asked to make a reservation. *Open Tues.-Sun. 10 AM-6 PM. Donation. Weekdays, take MUTC's regular bus No. 168 from the McGill, Bonaventure, and Victoria Metro stations. Weekends, take the free Museum Blue Bus. Pickups and returns are made at the McGill and Bonaventure Metro stations.*

For something completely different, head one block east of Lafontaine on rue Rachel. There stands a forgotten museum that is a must-see for those with a taste for the, well, slightly odd. The **Midget Palace** was purchased in 1913 and renovated by 3-foot-tall (92 centimeters) Phillipe Nicol as a home for him and his wife, the "Count and Countess of Lilliputian Royalty." It was later bought by Huguette Rioux, a midget and founder of the Canadian Midgets Association, who turned it into a museum and doll hospital. On either side of the entrance are stained-glass panels depicting midgets shaking hands over the caption, "Toward a New Future." Inside you can take a tour of eight rooms that have been shrunk for midget use. The doorknobs and the furniture, including a baby grand piano, have all been lowered, and the kitchen is replete with specially scaled-down appliances. Ms. Rioux conducts the tour. *961 Rachel E, tel. 514/527-1121. Admission: $3.50 adults, $2.50 senior citizens, handicapped, and children. Open Mon.-Thurs. 10-noon* and 1–5 PM, Sun. 1–5 PM; open daily in summer, Mon.–Sat. 10–noon and 1–5 PM, Sun. 1–5 PM.

Shopping

by Patricia Lowe

Montrealers *magasiner* (go shopping) with a vengeance, so it's no surprise that the city has 160 multifaceted retail areas encompassing some 6,200 stores. This rough estimate will increase substantially in 1990 when new downtown complexes will add even more boutiques, specialty shops, and outlets.

Visitors usually reserve at least one day to hunt for either exclusive fashions along Sherbrooke or bargains at the Vieux-Montréal flea market. But there are specific items that the wise shopper seeks out in Montreal.

Montreal is one of the fur capitals of the world. Close to 85% of Canada's fur manufacturers are based in the city, as are many of their retail outlets: **Alexandor** (2025 de la Montagne); **Shuchat** (2015 de la Montagne); **Grosvenor** (400 de Maisonneuve O); **McComber** (440 de Maisonneuve O); **La Baie** (Square Phillips); and **Birger Christensen at Holt Renfrew** (1300 Sherbrooke W) are a few of the better showrooms.

Fine English bone china, crystal, and woolens are more readily available and cheaper in metropolitan stores than in their U.S. equivalents, thanks to Canada's tariff status as a Commonwealth country. There are three **Jaeger** boutiques (Ogilvy downtown, Centre Rockland in the town of Mount Royal, and Centre Fairview in the West Island) selling traditional woolen sweaters along with $700 pure wool suits. Collectors of china and crystal will do well at any of the **Birks Jewellers** on Square Phillips or in shopping complexes and suburban shopping centers. With lower price tags, **Caplan Duval's** two branches (at Côte-St-Luc's Cavendish Mall and at 6700 Côte-des-Neiges) offer an overwhelming variety of patterns.

Today, only dedicated connoisseurs can uncover real treasures in traditional pine Canadiana, but scouting around for Quebec *antiquités* and art can be fun and rewarding, especially along increasingly gentrified Notre-Dame Ouest.

Montreal area has six major retail districts: the city center or downtown, Vieux-Montréal, Notre-Dame Ouest, the Plâteau Mont Royal–St-Denis area, the upper St-Laurent–Laurier Ouest areas of Outremont, and the city of Westmount.

Montreal stores, boutiques, and department stores are generally open from 9 or 9:30 to 6 Monday, Tuesday, and Wednesday. On Thursday and often on Friday, stores close at 9, Saturday at 5. A number of pharmacies are open six days a week until 11 PM or midnight, a few are 24-hour operations. Just about all stores, with the exception of some bargain outlets and a few selective art and antiques galleries, accept major credit cards. Buy your Canadian money at a bank or exchange bureau beforehand to take advantage of the latest rates on the dollar.

A Quebec sales tax of 9% applies to all clothing purchases over $500 and shoes and boots over $125. There is no sales tax on books, home furnishings, or clothing sold for under $500.

If you think you might be buying fur, it is wise to check with your country's customs officials before leaving to find out which

76

Canadian Guild of Crafts, **4**
Complexe Desjardins, **11**
Eaton, **7**
Faubourg Ste-Catherine, **1**
Holt Renfrew, **2**
La Baie (The Bay), **9**
Les Cours Mont-Royal, **5**
Les Promenades de la Cathédrale, **8**
Marché Aux Puces, **14**
Notre-Dame Ouest Antiquing District, **12**
Ogilvy, **3**
Place Bonaventure, **13**
Place Montreal Trust, **6**
Place Ville Marie, **10**

77

animals are considered endangered and cannot be imported. Do the same if you think you might be buying Eskimo carvings, many of which are made of whalebone and ivory and cannot be brought into the United States.

City Center

Central downtown is Montreal's largest retail district. It takes in Sherbrooke Street, boulevard de Maisonneuve, rue Ste-Catherine, and the side streets between them. Because of the proximity and variety of shops, it's the best shopping bet for visitors in town overnight or over a weekend.

Faubourg Ste-Catherine Several new or soon-to-open complexes have added glamour to the city center shopping scene. A good place to start is the **Faubourg Ste-Catherine,** Montreal's answer to Boston's Quincy Market. At the corner of rue Ste-Catherine Ouest and Guy, it is a vast bazaar housed in a former parking and auto body garage abutting the Grey Nuns' convent grounds. Three levels of clothing and crafts boutiques, as well as food counters selling fruits and vegetables, pastry, baked goods, and meats, surround the central atrium of tiered fountains and islands of café tables and chairs. This is the place to pick up a $30 original Peruvian wall hanging or a fine French wine, also about $30, at the government-run **Société d'alcools du Québec.** Prices at most stores are generally reasonable here, especially if you're sampling the varied ethnic cuisine at any of the snack counters.

Les Cours Mont-Royal Continuing east on Ste-Catherine, the ultraelegant **Les Cours Mont-Royal** dominates the east side of Peel Street between this main shopping thoroughfare and de Maisonneuve. This mall caters to expensive tastes, but even bargain hunters find it an intriguing spot for window-shopping. Of particular interest is the grand old Mont Royal Hotel, which fell on hard times in the '70s and emerged in the spring of 1988 in all, if not more, of its former glory. Now it hosts such Canadian designers as Alfred Sung and his two boutiques, the white-marble Alfred Sung boutique with day and evening wear and his sportswear boutique, **Club Monaco.** His white-marble salon is joined by fellow Canadian superstars Simon Chang's **La Cricca** boutique and Nicola Pelly and Harry Parnass's minimalist **Parachute** boutique, **Ferre's** sophisticated salon, **Lancia Uomo** for trendy young men, and **Aquascutum of London** for traditionalists. Montreal's popular gourmet kitchen shop, **Ma Maison,** displays splashy cookware and picnic baskets complete with flowered napkins. Les Cours' stores are temptingly arranged around a vaulted lobby that includes a meticulously restored pastel-and-gilt ceiling with its magnificent crystal chandelier (part of the original hotel decor). Curving white stairways wend their gracious way between shopping levels while one pianist after another plays soothing selections on the central level baby grand.

Place Montreal Trust Just two blocks away, Place Montreal Trust at McGill College is the lively entrance to an imposing glass office tower. Shoppers, fooled by the aqua-and-pastel decor, may think they have stumbled into a California mall. Prices at the 120 outlets range from hundreds (for designs by **Alfred Sung,** haute couture at **Gigi** or **Rodier,** or men's high fashion at **Bally**) to mere dollars (for sensible cotton boys' T-shirts, or beef-and-kidney pies or minced tarts at the British dry-goods and food store, **Marks &**

Shopping

Spencer). These imported goodies share the floor space with moderately ticketed ladies' suits, menswear, lingerie, and children's clothing. Marks & Spencer is a far cry from neighboring **Abercrombie and Fitch,** which stocks the offbeat and the outrageous, such as a fold-up miniature billiards table or a handsome $2,400 wooden rocking horse.

Les Cours Mont-Royal and this complex will have competition from the **Centre Eaton** and **Les Promenades de la Cathédrale.** All four of these centers will be linked to the Underground City retail network.

Always a favorite with visitors, the nearly 7-mile (11-kilometer) "city below" draws large crowds to its shop-lined corridors honeycombing between Les Promenades de la Cathédrale, Place Ville Marie, Place Bonaventure, and Complexe Desjardins.

Les Promenades de la Cathédrale Nestled between Eaton and La Baie department stores, this underground retail complex is already proving popular with Montrealers. Its unusual location makes it a sightseeing adventure as well. Connected to the McGill Metro and located directly beneath the stately and historic Christ Church Cathedral, a highlight (some say a travesty) of the retail mall's design is the replication of architectural details found in the cathedral above. The retail complex boasts some 150 stores, with many well-known international and Canadian chain stores among them. Look for **W.H. Smith** bookstore, **HMV Canada's** unique record outlet, **Caroline B.'s** and **Yü's** faux jewelry and accessories, **Au Coton, By American, Lacoste** and **Jacob** for reasonably priced fashions, as well as **Lily Simon, Parachute,** and **René Derhy** for the latest in *prêt-à-porter* and haute-couture apparel.

Place Ville Marie Weatherproof shopping began in 1962 beneath the 42-story cruciform towers of Place Ville Marie on boulevard René Lévesque (formerly Dorchester Boulevard) at University. A recent renovation has opened Place Ville Marie up to the light, creating a more cheerful ambience as well as adding stores. Ville Marie's pedestrian passageways lead to such interesting specialty shops as **Le Rouet Métiers d'Art,** one of eight city branches featuring fine Quebec crafts—wood carvings and toys, handcrafted silver jewelry, weaving, and ceramics. Souvenirs range from signed ceramic plates or wood carvings for around $50, designer jewelry at $25, and down to a scented bathcube for 29¢. The Canadian candy chain **Laura Secord** sells delicious chocolates (a half-pound box of mixed miniatures is $7.25), and, as in most complexes, the **Société des alcools** has an outlet here.

Stylish women head to Place Ville Marie's 85-plus retail outlets for the clothes: haute couture at **Lalla Fucci, Jacnel, Marie-Claire, Cactus,** as well as **Holt Renfrew's** branch store. Traditionalists will love **Heritage House** and **Aquascutum.** More affordable clothes shops include **Dalmy's, Gazebo, Reitman's,** and, for shoes, **Mayfair, Brown's, François Villon,** and **Cemi.**

Place Bonaventure From here it's an easy underground trip through Gare Centrale (the train station) to Place Bonaventure's mall beneath one of Canada's largest commercial buildings. It houses some 100 stores, ranging from the trendy (**Au Coton** and **Bikini Village**) to the exclusive (**Alain Giroux** boutique) to the romantic (the bridal salon **Pronuptia**). Moderately priced shoe stores abound—**Bally, Dack,** and **Pegabo**—and booths on every aisle sell candy, cosmetics, and gadgets.

Complexe Desjardins Still in the downtown area but a bit farther east on René Lévesque is Complexe Desjardins. It's a fast ride via the Metro at Bonaventure station; just get off at Place des Arts and follow the tunnels to Desjardins' multitiered atrium mall. Also home to the Meridien Hotel, Complexe Desjardins' opening coincided with the 1976 Summer Olympic Games and was an immediate hit. It is popular with a mainly French-speaking clientele, making it more typical of the city's cultural mix. Filled with splashing fountains and exotic plants, Desjardins exudes a Mediterranean joie de vivre, even when it's below freezing outside. Roughly 80 stores include budget outlets like **Le Château** for fashion and **Sarosi** for shoes, as well as the exclusive **Rodier of Paris,** where dresses start around $150. A pleasant art gallery, **France-Martin** on the lower level, features works by local and other Canadian painters.

Department Stores Still downtown, but above ground, department stores worth a browse are **La Baie, Eaton, Ogilvy,** and **Holt Renfrew** (dealing strictly in fashion). In fact, Ste-Catherine's best-shopped blocks start at La Baie on Phillips Square and Eaton at No. 677N (both are connected with the McGill Metro station and to even more stores in Galeries 2001 and 2020 University), ending at Splash Boutique (No. 1397 O) at the corner of Ste-Catherine and Bishop.

Eaton is the city's leading department store and part of Canada's largest chain. Founded in Toronto by Timothy Eaton, the first Montreal outlet appeared in 1925. It now sells everything—from the art decorating the top-floor restaurant entrance to zucchini loaves in the basement bakery. Floors in between sell Canadian crafts and souvenirs; Canadian designers like Leo Chevalier as well as labels by Nipon and Ports International; fine furnishings and accessories in addition to the bargain-basement variety; microwaves, VCRs, the whole gamut of department store selections. The main restaurant is an unusual Art Deco replica of the dining room aboard the old *Île de France* ocean liner, once Lady Eaton's favorite cruise ship. Construction has begun on the $120 million Eaton Centre, which will incorporate the present store and the adjoining Les Terrasses labyrinth of boutiques.

The nearby sandstone building housing **La Baie** opened in 1891, although the original Henry Morgan Company that founded it moved to Montreal as early as 1843. Morgan's was purchased in 1960 by the Hudson Bay Company, which was founded in 1670 by famous Montreal *voyageurs* and trappers Radisson and Grosseilliers. For more than 150 years, Hudson Bay held the monopoly on Canada's fur trade, so it follows that this store's fur salon has a reputation for quality. La Baie is also known for its Hudson Bay red-, green-, and white-striped blankets and duffel coats. It also sells the typical department store fare. Its ground floor has undergone a dramatic renovation. It now features "boutique" shopping à la Ogilvy, in which the fashion-conscious will find the latest in jewelry and accessories from Lancel Handbags, Beverley Hamburg, Yves St-Laurent cosmetics, and Boutique 317 For Men, among others.

Exclusive **Holt Renfrew,** at 1300 Sherbrooke West, is also known for its furs. The city's oldest store, it was established in

1837 as Henderson, Holt and Renfrew Furriers and made its name supplying coats to four generations of British royalty. When Queen Elizabeth II married Prince Philip in 1947, Holt's created a priceless Labrador mink as a wedding gift. Commoners, however, must be content with a brown-dyed blue fox for $14,750. Holt's also now carries the exclusive and pricey line of furs by Denmark's Birger Christensen, as well as the haute-couture and *prêt-à-porter* collections of perennial fashion favorite Yves St-Laurent (in a fabulously elegant new boutique devoted exclusively to the internationally lionized designer's designer). The **Gucci, Giorgio Armani,** and **Polo Ralph Lauren** boutiques on Holt's main and lower level, as well as the elegant men's shop in a separate shop next door, give a hint of the kind of prices you may expect here; even in the children's department, a size 6X velveteen dress can come to more than $200.

Around the corner and two blocks down de la Montagne, at **Ogilvy** (1307 Ste-Catherine O), a kilted piper regales shoppers every day at noon. An institution with Montrealers since 1865, the once-homey department store has undergone a miraculous face-lift. Fortunately, it has preserved its delicate pink glass chandeliers and still stocks traditional apparel—Aquascutum, Jaeger, tweeds for men, and smocked dresses for little girls. Every Christmas its main window showcases a fantasy world of mechanized animals busy with their holiday preparations, as it has since Steiff of Germany first made the display for Ogilvy in 1947. Style-conscious customers snap up designs by Valentino, Jean Muir, Don Sayres, and Raffinati, Joan & David shoes, and the unusual dyed coats in the fur salon. Crabtree & Evelyn sells toiletries in a quaint boutique on the second floor. The **David S. Brown Antique** boutique on the fifth floor specializes in mid- to late-18th-century and early-19th-century English furniture, silver, porcelain, and accessories.

This area—bounded by Sherbrooke and Ste-Catherine, and de la Montagne and Crescent—also boasts antiques and art galleries as well as designer salons. Sherbrooke is lined with an array of art and antique galleries. Notables include the **Galerie Samuel Lallouz** (No. 1620), showcase for international contemporary artists, especially the avant-garde; **Elca London Gallery** (No. 1616), with a large collection of Eskimo and contemporary art; **Franklin Silverstone** (No. 1618), which specializes in contemporary ceramics, sculpture, and other mixed media, as well as in artisan handicrafts; **Elena Lee-Verre d'Art** (No. 1518), with fabulous one-of-a-kind, contemporary glass and ceramics, as well as avant-garde jewelry designs; **Waddington & Gorce** (No. 1504), featuring contemporary pieces; the **Petit Musée** (No. 1494), selling ancient *objets* and *bijoux* from the Orient, Egypt, and Greece; **Galerie D'Art Eskimau** (No. 1434), one of the country's largest galleries specializing in Eskimo sculpture; **Dominion Gallery** (No. 1438), known for introducing sculptor Henry Moore to Canada; and **Walter Klinkhoff** (No. 1200). Clotheshorses strolling Sherbrooke stop at **Brisson & Brisson** (No. 1472), featuring elegant styles and accessories for men; **Bruestle** (No. 1490), for tailored women's classics; **Les Gamineries** (No. 1458), outfitting fashionable children; **Lily Simon** (No. 1480), for the haute couture of Armani and Valentino; **Ralph Lauren** (No. 1316), a house full of East Coast styles; **Ungaro** (No. 1430), high fashion by a top designer; **Bijouterie** (No. 1498); and recent arrival **Cartier** (at the corner of Sherbrooke and Simpson), where diamonds sparkle from showcase windows in the green marble facade.

Crescent is a tempting blend of antiques, fashions, and jewelry boutiques displayed beneath colorful awnings: **André Antiques** (No. 2125), for fine furniture; **Ferroni** (No. 2145), known for English antiques; and **Laura Ashley** (No. 2110), two stories of romantic clothes, linens, and fabric.

Fine-art lovers should take a detour two blocks west from Crescent to check out the galleries on Mackay. Notably, **Galerie Daniel** (No. 2159) features major Montreal, Canadian, and international contemporary artists (it also has a lovely sculpture courtyard adjacent to the premises); **Galerie Esperanza** (No. 2144) features mixed-media exhibitions of new and established artists from around the world; and **Galerie Barbara Silverberg** (No. 2148) enjoys the enviable reputation as *the* preeminent promoter of Quebec and international ceramicists and jewelry artists.

The highly regarded **Canadian Guild of Crafts** (2025 Peel St.), between Sherbrooke and de Maisonneuve, sells Inuit art and other Canadian crafts, weavings, glass, and ceramics in addition to displaying its own collection in a showroom open free of charge during business hours. Novice collectors are advised to consult guild personnel before investing in Inuit art at souvenir shops.

Vieux-Montréal

The second major shopping district, historic Vieux-Montréal, can be a tourist trap; but a shopping spree there can be a lot less expensive and more relaxing than shopping downtown. Both Notre-Dame and St-Jacques, from McGill to Place Jacques Cartier, are lined with low- to moderately priced fashion boutiques, garish souvenir shops slung with thousands of Montreal T-shirts, and shoe stores. **Tripp Distribution & Importation** (389 and 21 Notre-Dame O) has bargains on Ralph Lauren (polo shirts for $25) and other labels; the store prefers cash to credit cards. Quebec crafts are well represented at **Centre de Ceramique de Bonsecours** (444 St-Gabriel), which sells and shows ceramics and sculptures by local artisans from noon to 5. **Desmarais & Robitaille** (60 Notre-Dame), a store specializing in religious objects and vestments, also has lovely handcrafted souvenirs, knits, and weavings.

Cobblestoned rue St-Paul, the main historic street, has more souvenir and ice cream stands than necessary. But outdoor jewelry vendors and the range of art displayed here and along tiny rue St-Amable, off Place Jacques Cartier, make browsing fun, especially if shoppers sit for a portrait by a local caricaturist.

For finer art, go to **Galerie St-Paul** (4 St-Paul E), selling limited edition prints, sculptures, and works by local and international artists; or **La Guilde Graphique** (9 St-Paul O), for prints. **Les Artisans du Meuble Québeçois** (88 St-Paul E) has an artistic selection of Quebec-made crafts as well as silver, jewelry, and clothing. **Le Rouet Metiers d'Art,** which sells handcrafts, has its main store at 136 St-Paul Est, while the historic **Maison du Patriote** (165 St-Paul E) houses a specialty candy store featuring unusual gift items.

Along the edge of Vieux-Montréal is Montreal's rejuvenated waterfront, the Vieux-Port, which hosts a sprawling flea market, the **Marché aux puces,** on Quai King Edward (King Edward Pier). Dealers and pickers search for secondhand steals and antique treasures as they prowl through the huge hangar that is open Wednesday through Sunday from spring through early fall.

Notre-Dame Ouest

The place for antiquing is the city's third shopping sector, beginning at Guy and continuing west to Atwater Avenue (a 5-minute walk south from the Lionel-Groulx Metro station). Once a shabby strip of run-down secondhand stores, this area has blossomed beyond its former nickname of Attic Row. It now has the highest concentration of antiques, collectibles, and curiosity shops in Montreal. Collectors can find Canadian pine furniture—armoires, cabinets, spinning wheels, rocking chairs— for reasonable prices here. From Guy to Vinet streets, all outlets run along the south side of the artery; the north side is a new neighborhood of attractive brick town houses and landscaped gardens.

With rapid gentrification taking place about their ears, existing dealers have upgraded their wares, while many new shops have moved into what has become a serious shopping district. Saturday is busy, so some stores stay open on Sunday, a better day to visit as shopkeepers are more apt to offer sweet deals.

A westbound walk along this avenue takes in: **Portes & Vitraux Anciens du Grand Montreal** (No. 1500), which sells Canadian pine furniture and stained glass; **Danielle J. Malynowsky Inc.** (No. 1640), including Victorian and Chinese pieces with Canadiana; **Antiquités Marielle Moquin and Michelle Parent** (No. 1650), where silver tea services (sterling cream and sugar, $250) grace an inlaid buffet; **Martin Antiques** (No. 1732); **Antiquités Ambiance & Discernement** (No. 1654), blending old and new furniture designs; and **Antiquités G. M. Portal** (No. 1894), more Canadian pine. Eclectic collections (barber poles and suits of armor) crowd together at **Deuxièmement** (No. 1880). The jumbly attics of **Basilières** (No. 1904) and **Gisela's** (No. 1960) are for old dolls and teddy bears.

Antiques buffs might also want to explore a Montreal favorite—Place Bonaventure's much-touted annual three-day antiques show, held during June (tel. 514/933–6375).

Plateau–Mont Royal–St-Denis

Popular with students, academics, and journalists, this easterly neighborhood embraces boulevard St-Laurent, the longtime student ghetto surrounding the Prince Arthur mall, St-Denis and its Latin Quarter near the Université du Québec à Montréal campus, and the Plateau district. Plateau–Mont Royal–St-Denis attracts a trendier, more avant-garde crowd than the determined antiquers along Notre Dame.

St-Laurent—dubbed "The Main" because it divides the island of Montreal into east and west—has always been a lively commercial artery. It was first developed by Jewish merchants who set up shop here in the early 1900s. Cutting a broad swath across the island's center, this long boulevard has an international flavor, with its mélange of stores run by Chinese, Greek, Slav, Latin American, Portuguese, and Vietnamese immigrants. Lower St-Laurent is lined with discount clothing and bric-a-brac stores, secondhand shops, electronics outlets, and groceries selling kosher meats, Hungarian pastries, Peking duck, and natural foods. Also off this boulevard, at 74 Roy Est, is **Waldman's** fish market, a mecca for serious cooks who delight in Gaspé salmon or *moules* (mussels). Fashionable clothing shops join this colorful bazaar, though none has been as successful as the now-international **Parachute Boutique** (No. 3526), which began its career in Montreal.

While St-Laurent's personality is multiethnic, St-Denis's is distinctly French. (Both are lengthy arteries, so make use of Bus 55 for St-Laurent, Bus 31 along St-Denis.) More academic in makeup, its awnings shelter bookstores (mostly French), with **Librairie Flammarion Scorpion** (No. 4380) being one of the best. Rare and used-book stores are scattered along the street from **Librairie Kebuk** (No. 2048) to **Librairie Delteil** (No. 7348). **Musique Archambault** (off St-Denis at 500 Ste-Catherine) caters to the city's music students. Bookstores are complemented by scattered art galleries (**Michel Tétrault**, No. 4260; **Morency**, No. 4340; **Art Select**, No. 6810) and antiques stores (**Antiquités Je Me Souviens**, No. 8254-A, and **Puces Libres**, No. 4240). **Le Château** has one of its many trendy fashion boutiques at No. 4201; **Thalie** (No. 4203) has inexpensive, high-quality, and fashion-forward men's and women's knitwear; and Maurice Ferland's designs are available at **Un Brin d'Elle** (No. 4417). Denim sportswear by Canadian designers at **Revenge** (No. 3852) and international fashions at **Orphee** (No. 3997) are among a wide range of other boutiques. Modern furnishings, such as colorful art clocks for $85, brighten up the showroom at **Dixversions** (No. 4361), **Zone** (No. 4246), and **Après L'Eden** (No. 4201). **Le Sieur Duluth chapeaux, bijoux et accessoires** (No. 4454) is an absolute must for mad hatters of either sex. Many of the creations are designed in-house; custom orders are also accepted. And the array of ready-to-wear (or just waiting to be bought) hats, jewelry, and accessories will delight the eye.

Upper St-Laurent and Laurier Ouest

Upper St-Laurent (for our purposes, roughly from Mont Royal north to St-Viateur), intersecting with Laurier Ouest and climbing the mountain to Bernard, has blossomed into one of Montreal's most chic *quartiers* in recent years. It's not entirely surprising, given that much of this area lies within or adjacent to Outremont, traditionally the enclave for wealthy Francophone Montrealers, with restaurants, boutiques, nightclubs and bistros catering to the upscale visitor. In addition, the influx of a new generation of multiethnic professionals, artists, and entrepreneurs is making its mark on the area.

Upper St-Laurent now rivals St-Denis, the downtown, and Laurier Ouest as a cultural hot spot, and it is reminiscent of New York City's SoHo. Here you'll find the lusciously colored, butter-soft suede and leather fashions for men and women designed by Montrealer **Robert Krief** at his showroom storefront of the same name (No. 5226), as well as his more rugged "Western" leather and denim unisex fashions at his boutique, **Paris, Texas** (No. 5251). If those are too pricey, check out **Le Château's** own label—knockoffs of the latest designer styles and retro fashions at its two-floor boutique (No. 5160); **Trois & Un** (no. 5129) for sportswear; **Luna** (No. 5155) or **Le Lotus Blanc** (No. 5163) for soft, brightly colored cotton and rayon knit jersey wear; **Double Vé** (No. 5145) for Annie Coriat-Ropsard sportswear; and **Atout Fringues** (No. 5183) for NafNaf, Paris's latest casual wear.

If it's home fashions you're after, you'll find both the avant-garde and the retro on St-Laurent. Practical but unusual and beautiful hardware for dressing up doors and windows can be found at **Par le trou de la Serrure** (No. 5101), and one-of-a-kind furniture from the '30s through the '50s is at **M.A.D. objets de collection** (No. 5330).

Laurier Ouest, from St-Laurent to Cote Ste-Catherine—roughly an eight-block stretch, which you'll crisscross many times as you flit in and out of the many cafés, boutiques, galleries, and restaurants lining both sides of the street—is a shopper's paradise.

Choose from home furnishings: outré wall coverings at **Griffe** (No. 92 O); French-Canadian pine antiques at **Boutique Confort** (No. 201 O); or unusual handcrafted ceramics and pottery at **Cache-Cache** (No. 1051 O).

Head-to-toe fashion choices for men and women of all ages—from haute couture to the internationally marketed same-as-everywhere fashions by Benetton (No. 1068 O)—can also be found on Laurier Ouest. Canadian designers include **Les Tricots d'Ariane** (No. 207 O) for knits by Ariane Carle, and **Revenge** (No. 111 O) for Québécois rising designer stars Denommé-Vincent, Dagisco, Jean-Claude Poitras, and Alain Thomas.

The more culturally inclined can discover the reigning literary stars of Quebec and French literature at **Librairie Lettre Son** (No. 1005 O) or Quebec's contemporary artists at **Artes** (No. 102 O), devoted exclusively to promoting works in every medium by Quebec's established and up-and-coming artistic talent.

Westmount Square and Greene Avenue

Visitors with time to shop or friends in the elegant residential neighborhood of Westmount, a separate municipality in the middle of Montreal Island, should explore Westmount Square and adjacent Greene Avenue. Next door to downtown, these malls are on the Angrignon Metro line, easily accessible via the Atwater station, which has an exit at Westmount Square. Just follow the tunnel to this mall's 20 or so exclusive shops, including **Cacharel,** for Liberty prints; **Guy Laroche; Chacok,** for the avant-garde; **Diaghilev,** for romantic formal gowns; **Lily Simon,** for French and Italian haute-couture, *prêt-à-porter* and sportswear designer fashions; and **Victoire Paris.** Indulgent grandmothers like the **Toy Box** for its imported dolls.

The square's plaza opens onto Greene Avenue, which is two blocks long and lined with trees and flowers. Its redbrick row houses and even the renovated old post office are home to a wealth of boutiques and shops. All make newcomers glad they strayed off the tourist beaten path. The food could be one reason. Costumed salespeople at the epicurean shop **By George** (No. 1343) don't mind cheering a tired nine-year-old with free samples of gingerbread while Mom settles on $5 gift boxes of maple sugar candy and a fresh *baguette*. The deli at the post of-

Montreal

fice on the corner of de Maisonneuve is always busy, as is the **Cinq Saisons** gourmet food store across the street.

Other shops include the **Double Hook** bookstore (No. 1235A), which sells works by Canadian authors only; **Avenue Books** (No. 1368), which has an excellent selection of fiction and nonfiction by British (read English, Irish, and Scottish) authors but isn't confined to them alone; **Coach House Antiques** (No. 1325), with fine furniture such as its Louis Philippe Semainier, circa 1875; and **Connaisseur Antiques** (No. 1312), featuring china and silver. **Crisma Toys** (No. 1230) has unusual Olive Oyl dolls and puppet stages (both for $24), large $127 teddy bears, and a tantalizing range of items for less than $1.

Sports and Fitness

The range of sporting activities available in Montreal is testament to Montrealers' love of the outdoors. With world-class skiing in the Laurentians less than an hour away and dozens of skating rinks within the city limits, they revel in winter. When the last snowflake has melted, they store away skis, poles, and skates and dust off their bikes, tennis rackets, and fishing poles. And year-round they watch the pros at hockey matches, baseball and football games, car races, and tennis tournaments.

Participant Sports

Bicycling   The island of Montreal—except for Mont Royal itself—is quite flat, and there are more than 20 cycling paths around the metropolitan area. Among the most popular are those on Île Ste-Hélène, along rue Rachel, and in Maisonneuve and Mont Royal parks. You can rent 10-speeds at **Cycle Peel** (6665 St-Jacques, tel. 514/486–1148).

Parks Canada conducts guided cycling tours along the historic **Lachine Canal** (1825) every summer weekend. Tours leave from the corner of McGill and de la Commune streets at 10:30 AM, in English on Saturdays, in French on Sundays. For more details, call 514/283–6054 or 514/872–6211.

Curling   The oldest curling club in North America—the **Royal Montreal Curling Club** (1850 de Maisonneuve O, tel. 514/935–3411), begun in 1807—is only one of many such organizations in the city.

Golf   For a complete listing of the many golf courses in the Montreal area, call **Tourisme Quebec** at 514/873–2015. Here are some of the city's public courses:

Club de Golf de la Rive-Sud (415 rue Bella Vista, Saint-Basile-le-Grand, tel. 514/653–2471).

Club de Golf Île des Soeurs (301 ave. Golf, Île des Soeurs, tel. 514/761–5900).

Fresh Meadows Golf Club (505 ave. Golf, Beaconsfield, tel. 514/697–4036).

Health Clubs   Most major hotels have pools/exercise facilities on the premises. **Club La Cité** (3625 ave. du Parc, tel. 514/288–8221), adjacent to the Ramada Renaissance du Parc, has an indoor-outdoor pool (heated in winter), squash and tennis courts, Nau-

Sports and Fitness

tilus equipment, aerobic dance studio, sauna, whirlpool, and steamroom.

Members of the New York Athletic Club, the Buffalo Athletic Club, and the Mohawk Club in Schenectady, NY, have guest privileges at the Montreal Amateur Athletic Association (2070 Peel, tel. 514/845-2233). Facilities include everything but indoor tennis. Montreal's YMCA branches (main downtown location, 1450 rue Stanley, tel. 514/849-8393), YWCA (1355 blvd. René Lévesque O, tel. 514/866-9941) and YM-YWHA branches (main branch, 5500 Westbury, tel. 514/737-6551) have day passes for out-of-town members or nonmembers, entitling users to most sports and recreational facilities and activities.

Horseback Riding For information, call **Québec à Cheval** (tel. 514/252-3002) or the **Fédération Equestre du Québec** (tel. 514/252-3053).

Hunting and Fishing Quebec's rich waters and forests are filled with fish and wildlife. Before you begin the chase you need to purchase the appropriate license from the Ministère des Loisirs de la Chasse et de la Pêche or from an authorized agent. The lakes and rivers around Montreal teem with fish, and a number of guides offer day trips. For hunting you'll have to go farther afield, to the Laurentians or l'Estrie (the Eastern Townships). For complete information, call **Tourisme Québec** (tel. 514/873-2015).

Ice-Skating There are at least 30 outdoor and 21 indoor rinks in the city. You'll probably find one in the nearest park. Call parks and recreation (tel. 514/872-6211). A few of the more popular outdoor rinks include:

Parc Angrignon. Night skating. 7050 boulevard de la Verendrye.

Île Notre-Dame. Olympic rowing basin.

Parc Lafontaine. Sherbrooke E at Calixa-Lavallée.

Parc Mont Royal. Night skating on Beaver Lake.

Jogging Montreal became a runner's city following the 1976 Olympics. There are paths in most city parks, but for running with a panoramic view, head to the dirt track in **Parc Mont Royal** (take Peel, then the steps up to the track).

Rafting Montreal is the only city in the world where you can step off a downtown dock and minutes later be crashing through Class V whitewater in a sturdy aluminum jet boat. The Lachine Rapids, just south of Vieux-Montréal, were responsible for the founding of Montreal. The roiling waves were too treacherous for the first settlers to maneuver, so they founded Ville Marie, the forerunner of Vieux-Montréal. Modern voyageurs suit up for the 45-minute jet-boat trip in multiple layers of wool and rain gear, but it's nearly impossible to stay dry—or to have a bad time. *Lachine Rapids Tours Ltd. 105 de la Commune, Vieux-Montréal, tel. 514/284-9607. 5 trips daily departing from Victoria Pier May–Sept. 10 AM, noon, 2, 4, and 6 PM. Trips are narrated in French and English and reservations are necessary. Rates: $30 adults; $22 children 11–18, $10 6–10; $25 senior citizens.*

Nouveau Monde Expédition en Rivière. *5475 Paré, Suite 221, tel. 514/733-7166. 4- to 5-hr. expedition on rivers outside Mont-*

real, daily mid-Apr.–late Sept. 9–6. Closed Tues. Rates: weekdays $59, weekends $75.

Skiing With the Laurentians in their backyard, it's no surprise that skiing is the sport of choice for most Montrealers. (*See* Excursions, Chapter 4, for details on downhill and cross-country facilities in the Laurentians and l'Estrie.)

Alpine For the big slopes you'll have to go northwest to the Laurentians or south to l'Estrie, an hour or two away by car. There is a small slope in Parc Mont Royal. Pick up the Ski-Quebec brochure at the Tourisme Québec offices.

Nordic Trails crisscross most of the city's parks, including Notre-Dame and Île Ste-Hélène, Angrignon, Maisonneuve, and Mont Royal.

Squash You can reserve court time for this fast-paced racquet sport at **Nautilus Centre St-Laurent Côte de Liesse Racquet Club** (8305 Côte de Liesse Rd., tel. 514/739-3654).

Swimming There is a large indoor pool at the **Olympic Park** (Metro Viau, tel. 514/252-4622) and another at the **Centre Sportif et Loisirs Claude-Robillard** (1000 Emile Journault, tel. 514/872-6900). The free outdoor pool on Île Ste-Hélène is an extremely popular (and crowded) summer gathering place. Open June–Labor Day.

Tennis There are public courts in the Jeanne Mance, Kent, Lafontaine, and Somerled parks. For details call Montreal Sports and Recreation (tel. 514/872-6211).

Windsurfing and Sailing Sailboards and small sailboats can be rented at **L'École de Voile de Lachine** (2105 St. Joseph, Lachine, tel. 514/634-4326) and the **Club Nautique de Pleine Air de Montréal** (Île Notre-Dame, tel. 514/872-6093).

Spectator Sports

Baseball The National League **Montreal Expos** play at the Olympic Stadium from April through September. For information, call 514/253-3434 or 800/351-0658; for credit card reservations, call 514/253-0700.

Cycling **La Classique Cycliste de Montréal** is a professional cycling competition through the Lafontaine, Mont Royal and Olympic parks held in early June (tel. 514/251-6946).

Le Tour de L'Île de Montréal has made the *Guinness Book of Records* for attracting a great number of participants for the past four years. More than 30,000 amateur cyclists participate in "North America's most important amateur cycling event" each June, wending their way through the streets and parks of Montreal (514/251-6955).

In early August, **Le Grand Prix cyclistes** brings together professional cyclists from around the world to compete in this 124-mile (200-kilometer) cycling competition (tel. 514/879-1027).

Grand Prix The annual **Molson Grand Prix du Canada,** which draws top Formula 1 racers from around the world, takes place every June at the Gilles Villeneuve Race Track on Île Notre-Dame (tel. 514/392-0000 for tickets, tel. 514/392-9022 for information).

Harness Racing	**Hippodrome Blue Bonnets.** *7440 boulevard Decarie (Metro Namur), tel. 514/739–2741. Admission: $3–$4. Open year-round; closed Tues., Thurs.*
Hockey	The **Montreal Canadiens,** winners of 22 Stanley Cups, meet National Hockey League rivals at the Forum (2313 rue Ste-Catherine O, tel. 514/932–6131) from October to April.
Marathon	More than 12,000 runners do the grueling 26.2-mile **Montreal International Marathon** each September through the streets of Montreal (tel. 514/879–1027).
Tennis	The **Player's Challenge tennis championships** are held during the first two weeks of August on the courts of Jarry Tennis Stadium (rue Jarry and blvd. St-Laurent, tel. 514/273–1515). The men compete in odd years, the women in even years.

Dining

by Josée Blanchette and Andrew Coe

Josée Blanchette is a restaurant critic for Montreal's French daily newspaper, Le Devoir, and for Radio Canada (CBC French network). She takes a special interest in traditional Canadian and ethnic cooking.

The promise of a good meal is easily satisfied in Montreal. Les Montrealais don't "eat out"; they "dine." And they are passionate about dining. The city has more than 7,000 restaurants of every price representing more than 35 ethnic groups. It has culinary institutions like Les Mignardises, Le Paris, and the Beaver Club, which emphasize classic cuisine and tradition. Delicatessens such as Briskets, Schwartz's, and Wilensky's are mainstays for budget dining. In between there are ethnic eateries featuring the foods of China, Greece, India, Morocco, and Italy. Then there are the ubiquitous inexpensive fast-food outlets and coffee shops. But above all, Montreal is distinguished by the European ambience of its restaurants. Catch a glimpse of the eateries' terraces from midday to 2 PM for a look at the hours that Montreal diners take most seriously. Each of the city's well-known bistros is more Parisian than the next. The challenge to dining in Montreal is choosing from among the thousands of restaurants and the varieties of cuisine.

Places to dine or catch a bite are scattered throughout every neighborhood of Montreal. The most famous area—Restaurant Row—is Crescent Street (and the neighboring Bishop and Mountain streets) between boulevard René Lévesque and Sherbrooke Street. Dozens of eateries of all types of cuisine line both sides of the street. Both boulevard St-Laurent and rue St-Denis from rue St-Antoine (near Vieux-Montréal) north for several miles are chock-full of restaurants of various types and coffee houses. The former tends to have the cheaper, more ethnic eateries, while along St-Denis can be found more Francophile and chic cafés and cookeries. If you want to eat authentic Chinese food (mostly Cantonese), head to Chinatown between avenue Viger and boulevard René Lévesque, east of the convention center. Prince Arthur Street and Duluth Avenue, in certain stretches, are pedestrian malls lined with ethnic restaurants, mostly Greek and Vietnamese. Vieux-Montréal has both high-class French and second-class tourist eateries. By law, all restaurants must post their menus outside, so you can window-shop for your dining spot.

Many expensive French and Continental restaurants offer two options, which can be a blessing or a burden to your wallet. Either choice guarantees you a great meal. Instead of ordering *à la carte*—you select each dish—you can opt for the *table d'hôte* or the *menu de dégustation*. The table d'hôte is a complete two- to four-course meal chosen by the chef. It is less expensive than a complete meal ordered à la carte and often offers interesting special dishes. It also may take less time to prepare. If you want to splurge with your time and money, indulge yourself with the menu de dégustation, a five- to seven-course dinner executed by the chef. It usually includes, in this order, salad, soup, a fish dish, sherbet, a meat dish, dessert, and coffee or tea. At the city's finest restaurants, this menu for two and a good bottle of wine can cost $170 and last three or four hours. But it's worth every cent and every second.

At the low end of the price spectrum, budget restaurants are everywhere in Montreal. You can get a satisfying meal at the ubiquitous sandwich-souvlaki-spaghetti-pizza establishments or some delicious baked goods, café au lait, and salads at the many *croissanteries*. American fast-food spots—Burger King, McDonalds, Kentucky Fried Chicken, etc.—are hard to miss. Another option is Quebec's homegrown chains like St. Hubert (barbecue chicken). Excellent meat and produce is available if you want to buy your own food. Surprisingly, a wide variety of tropical fruits and vegetables is sold at relatively low prices.

Montreal restaurants are refreshingly relaxed. Although many of the hotel restaurants require a jacket and tie, neatness (no torn T-shirts and scruffy jeans) is appreciated in most of the other restaurants. Lunch hour is generally from noon to 2:30 PM and dinner from 6 to 11 PM or midnight. (Montrealers like to dine late, particularly on summer weekends.) Some restaurants are closed on Sunday or Monday. Since there is no consistent annual closing among Montreal eateries—some will take time off in August, while others will close around Christmas and January—call ahead to avoid disappointment.

Highly recommended restaurants in each price category are indicated by a star ★ .

Category	Cost*
Very Expensive	over $30
Expensive	$20–$30
Moderate	$10–$20
Inexpensive	$5–$10

per person without tax (10% for meals over $3.25), service, or drinks

Chinese

Moderate **Cathay Restaurant.** Hong Kong investors, fearful of their city's future, are pouring money into Montreal's and other Chinatowns in North America. Among other businesses, they're opening slick, Hong Kong–style restaurants and competing with the older Chinese eateries. The consumer wins in these restaurant wars. The 15-year-old Cathay was remodeled and expanded in 1985, and is now the most popular and largest dim sum restaurant in the city. The two floors are both huge rooms with institutional dropped ceilings and the usual red and gold Chinese stage decorations. From 11 AM to 2:30 PM waitresses emerge from the kitchen pushing carts laden with steaming beef dumplings in bamboo steamers, spicy cuttlefish, shrimp rice noodles, bean curd rolls, and on and on. You point to what you want. Each plate costs between $1.40 and $3.75. At the end of the meal a waiter tallies your empty plates and presents you with the bill, which is usually very reasonable considering the amount of food you eat. The more crowded the restaurant is—Sunday mornings are the busiest—the greater the variety of dim sum. In the evening a standard Chinese menu is served. Wine, cocktails, and a number of Polynesian drinks, including something called à Go Go Loco (rum and coconut, $5.25), are available. *73 rue de la Gauchetière O, Chinatown, tel. 514/866-3131. No reservations on weekends, so be prepared to wait on Sun. morning. Dress: informal. AE, DC, MC, V.*

Delicatessens

Inexpensive **Bens.** On the menu of this large, efficient, and charming deli, all the items with "Bens" in the name are red or are covered in red. "Bens Cheesecake" is smothered in strawberries; "Bens Ice Cold Drink" is the color of electric cherry juice; and the specialty, the "Big Ben Sandwich," is two slices of rye bread enclosing a seductive, pink pile of juicy smoked meat (Montreal's version of corned beef). According to Bens lore, the founder, Ben Kravitz, brought the first smoked-meat sandwich to Montreal in 1908. The rest, as they say, is history. A number of the walls are devoted to photos of celebrities who have visited Bens. The decor is strictly '50s, with yellow and green walls and vaguely Art Deco, institutional furniture. The waiters are often wisecracking characters but are nonetheless incredibly efficient. Beer, wine, and cocktails are served. Bens motto: "But for life the Universe were nothing, and all that has life requires nourishment." *990 blvd. de Maisonneuve O, downtown, tel. 514/844-1000. Reservations accepted. Dress: informal. MC, V. Closed Sun.*

Briskets. The neo-student-hangout-style decor—old advertising posters and college banners on the walls and thick wood tables for carving your initials—is appropriate since it's next to Concordia University. Briskets serves a variety of burgers and sandwiches, but the emphasis is on smoked meat, lean, medium, and fatty. Lean is too dry and flaky, fatty is just that. So medium is the way to go: tender and juicy. A "king-size" sandwich is served with fat, red, pickled peppers, a slightly sweet, crisp slaw, and a sour dill pickle. There is also steak with sides of fries, onion rings, and "Munchy Mushrooms." Briskets serves draft beer and house wine but no harder stuff. The service is fast, and takeout is available. *Three downtown locations: 4006 Ste-Catherine O, 1073 Beaver Hall, and 2055 Bishop, near Metro Guy, tel. 514/843-3650. No reservations. Dress: informal. AE, MC, V.*

★ **Schwartz's.** There's intense competition for the title as the best smoked-meat restaurant in Montreal. Briskets and Schwartz's seem to bobble the crown between themselves. Schwartz's is definitely the more traditional of the two. It occupies a storefront in the heart of The Main, the old Jewish section, and inside there's a short counter and seven or eight rows of tables. The kitchen serves up smoked-meat sandwiches, steak, liver steak, frankfurters, and pickled pimiento peppers. That's it. As at Briskets, the choices are lean, medium, and fatty, and the medium is the best ("Only a fool would order rare," say Schwartz's owners). The meat is more peppery on the outside

Auberge le Vieux St-Gabriel, **36**
Bagatelle, **9**
Beaver Club, **31**
Ben's, **19**
Bocca d'Oro, **28**
Brisket's, **24, 30, 32**
Cathay, **33**
Chez Delmo, **34**
Il Était une Fois, **39**
Katsura, **23**
La Binerie Mont-Royal, **10**
La Chartreuse, **15**
La Desserte, **7**
La Paryse, **17**
La Sucrerie de la Montagne, **1**
Laurier BBQ, **4**
Le Café de Paris, **21**
Le Lutetia, **22**
Le Mitoyen, **2**
Le Paris, **29**
Le Restaurant, **18**
Les Filles du Roy, **37**
Les Halles, **26**
Les Mignardises, **16**
L'Etang des Moulins, **41**
Le Taj, **20**
L'Express, **14**
Manoir Rouville Campbell, **40**
Milos, **5**
Moishe's, **12**
Pizzaiole, **3, 25**
Prego, **8**
Schwartz's, **11**
Stash's, **35**
Toman, **27**
Wilensky's, **6**
Xuan, **13**
Zhivago, **38**

93

than the offerings of other smoked-meat eateries, and as tender as any inside. The service is fast, if unadorned. *3895 rue St-Laurent, near Metro Mont Royal, tel. 514/842-4813. No reservations. Dress: informal. No credit cards, no alcohol.*

Wilensky's Light Lunch. Since 1932 the Wilensky family has served up its special: Italian-American salami on a Jewish roll, generously slathered with mustard. Served hot, it's a meal in itself. You can also get hot dogs or a grilled sandwich, which comes with a marinated pickle and an old-fashioned sparkling beverage. The regulars at the counter are among the most colorful in Montreal. A visit here is a must. This neighborhood haunt was the setting for the film *The Apprenticeship of Duddy Kravitz*, from the novel by Mordecai Richler. The service, which is not very friendly, does not prompt one to linger, but the prices make up for it. To satisfy your sweet tooth, take a short walk over to Chez L-G (5181 blvd. St-Laurent), where you will find the best cookies in town. *5167 Clark, tel. 514/271-1247. Dress: informal. No credit cards. No liquor license. Closed weekends.*

French

Very Expensive

The Beaver Club. Early fur traders started the Beaver Club in a shack during Montreal's colonial days. In the 19th century it became a social club for the city's business and political elite. It still has the august atmosphere of a men's club devoted to those who trap: pelts of bear, raccoon, and beaver still line the walls and members' engraved brass plates gleam from a sideboard near the entrance. The Beaver Club is a gourmet French restaurant open to anyone with a reservation who arrives in the proper attire. Master chef Edward Merard was among the first to introduce nouvelle cuisine to Montreal, and he has a large and devoted following. The luncheon table d'hôte includes such dishes as terrine of duckling with pistachios and onion-and-cranberry compote. For more mundane tastes, the restaurant also specializes in meaty dishes like roast prime rib of beef au jus. The Beaver Club always offers one or two low-fat, low-salt, low-calorie plates. The waiters are veteran to the point of being antiques (Charles, the maître d', has been faithfully at his post for more than 20 years), and the service is as excellent as the food. *The Queen Elizabeth Hotel, 900 blvd. René Lévesque O, downtown, tel. 514/861-3511. Reservations a must. Jacket and tie. AE, DC, MC, V.*

Le Café de Paris. This restaurant is a masterpiece of atmosphere. You sit at large, well-spaced tables in a room ablaze with flowers with the light streaming in the French windows. During the summer you can sit outside under a canopy and dine beside a flower-filled garden and a pool complete with ducks. Inside or outside the waiters provide perfect, unobtrusive service. The menu opens with a selection of fresh caviar flown in from Petrossian in New York City. Then you turn to the seven-course menu de dégustation, a meal of small, exquisite dishes, such as quail salad with grapes, that adds up to a sumptuous repast. If you can't spend a couple of hours over dinner, you can choose from classics like calf sweetbreads with a slightly bitter endive sauce or the flambéed fillet of buffalo with green peppercorns. At meal's end the waiter will trundle over the dessert cart; the crème brûlée with raisins is a favorite. The wine list includes everything from reasonably priced bottles to extremely expensive vintages. The table to the right rear of the dining room as you enter is where the prime minister dines when he's in town. If he's not there, you are likely to see other national political and financial figures supping or schmoozing between tables. *Ritz-Carlton Hotel, 1228 Sherbrooke St. W, tel. 514/842-4212. Reservations required. Jacket required at lunch and dinner. AE, MC, V.*

★ **Les Halles.** Definitely French, this restaurant took its name from the celebrated Parisian market immortalized by the pen of Émile Zola in *Le Ventre de Paris.* Its old France character, enhanced by mirrors and typical bistro inscriptions, will give you the feeling of having gone from busy Crescent Street to even busier rue Montorgueil. However, dependable cuisine and tradition make Les Halles very efficient. The fussy waiters, with their white aprons and towels on their arms, seem to come straight out of a '40s French film. The wine cellar is exceptional and contains around 250 different bottles, from $11 to $475. The menu shows a lot of imagination without ignoring the classics: terrine of venison with a walnut sauce, fish stew with croutons, snails in all kinds of sauces, *plaice* (lemon sole) in cider, chicken *forestière,* and duck with foie gras in port sauce sit comfortably beside the chef's ventures into nouvelle cuisine such as his lobster with ginger and coconut. The desserts are classic, delicious, and remarkably fresh. The Paris-Brest, a puff pastry with praline cream inside, is one of the best in town. *1450 Crescent, tel. 514/844-2328. Reservations recommended. Dress: informal but chic. AE, DC, MC, V. Closed Sun.-Mon., Sat. lunch.*

Le Lutetia. This magnificent restaurant is worth a little detour, if only for the piano bar happy hour. The plethora of styles—rococo, Renaissance, empire, fin de siècle, and baroque—is a spectacle in itself. This outrageously romantic restaurant is the perfect choice for a tête-à-tête by candlelight. The French cuisine, sometimes nouvelle, sometimes classic, is always served under a silver cover. Behind their glass partition, the cooks busy themselves and give the clientele an appetizing show, even at the busiest moments. The menu gastronomique changes each week according to the market and the seasons. À la carte half portions are available, which enables the diners to taste many dishes in one meal. Shrimp with fennel in puff pastry, ballotine of pheasant in a brioche dough, noisettes of veal *périgourdine* (with truffles), or medallion of beef with coarse mustard precede the cheese or the dessert cart. There is a very good wine list and champagne cart. *1430 rue de la Montagne, tel. 514/288-5656. Reservations recommended. Dress: informal but chic. Terrace on the roof in summer. AE, CB, DC, MC, V.*

★ **Les Mignardises.** Chef Jean-Pierre Monnet used to run the kitchen at Les Halles. Now that he has his own place, his talents are given free range. Les Mignardises is considered the finest and certainly the most expensive restaurant in town. You enter via the bar and climb up one flight to the simple, elegant dining room decorated with copper pans hanging from the exposed brick walls. The dining area holds only about 20 tables, so reservations are a must. If your wallet is full, you can choose the seven-course menu de dégustation ($58.95, or $71.50 if you allow the chef to choose the dishes for you). But if you're on a budget, it's still possible to enjoy a full meal. The three-course table d'hôte lunch menu allows you to sample delicious dishes like fish salad on gazpacho or marinated duck breast with vinegar sauce. The latter is sliced rare duck breast artfully arranged on a bed of oyster mushrooms with a slightly sweet vinegar sauce. The former is an appetizer of marinated raw salmon, tuna, and swordfish with tarragon and pink peppercorns on a light tomato gazpacho. Delicious potatoes sautéed with bouillon and onions in a little copper pot accompany the dishes. One of the house special desserts is crepes with honey ice cream. The presentation always takes a back seat to the taste. As you would expect, the wine list is large and pricey (the least expensive bottle is $24.50). The waiters and waitresses are prompt, knowledgeable, and friendly. *2035–37 St-Denis, near Berri and Sherbrooke metros, tel. 514/842–1151. Reservations required. Dress: informal, but no jeans or T-shirts. AE, CB, DC, MC, V. Closed Sun. and Mon.*

Expensive– Very Expensive **Le Restaurant.** Le Quatre Saisons' management claims to have invented Montreal's version of "power" dining here. (The competition with the Ritz-Carlton continues.) Le Restaurant certainly has the power look. The choicest seats are on a raised circular platform, encircled by a white Hellenistic colonnade. They are comfortable, but very businesslike, executive chairs. In these impressive surroundings Quebec's political and business leaders dine on first-class nouvelle cuisine. Many must suffer from high blood pressure, because the menu features "alternative cuisine" dishes with reduced salt, cholesterol, and calories. The fricassee of sweetbreads and prawns with lobster butter is not on this list. If you suffer from chronic low wallet weight, you can stop in for lunch and have the onion soup with a ham-and-cheese sandwich on French bread. Power breakfasts start at 7 AM. The standard of service here, as in the rest of the hotel, is high. The wine list is expensive and excellent, of course. *Le Quatre Saisons, 1050 Sherbrooke St. W, tel. 514/284–1110. Reservations required. AE, CB, DC, MC, V.*

Expensive **Auberge le Vieux St. Gabriel.** Established in a big stone house in 1754, this restaurant claims to be the oldest in America. The interior is lined with rough stone walls, and enormous old beams hold up the ceilings. In late 1987 it reopened with new owners who plan to expand both the menu and the dining space. At this writing the fare was hearty yet unadventurous French, with a bit of local Québécois flavor. The pea soup à la Canadienne is yellow and chunky rather than the American-style bland green puree. The perch fillets sautéed in dill butter are morsels of tender fish on top of mushy, overly rich creamed mushrooms. Other entrées include beef tenderloin with morels in a brandy-and-cream sauce and a terrine of rabbit with prunes and apples in a honey cream. If you're worried about your cholesterol, watch out. Waitresses in colonial costumes provide prompt service. The restaurant seats close to 500 people, but you'd never guess it because there are so many separate dining rooms. *426 rue St-Gabriel, Vieux-Montréal, tel. 514/878–3561. Reservations suggested. Dress: informal. AE, DC, MC, V. Closed Sun. except in summer.*

Moderate–Expensive **L'Express.** The crowd is elbow to elbow, and the animated at★ mosphere is reminiscent of a Paris train station at this earnest establishment. L'Express has earned the title "best bistro in town." It is also the best-stocked. Popular media figures come here to be seen, a task made easier by the mirrored walls. The atmosphere is smoky, and the noise level at its peak on weekend evenings. The cuisine is always impeccable, the service is fast, and the prices are very good. L'Express has one of the best and most original wine cellars in town. Wine and champagne are available by the glass as well as by the bottle. The steak tartare with french fries, the salmon with sorrel, the calf's liver with tarragon, the first course of chicken livers with pistachios, or even the modest smoked salmon, are all marvelous year-round. There are specials of the day to give the many regulars a change of pace. Jars of gherkins and fresh *baguettes*, cheeses aged to perfection, and quality eaux-de-vie make the pleasure last longer. *3927 rue St-Denis, tel. 514/845-5333. Reservations a must. Dress: casual but studied. AE, CB, DC, MC, V.*

★ **Le Paris.** This is a true bistro, where old Francophone couples dressed to the nines sit side by side on red banquettes, sip *vin rouge*, and fork down the *choucroute garnie* (sausages and ham on a huge mound of sauerkraut—a hearty meal on a winter's night). The decor is tacky French; the walls are hung with old theater posters and maritime scenes by pseudo-Impressionists, but the fare is simple, reasonably priced, and excellent. It serves steak grilled, with Bordelaise sauce or *au poivre;* fresh skate with *beurre noir;* and salmon poached with *beurre blanc*. Desserts include praline cake, and rhubarb compote cooked in syrup. The surroundings are homey and comfortable, unless you're near the kitchen door, which swings open every 10 seconds. *1812 rue Ste-Catherine O, 1 block from Metro Guy, tel. 514/937-4898. Reservations suggested. Dress: informal but neat. AE, MC, V. Closed Sun.*

Greek

Expensive
★ **Milos.** Nets, ropes, floats, and lanterns—the usual clichéed symbols of the sea—hang from Milos's walls and ceilings. The real display, however, is in the refrigerated cases and on the beds of ice in the back by the kitchen: fresh fish from all over the world; octopus, squid, and shrimp; crabs, oysters, and sea urchins; lamb chops, steaks, and chicken; and vegetables, cheese, and olives. In short, all the makings of your meal are there for you to inspect before you make your choice. The seafood is flown in from wholesalers in Nova Scotia, New York, Florida, and Athens. A meal can start out with chewy, tender, and hot octopus, or if you're adventurous, you might try the cool and creamy roe scooped from raw sea urchins. The main dish at Milos is usually fish—pick whatever looks freshest—grilled over charcoal and seasoned with parsley, capers, and lemon juice. It's done to a turn and is achingly delicious. The fish are priced by the pound, and you can order one larger fish to serve two or more. Don't be afraid to use your fingers: hot towels are provided at the end. The bountiful Greek salad (enough for two) is a perfect side dish or can be a meal itself. For dessert you might try a *loukoumad* (honey ball), a deep-fried puff of dough doused in honey, chopped nuts, and cinnamon. The waiters are professional but not always knowledgeable about the whole array of exotic seafood available. Milos is a healthy walk from Metro Laurier. You can also take Bus 51 from the same Metro stop and ask the driver to let you off at avenue du Parc; Milos is halfway up the block to the right. *5357 ave. du Parc, tel. 514/272-3522. Reservations required. Dress: informal. AE, MC, V.*

Hamburgers

Inexpensive **La Paryse.** This Montreal institution offers *hambourgeois*, so-
★ named by the "Office de la langue française." Very '50s, this
modest greasy spoon attracts a colorful and ever-famished collection of characters. Indeed, Paryse Taillefer makes the best
hamburgers in town. The misshapen meat patties, the hand-cut
french fries, and the dripping bacon and cheese are guarantees
of authenticity. The "regular" consists of Viennese bread, a
quarter pound of good lean ground beef, mozzarella cheese,
pickles, onions, tomatoes, lettuce, and mayonnaise. Also try
the "special," with cream cheese and bacon. Five-cent candy
and old-fashioned cake complete the illusion of going back in
time. *302 Ontario E, tel. 514/842-2040. Dress: informal. No
credit cards.*

Il était une fois. Near the principal touristic attractions of
Vieux-Montréal, this old train station has been transformed
into a dining car. The historical decor with antique ornaments
is amusing and familiar. A small terrace at the back enables the
diner to enjoy the good weather with his meal. Hamburgers
weighing half a pound are served in baskets with enormous
french fries. There is nothing better to satiate hungry appe-
tites. Grand Trunk Burger, Chili Burger, and Végé Burger are
among the more than 10 choices. There is local beer on tap or
old-fashioned floats. *600 d'Youville, tel. 514/842-6783. Dress:
informal. MC, V.*

Indian

Expensive **Le Taj.** One of the rare Indian restaurants in town in which the
decor and the music are appropriate. The cuisine of the north of
India is honored here, less spicy and more refined than that of
the south. The tandoori ovens seal in the flavors of the grilled
meat and fish, the *nan* bread comes piping hot to the table, and
behind a glass partition the cook retrieves the skewers with his
bare hands from the hot coals just like an experienced fakir.
There are a few vegetarian specialties on the menu; for example, the *taj-thali*, consisting of lentils, chili *pakoras*, *basmati*
rice, and *saag panir*—spicy white cheese with spinach. The
tandoori quail and the nan stuffed with meat go well together,
as does a whole series of dry curries, from lamb to chicken and
beef with aromatic rice. The desserts, coconut ice cream or
mangoes (canned) are sometimes decorated with pure silver
leaves if the patron so desires. Other cultures, other mores!
The tea scented with cloves is delicious; it cleans the palate,
warms in winter, and cools in summer. *2077 Stanley, tel. 514/
845-9015. Reservations recommended on weekends. Dress: informal but chic. AE, MC, V. Closed Sat. lunch.*

Italian

Expensive **Prego.** European chic lives at Prego. So does excellent nouvelle
★ Italian cuisine. The clientele looks old and wealthy and is outfit-
ted in the latest fashions. They sit on *faux* zebra-skin chairs or
black banquettes and watch the flames in the high-tech black
kitchen (if they aren't watching themselves in the mirror). Every dish is relatively light and absolutely fresh. The *Insalata
Caprese* is a simple, satisfying salad of tomatoes, basil, olive
oil, and bocconcini cheese. Between courses you are given a

Dining

small serving of sorbet; if you're lucky, it will be the tarragon sorbet with poppy seeds sprinkled in it. The linguine with tuna, tomatoes, and capers is warm, light, and redolent of summer, even on a winter night. An excellent main dish is *medaglione di vitello ai pistacchi*—veal with cream, pistachios, fresh fruits, and Frangelico (hazelnut liqueur). Keep some room for dessert, because Prego serves one that should be in a hall of fame somewhere: *tiramisu*, a light cake with a filling of sweet, creamy mascarpone cheese and a chocolate icing dusted with cocoa. On the serving plate it sits next to a pool of sweet vanilla and chocolate crème in a sunburst design crowned with a single candied violet. It's a feast for the eyes and the mouth. The service and wine list are first rate. *5142 blvd. St-Laurent, 5 blocks from Metro Laurier, tel. 514/271-3234. Reservations a must. Dress: informal but chic. AE, CB, DC, MC, V. Closed lunch.*

Moderate–Expensive **Bocca d'Oro.** This four-year-old Italian restaurant next to Metro Guy has a huge menu offering a wide variety of appetizers, pastas, and veal and vegetarian dishes. One pasta specialty is *tritico di pasta*, which is one helping each of spinach ravioli with salmon and caviar, shells marinara, and spaghetti primavera. A good choice from the dozen or so veal dishes is scaloppine *zingara* with tomatoes, mushrooms, pickles, and olives. With the dessert and coffee the waiters bring out a big bowl of walnuts for you to crack at your table (nutcrackers provided). The two floors of dining rooms are decorated with brass rails, wood paneling, and paintings, and Italian pop songs play in the background. The staff is extremely friendly and professional; if you're in a hurry, they'll serve your meal in record time. *1448 rue St-Mathieu, downtown, tel. 514/933-8414. Reservations suggested. Dress: informal but neat. AE, CB, DC, MC, V. Closed Sun.*

Moderate **Pizzaiole.** The wood-fired oven pizzas have had no respite since they started to appear in Montreal in the beginning of the 1980s. Pizzaiole, the pioneer in the field, is still by far the best. The two branches have somewhat adopted the same fresh decor emphasizing the brick oven, but the clientele and the ambience of the Crescent place are a bit younger. In both places, there are about 20 possible combinations, without counting the toppings and extras which personalize a pizza in no time at all. Whether you choose a simple tomato-cheese, a "Monalisa" with onions, ham, tomato, cheese, and eggs on crackling "half-dough" (actually half the weight of the regular pizza dough), one with smoked salmon, béchamel sauce, and capers, or a ratatouille on a whole-wheat crust, you'll find that all the pizzas are made to order and brought immediately to the table. The calzone, a turnover filled with a variety of meats and cheeses, is worth the trip. Try the thirst-quenching Massawipi beer from a local brewery, perfect with a pizza. As for the desserts, the chocolate terrine is delicious and easily shared by two people, but it is even better when eaten by one. *Two locations: 1446-A Crescent, tel. 514/845-4158; 5100 Hutchison, tel. 514/274-9349. AE, MC, V.*

Japanese

Expensive–Very Expensive **Katsura.** This cool, elegant Japanese restaurant introduced sushi (Japanese raw fish) to Montreal and is the haunt of business people who equate raw food with power. If you're with a group or just want privacy, you can reserve a tatami room closed off from the rest of the restaurant by rice-paper screens. Tatami are the straw mats you sit on (sans shoes) for a traditional Japanese dining experience. The sushi chefs create an assortment of raw seafood delicacies, as well as their own delicious invention, the Canada roll (smoked salmon and salmon caviar) at the sushi bar at the rear. Sushi connoisseurs may find some offerings less than top quality. The California rolls, for instance, are prepared in advance and refrigerated for a little too long. Katsura also serves some nonsushi dishes, like *Shabu-shabu*, a boiling hot pot of broth in which thin slices of beef and vegetables are dipped. Teriyaki and tempura dishes tempt the less adventuresome. Katsura offers wine, sake, Japanese beer, and a number of house cocktails. The service is excellent, but if you sample all the sushi, the tab can be exorbitant. *2170 rue de la Montagne, downtown between Peel and Guy metros, tel. 514/849-1172. Reservations necessary, but you might get a seat at the sushi bar without them. Dress: informal but neat. AE, CB, DC, MC, V. No lunch weekends.*

Polish

Moderate ★ **Stash's.** This Montreal institution is also the preferred refuge for pilgrims and tourists visiting the Notre-Dame church. A way to renew one's ties with the native Poland of the Pope, this unpretentious little restaurant offers a cuisine totally adapted to the hard winters of Quebec. Pork, potatoes, and cabbage are the basis of this Eastern European cuisine, just as they were in Quebec not so long ago. The soup of the day is generously served in a big bowl and accompanied with slices of buttered rye bread. More like a stew, it is a meal in itself. The specials of the day—stuffed cabbage, stuffed peppers, or goulash—share the bill with the à la carte dishes, either veal scallops topped with an egg or the famous pierogis stuffed with cheese or meat. The desserts also deserve an honorable mention and are a reminder of family cooking. The apple and peach croustade with vanilla cream will make your mouth water, and the lemon, poppy, coffee, hazelnut, and chocolate cakes invite a coffee break. Vodka is served with every meal, just to make all of this hearty food go down easily. *461 rue St-Sulpice, tel. 514/861-2915. Dress: informal. AE, MC, V.*

Québécois

Moderate–Expensive ★ **Les Filles du Roy.** This restaurant serves fine Québécois cuisine, a blend of 17th-century French recipes, North American produce and game, and some culinary tips picked up from Native Americans . . . with a lot of maple syrup poured over everything. The Trottier family opened Les Filles du Roy (the name refers to the women brought over to New France by Louis XIV to marry settlers) in an 18th-century stone mansion in 1964. If you want to go the native route—and you can eat excellent classic French cuisine as well—start with the "caribou," which is an eye-popping drink made of grain alcohol, sweet local wine, a dash of scotch, and Drambuie. The original recipe was concocted by hunters; it called for real caribou blood and homemade alcohol and provided warmth as well as vitamins. A traditional Québécois meal starts with an appetizer like Canadian-style pork and beans or pea soup. If you like sweet meat dishes, try the ham with maple syrup. More refined dishes using local game and produce include wild lake duck with blueberries and *cipaille du Lac St-Jean*, which is a combination of six different meats, some wild, in a pie crust with vegetables. A large variety of maple syrup desserts are available: *trempette au sirop d'érable*, pieces of bread that have been dipped in boiling maple syrup in a bowl of heavy cream; sugar pie; and *oeuf cuit dans le sirop d'érable*, an egg poached in maple syrup. The popular Sunday brunch, served from 11 to 3, attracts groups of Japanese tourists wolfing down the ham and maple syrup dishes. The interior of Les Filles du Roy is all stone and wood, and the furniture looks authentic; the staff wears the usual colonial-era dress. The service is knowledgeable and friendly. *415 rue Bonsecours, 3 blocks from Metro Champs de Mars in Vieux-Montréal, tel. 514/849-3535. Reservations required. Dress: informal but neat. AE, DC, MC, V.*

Moderate **Laurier BBQ.** At its post for 50 years, this family-run restaurant is still famous for its roast chicken with clove-scented barbecue sauce. Laurier has been the Sunday-night meeting place of French-Canadian families for generations, and its recipes have remained faithful to the culinary heritage of their grandmothers. The pea soup and the vegetable soup are the first courses par excellence, and the Laurier salad has been presented in the same way for 50 years, with a spicy vinaigrette. The tasty and juicy chicken, the french fries (frozen), and the cole slaw form an inseparable trio baptized with barbecue sauce. Many house specialties are prepared, like chicken pâté or chicken pot pie, that are available in small or large portions. A meal here is not complete without dessert: warm sugar pie with ice cream or warm mocha cake with a big glass of milk are worth the best childhood memories. The waitresses are so maternal they'll make you homesick. *381 ave. Laurier O, tel. 514/273-3671. Dress: informal. AE, MC, V.*

Inexpensive **La Binerie Mont-Royal.** The name of this Plateau Mont-Royal haunt is used to describe the unpretentious little neighborhood restaurants of the "belle province." The *bineries* offer everything and nothing, breakfast with the newspaper, or the special of the day with a bit of free conversation. The name also refers to the national dish of the Québécois: the *bines* (beans), or pork and beans. The restaurant knows its business: it serves 27 tons of pork and beans each year! This binerie was at the center of the novel *Le Matou* (the Quebec best-seller by Yves Beauchemin) and is still today the meeting place of incorrigible nostalgists. From morning to night it serves *rôties* (toasts) with *minoune* (roast drippings), *tourtière*, Chinese pâté (a Quebec specialty), beef with vegetables, and the famous pork meatball stew. Everything is generously covered with Heinz ketchup. Rice pudding and *pouding chômeur* (poor man's pudding) are usually served as well. There's lots of coffee, no alcohol, and ultrafast service. Its lack of space accounts for the fact that everybody squeezes at the counter, which has only 10 seats. La Binerie is a historical sight not to be missed. *367 rue Mont-Royal E, tel. 514/285-9078. No reservations. Dress: informal. No credit cards. Closed Sun. and Sat. after 2 PM.*

Russian

Very Expensive **Zhivago.** Ideally, you should arrive here by horse-drawn car-
★ riage in the middle of winter. Tucked behind the heavy draperies of the entrance hall, this restaurant attracts lovers of

19th-century Russia as well as caviar-and-vodka devotees. Indeed, nobody leaves this private house without having downed an icy cold Polish vodka. *Nasdrovie!* Once warmed up, don't miss the excellent "made in Quebec" caviar, a lot less expensive than its Russian or Iranian counterparts. The smoked wild salmon with coriander is paired on your plate with the *zakouski* (small sour-cream-covered hors d'oeuvres). The spectacular rack of lamb flambéed with vodka and the simpler beef Stroganoff, with sour cream and mushrooms, are wholesome dishes that derive more from the splendor of French cuisine than from the economy of Russian cooking. For dessert, the crepes Manouch (glorified crepes Suzette) or the chocolate Sacher torte are beautiful endings to the meal, and the *tzigane* singers and heartrending music will leave an indelible impression. Reserve one of the private loges (for two) with heavy draperies, but keep in mind that these rooms are separated by a glass partition . . . no exhibitionists, please. *419 rue St-Pierre, tel. 514/284-0333. Reservations strongly recommended. Dress: informal but chic. AE, CB, DC, MC, V. Closed Sun., Mon., and daily for lunch.*

Seafood

Expensive **Bagatelle.** The decor of this bistro has been entirely imported from Belgium, from the wood-paneled counter, where solitary diners gather at noon, to the engraved mirrors. This does not make Bagatelle a Belgian restaurant, though. Chef Pascal Gellé, a Frenchman, took over this pseudo-chic bistro and changed it into a restaurant in which fish is treated with deference. (There are also offals and nouvelle-cuisine meat preparations on the menu.) With each fish dish (seven or eight specials each day), you can choose from a variety of sauces: sorrel, tomato, sweet peppers, coarse mustard, or saffron. Select one or many, depending upon your mood. Pollack, salmon, trout, swordfish, whitefish, monkfish, and grouper are all very fresh and at unbeatable prices. The light wines are of good quality and are reasonably priced. Some wines are available by the glass. The service is first class, but the noise level is a bit high when the restaurant is full. The desserts are fine and when the chef is not overwhelmed they can be extraordinary. The *gâteau de crêpes* will take your breath away. *4806 ave. du Parc, tel. 514/273-4088. Reservations recommended. Dress: bohemian but studied. AE, MC, V. Closed Sat., and Sun. for lunch.*

★ **Chez Delmo.** This stretch of rue Notre-Dame is halfway between the courts and the stock exchange, and at lunchtime Chez Delmo is filled with professionals gobbling oysters and fish. The first room as you enter is lined with two long, dark, wood-and-brass bars, which are preferred by those wishing a fast lunch. Above both are murals depicting a medieval feast. The back room is a more sedate and cheerful dining room. In either room the dining is excellent and the seafood fresh. A good first course, or perhaps a light lunch, is the seafood salad, a delicious mix of shrimp, lobster, crab, and artichoke hearts on a bed of Boston lettuce, sprinkled with a scalliony vinaigrette. The poached salmon with hollandaise is a nice slab of perfectly cooked fish with potatoes and broccoli. The lobsters and oysters are priced according to market rates. Chez Delmo was founded at the same address in 1910. The service is efficient and low-key. *211-215 rue Notre-Dame O, Vieux-Mon-*

tréal, tel. 514/849-4061. Reservations suggested for dinner. Dress: informal but neat. AE, CB, DC, MC, V. No dinner Mon., no lunch Sat., closed Sun.

Steaks

Expensive Moishe's. A paradise for carnivores, Moishe's is the last place to
★ receive dietetic advice. The meat portions are as large as a pound, which will no doubt send your cholesterol level way up. Rib steak, T-bone, and filet mignon are all grilled on wood and presented with dill-scented pickles, cole slaw, french fries or baked potato. The meat, imported from West Canada, is juicy and tender, marbled and delectable, and aged 21 days in the restaurant's cold chambers. Moishe's grouchy service, its decor (reminiscent of an all-male private club), and its tasteless desserts don't seem to frighten away the real meat eaters. For those with a smaller appetite, the portions can be shared, but it will cost you an additional $4 and the waiter's reproachful look. *3961 blvd. St-Laurent, tel. 514/845-1696. Reservations for parties of 3 or more. Dress: informal. AE, MC, V.*

Vietnamese

Moderate Xuan. Near the pedestrian zone of Prince Arthur Street, this
★ little restaurant strives to perpetuate real Vietnamese cuisine beyond the popular brochettes formula so popular with competitors. The owners lived in France for many years before settling in the province of Quebec. They have included in the menu typical dishes such as the Vietnamese crepe with vegetables and mint, the five-flavor stuffed quail, honey and citronella pork, and numerous soups at noontime that are hearty enough to be meals. The cold spring rolls in Hoisin sauce are particularly filling. For dessert, there is a delicious *assiette maison* (house plate) consisting of fruit puffs and rice-alcohol-scented ice cream, decorated with little Chinese umbrellas and flambéed in the French style. *26 Prince Arthur W, tel. 514/849-4923. AE, MC, V. Closed Mon.*

Tearooms

Inexpensive La Chartreuse. This tiny tearoom, in the Viennese tradition, has big surprises in store. On the counter are exhibited heavy and filling cakes, sparsely decorated but mouth-watering. *Nusstorte* with hazelnut buttercream, *Dobostorte* with chocolate layers and caramel icing, Sacher torte garnished with apricot jam, and Rigo Jancsi with chocolate ganache, fresh nuts and coffee syrup contribute to make your time at La Chartreuse well spent. One moment on the lips, forever on the hips! The coffee (there is no espresso or cappuccino for lack of the appropriate equipment) is served with liqueurs, chocolate, cinnamon, or cream (whipped or not). Mozart is played discreetly in the background. *3439 rue St-Denis, tel. 514/842-0793. Dress: informal. No credit cards. Open 4 PM-midnight. Closed Mon.*

★ La Desserte. Here are without a doubt the best cheesecakes in town. This tiny tearoom offers its cakes by the slice or in combinations of three. The ingredients are first class; the nuts are ground by hand and the purees of fresh fruit make these cakes handicraft showpieces. Valrhona chocolate (there is no richer brand) is used in the pistachio-and-black chocolate cake, in the chestnut-and-brown chocolate cake, and in the white-and-black chocolate cake. The plum and nut cake and the Italian-style ricotta cake are also worth trying. The cakes with fruit are more subtle but also delicious. There are also different kinds of Swiss tarts (the nut tart will make you cry with joy), English cakes, and Austrian pastry (the chocolate Rigo Jancsi is a triumph). The proprietress does not hide her predilection for good hot chocolate and good teas. We forgive her. *5380 ave. du Parc, tel. 514/272-5797. Dress: informal. No credit cards. No alcohol. Closed Mon.*

Toman Pastry Shop. This pleasant small haven on the second floor of an old house in the center of the city is the ideal location to take a break between intensive shopping sprees. Very Old Europe, Toman is in fact of Czech origin. The pastry is honest, without frills, and the service without ceremony. A Czech specialty, little cubes covered with chocolate and filled with marzipan, hazelnuts or liqueur, make a guilt-free little snack. For the incorrigibles, the apple strudel, the strawberry shortcake, the hazelnut cake, the Black Forest cake, the chestnut cake, and the orange cake are there to help you cope once and for all with one of the seven deadly sins. Light meals and soups of the house are also available. *1421 Mackay, tel. 514/844-1605. Open Tues.-Sat. 9-6. Open Mon. Oct.-April. No credit cards. No liquor license.*

Bagels

Bagel Factory (74 Fairmount Ave. W, tel. 514/272-0667).
The Bagel Place (1616 rue Ste-Catherine O, tel. 514/931-2827).
Bagel Shop (263 rue St-Viateur O, tel. 514/276-8044; 158 rue St-Viateur O, tel. 514/270-2972).

Chocolate

La Brioche Lyonnaise (1593 rue St-Denis, tel. 514/842-7017).
Léonidas (605 blvd. de Maisonneuve O, tel. 514/849-2620; 5111 ave. du Parc, tel. 514/272-3447).
Chocolat Heyez (Passage CN, Place Bonaventure, 1000 Lagauchetière O, tel. 514/392-1480).
Lenôtre (1050 ave. Laurier O, tel. 514/270-2702).

Restaurants Near Montreal

Very Expensive **Le Mitoyen.** North of the city, in the small village of Ste-Dorothée (today part of the city of Laval), this great French restaurant leans resolutely in favor of nouvelle cuisine. People come from everywhere (mostly from Montreal) to taste the inventions of the self-taught chef. Meticulously decorated, this old house with the red roof is a haven for gourmands. Try the galette of smoked salmon, sweetbreads *ragout* (stew) with artichoke hearts, Guinea hen with sherry wine vinegar, or quail with juniper berries in puff pastry. All are heavenly. For dessert, the maple nougat glacé or the poached pears in red wine and pepper end the meal elegantly. *Place publique Ste-Dorothée, Laval (Rte. 15 N), tel. 514/689-2977. Reservations required. Dress: informal but chic. Closed Mon., and lunch daily (except for parties).*

Expensive– **L'Étang des Moulins.** In the charming small village of
Very Expensive Terrebonne, only 30 minutes from the center of Montreal, the

restaurant of chef Jean Cayer is an oasis in a gastronomic desert. Facing the pond with its splashing ducks, the terrace offers a bucolic feast for the urban crowd at noontime. In the evening, the cozy interior of this old fieldstone house built in 1820 provides comfortable intimacy. But it is mostly for the cuisine of this great chef that people converge here, away from the city's chaos. Cayer's specialty is offals, and he is marvelous at preparing sweetbreads with tarragon and kidneys with port. The little pâté Québécois, the confit of honey-lacquered duck and lemon marmalade, and the rack of lamb with herbs are done with genius, love, and passion. The classic desserts of fruit over *crème anglaise* (light custard sauce) are ravishing, especially during berry season. The service and wine list are equally impeccable. *888 chemin St-Louis, Terrebonne (Rte. 440 E or 25 N), tel. 514/471-4018. Reservations and directions recommended. Dress: informal but chic. AE, MC, V. Closed Mon.*

Expensive **La Sucrerie de la Montagne.** On the road to Rigaud in the direction of Ottawa, maple syrup flows from carafes year-round and seasons the plates of pork and beans, *tourtière*, maple ham, omelet soufflés, and crepes cooked over wood fires at this old-fashioned sugar hut. Even the bread is baked on the premises in the old brick ovens fired with maple wood. Everything in this young maple grove is intended to re-create the atmosphere of the sugar season: from the sap flowing in the snow (in season) to the workhorses to men collecting the sap bucket by bucket. Pierre Faucher, the owner of this immense sugar cabin, who looks more like a lumberjack than a restaurateur, greets the Sunday passersby as well as the buses overflowing with Japanese tourists in the middle of July. The food is good, but do not buy the souvenir syrup here; you will find syrup as good in any grocery in Montreal for a lot less money. Complete meal: $25 for adults (tax and sleigh ride included). *300 rang St-Georges, Rigaud (Rte. 40, exit 17), tel. 514/451-5204. Reservations a must. Dress: informal. No credit cards.*

Manoir Rouville Campbell. East of Montreal, facing the Richelieu River, this 17th-century manor has been entirely renovated. It has become one of the most comfortable *relais et châteaux* and is sought after by foreign visitors. This was the home of French and Scottish lieutenants successively, then the home of the Québécois painter Jordi Bonet. The Manoir Rouveille Campbell is a haven of calm and offers classical concert dinners every Sunday evening ($45). The dining room is under the staff of Jean-Pierre Curtat, a very talented young chef who worked for a few years in Paris. From the breadbasket to the voluptuous desserts, nothing is overlooked, and everything is made on the premises. Lobster with ginger, partridge with cabbage, sautéed shrimp with lukewarm *pétoncles* (oysters), and the terrine of sweetbreads in a tart sauce are appetizing propositions. The wine list is rather interesting and affordable. The Sunday brunch is abundant and pleasant for $19.95. *125 chemin des Patriotes S, Mont St-Hilaire (Rte. 20 E), tel. 514/464-5250. Reservations and directions recommended. Dress: informal but chic. AE, CB, DC, MC, V.*

Lodging

On the island of Montreal alone there are more than 15,000 rooms available in every type of accommodation, from world-class luxury hotels to youth hostels, from student dormitories to budget executive motels. Keep in mind that during peak season (May–Aug.), it may be difficult to find a bed without reserving.

Connoisseurs of luxury hotels go to Montreal to enjoy the six-star service of two world-class properties: the Ritz-Carlton and Le Quatre Saisons. Now the subject of a book commemorating its 75th anniversary, the former occupies a central place in Montreal culture because of its age, its historical importance, and its position as a meeting place for the nationally and internationally powerful. Its grande-dame status is a result of its top-notch service and renowned gourmet restaurants. Its only competitor is the Le Quatre Saisons, which offers ultramodern facilities, impeccable service, and comparable cuisine. Of the less expensive (but still pricey) convention-oriented hotels, the Queen Elizabeth (La Reine Elizabeth) and the Bonaventure Hilton International both stand out for having more individuality and less utilitarian corporate style than others in their class. Some may find the Hôtel de la Montagne overdecorated, but it is relatively inexpensive and features one of the city's top restaurants, Lutetia. In the moderate price range, the elegant and friendly Château Versailles is a gem. There are many small, cheap hotels on rue St-Hubert in both directions from the Voyageur bus station. Don't forget the hundreds of homes that provide inexpensive beds and breakfasts. The youth hostel, of course, has the cheapest bed in town.

Peak tourist season runs from May 1 to October 31, when many, but not all, hotels raise their prices. Thus prices often drop from mid-November to early April. Throughout the year a number of the better hotels have two-night, three-day, double-occupancy packages that offer substantial discounts. During the off-season some hotels offer the "Montreal Hospitality Package," with up to a 50% discount on all rooms from Thursday to Sunday inclusive. Montreal tourism offices can provide details on both of these hotel packages. If the hotel you're interested in does not have either plan, it may have its own weekend or special package.

If you arrive in Montreal without a hotel reservation, the tourism information booths at either airport can provide you with a list of hotels and room availability. You must, however, make the reservation yourself. There are no information booths at the Voyageur bus terminal, but the Gare Centrale is directly behind Queen Elizabeth Hotel and a block from the Tourisme Québec center at Place Ville Marie.

The following list is composed of recommended lodgings in Montreal for various budgets. Almost all of them are in the downtown area. There are no hotels in Vieux-Montréal (at least not until the World Trade Centre opens in late 1990), although you will find some bed-and-breakfasts there.

The rates quoted are for a standard double room in May 1989; off-season rates are almost always lower.

Highly recommended hotels in each price category are indicated by a star ★.

Category	Cost*
Very Expensive	over $130
Expensive	$90–$130
Moderate	$70–$90
Inexpensive	under $70

All prices are for a standard double room, excluding an optional service charge.

Downtown

Very Expensive
★
Bonaventure Hilton International. This 394-room Hilton—situated atop a metro station, the Place Bonaventure exhibition center, and a mall crowded with shops and restaurants—is, first and foremost, a resort hotel, and it's 17 floors above the street. When you exit the elevator at 17, you find yourself in a spacious reception area flanked by an outdoor swimming pool (heated year-round) and 2½ acres of gardens, complete with ducks. Also on this floor is a complex of three restaurants and a nightclub that features well-known international entertainers. Le Castillon is the flagship restaurant, known for its three-course, 55-minute businessman's lunch. On Sunday, Gypsy night, the fare is Russian. All rooms have fully stocked minibars and black-and-white TVs in the bathrooms. The Bonaventure has excellent access to the Metro station of the same name beneath it and to all the shops at Place Ville Marie through the Underground City. *1 Place Bonaventure H5A 1E4, tel. 514/878 -2332 or 800/445-8667. 394 rooms. Facilities: 3 restaurants, nightclub, health club with sauna, outdoor pool, rooftop garden, gift shop (hotel is located in a building with a shopping mall), 24-hr room service. AE, CB, DC, MC, V.*

La Citadelle. There's a small pack of hotels on Sherbrooke Street, all of them convenient to Place des Arts, shopping, and the financial district; the Citadelle, a Quality Inn property, is one of them. This relatively small business hotel offers four-star elegance in a low-key atmosphere and service, along with all the features of its better-known brethren: minibars, in-room movies, a small health club with an indoor pool, etc. There's also a passable French restaurant, Le Châtelet. *410 Sherbrooke St. WH3A 1B3, tel. 514/844-8851 or 800/361-7545. 180 rooms. Facilities: restaurant, lounge with entertainment, health club with Nautilus, sauna, and steam room, indoor pool, gift shop. AE, DC, MC, V.*

Le Centre Sheraton. In a huge 37-story complex well placed between the downtown business district and the restaurant streets of Crescent and Bishop, this Sheraton offers a wide variety of services to both the business and tourist crowds. It's also a favorite with international entertainment celebrities. There are three restaurants, five lounges, a nightclub, an indoor pool, a health club, and indoor parking for 600 cars. The elite, five-story Towers section is geared toward business travelers. The Sheraton caters to conventions, so expect to encounter such groups when you stay here. Though the decor is beige and unremarkable (once inside you could be in any large,

Montreal Lodging

Auberge de Jeunesse Internationale de Montréal, **14**
Bonaventure Hilton International, **21**
Château Versailles, **2**
Delta Montreal, **17**
Holiday Inn Crowne Plaza, **18**
Holiday Inn Le Richelieu, **25**
Hôtel de la Montagne, **5**
Hôtel de l'Institut, **24**
Hôtel Maritime, **4**
La Citadelle, **19**
La Reine Elizabeth (Queen Elizabeth), **20**
Le Baccarat Comfort Inn, **16**
Le Centre Sheraton, **9**
Le Château Champlain, **10**
Le Grand Hôtel, **22**
Le Meridien, **23**
Le Nouvel Hôtel, **3**
Le Quatre Saisons (Four Seasons), **12**
Le Royal Roussillon, **26**
Le Shangrila, **11**
Lord Berri, **27**
McGill Student Apartments, **13**
Ramada Renaissance du Parc, **15**
Ritz-Carlton, **6**
Université de Montréal Residence, **1**
YMCA, **8**
YWCA, **7**

109

modern hotel in any North American metropolis), the location's the thing. *1201 blvd. René Lévesque O, H3B 2L7, tel. 514/878–2000 or 800/325–3535. 824 rooms. Facilities: 3 restaurants, 5 lounges, nightclub, health club with whirlpool and sauna, indoor pool, unisex beauty parlor, gift shop. AE, CB, DC, MC, V.*

Le Château Champlain. In the heart of downtown Montreal, at the southern end of Place du Canada, Le Château Champlain is a 36-floor skyscraper with distinctive half-moon-shaped windows. The decor of this Canadian Pacific hotel is glitzy-modern, and the scale is big; the hotel specializes in the convention crowd. Five restaurants offer different ways of entertaining expense-account clients, from formal gourmandizing or tropical-style dining and dancing to high-stepping can-can girls. You can work off the excesses of appetite at Le Spa, a health club with an exercise room, saunas, and a large indoor pool. Two floors are reserved for nonsmokers. Underground passageways connect the Champlain with the Bonaventure Metro station, the Bonaventure Hilton International, and Place Ville Marie. *1 Place du Canada H3B 4C9, tel. 514/878–9000 or 800/828-7447. 614 rooms. Facilities: 3 restaurants, lounge with entertainment, health club with sauna and whirlpool, large indoor pool, movie theater, gift shops. AE, CB, DC, MC, V.*

★ **Hôtel de la Montagne.** The reception area of the Hôtel de la Montagne greets you with a naked, butterfly-winged nymph rising out of a fountain. An enormous crystal chandelier hangs from the ceiling and tinkles to the beat of disco music played a little too loudly. The decor says Versailles rebuilt with a dash of Art Nouveau by a discotheque architect circa 1975. Some puritanical tastes might find it overdone ("Naked nymphs!"), but others will find it fun. The rooms are tamer but large and comfortable. Another excellent reason to stay in or visit this hotel is the food. The main restaurant, Le Lutetia, is known as one of the best and most innovative gourmet eateries in Montreal (*see* Dining, above). There are three other restaurants offering less expensive, faster meals and an extremely popular dance club called Thursday's. Most of the guests are French-speaking, and the restaurants and Thursday's attract a big local crowd. If you're staying elsewhere, the reception area is at least worth a visit. *1430 de la Montagne, H3G 1Z5, tel. 514/288–5656 or 800/361–6262. 132 rooms. Facilities: 2 restaurants, disco-bar, outdoor pool. AE, DC, MC, V.*

Le Meridien. This Air France property rises from the center of the Complexe Desjardins, a boutique-rich mall in the center of the plushest stretch of the Underground City. The Place des Arts and the metro stop of the same name are mere meters in one direction, the Complexe Guy-Favreau mall and the Palais des Congrès convention center the same distance in the other. The hotel caters to businesspeople and tourists who want ultramodern European style and convenience. Le Meridien is designed on a plan of circles of privilege within these already-exclusive surroundings. For instance, within Le Café Fleuri French restaurant there's a chicer, pricier enclave called Le Club. The ninth floor of the hotel, Le Club President, is reserved for businesspeople who demand *ne plus ultra* service. Toiletries are by Hermès throughout. There's also a no-smoking floor and an indoor pool, sauna, and whirlpool facility. And if the atmosphere ever seems too confining, you can always burst out the door and go to Chinatown, a block away. *4 Complexe Desjardins, H5B 1E5, tel. 514/285–1450 or 800/543–*

4300. 601 rooms. Facilities: 3 restaurants, piano bar, indoor pool, sauna, whirlpool, guest passes to nearby YMCA and YWCA, baby-sitting services; located in complex with shops and boutiques. AE, CB, DC, MC, V.

★ **Le Quatre Saisons (Four Seasons).** The "Golden Square Mile" of Sherbrooke Street West—Montreal's Fifth Avenue—is decorated by the city's two best hotels. The Ritz-Carlton and this property are engaged in a constant battle to see which can give its clients the best and most in services. Even the least expensive room, known as a "Superior," has amenities galore: three phones, bathrobes, silk hangers, a minibar, a hair dryer, a clock-radio, and a safe. The more expensive suites have even more phones, and some are graced with marble bathtubs like the one Michael Jackson presumably floated in when he was a guest. Le Quatre Saisons is renovated frequently, and the latest decor is at the same time slickly modern and filled with "stately English manor" furnishings. The white-columned Le Restaurant is known as one of Montreal's best places for nouvelle cuisine (*see* Dining, above). The other two eateries are more informal. The Gym Tech Fitness center, filled with strange-looking machines, is available for guests' use for a fee, and there's also a heated, year-round, outdoor pool. Le Quatre Saisons is one block from Metro Peel in the heart of Montreal's fanciest shopping district. *1050 Sherbrooke St. W H3A 2R6, tel. 514/284–1110 or 800/332–3442. 302 rooms. Facilities: 3 restaurants, lounge, health club with whirlpool and sauna, outdoor pool, 24-hr room service. AE, CB, DC, MC, V.*

Ramada Renaissance du Parc. The Ramada chain bought the old Hôtel du Parc in July 1987 and has made it the most luxurious of its four Montreal properties. Half a block away from the acres of greenery in Parc Mont Royal, this Ramada's locale is prime. The hotel itself aims its services mainly at a corporate clientele. The rooms are large, and the decor is modern and well maintained. Health-minded guests may use the adjoining Club La Cité, which has squash and tennis courts, whirlpools and saunas, weight room, exercise classes, and an indoor-outdoor pool. From the lobby you can descend to a shopping mall with many stores and a movie theater. The nightlife of Prince Arthur Street is six blocks away. *3625 ave. du Parc, H2X 3P8, tel. 514/288–6666 or 800/228–9898. 456 rooms. Facilities: restaurant, café-bar, lounge, health club with Nautilus, sauna, whirlpool, squash and tennis courts, indoor-outdoor pool, 24-hr room service, gift shop. AE, CB, DC, MC, V.*

★ **La Reine Elizabeth (Queen Elizabeth).** If the Ritz-Carlton is a stately old cruise ship, then the Queen Elizabeth, also called La Reine Elizabeth, is a battleship. Massive and gray, this hotel sits on top of the Gare Centrale train station in the very heart of the city, beside Mary Queen of the World Catholic cathedral and across the street from Place Ville Marie. The lobby is a bit too much like a railway station—hordes march this way and that—to be attractive and personal, but upstairs the rooms are modern, spacious, and spotless, especially in the more expensive Entrée Gold section. All the latest gadgets and other trappings of luxury are present. The Beaver Club (*see* Dining, above), the flagship restaurant, is such an institution that there is a small museum devoted to it on the lobby level. There's a cheaper restaurant, too, as well as Arthur's supper club, and four lounges. Conventions are a specialty here. *900 blvd. René Lévesque H3B 4A5, tel. 514/861–3511 or 800/268–9143. 1,045 rooms. Facilities: 2 restaurants, supper club, 4 bars/lounges,* *beauty salon, boutiques, indoor swimming pool, gift shops. AE, CB, DC, MC, V.*

★ **Ritz-Carlton.** This property floats like a stately old luxury liner along Sherbrooke Street. It was opened in 1912 by a consortium of local investors who wanted a hotel in which their rich European friends could stay and indulge their champagne-and-caviar tastes. Since then many earth-shaking events have occurred here, including one of the marriages of Elizabeth Taylor and Richard Burton. Power breakfasts, lunches, and dinners are the rule at the elegant Café de Paris, and the prime minister and others in the national government are frequently sighted eating here. A less heady atmosphere prevails at the Ritz-Carlton's three other excellent restaurants. Guest rooms are a successful blend of Edwardian style—working fireplaces—with such modern accessories as electronic safes. Careful and personal attention are hallmarks of the Ritz-Carlton's service. Even if you're not a guest, stop by the Ritz's Hotel Courtyard for afternoon tea and to see the duck pond, a Ritz tradition since 1912. *1228 Sherbrooke St. W, H3A 2R6, tel. 514/842-4212 or 800/223-9868. 240 rooms. Facilities: 4 restaurants, piano bar, giftshop, beauty salon, barber shop, 24-hr room service. AE, CB, DC, MC, V.*

Le Shangrila. If you're a frequent traveler to Montreal, you may want to try something different: an Oriental-style hotel. Le Shangrila is situated across the street from Le Quatre Saisons on Sherbrooke, one block from Metro Peel. Owned by a businesswoman from Singapore of Chinese descent, the hotel's decor from reception to restaurant to rooms is modern with an amalgam of Korean, Chinese, Japanese, and Indian motifs and artwork. The management claims that its rooms are among the largest in square footage in downtown Montreal. There is a large Szechuan-style restaurant, Dynastie de Ming, on the lobby level. The Shangrila has no health club or pool; for these you'll have to go across the street to Le Quatre Saisons and pay. During the week the clientele is corporate, while on weekends most of the guests are tourists from the United States and Ontario. *3407 Peel St., H3A 1W7, tel. 514/288-4141 or 800/361-7791. 166 rooms. Facilities: café, restaurant, bar. AE, CB, DC, MC, V.*

Expensive **Delta Montreal.** One of Montreal's newest hotels, the French-styled Delta is making a bid to break into the ranks of Montreal's world-class hotels. Many of the spacious guest rooms have balconies and excellent views of the city. The Le Bouquet restaurant and the piano lounge are designed like 19th-century Parisian establishments with dark wood paneling and brass chandeliers. The cuisine is Continental and not above trendy touches like grilling over mesquite. The Delta has the most complete exercise and pool facility in Montreal. There are indoor and outdoor pools, two international squash courts, an exercise room, a sauna, and a whirlpool. The innovative Children's Creative Centre lets your children play (under supervision) while you gallivant around town. *450 Sherbrooke St. W H3A 2T4 (entrance off President-Kennedy), tel. 514/286-1986 or 800/268-1133. 458 rooms. Facilities: restaurant; jazz bar (which also serves lunch Mon.–Fri.); indoor and outdoor pools; health club with whirlpool, sauna, squash courts, aerobics classes; children's center; gift shop. AE, CB, DC, MC, V.*

★ **Le Grand Hôtel.** Le Grand abuts the stock exchange; Place Bonaventure is half a block one way, the western fringe of Vieux-

Lodging

Montréal one block the other, and the Metro Square Victoria can be reached via an underground passage. In the midst of all this, Le Grand rises above a stunning three-story atrium-reception area. It's yet another large, modern hotel attractive to meeting planners. With the same owners as the Copley Plaza in Boston, Le Grand offers the usual health club and pool facilities, a more exclusive floor for higher-paying guests, and a shopping arcade on the underground level. Its most outstanding feature: the restaurants. The Tour de Ville on the top floor is the city's only revolving restaurant, and its bar has live jazz nightly. The newly renovated Chez Antoine is an Art Nouveau-style bistro with grilled meats a specialty. *777 University, H3C 3Z7, tel. 514/879-1370 or 800/361-8155. 737 rooms. Facilities: 2 restaurants, bar, health club with spa and steam room, aerobics classes, indoor pool, gift shop. AE, DC, MC, V.*

Holiday Inn Crowne Plaza. The flagship of the Holiday Inn chain's downtown Montreal hotels, the Crowne Plaza could just as well have been plopped down in Las Vegas or Atlanta. On the other hand, one doesn't stay in Holiday Inns for originality of design. This hotel *does* sparkle: It was recently renovated from top to bottom. Indoor pool, health club, café-restaurant, two bars: It's all here. Popular for conventions, this hotel is near Metro Place des Arts, Sherbrooke Street shopping, and downtown. *420 Sherbrooke St. W, H3A 1B4, tel. 514/842-6111 or 800/465-4329. 487 rooms. Facilities: café-restaurant, 2 bars, indoor pool, health club with sauna and whirlpool, unisex beauty parlor, gift shop. AE, DC, MC, V.*

Holiday Inn Le Richelieu. Chocolate brown is the predominant color in Le Richelieu. This hotel is near Metro Sherbrooke, the Square St-Louis, the restaurants of St-Denis, and the summertime nightlife of Prince Arthur Street. Le Richelieu has an indoor pool, a restaurant, and a bar. Its good location makes you want to spend a lot of time outdoors. *505 Sherbrooke St. E, H2L 1K2, tel. 514/842-8581 or 800/465-4329. 330 rooms. Facilities: restaurant, bar, indoor pool, sauna, gift shop. AE, CB, DC, MC, V.*

Hôtel de l'Institut. The Quebec Institute of Tourism and Hôtellerie, an official government agency, owns and operates the Hôtel de l'Institut, a training academy for future hotel and restaurant managers. The exterior looks like a prefab office building constructed by the phone company; the interior is more attractive, although still a bit institutional. The service, however, is excellent (after all, they're getting graded on it). The rooms are small and comfortable, but a bit outmoded. Both the hotel and the restaurant are good values, and reservations may be difficult to get. Hôtel de l'Institut is on top of the Metro Sherbrooke station and near the Prince Arthur Street pedestrian mall. *3535 St-Denis H2X 3P1, tel. 514/282-5120. 42 rooms. Facilities: restaurant (closed except for breakfast May 15-Labor Day), free Continental breakfast. AE, CB, DC, MC, V.*

Moderate **Le Baccarat Comfort Inn.** Completely renovated in 1988, this medium-size, medium-price hotel, next to the McGill campus, caters to the business trade. A spa with whirlpool, sauna, and exercise machines has been added and the lobby was redone. The decor of the restaurant is Italianate, with lots of brass and marble and with bay windows overlooking the street. There's also a terrace for summer dining outdoors. The new chef presents Continental cuisine. Le Baccarat is handy to downtown

Montreal 114

business and shopping areas. *475 Sherbrooke St. W, H3A 2L9, tel. 514/842-3961 or 800/361-4973. 200 rooms. Facilities: restaurant, café. AE, CB, DC, MC, V.*

★ **Château Versailles.** This small, charming hotel occupies a row of four converted mansions in an excellent location on Sherbrooke Street West. The owners have decorated it with many antique paintings, tapestries, and furnishings; some rooms have ornate moldings and plaster decorations on the walls and ceilings. Each room also has a full bath, TV, and air-conditioning. The reception area is designed to look like a European pension. There's no restaurant at the Versailles, though breakfast is served in the Breakfast Room, and afternoon tea is available from room service. The staff is extremely helpful and friendly. The Versailles is unassuming, not too expensive, and classy. *1659 Sherbrooke St. W (near Metro Guy-Concordia) H3H 1E3, tel. 514/933-3611 or 800/361-3664. 70 rooms. Facilities: breakfast room; room service offers tea and biscuits in the evening. AE, MC, V.*

Hôtel Maritime. This medium-size hotel next to the Grey Nun's Museum and Convent on boulevard René Lévesque was recently overhauled. The decor is now somewhat Spartan and ultramodern, with recessed colored lights casting pastel glows around the mirrored reception area. There's an indoor pool and a circular French restaurant, Le Beau Rivage, with a mediocre reputation. The rooms are painted from a palette of cream, peach, and pale caramel. The Maritime's clientele is mainly French-speaking. *1155 Guy St. (2 blocks from Metro Guy-Concordia), H2H 2K5, tel. 514/932-1411 or 800/363-6255. 215 rooms. Facilities: restaurant, piano bar, indoor pool, boutique, barber shop, indoor parking. AE, CB, DC, MC, V.*

Le Nouvel Hôtel. The Nouvel Hôtel is what hotel managers like to call a "new concept"—it offers a little of everything: studios, suites, 2½- to 4½-room apartments. It's not very classy, but it's all new, brightly colored, and functional. Le Nouvel Hôtel is near the restaurant district, five or six blocks from the heart of downtown, and two blocks from the Guy-Concordia Metro station. *1740 blvd. René Lévesque O H3H 1R3, tel. 514/931-8841 or 800/567-2737. 481 rooms. Facilities: restaurant, bar, free Continental breakfast, gift shop. AE, DC, MC, V.*

Inexpensive **Lord Berri.** Next to the University of Quebec–Montreal, the Lord Berri is a new, moderately priced hotel convenient to the restaurants and nightlife of rue St-Denis. It offers some of the services of its more expensive competition: minibars, in-room movies, and nonsmoking floors. The De La Muse restaurant serves good bistro food and is popular with a local clientele. The Berri-UQAM Metro stop is a block away. *1199 Berri St. H2L 4C6, tel. 514/845-9236 or 800/363-0363. 154 rooms. Facilities: restaurant, gift shop. AE, DC, MC, V.*

Le Royal Roussillon. This hotel is adjacent to the Terminus Voyageur bus station (buses park directly beneath one wing of the hotel) and some of the bus station aura seems to rub off on the Roussillon; it's a little dingy. But if you're stumbling after a long bus ride and want somewhere to stay, *now*, the Roussillon's rooms are large and clean, the service is friendly, and the price is right. It's also handy to the Berri-UQAM Metro station. *1610 rue St-Hubert H2L 3Z3, tel. 514/849-3214. 104 rooms. Facilities: restaurant. AE, DC, MC, V.*

YMCA. This clean, modern Y is downtown, next to Peel Metro station. Book at least two days in advance. Women should book seven days ahead—there are fewer rooms with showers for women. Anyone staying summer weekends must book a week ahead. *1450 Stanley St. H3A 2W6, tel. 514/849-8393. 352 rooms. MC, V.*

YWCA. Very close to dozens of restaurants, the Y is three blocks from downtown. *1355 blvd. René Lévesque H3G 1P3, tel. 514/866-9941. 117 rooms. Facilities: recently renovated hotel and fitness facilities. Accepts women only. Men may use café. Rooms with sink or bath available. (Reserve for best choice.) Oct.–May, stay 7 nights, pay for 6. Café open 7:30 AM–7 PM. Pool, sauna, whirlpool, weight room, fitness classes—no extra charge for hotel guests. MC, V.*

McGill University Area

Inexpensive **Auberge de Jeunesse Internationale de Montréal.** The youth hostel near the McGill campus in the student ghetto charges $9.50 for members, $12.50 for nonmembers, per night per person. Reserve early during the summer tourist season. *3541 Aylmer St. H2X 2B9, tel. 514/843-3317. 108 beds. Facilities: rooms for 4 to 12 people (same sex); a few rooms available for couples and families. No credit cards.*

McGill Student Apartments. From mid-May to mid-August, when McGill is on summer recess, you can stay in its dorms on the grassy, quiet campus in the heart of the city. Nightly rates: students $21; nonstudents $28.50 (single rooms only). *3935 University St. H3A 2B4, tel. 514/398-6367. 1,000 rooms. Facilities: campus swimming pool and health facilities (visitors must pay to use them).*

Université de Montréal Area

Inexpensive **Université de Montréal Residence.** The university's student housing accepts visitors from May 9 to August 22. It's on the other side of Mont Royal, a long walk from downtown and Vieux-Montréal, but there's the new Université de Montréal Metro stop right next to the campus. Nightly rates: students $17; nonstudents $27. *2350 blvd. Édouard Montpetit H3C 3J7, tel. 514/343-6531. 1,171 rooms. Facilities: campus sports center with pool and gym (visitors must pay to use it). AE, MC, V.*

Bed-and-Breakfasts

Bed and Breakfast à Montréal. Founded in 1979, this is the oldest B & B agency in Montreal. Most of the more than 50 homes are downtown or in the elegant neighborhoods of Westmount and Outremont. Some of them can be quite ritzy. Others are less expensive, but all provide breakfast and a wealth of information about the city. Visitors who take a Gray Line tour get a 15% discount. *Contact: Marian Kahn, 4912 Victoria, Montreal H3W 2N1, tel. 514/738-9410. Single $30–$50, double $45–$100. "Unhosted" apartments also available, minimum 4-night stay, rates $90 and up. AE, MC, V accepted for deposits only; the balance must be paid with cash or traveler's checks.*

Downtown B & B Network. This organization will put you in touch with 75 homes and apartments, mostly around the downtown core and along Sherbrooke Street, that have one or more rooms available for visitors. These homes generally are clean, lovingly kept-up, and filled with antiques. The hosts generously dole out, with breakfast, recommendations about what to see and do during your stay in Montreal. Even during the height of the tourist season, this organization has rooms open. *Contact: Bob Finkelstein, 3458 rue Laval (at Sherbrooke St.), Montreal H2X 3C8, tel. 514/289-9749. Single $25-$40, double $35-$55. AE, MC, V.*

The Arts and Nightlife

When it comes to entertainment, Montreal has a superiority complex. It can boast of serious culture—symphony orchestras, opera and dance companies. At the pinnacle of the High Art scene stands the Orchestre Symphonique de Montréal, led by Charles Dutoit, and l'Opéra de Montréal. The city is known for its adventurous theatrical companies; unfortunately for the English-speaking visitor, most presentations are in French. Montreal is also the home of a small group of filmmakers who regularly bring home accolades from international festivals. On the low-life side of the tracks, the city is filled with all types of bars and clubs, including jazz and rock clubs, discos, cabarets, singles bars, and strip clubs. Puritanism is definitely not in fashion here. There are also a number of larger halls where international pop and rock stars regularly perform. Summer is the time for the most action—more events, bigger crowds, later hours—but if you visit during the off-season there's sure to be something going on.

The entertainment section of the *Gazette*, the English-language daily paper, is a good place to find out about upcoming events. The Friday weekend guide has an especially good list of all events at the city's concert halls, theaters, clubs, dance spaces, and movie houses. The "Best Bets" column goes beyond the listings to descriptions of the most interesting shows. *Montreal Scope*, which is provided to hotel patrons or can be bought at most newsstands, points you to the strictly "tourist" entertainment, shopping, and restaurants. The city cultural authorities distribute a free brochure to concerts and other events in the Place des Arts complex. The brochure is available at tourist information centers and at the larger hotels. For more offbeat events, experimental theater productions, and "insiders" dining choices, look for the *Montreal Mirror* (English) or *Voir* (French). These can be picked up free in almost any bar, restaurant, magazine outlet, or bookstore throughout Montreal.

For tickets to major pop and rock concerts, shows, festivals, and hockey, baseball, and football games, go to the individual box offices or call **Ticketron** (tel. 514/288-3651). Ticketron outlets are located in La Baie department store, in all Sears stores, and downtown at Phillips Square. Place des Arts tickets may be purchased at its box office underneath the Salle Wilfrid Pelletier, next to the Metro station. **Les Enterprises Dupont et Dupont** (tel. 514/845-3535) sells restaurant-theater ticket packages that get you a reservation at a restaurant near the theater and a good seat for the show.

The Arts

Music The **Orchestre Symphonique de Montréal** has gained world renown under the baton of Charles Dutoit. When not on tour its

The Arts and Nightlife

regular venue is the Salle Wilfrid Pelletier at the Place des Arts. The orchestra also gives Christmas and summer concerts in the Notre-Dame Basilica and pops concerts at the Arena Maurice Richard in the Olympic Park. For tickets and program information, call 514/842-2112. Also check the *Gazette* listings for its free summertime concerts in Montreal's city parks. Montreal's other orchestra, the Orchestre Métropolitain de Montréal (tel. 514/598-0870), also stars at Place des Arts most weeks during the October-May season. McGill University, at Pollack Concert Hall (tel. 514/398-4547) and Redpath Hall (tel. 514/398-4539 or 398-4547), is also the site of many classical concerts. The most notable are given by the **McGill Chamber Orchestra,** which also occasionally plays at Place des Arts with guest artists. **L'Opéra de Montréal,** founded in 1980, stages four productions a year at Place des Arts (tel. 514/521-5577).

The 20,000-seat **Montreal Forum** (tel. 514/932-6131) and the much larger Olympic Stadium are where rock and pop concerts are staged. More intimate concert halls include the **Théâtre St-Denis** (1594 St-Denis, tel. 514/849-4211) and the **Spectrum** (318 Ste-Catherine O, tel. 514/861-5851).

Theater French-speaking theater lovers will find a wealth of dramatic productions. There are at least 10 major companies in town, some of which have an international reputation. Best bets are productions at **Théâtre Denise Pelletier** (4353 Ste-Catherine E, tel. 514/253-8974), **Théâtre de Quat-Sous** (100 ave. des Pins E, tel. 514/845-7277), **Théâtre du Nouveau Monde** (84 Ste-Catherine E, tel. 514/861-0563), and **Théâtre du Rideau Vert** (4664 St-Denis, tel. 514/845-0267). Anglophones have less to choose from, unless they want to chance the language barrier. **Centaur Theatre,** the best-known English theatrical company, stages productions in the beaux arts-style former stock exchange building at 453 St-Francis-Xavier in Vieux-Montréal (tel. 514/288-3161). English-language plays can also be seen at the **Saidye Bronfman Centre** at 5170 Côte Ste-Catherine. Michel Tremblay is Montreal's premier playwright, and all of his plays are worth seeing, even if in the English translation. Touring companies of Broadway productions can often be seen at the **Théâtre St-Denis** on rue St-Denis (tel. 514/849-4211), as well as at Place des Arts (tel. 514/842-2112)—especially during the summer months.

Dance Traditional and contemporary dance companies thrive in Montreal, though many take to the road or are on hiatus in the summer. Among the best-known are **Ballets Classiques de Montréal** (tel. 514/866-1771), **Les Grands Ballets Canadiens** (tel. 514/849-8681), **Les Ballets Eddy Toussaint** (tel. 514/524-3749), **Montréal Danse** (tel. 514/845-2031), **LaLaLa Human Steps** (tel. 514/288-8266), **Les Ballets Jazz de Montréal** (tel. 514/875-9640), **Michael Montanaro Dance Company,** soloist **Margie Gillis,** and **Tangente** (tel. 514/842-3532)—a nucleus for many of the more avant-garde dance troupes. When not on tour, many of these artists can be seen at Place des Arts or at any of the Maisons de la Culture performance spaces around town. As of September 1990, Montreal's dancers will have a brand new downtown performance and rehearsal space, the Agora Dance Theatre, affiliated with the Université de Montréal dance faculty (840 Chérrier E). Check newspaper listings for details. Every other September (that is, in the odd years, such as 1991), the **Festival International de Nouvelle Danse** brings "new"

Film While not quite Hollywood, Montreal is the site of at least five major film festivals—the **Montreal World Film Festival** in late August is the most notable—and thus is the heart of Canada's film industry. Many U.S. producers like to film here because costs are lower. Local filmmakers frequently garner praise at international competitions and, of course, have an avid following. There are well over 75 first-run movie houses in town—see the *Gazette* for listings—with films in both French and English. Read the ads carefully or you may find yourself watching a recent Hollywood release, like *Cocktail*, dubbed in French. There are also many revival cinemas in Montreal, a sample of which includes **Cinémathèque Québécoise** (335 de Maisonneuve E, tel. 514/842–9763), **Ouimetoscope** (1204 Ste-Catherine E, tel. 514/525–8600), **Cinéma de Paris** (896 Ste-Catherine O, tel. 514/866–3636), and the **Rialto Cinema**—the city's only English repertory film house (5723 ave. du Parc, tel. 514/274–3550).

Nightlife

Bars and Clubs Elegant dinner-theater productions have revitalized Montreal's English theater. Prices range from about $12 for the show alone to more than $40 for the show and dinner (not including drinks—which can run up to about $4.50 each—tips, or tax). Enthusiasts find this a great excuse to dress up for a night on the town. Small, cabaret-type shows can be found at a few major hotels. **Arthur's Café Baroque** at the Queen Elizabeth (tel. 514/861–3511) stages a can-can/Charleston revue that rates a PG; **Le Café Conc** at the Château Champlain (tel. 514/878–9000) is a bit more risqué. **La Diligence** (tel. 514/731–7771) has two dinner theaters and a solid reputation for presenting polished performances of popular productions—usually Broadway hits, as well as light musical comedies and plays in English. **Le Festin du Gouverneur** at the old fort on Île Ste-Hélène (tel. 514/879–1141) offers a unique dinner-theater experience. Light operatic airs are beautifully rendered as a merry 17th-century frolic in the military barracks mess hall is served up with copious amounts of food and drinks. Great for group outings. **Broadway Theatre** (514/483–5426), Montreal's newest dinner-theater venture in Vieux-Montréal, offers up musicals, lighthearted contemporary spoofs of topical interest, and popular Broadway shows, presented by a "resident" group, Foolhouse Theatre Company, among other Montreal theatrical high jinkers.

Aside from full-fledged cabarets and dinner theater, most of the big hotels offer some kind of live entertainment, including music and dancing to live music between shows. The Ritz-Carlton (tel. 514/842–4212) has a ground-floor bar (*très élégant*), with a pianist in evening dress, in which you can nibble on smoked salmon. There is music and slow dancing at **Puzzle's Jazz Bar** in the Ramada Renaissance (tel. 514/288–3733), the Sheraton's **L'Impromptu** (tel. 514/878–2000), and the **Tour de Ville,** atop Le Grand Hôtel (tel. 514/879–1370).

Jazz Montreal has a very active local jazz scene. The best-known club is Vieux-Montréal's **L'Air du Temps** (191 St-Paul O, tel. 514/842–2003). This small, smoky club presents 90% local talent and 10% international acts from 5 PM on into the night. There's a cover charge Thursday through Saturday. If you like jazz and you're downtown, duck into **Biddle's** (tel. 514/842–8656) at 2060 Aylmer Street, where bassist Charles Biddle holds forth most evenings when he's not appearing at a local hotel. Bernard Primeau's Trio are weekend regulars and Montreal's own Oliver Jones can occasionally be found tickling the ivories on those rare occasions when he's in town. This upscale club is also a restaurant that serves ribs and chicken, so lick the bones clean and start drumming. There's a cover charge for the big acts. You also might try **Club Jazz 2080** (tel. 514/285–0007) at 2080 Clark, where jazz legend Sonny Greenwich can often be heard, or **Le Grand Café** (tel. 514/849–6955) at 1720 St-Denis. **Le Bijou** (tel. 514/288–5508), at 300 rue Lemoyne, is another sure bet. This popular jazz club in Vieux-Montréal has launched the career of many local jazz and rhythm-and-blues musicians. Montreal Festival jazz greats like Pat Metheny sometimes turn up for impromptu jam sessions.

Rock Rock clubs seem to spring up, flourish, then fizzle out overnight. **Club Soda** (tel. 514/270–7848) at 5240 avenue du Parc, the granddaddy of them all, sports a neon martini glass complete with neon effervescence outside. Inside it's a small hall with a stage, three bars, and room for about 400 people. International rock acts play here as well as local talent. It's also a venue for the comedy and jazz festivals. Open seven nights from 8 PM to 3 AM; admission ranges from nothing up to $20, depending. **Foufounes Electriques** (tel. 514/845–5484)—which translates as "electric buns"—at 97 Ste-Catherine Est in the Latin Quarter is the downscale, more avant-garde competitor of Club Soda. Foufounes is the center for the local band scene and also attracts up-and-coming acts from the United States. There's a "quiet" section for conversation and a "loud" section for music and dancing. Open weekdays 1 PM–3 AM, weekends 7 PM–3 AM, admission variable. Other clubs include **Déjà Vu** (1224 Bishop St., tel. 514/866–0512), **Station 10** (2071 Ste-Catherine O, tel. 514/934–0484), **Secrets** (40 ave. des Pins O, tel. 514/844–0004) and **Nuits Magiques** (22 St-Paul E, tel. 514/861–8143) in Vieux-Montréal.

Discos Montrealers are as into discos as you could imagine. The newest and the glitziest is **Metropolis** (tel. 514/288–5559) at 59 rue Ste-Catherine Est. The crowd is young, primarily French-speaking, and clad in black. This club is reminiscent of New York's Palladium in that the enormous space (a former theater where Sarah Bernhardt performed) has been given a complete workover by local architects, and it has high-powered light and sound systems. It's open Thursday through Sunday, and the admission is $5 unless a band is appearing. Many of the hotels have discos, and they're scattered throughout the nightlife areas around Crescent and St-Denis. The more popular ones are **Thunder Dome** (1254 Stanley St., tel. 514/397–1628), **Le Business** (3500 blvd. St-Laurent, tel. 514/844–3988), and the **Diamond Club** (1186 Crescent St., tel. 514/866–4048).

Singles Bars Singles bars center on Crescent, Bishop, and de la Montagne. The two mainstays are **Thursday's**—the city's best-known—and the **Sir Winston Churchill Pub** at Nos. 1449 and 1459 Crescent Street. Emulators of the former are **Thirsty's** (1187 Bishop St.) and **Friday's** (636 Cathcart St.). The athletic set unwinds at **La Cage aux Sports,** not too far from the Forum at 2250 Guy

Street. Another bar scene takes place on Prince Arthur Street. The French-flavored **Vol de Nuit** at No. 14 and **Du Côté de Chez Swann** at No. 54 are the *classiest* joints there. Nearby on St-Laurent is **Lola's Paradise** (No. 3604)—a trendy, lively all-night hideaway conveying the glitz and glamour of the '30s. Bar service til 3 AM; it also serves dinner daily 5 PM–6 AM. **Le Keg** (25 St-Paul E) is known as a place for raucous carousing in Vieux-Montréal. A quieter, more sophisticated (and probably more expensive) evening can be had at one of the bars in the better hotels, the **Grand Prix Bar** in the Ritz-Carlton being the classiest.

4 Excursions from Montreal

by Mary Kelly and Patricia Lowe

Mary Kelly runs her own communications consulting business in Montreal. She is a contributor to Fodor's Canada and Quebec travel guides, as well as coauthor of A Gringo's Guide to Doing Business in Montreal, *a guidebook for the executive business traveler.*

Montreal has two major attractions beyond its city limits: les Laurentides (the Laurentian) mountain range to the north, and l'Estrie (the Eastern Townships) between Montreal and the Vermont and New York borders. The Laurentians are characterized by thousands of miles of unspoiled wilderness and world-famous ski resorts. The Townships have rolling hills and farmlands. As major vacation areas in both winter and summer, they offer outdoor activities on ski slopes and lakes and in their provincial parks. All hotels, restaurants, and resorts in this chapter are categorized according to Montreal's dining and lodging price charts (*see* Chapter 3, Dining).

Les Laurentides (the Laurentians)

Avid skiers might call Montreal a bedroom community for the Laurentians; just 35 miles (56 kilometers) to the north, they are home to some of North America's best-known ski resorts. The Laurentian range is ancient, dating to the Precambrian era (600,000 years ago). These rocky hills are relatively low, worn down by glacial activity, but they include eminently skiable hills, with a few peaks above 2,500 feet (760 meters). World-famous Mont Tremblant, at 3,150 feet (960 meters), is the tallest.

The **P'tit Train du Nord** made it possible to easily transport settlers and cargo to the Upper Laurentians. It also opened them up to skiing by the turn of the century. Before long, trainloads of skiers replaced settlers and cargo as the railway's major trade. The Upper Laurentians soon became known worldwide as the number one ski center in North America—a position that it still holds today. Initially a winter weekend getaway for Montrealers who stayed at boarding houses and fledgling resorts while skiing its hills, the Upper Laurentians began attracting an international clientele, especially with the advent of the Canadian National Railway's special skiers' train, begun in 1928. (Its competitor, the Canadian Pacific Railway, jumped on the bandwagon soon after, doubling the number of train runs bringing skiers to the area.)

Soon, points north of Saint-Jérôme began to develop as resort areas: Saint-Sauveur-des-Monts, Saint-Jovite, Sainte-Agathe-des-Monts, Mont Tremblant, and points in between became major ski centers.

Roads north of Saint-Jérôme weren't kept open in winter before the end of World War II, so travel by car was virtually impossible and very hazardous. However, an intrepid few had already penetrated deep into the Upper Laurentians' wilderness, staking out their claims for prime resort locations. The founders of **Gray Rocks Inn** in Saint-Jovite were the grandparents of them all. Nearly a hundred years ago, so the story goes, New Yorker George Ernest Wheeler fell for one Lucile Aldridge of Chicago. Though her family promised her a life of luxury if she would forgo marrying Wheeler, Aldridge spurned her family's offer and set out with him for the wilds of Quebec, lured by the tales of lumber fortunes. In 1906, their lumber stake went up in smoke, literally. But the enterprising couple decided to open a wilderness retreat for city folk.

Gray Rocks Inn—named after the granite boulders of the Canadian Shield on which it stood—opened on the shores of Lac Ouimet. By 1938, the by then gentrified country inn was attracting an international clientele, including movie stars flown in by the Wheelers' eldest son. Ever the innovator, Gray Rocks was the first resort to hire professional ski instructors. The Snow Eagle Ski School celebrated its 50th anniversary in 1988. Granddaughter Lucile Wheeler, who began skiing at the age of two under the tutelage of Tyrolean cousins Hermann Gadner and Hans Falkner, became North America's first champion skier and Canada's first Olympic medalist in the sport. Other Olympians have trained there since but not one has yet surpassed her international accomplishments.

Another pioneer who helped build the Laurentians' reputation for skiing was the late legendary cross-country skiing champion, Norway native "Jackrabbit" Herman Smith Johannsen. He began his Canadian trailblazing career in this region in 1918. A devout missionary for skiing, he considered it not only a sport but also a philosophy of life. Among his converts were members of the Red Birds Ski Club, all graduates of McGill University. In 1928, they established one of the first ski clubs at Saint-Sauveur-des-Monts on Hill 70—the central part of Mont Saint-Sauveur. Their award-winning exploits and championing of the sport made Hill 70 one of the Laurentians' early ski centers. Here both downhill and slalom races were introduced, and competitions were held annually. Competitors who couldn't fit into the "sleigh taxis" coming from Saint-Sauveur's nearby train station would ski the half-mile trip to the site.

Johannsen also opened up the famous Maple Leaf Trail linking Shawbridge (Prévost) to Mont Tremblant between 1932 and 1935. Before his death in 1987 at the age of 111, he personally participated in expanding the Laurentians network of cross-country ski trails, which today cover about 625 miles (1,000 kilometers). Inducted into the Temple de la renommée du ski des Laurentides (Laurentian Hall of Ski Fame) in 1982 at the age of 107, he continues to be celebrated by lovers of the sport.

The Upper Laurentians also began to grow as a winter haven for prominent Montrealers, who traveled as far north as Sainte-Agathe-des-Monts to establish private family ski lodges. A number of these properties continue to be preserved in their rustic turn-of-the-century wilderness settings. Proud of their heritage, these families consider their retreats a privilege to maintain, spending as much time there as possible year-round and enjoying the same outdoor pursuits as their forebears, though with considerably more ease.

Accessible only by train until the 1930s, when the highway was built, these were used primarily as winter ski lodges. But once the road opened up, cottages became year-round family retreats. Today, there is an uneasy alliance between the long-time cottagers and resort-driven entrepreneurs. Both recognize the other's historic role in developing the Upper Laurentians, but neither espouses the other's cause. At the moment, commercial development seems to be winning out. A number of large hotels have added indoor pools and spa facilities, and efficient highways have brought the country closer to the city—45 minutes to Saint-Saveur, 1½ to 2 hours to Mont Tremblant. Montrealers can drive up to enjoy the fall foliage or engage in spring skiing and still get home before dark. The only

Excursions from Montreal 124

slow periods are early October, when there is not much to do, and June, when there is plenty to do but also a lot of black flies.

Getting Around

By Car Autoroute des Laurentides 15, a six-lane highway, and the slower but more scenic secondary road, Route 117, lead to this resort country. Try to avoid traveling to and from the region on Friday evenings or Sunday afternoons, as you're likely to sit for hours in bumper-to-bumper traffic.

By Bus Frequent bus service is available from the Terminus Voyageur (505 blvd. de Maisonneuve E, tel. 514/842–2281) in downtown Montreal. **Limocar Laurentides'** service departs regularly for Sainte-Adèle, Ville d'Esterel, Sainte-Agathe-des-Monts, Saint-Jovite, and Mont Tremblant, among other stops en route. Limocar also has a service (tel. 514/383–6410) to the Basses Laurentides (Lower Laurentians) region, departing from the bus terminal at the Metro Henri-Bourassa stop in north Montreal, stopping at Sainte-Thérèse and Saint-Jérôme. In winter, **Aerocar** offers a special Aeroski bus service (tel. 514/397–9999) that operates from both Dorval and Mirabel airports. Likewise, **Limocar** (tel. 514/842–4281), **Murray Hill** (tel. 514/937–5311), and **Tour Autocar** (tel. 514/476–2514) operate ski express bus service to many of the Laurentians' resorts. Advance reservations are required.

Important Addresses and Numbers

Tourist Information The region's major tourist office is the **Maison du Tourisme des Laurentides** at Saint-Jérôme, just off the Autoroute des Laurentides 15 at exit 39. *14 142 rue de Lachapelle, R.R. 1, Saint-Jérôme, Quebec, J7Z 5T4, tel. 514/436–8532. Open daily 9–5 year-round.*

You can also get information at the **Tourisme Québec** office in Montreal (2 Place Ville Marie, plaza level near the corner of Cathcart and University streets). Year-round regional tourist offices are located in the towns of Carillon, L'Annociation, Mont-Laurier, Mont-Tremblant, Saint-Antoine, Saint-Eustache, Saint-Sauveur-des-Monts, Saint-Jovite, Sainte-Adèle, and Sainte-Agathe-des-Monts. Seasonal tourist offices (mid-June–Labor Day) are also located in Labelle, Lachute, Morin-Heights, Notre-Dame-du-Laus, Piedmont, Saint-Adolphe-Howard, and Val David.

Ski Information *The Gazette* operates **SkiLine,** a telephone service that gives daily information about ski slope conditions (tel. 514/875–SNOW). The paper also prints a column, **"The Snow Report,"** that appears daily throughout the ski season.

Outfitters

There are more than 60 outfitters (a.k.a. innkeepers) in the northern Laurentians area, where provincial parks and game sanctuaries abound. Pike, walleye, lake and speckled trout, moose, deer, partridge, and rabbit are plentiful just a three-hour drive north of Montreal. Outfitters provide the dedicated hunter or angler with accommodations and every service wildlife and wilderness enthusiasts could possibly require. Open year-round in most cases, their lodging facilities range from the most luxurious first-class resort to the log-camp type "back of beyond." As well as supplying trained guides, all offer services and equipment to allow neophytes or experts the best possible hunting and fishing in addition to boating, swimming, river rafting, windsurfing, ice-fishing, cross-country skiing, hiking, or just relaxing amid the splendor of this still spectacularly unspoiled region.

Outfitters recommended by the Laurentian tourist association include **Pourvoirie des 100 Lacs Nords,** run by Claude Lavigne (tel. 514/659-4155); **Club de Chasse and Pêche du Lac Beauregard** in Saint-Jovite (tel. 819/425-7722); and **Club des Guides** at Lac-du-Cerf, run by Raymond Webster (tel. 819/597-2486). Before setting off into the wilds, consult the Association des Pourvoyeurs du Québec (Quebec Outfitters Association, 2900 blvd. St-Martin O, Laval, Quebec, H7T 2J2, tel. 514/687-0041) or ask for its list of outfitters available through tourist offices.

Don't forget: Hunting and fishing require a permit, available from the regional offices of the Ministère du Loisir, de la Chasse et de la Pêche (C.P. 22,000, Quebec, Quebec, G1K 7X2) or inquire at any Laurentians sporting-goods store displaying an "authorized agent" sticker.

River Rafting

The Rivière Rouge in the Laurentians rates as one of the best in North America, according to expert river rafters, so it's not surprising that this river has spawned a miniboom in the sport. Just an hour's drive north of Montreal, the Rouge cuts across the rugged Laurentians through rapids, canyons, and alongside beaches. From April through October, the adventurous can experience what traversing the region must have meant in the days of the *voyageurs* and *coureurs du bois*, though today's trip, by comparison, is much safer and more comfortable.

Four companies specializing in white-water rafting are on-site at the trip's departure point near Calumet. (Take Rte. 148 past Calumet; turn onto chemin de la Rivière-Rouge until you see the signs for the access road to each rafter's headquarters.) **Aventures en eau vive** (tel. 819/242-6084), **Nouveau Monde** (tel. 514/733-7166), **Propulsion** (tel. 514/382-0553), and **W-3 Rafting** (tel. 514/638-3437) all offer four- to five-hour rafting trips. All provide transportation to and from the river site, as well as guides, helmets, life jackets, and, at the end of the trip, a much-anticipated meal. Most have facilities on-site or nearby for dining, drinking, camping, bathing, swimming, hiking, and horseback riding. Propulsion even offers helicopter transportation. The only prerequisite: You must weigh at least 88 pounds (40 kilograms).

Deltaplaning

If white-water rafting isn't adventure enough, there is always deltaplaning, in which man and machine become one. The **Vélidelta au Mont Christie School** in Mont Rolland (C.P. 631, Mont-Rolland, J0R 1G0, tel. 514/229-6887) offers lessons on free-flying, flight simulation, plus the more advanced tricks of the trade you'll need to earn the required deltaplane pilot's license—flight maneuvers, speed, and turns. Equipment is provided. You can choose a half-day initiation lesson, one-day flying lesson or four-day course.

Exploring the Laurentians

Numbers in the margin correspond with points of interest on the Laurentians map.

Les Basses Laurentides (the Lower Laurentians) The Laurentians are actually divided into two major regions, les Basses Laurentides (the Lower Laurentians) and les Hautes Laurentides (the Upper Laurentians). But don't be fooled by the designations; they don't signify great driving distances.

The Lower Laurentians start almost immediately outside Montreal. Considered the birthplace of the Laurentians, this area is rich in historical and architectural landmarks. Beginning in the mid-17th century, the governors of New France, as Quebec was then called, gave large concessions of land to its administrators, priests, and top-ranking military, who became known as *seigneurs*. In the Lower Laurentians, towns like Terrebonne, Saint-Eustache, Lac-des-Deux-Montagnes, and Oka are home to the manors, mills, churches, and public buildings these seigneurs had built for themselves and their *habitants*—the inhabitants of these quasi-feudal villages.

❶ Two of the most famous seigneuries are within an hour of Montreal: **La Seigneurie de Terrebonne,** on l'Île-des-Moulins, is about 20 minutes from Montreal, and **La Seigneurie du Lac-des-Deux-Montagnes,** in St-Scholastique, is 40 minutes from Montreal. You reach Terrebonne by taking boulevard Pie-IX in Montreal to the bridge of the same name. From the bridge take Highway 25 N. Exit at Terrebonne to Highway 440.

Governor Frontenac gave the land to Sieur André Daulier in 1673. Terrebonne was maintained by a succession of seigneurs until 1832, when Joseph Masson, the first French-Canadian millionaire, bought it. He and his family were the last seigneurs de Terrebonne; their reign ended in 1883.

Today, Terrebonne offers visitors a bona fide glimpse of the past. Now run by the Corporation de l'Île-des-Moulins rather than a French aristocrat, the seigneurie's mansions, manors, and buildings have all been restored. Take a walk through Terrebonne's historical center and then stop at the **centre d'interprétation historique de Terrebonne Museum.** It features a large collection of artifacts from the life and times of Joseph Masson and his family. There is also the Île-des-Moulins art gallery, which presents exhibitions of works by local artists, a year-round theater presenting English and French plays as well as musical matinees and outdoor summer shows. Most activities are free. *Corner of blvd. des Braves and rue St-Pierre, tel. 514/471–0619. Admission free. Open daily 10–8, summer only.*

La Seigneurie du Lac-des-Deux-Montagnes was allotted to the Sulpician priests in 1717. Already appointed the seigneurs of the entire island of Montreal, the priests used this as the base from which to establish an Amerindian mission. To reach this mission, take Highway 13 or 15 N out of Montreal to Highway 640 W. Exit 640 W at Highway 148. Take this road directly into the town of St-Scholastique. A highlight of the seigneurie is the Sulpicians' seignorial manor on rue Belle-Rivière, erected be-

The Laurentians

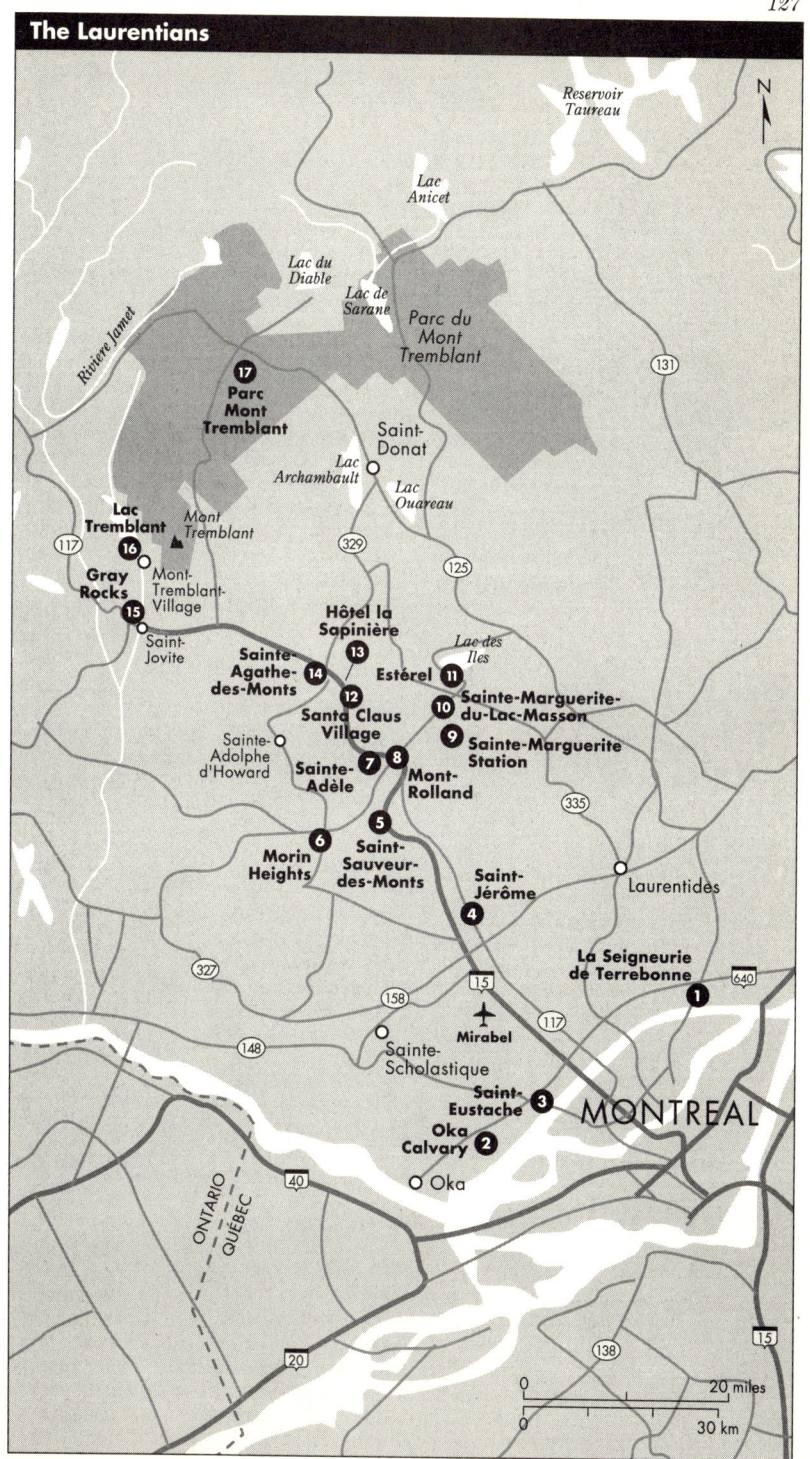

tween 1802 and 1808 in the village of Saint-Scholastique. Recently, it was used as part of the set for the late Claude Jutra's acclaimed film, *Kamouraska*, based on the novel by Quebec's prize-winning author, Anne Hérbert.

❷ To promote piety among the Amerindians, the Sulpicians erected the **Oka Calvary (Stations of the Cross)** between 1740 and 1742. Three of the seven chapels are still maintained, and every September 14 since 1870, Québécois pilgrims congregate here from across the province to participate in the half-hour ceremony on foot to the Calvary's summit. A sense of the divine is inspired as much by the magnificent view of Lac-des-Deux-Montagnes as by religious fervor.

In 1887, the Sulpicians gave about 350 hectares (865 acres) of their property located by the Oka Calvary to the Trappist monks, who had arrived in New France in 1880 from the Bellefontaine Abbey in France. Within 10 years they had built their monastery, the **Abbaye cistercienne d'Oka,** and transformed this land into one of the most beautiful domains in Quebec. The abbey is one of the oldest in North America. Famous for creating Oka cheese, the Trappists established the Oka School of Agriculture, which operated up until 1960. Today, the Monastery is a noted prayer retreat. Tour the miller's modest home, where the Trappists stayed when they first arrived here, and visit the gardens and the chapel. *1600 chemin d'Oka, tel. 514/479–8361. Admission free. Chapel open daily 4 AM–9 PM; gardens and boutique open daily 9:30–11:30 and 1–4.*

Close by is the **ferme avicole d'Oka,** one of Quebec's largest poultry farms, also developed by the Trappists. Tours of the breeding grounds for exotic pheasant, partridge, and guinea hen fowl, as well as for the ordinary variety, are given, and there is a slide show of the transition from farm to table—an interesting encounter for city kids. Bonuses are the fresh eggs and fowl that can be bought on site, presumably later to be roasted over the campfire or barbecue. *1525 chemin d'Oka, tel. 514/479–8394. Store open Mon.–Sat. 1–5, Sun. 1–5.*

❸ Nearby **Saint-Eustache** is another must for history buffs. One of the most important and tragic scenes in Canadian history took place here: the 1837 Rebellion. Since the British conquest of 1760, French Canadians had been confined to preexisting territories while the new townships were allotted exclusively to the English. Adding to this insult was the government's decision to tax all imported products from England, which made them prohibitively expensive. The end result? In 1834, the French Canadian Patriot party defeated the British party locally. Lower Canada, as it was then known, became a hotbed of tension between French and English, with French resistance to the British government reaching an all-time high. Rumors of rebellion were rife, and in December 1837, some 2,000 English soldiers led by General Colborne were sent in to put down the "army" of North Shore patriots by surrounding the village of Saint-Eustache. Jean-Olivier Chénier and his 200 Patriots took refuge in the local church, which Colborne's cannons bombed and set afire. Chénier and 80 of his comrades were killed during the battle, and more than 100 of the town's houses and buildings built during the seignorial regime were looted and burned down by Colborne's soldiers. Even today, traces of the bullets fired by the English army cannons are visible on the facade of Saint-Eustache's church at 123 rue St-Louis. Most of the town's

Les Laurentides (the Laurentians)

period buildings are open to the public. Note especially **Manoir Globenski** and **Moulin Légaré**, the only water mill still in operation in Canada. For a guided tour or for a free brochure that gives a good walking-tour guide, visit the town's Arts and Cultural Services Center, at 235 rue St-Eustache (tel. 514/472–4440).

Time Out Before heading north, stop at **Pâtisserie Grande-Cote** (367 chemin de la Grande-Cote, tel. 514/473–7307) to sample the wares of St-Eustache's most famous bakery and pastry shop.

Les Hautes Laurentides (the Upper Laurentians) ❹ Rivaling Saint-Eustache in Quebec's historic folklore is **Saint-Jérôme**, founded in 1830. Today a thriving economic center and cultural hub off Route 117, it first gained prominence in 1868 when Curé Antoine Labelle became pastor of this parish on the shores of Rivière du Nord. Of legendary stature, this charismatic priest was instrumental in the colonization of St-Jérôme and points beyond in what are now known as the Upper Laurentians. Messianic in his mission, Curé Labelle devoted himself to opening up northern Quebec to French Canadians. Between 1868 and 1890, he founded 20 parish towns—an impressive achievement given the harsh conditions of this vast wilderness. But his most important legacy was the famous P'tit Train du Nord railway line, which he persuaded the government to build in order to open Saint-Jérôme to travel and trade.

Not surprisingly, he is still fervently admired by the Québécois, and many monuments and roads in Saint-Jérôme and elsewhere bear his name: boulevard Labelle, the municipality of Labelle, the Papineau-Labelle wildlife reserve, and the statue of Curé Labelle in Parc Antoine-Labelle facing Saint-Jérôme cathedral.

Follow Saint-Jérôme's **promenade,** a 4-kilometer-long (2½-mile) boardwalk alongside the Rivière du Nord from rue De Martigny bridge to rue St-Joseph bridge for a walk through the town's history. Descriptive plaques en route highlight episodes of the Battle of 1837. The **Centre d'exposition du Vieux-Palais** housed in St-Jérôme's old courthouse exhibits shows focusing on the town's history. The museum also houses a permanent art exhibit and offers some activities for children, and concerts. *185 rue du Palais, tel. 514/432–7171. Admission free. Open Tues.–Fri. Noon–5, Sun. 1–5.*

Saint-Jérôme's **Parc régional de la Rivière-du-Nord** (1051 blvd. Industriel, tel. 514/431–1676) was created as a nature retreat. Paths throughout the park lead to the spectacular Wilson Falls (*chutes, en français*). Rain or shine, the Pavillon Marie-Victorin is open daily, with summer weekend displays and workshops devoted to nature, culture, and history.

The resort vacation area truly begins at Saint-Sauveur-des-Monts (Exit 60) and extends as far north as Mont Tremblant. Then it turns into a wilderness of lakes, some with private chalets and fishing camps, and forests best visited with an outfitter. Laurentian guides planning fishing and hunting trips are concentrated around Saint Donat near Parc Mont Tremblant.

To the first-time visitor, the hills and resorts around Saint-Sauveur, Sainte-Marguerite Station, Morin Heights, Val Morin and Val David, up to Sainte-Agathe, form a pleasant hodgepodge of villages, hotels, and inns that seem to blend one into another.

❺ Saint-Sauveur-des-Monts, exit 60 off the Autoroute, is the focal point for area resorts. During the past decade this town has grown so swiftly that vacationers who once camped on its outskirts say they barely recognize it.

The surrounding ski hill complexes of Mont-Habitant and Mont-St-Sauveur offer ever-increasing condo developments, lodges, hotels, motels, and inns at the foot of, or just a mile or so from, mountain slopes. Mont-Habitant alone features two 40-room and six 100-room lodges in addition to 125 motel rooms. Mont-St-Sauveur's slopes are dotted with modern condo units.

Despite all this development, Saint-Sauveur has managed to add more than 60 good restaurants and a shopping mall without totally ruining its character. It has gone from a 1970s sleepy Laurentian village of 4,000 residents that didn't even have a traffic light to a thriving year-round town attracting some 30,000 cottagers and visitors on weekends. Its main street, rue Principale, once dotted with quaint French restaurants, now boasts *brochetteries* and sushi bars, and the narrow strip is so choked in summertime by cars and tourists that it has earned the sobriquet "Crescent Street of the North." Residents here once won the battle against a McDonald's opening. Now the parking lots of major franchise fast-food eateries are always packed.

The gleaming white spires of **Saint-Sauveur Church** still dominate rue Principale, but Saint Francis of the Birds has not been so lucky. Built in 1951 with support from Montreal's Molson family, this sturdy, rustic log church with its fine stained-glass-window portraits of the Laurentian countryside no longer offers the worshiper or visitor a secluded and peaceful spiritual retreat. Where only two years ago its immediate neighbors were modest chalets dotting the forest, today the new Delta Hotel complex sits in the church's backyard. However, classical concerts can still be heard in the church every Tuesday evening during July and August (tel. 819/227-2663).

But for those who like their vacations—winter or summer—lively and activity-filled, Saint-Sauveur is *the* place where the action rolls nonstop. In winter, skiing is the main thing. (Mont-Saint-Sauveur, Mont Avila, Mont Gabriel, and Mont Olympia all offer special season passes and programs, and some ski-center passes can be used at more than one center in the region.) From Mont-Saint-Sauveur to Mont Tremblant, the area's ski centers (most situated in or near Saint-Sauveur, Sainte-Adele, Sainte-Agathe, and Saint-Jovite) offer night skiing—a perk for Montrealers and town residents who are fanatical about cramming as much skiing as possible into each season. All boast ski instructors—many are members of the Canadian Ski Patrol Association.

Mont-Saint-Sauveur is the new site of the **Pepsi Celebrity Ski Invitational,** in which Hollywood celebrities compete on and off the hills in this annual charity fund-raiser. It attracts at least 10,000 skiing and nonskiing stargazers to the popular weekend events held in mid-March.

For fine dining, try **Auberge Saint-Denis,** a classic Quebec inn that has earned the title of "Relais Gourmand" for its cuisine.

Les Laurentides (the Laurentians)

Don't eat and run . . . it is one of the nicer places from which to base a Laurentian visit. *62 St-Denis, Saint-Sauveur-des-Monts, Quebec J0R 1R0, tel. 514/227-4602. 23 rooms. AE, MC, V. Very Expensive.*

To break from the slopes, consider a stroll along rue Principale amid shops, fashion boutiques, and outdoor café terraces decorated with bright awnings and flowers. Housed in a former bank, **La Voute Boutique** (239B rue Principale, tel. 514/227-4144) carries such international labels as Byblos and an up-to-the-minute all-season selection of coordinates in cotton, knits, suede, and leather, plus sequin-styled dresses, sweaters, pants, jackets, and suits from France, Italy, and Spain. Montreal's queen of knitwear, Ariane Carle, has also opened a boutique in Saint-Sauveur, **Tricots d'Ariane** (248 rue Principale, tel. 514/227-6666). Her beautifully fluid knitwear collections (mostly woven jersey, linen, cotton, silks, and wool-acrylic blends) are known for their timeless quality. One other Montreal institution has recently arrived in Saint-Sauveur, the newest offspring of rue Ste-Catherine's **Dunn's Famous Smoked Meat Shoppes and Delis** (chemin Lac Milette, tel. 514/227-1881).

Arguably, such deluxe new digs as the **Delta St-Sauveur,** with its luxuriously appointed 215-room hotel, offer creature comforts rarely experienced at home but certainly welcome after a day on the slopes. Aside from special ski packages and multiday ski passes to Saint-Sauveur's many hills, this four-star hotel has an indoor swimming pool, whirlpool, squash, sauna, exercise room, games room, and a children's activity center. It also has excellent restaurants and bar-lounges on-site. *246 chemin du Lac Millette, Quebec, J0R 1R0, tel. 514/227-1811, 800/268-1133 elsewhere in Quebec and Canada, 800/877-1133 from the United States. AE, DC, MC, V. Very Expensive.*

Just outside of Saint-Sauveur, the $7 million Mont-St-Sauveur **Aquatic Park** (tel. 514/871-0101 or 800/363-2426) and tourist center (exits 58 or 60) will keep children happy with slides, wave pools, snack bars, etc. Its latest attraction is the $1.7 million man-made "Colorado" rafting river, which follows the natural contours of the steep hills. The nine-minute ride requires about 12,000 gallons of water to be pumped per minute.

❻ Nearby in **Morin Heights,** there's a new spin on an old sport at **Ski Morin Heights** (exit 60, Autoroute 15 N, tel. 514/226-1333 or 800/363-2527) where snowboarding is the latest craze. Likened to surfing a big wave, riding a skateboard down a hill, or windsurfing on a white-capped lake, snowboarding demands similar skills and dexterity, not to mention the fearlessness of the lion-hearted. Nonetheless, it is carefully supervised by Ski Morin Heights' instructors. Would-be snowboarders are required to pass a test by the center's ski patrol. Although it doesn't have overnight accommodations, the Ski Morin Heights boasts a 44,000-square-foot chalet with a full range of hospitality services and related facilities. Eateries include the Après-Vous Pub and cafeteria, a new 300-seat restaurant (pizza and deli food are the specialties), and La Croissanterie for fresh croissants, danish, and muffins. Après-ski activities include Mardi Gras Pub nights and a new health club for those over age 18. Season ski-pass holders get reduced rates in club membership, which includes use of the international-size squash courts, gym with exercise equipment, Jacuzzi, and sauna.

There's also a large nursery on-site and special ski lesson programs for children age 3 and up. The nursery slope school emphasizes the fun of skiing with these youngsters. A Disneyland theme quickly wins over the most shy preschoolers, who are soon happily greeting ski instructors dressed as Mickey Mouse, Donald Duck, and Roger Rabbit as they advance through their lessons in Looney Toon station, encountering new toys, tunnels, and ski tracks en route.

The town's architecture and population reflect its English settlers' origins. Most residents are English-speaking. Morin Heights has escaped the overdevelopment of Saint-Sauveur but still offers the visitor a good range of restaurants, bookstores, boutiques, and craft shops to explore. During the summer months, windsurfing, swimming, and canoeing on the area's two lakes are popular pastimes. The most recent addition, now entering its fifth season to popular and critical acclaim, is **Théâtre Morin Heights** (tel. 514/226-5863) whose productions are presented at Ski Morin Heights during the summer months. Popular musicals, lighthearted comedies, mysteries, and children's plays are in the repertoire. Run by a dedicated coterie of Morin Heights residents on a volunteer basis, the theater falls into the "highly professional amateur group" category. Ticket reservations are a must, especially since the theater offers a dinner-show package for only $25 per person. Both parts of the package have won kudos consistently.

In the summer holiday goers make for its golf courses (two of the more pleasant are 18-hole links at Sainte-Adèle and Mont Gabriel), campgrounds at Val David, Lacs Claude, and Lafontaine and beaches; in the fall and winter, they come for the foliage as well as alpine and nordic skiing.

An old favorite with Montrealers, the 300-room **Le Chantecler** on Lac Rond in Sainte-Adèle is nestled at the base of a mountain with 22 downhill ski runs. Skiing is the obvious draw—trails begin almost at the hotel entrance. (It's the official training site of the National Alpine Ski Teams.) Summer activities include tennis, golf, and boating. An indoor pool and spa, as well as a beach, make swimming a year-round possibility. There are a number of rate plans available, like a special summer package starting at $105 per day, but expect to pay between $240 and $309 double. *Box 1048, Sainte-Adèle, J0R 1L0, tel. 514/229-3555, 800/363-2420 in Quebec. AE, DC, MC, V.*

For those whose pocketbooks are not inclined to the deluxe, **Pension Ste-Adèle en Haut Bed and Breakfast** is a good alternative. This European-style B&B is located in a charming house. Inexpensive, cosy, and intimate, it has five rooms for overnight accommodations, B&B-style or dinner included. *151 rue Lesage Ste-Adèle, Quebec, J0R 1L0, tel. 514/229-2624. No credit cards. Inexpensive.*

The town also has a number of *auberges* (inns) for overnight stays. Inexpensive rates still mean quality service and facilities here.

The Auberge Swiss Inn *796 rte. St-Adolphe, Quebec, J0R 1H0, tel. 514/226-2009. 10 rooms. AE, MC, V. Inexpensive.*

The Carriage House *Rte. 329 N, 486 rte. St-Adolphe, Quebec, J0R 1H0, tel. 514/226-3031. 15 rooms. AE, MC, V. Inexpensive–Moderate.*

Les Laurentides (the Laurentians)

❼ The busy town of **Sainte-Adèle** is full of gift and Quebec-craft shops, boutiques, and restaurants. It also has an active nightlife, including a few discos. The town locals are a dynamic bunch who participate wholeheartedly in the special events held year-round. Take the **Défi sur Neige,** for example—held annually in early September, thanks to the modern miracle of snow machines. This two-day festival (tel. 514/229-2921) features acrobatic, downhill, and cross-country skiing competitions up and down the town's main streets.

Just as much of a rave with adults and children are the **Super Splash** water slides and the **Super glissades de glace.** *1791 blvd. Ste-Adèle, tel. 514/229-2909. 2 giant slides for adults, 3 for children. Admission: Mon.-Thurs., adults $7.50, children under 13 $6.50; Fri.-Sun. adults $9, children under 13 $7.50. Open Dec. 15-April, 9AM-10PM.*

Sainte-Adèle is also the site of Tennis Canada's annual international tournament (tel. 514/229-3555) in early July, when 200 competitors from 15 countries vie for the championships and upgrading of their ranking for the international circuit.

Sainte-Adèle offers culinary experiences of the extraordinary kind. In particular **L'Eau à la Bouche** has been a consistent award winner in gastronomic circles. It picked up Quebec's 1988 Ordre du mérite de la restauration top award among the Laurentians region's auberge/restaurants for its superb marriage of nouvelle cuisine and traditional Quebec dishes. Nonetheless, such superb supping doesn't come cheaply. L'Eau à la Bouche is one of the region's most expensive restaurants. However, the care and inventiveness of chef-proprietor Anne Desjardins, who opened the Bavarian-style restaurant nine years ago with her husband, Pierre Audette, is extraordinary. Such dishes as *chèvre* cheese tart, saddle of rabbit with onions, *baluchon* of lobster and scallops, roast partridge stuffed with oyster mushrooms in a cream sauce, *pavé* of dark chocolate with English cream or *cachette* of rhubarb and strawberries, leave dinner guests clamoring for more. *3003 blvd. Ste-Adèle, Rte. 117, tel. 514/229-2991. Reservations necessary. Dress: casual, but neat. AE, MC, V. No lunch. Very Expensive.*

Likewise, its 26-room auberge has received kudos for superb service, luxurious appointment and first-class status as an intimately scaled resort, perfect for weekend getaways or business retreats. Opened five years ago, it has attracted steady crowds since. The auberge faces Le Chantecler's ski slopes, so skiing is literally at the door, as is a golf course. Tennis, sailing, and horseback riding are nearby. Package rates are available. *3003 blvd. Ste-Adèle, Ste-Adèle, Quebec, J0R 1L0, tel. 514/229-2991, 514/229-4151, or 800/363-2582. Facilities: heated pool, whirlpool, flower garden terrace, wine cellar, handicapped facilities. Some suites with fireplaces. AE, DC, MC, V. Expensive-Very Expensive.*

You won't find accommodations at **Restaurant Les Cent-Ciels,** but the French cuisine prepared by chef Pascal Lemonnier (originally from Paris) rivals that of L'Eau à la Bouche. House specialties include pork tenderloin, fish and seafood in such delectable concoctions as *rillette de saumon fumé* (fresh and smoked salmon marinated in wine, shallots, and lemon and served with pickled baby onions and capers), and *filet de porc dijonnais à la crème. 430 chemin Ste-Marguerite, tel. 514/229-*

4164. Reservations suggested. AE, DC, MC, V. No lunch. Moderate–Expensive.

A couple of miles north on Highway 117, the reconstructed **Village de Seraphin's** 20 small habitant homes, grand country house, general store, and church recall the settlers who came to Sainte-Adèle in the 1840s. This award-winning historic town also features a train tour through the woods. *Tel. 514/229–4777. Admission: $6.50 adults, $3 children 5–11. Open late May–early Oct.*

❽ In **Mont-Rolland, Station touristique de Mont Gabriel** offers superb skiing, primarily for intermediate and advanced skiers. Most popular runs are the Tamarack and O'Connell trails for advanced skiers, the Obergurgl for intermediates. Mont Gabriel is also the annual site of the Free-Style World Cup Ski Championships (tel. 514/229–3547), in which more than 200 athletes from 20 countries compete every January. There's a lodge on site, with six-night ski-week packages (including all breakfasts and dinners, as well as unlimited day and night skiing available). Weekend ski packages are also available; ski lessons for both are extra. *Autoroute 15, exit 64, Mont-Rolland, Quebec, J0R 1G0, tel. 514/861–2852. 132 rooms. Facilities: Indoor/outdoor pools, tennis. AE, MC, V. Expensive.*

Auberge Mont Gabriel is worth a stay—overnight or for longer. This deluxe resort located on a 1,200-acre estate has 159 rooms and offers superb dining. Tennis, ski-week and weekend packages are also available, as is the Modified American Plan (MAP). *Autoroute 15, exit 64, Mont-Rolland, Quebec, J0R 1G0, tel. 514/229–3547. AE, MC, V. Very Expensive.*

Aside from the usual outdoor activities common to the Laurentians, Mont-Rolland's summer theater presents lighthearted entertainment for the whole family. Comedy, musicals, children's theater, and even circus acts may be part of the lineup. Your best bet is to check local newspapers or call **Théâtre de Mont-Rolland** (2525 chemin de la Rivière, tel. 514/229–5171).

❾ **Sainte-Marguerite Station** is home to the large family-style **Alpine Inn**, a log cabin main house with separate chalets for rent. Surrounded by rolling ski hills and manicured grounds, it features good dining, golf (CPGA pro for lessons), a putting green, swimming pools (indoor and out), skating rink, and one of the Laurentians' most scenic cross-country ski trails.

The social director organizes folksy summer barbecues around the pool and there are two-night packages available. *Chemin Sainte-Marguerite, J0T 2K0, tel. 514/229–3516 or 800/363–2577. Very Expensive.*

For dining, La Clef des Champs offers a charming alternative to even the most superbly prepared hotel fare. This family-owned hillside restaurant is well-known for its gourmet French cuisine. *875 chemin Ste-Marguerite, tel. 514/229–2857. Reservations advised. AE, MC, V. Closed Easter week. Moderate.*

❿ Neighboring community **Sainte-Marguerite-du-Lac-Masson** will be in the midst of its 125th-anniversary celebrations in 1990, with shows, parades, dances, carnivals, and special sports activities planned for the year-long fest. The town's Service des Loisirs (tel. 514/228–2543) is the place to call for details about events, schedules, and locations.

Les Laurentides (the Laurentians)

⓫ The permanent population of the town of **Estérel** is a mere 83 souls. But visitors to **Ville d'Estérel**, a 135-room resort at Autoroute 69, near Sainte-Marguerite Station, swells that number into the thousands. Founded in 1959 on the shores of Lac Dupuis, Fridolin Simard bought this 5,000-acre domain from Baron Louis Empain. Named Estérel by the baron because it evoked memories of his native village in Provence, Ville d'Estérel soon became a household word for holiday goers in search of a first-class resort area. The hotel features a private 18-hole golf course, beach, marina, swimming pool, tennis courts, and downhill skiing facilities. If this all-inclusive resort were in the Caribbean, it would probably be run by Club Med, given the nonstop activities. In particular, its sports complex and convention facilities make it a busy resort. *Fridolin Simard Blvd., Estérel, tel. 514/228-2571 or 800/363-3623. AE, DC, MC, V. Very Expensive. All-inclusive packages available.*

⓬ Children know **Val David** for its **Santa Claus Village.** *Tel. 819/322-2146. Admission: adults $6, children 2-12 $3. Open late May-early Oct.*

⓭ Discriminating adults come for the **Hôtel la Sapinière,** Canada's first member of the French association of fine country hotels, the Relais et Châteaux. This homey, dark-brown frame hotel with its bright country flowers provides comfortable accommodations but is best known for its fine dining room and wine cellar. Under Chef Marcel Kretz, who makes occasional TV appearances touting a certain brand of coffee, it has become one of Quebec's, if not Canada's, better restaurants. In peak season, nonhotel diners should make reservations a week or two in advance. La Sapinière is a major convention center, catering to government summits and high-level meetings. *1244 chemin de la Sapinière, Quebec, J0T 2N0, tel. 819/322-2020 or 800/567-6635. Moderate.*

Home to Passe-Montagne, a leader in outdoor adventure tours, Val David is a rendezvous for mountain climbers, ice scalers, dogsledders, hikers, and summer or winter campers. For equipment rentals and other information, contact the Maison du Tourisme des Laurentides (tel. 514/436-8532), Val David also has three campgrounds, all along Route 117, La Belle Étoile, Camping Laurentien, and Le Montagnais.

Val David is also a haven for artists, many of whose studios are open to the public. Most of their work is for sale. **Les Créateurs associés** (2495 rue d'Église, tel. 819/322-2043) boutique and art gallery features a wide range of artisan handicrafts. **Atelier Bernard Chaudron, Inc.** (2449 chemin de l'Île, tel. 819/322-3944), sells hand-shaped and hammered lead-free pewter objets d'art.

⓮ About 60 miles (96 kilometers) from Montreal, overlooking Lac des Sables, is **Sainte-Agathe-des-Monts,** the largest commercial center for ski communities farther north. This lively resort area attracts campers to its spacious **Camping Ste-Agathe** (Rte. 329, CP156 Sainte-Agathe-des-Monts, Quebec, J8C 383, tel. 819/326-5577); bathers to its municipal beach; and sailors to its lake cruises on the *Alouette* (tel. 819/326-3656) touring launch. Sailing is the favorite summer sport, especially during the "24 heures de la voile" sailing competition (tel. 819/362-0457) each Canada Day weekend in July.

Skin-diving is also popular here, with local headquarters for equipment rentals, guides, etc., at the Centre de plongée sous-marine (124 rue Principale, tel. 819/326–4464).

But mountain-climbing may be one of the best ways to view the scenery of the Upper Laurentians. The Fédération québécoise de la montagne (4545 rue Pierre-de-Coubertin, C.P. 1000, Succursale M, Montreal, Quebec H1W 3R2, tel. 514/252–3004) can give you information about this, as can the region's tourist offices.

Also popular is the summertime festival "Le Nord en fête" (tel. 819/425–0457), which takes place for two weeks in late July and early August under the Big Top on the shores of Lac des Sables. Six months later, the town celebrates "L'hiver en Nord" (tel. 819/326–0457), a four-month festival of sports competitions, tournaments, and entertainment every weekend from mid-December to mid-March.

About ½- mile north of Sainte-Agathe-des-Monts is the **Village du Mont-Castor,** an attractive re-creation of a turn-of-the-century Québécois village; more than 100 new homes have been built here in the traditional fashion of full-length logs set *pièce sur pièce* (one upon the other).

Sainte-Agathe offers many types of accommodations. Choices range from the inexpensive but charming fin-de-siècle manor house, **Manoir d'Ivry** (3800 chemin Renaud, Ste-Agathe-Nord, Quebec, J8C 2Z8, tel. 819/326–3564. MC, V. Open year-round), to the more expensive **Auberge du Lac des Sables** (230 St-Venant, Box 213, Quebec, J8C 383, tel. 819/326–7016, MC, V), a new 19-room country inn offering such amenities as a whirlpool, domed pool, color TV, living room with fireplace and piano and all-you-can-eat buffet brunches.

Sainte-Agathe also has two superb restaurants. Eberhards' **Chatel Vienna** (6 rue Ste-Lucie, tel. 819/326–1485) is run by proprietor Eberhards Rado and his wife, who is also the chef. Winner of the 1988 Ordre du merité de la restauration award for outstanding cuisine, moderately priced, this Austrian restaurant offers Viennese and other Continental dishes served up in a lakeside setting. House specialties include Gulyas Suppe mit spaetzli (goulash soup with dumplings) and Bauernschmaus (mixed plate of German and Swiss sausages, roast pork, sauerkraut, and potatoes). Meals are accompanied by hot spiced wine, Czech pilsner beer, or dry Austrian and Alsatian white wines. **Chez Girard** (18 rue Principale O, tel. 819/326–0922) serves up moderately priced, excellent French cuisine in an auberge on the shores of Lac des Sables.

Farther north lie two of Quebec's best known ski resorts, Gray Rocks, and Mont Tremblant Lodge, now part of Station Touristique de Mont Tremblant.

Exiting off the end of the Autoroute, motorists first come to **Gray Rocks,** in Saint-Jovite. The oldest ski resort in the Laurentians, it was founded by the Wheeler family more than three generations ago. A sprawling wooden hotel with modern chalets and units, it overlooks Lac Ouimet. Gray Rocks has its own private mountain ribboned by 18 ski runs. The winter ski weeks and weekends, including cross-country, are good value for the money, as are the summer tennis packages. Gray Rocks also runs the more intimate Auberge Le Château with 36 rooms

Les Laurentides (the Laurentians)

farther along on Route 327 North. *Rte. 327 N, St-Jovite, Quebec, J0T 2HQ, tel. 819/425-2771 or 800/567-6767. 252 rooms. Facilities: courts, tennis school, riding stables, marina, La Spa fitness center with hot tubs, indoor swimming pool, and sports-medicine clinic, children's activity programs, private airstrip and seaplane anchorage, gourmet restaurant. AE, MC, V. Full winter ski package available. Expensive.*

Gray Rock's 72-year-old neighbor, **Auberge Villa Bellevue** on Lac Ouimet, is an equally venerable and less-expensive alternative to the former. Run by the Dubois family for more than three generations, this inn has made its reputation as a family resort—so much so that accommodations for children are free if they share a room with their parents. (Meal plans are also scaled down accordingly: children age 3–10 pay about $50, while children 11–14 pay about $65 for vacation packages.) In winter, weekend packages include transportation to nearby Mont Tremblant, baby-sitting services, and a full program of children's activities. Accommodations range from hotel rooms to chalets and condominiums. In summer, special tennis-school packages for adults and children are available. Sailing, windsurfing, water-skiing, and lounging about on the outdoor terrace lakeside are other possible summer pastimes at Villa Bellevue. The indoor swimming pool and fitness center offer nonskiers plenty of physical activity during the winter without stepping outdoors. *845 Principale, Mont Tremblant, J0T 1Z0, tel. 819/425-2734 or 800/567-6763. 108 rooms. AE, DC, MC, V. Closed mid-Oct.–Thanksgiving, mid-Apr.–mid-May. Expensive.*

Only 90 minutes from Montreal, **Station Mont Tremblant Lodge** on 9-mile-long **Lac Tremblant** is the northernmost resort that is easily accessible in the Upper Laurentians. Considered the crown jewel of the Laurentians, it is busiest in winter. With the longest vertical drop 2,131 feet (650 meters), in Eastern Canada, Mont Tremblant offers a wide range of ski trails. Beginners favor the 3-mile (5-kilometer) long Nansen trail, while intermediate skiers head for the steeply sloped Flying Mile and Beauchemin runs. Experts choose the challenging Duncan and Expo runs on the mountain's north side. Mont Tremblant is a favorite ski destination of former Canadian Olympic Ski Jumping Team member Horst Bulau, who likes the variety of hills (33 trails in all), great snow conditions, and accommodations packages. Five-time World Cup downhill racer and former Canadian National Alpine Ski Team member Laurie Graham can also be found on the slopes.

The partying is lively in the winter, with lots of après-ski bars in the hotel and the immediate area. In summer, guests swim, windsurf, and sail. Mont Tremblant Lodge has a nine-hole golf course, and horseback riding and tennis are also available. *Lac Tremblant, Quebec, J0T 1Z0, tel. 819/425-8711 or 800/567-6761. 231 rooms. AE, DC, MC, V. Very Expensive.*

Across the lake is **Cuttle's Tremblant Club,** a hotel and condominium complex that uses the mountain for its skiing. Built as a private retreat in the 1930s by a wealthy American, the original large log cabin lodge is furnished in Colonial style, with wooden staircases and huge stone fireplaces. The rustic but comfortable main lodge has excellent facilities and a dining room with four-star gourmet cuisine. Both the main lodge and the deluxe condominium complex (fireplaces, private balconies, kitchenettes, and split-level design de rigueur), built just up the hill from the lodge, offer magnificent views of Mont Tremblant and its ski hills. Bordering Lac Tremblant, summer activities include swimming, fishing, boating, tennis, and golf. An indoor pool and exercise facility are planned for 1990. *Chemin Lac Tremblant Nord, Quebec, J0T 1Z0, tel. 819/425-2731. 67 rooms. AE, MC, V. Expensive-Very Expensive.*

Auberge du Coq de Montagne has in just 10 years earned a favorable reputation for its owners Nino and Kay Faragalli. Moderately priced, this cosy family-run inn is touted for its friendly service, great hospitality and modern accommodations. Kudos have also been garnered for the great Italian cuisine served up nightly, which also draws a local crowd, so reservations are a must. Situated on Lac Moore, year-round facilities and activities on-site or close by include canoeing, kayaking, sailboarding, fishing, badminton, sauna, exercise room, tennis, horseback riding, skating, and skiing. *324 chemin Principale, Lac Moore, Mont Tremblant, Quebec, J0T 1Z0, tel. 819/425-3380 or 819/425-7311. 27 rooms. MC, V. Moderate.*

Mont Tremblant is also car-racing country. Racing champion Jackie Stewart has called Mont Tremblant "the most beautiful racetrack in the world." Though Stewart didn't win the Canadian Grand Prix at Mont Tremblant in 1970 (his car fell apart), he did win a Can-Am race there in 1971 and came back in 1972 to win the Canadian Grand Prix. Nowadays, the **Formula 2000 "Jim Russell Championships"** of the Canadian Car Championships (tel. 819/425-2739) take place here on weekends in June, July, August, September, and October, as do three of the eight stock-car races for the **Rothmans-Porsche Turbo Cup.**

17 The mountain and the hundreds of square miles of wilderness beyond it comprise **Parc Mont Tremblant.** Created in 1894, this was once the home of the Algonquin Indians, who called this area Manitonga Soutana, meaning "mountain of the spirits." Today it is a vast wildlife sanctuary of more than 500 lakes and rivers protecting some 230 species of birds and animals, including moose, deer, bear, and beaver. In the winter, its trails are used by cross-country skiers, snowshoers, and snowmobile enthusiasts. Moose hunting is allowed in season, and camping and canoeing are the main summer activities. There are three campgrounds with a total of 1,500 sites: Lac Monroe (which also has a park reception center), Lac Chat, and Lac Lajoie. In addition there are approximately 20 cottages for rent. Other park reception centers are in Saint-Donat and Saint-Come (tel. 819/688-2281).

L'Estrie

L'Estrie (before Bill 101, known as the Eastern Townships) refers to the area in the southeast corner of the province of Quebec, bordering Vermont and New York State. Its northern Appalachian hills, rolling down to placid lakeshores, were first home to the Abenaki Indians, long before "summer people" built their cottages and horse paddocks here. The Indians are gone, but the names they gave to the region's recreational lakes remain—Memphremagog, Massawippi, Megantic.

L'Estrie

L'Estrie, known as the garden of Quebec, was left largely unsettled by the early French colonists, who, save for a few trappers, concentrated on northern Quebec.

L'Estrie was initially populated by United Empire Loyalists fleeing the American War of Independence and, later, the newly created United States of America, to continue living under the English king in British North America. It's not surprising that L'Estrie is reminiscent of New England with its covered bridges, village greens, white church steeples, and country inns. They were followed, around 1820, by the first wave of Irish immigrants, ironically, Catholics fleeing their country's union with Protestant England. Some 20 years later the potato famine sent more Irish pioneers to the townships.

L'Estrie became more Gallic after 1850, as French Canadians moved in to work on the railroad and in the lumber industry, and later to mine asbestos at Thetford. After the American Civil War, Lac Massawippi became a favorite summer haunt of wealthy Southerners, whose homes have since been converted into gracious inns, including the Manoir Hovey and the Hatley Inn. Around the turn of the century, English families from Montreal and Americans from the border states discovered the region and began summering at cottages along the lakes.

Today the summer communities fill up with equal parts French and English visitors, though year-round residents are primarily French. Nevertheless, townshippers are proud of both their Loyalist heritage and Quebec roots. They boast of "Loyalist tours" and Victorian gingerbread homes, and in the next breath, direct visitors to the snowmobile museum in Valcourt, where, in 1937, native son Joseph-Armand Bombardier built the first *moto-neige* in his garage. (Bombardier's inventions were the basis of one of Canada's biggest industries, supplying New York City and Mexico City with subway cars and other rolling stock.)

Over the last two decades, l'Estrie has developed from a series of quiet farm communities and wood-frame summer homes to a thriving all-season resort area. In winter, skiers flock to nine downhill centers and 26 cross-country trails. By early spring, the sugar huts are busy with the new maple syrup. L'Estrie's southerly location makes this the balmiest corner of Quebec, notable for its spring skiing. In summer, boating, swimming, sailing, golf, and bike riding take over. And every fall the inns are booked solid with "leaf peepers" eager to take in the brilliant foliage.

Getting Around

By Car Take Autoroute 10 East from Montreal or from New England on U.S. 91, which becomes Autoroute 55 as it crosses the border at Rock Island.

By Bus Buses depart almost hourly, daily from the Terminus Voyageur in Montreal (505 blvd. de Maisonneuve E, tel. 514/842–2281), with routes to Granby, Lac-Mégantic, Magog, Sherbrooke, and Thetford Mines.

Important Addresses and Numbers

Tourist Information
In Montreal, information about l'Estrie is available at the **Tourisme-Québec Office** (2 Place Ville Marie, plaza level near the corner of Cathcart and University Sts., tel. 514/873-2015). Year-round regional provincial tourist offices are located in the towns of Bromont, Granby, Lac-Brome, Lac-Mégantic, La Patrie, Magog, Mansonville, Sherbrooke, Sutton, and Thetford Mines. Seasonal tourist offices (June-Labor Day) are also located in Asbestos, Ayer's Cliff, Black Lake, Coaticook, Cowansville, Danville, North Hatley, Notre-Dame-des-Bois, Richmond, St-Denis-de-Brompton, and Sutton.

For lodging information, contact: Association Touristique de l'Estrie (2338 King St. W, Sherbrooke, PQJ11C6, tel. 819/566-7404).

Exploring L'Estrie

Numbers in the margin correspond with points of interest on the l'Estrie map.

① **Granby**, about 50 miles (80 kilometers) from Montreal, is considered to be the gateway to l'Estrie. This town is best known for its zoo, the **Jardin Zoologique de Granby**. It houses some 1,000 animals from 200 species. Two of its newest inhabitants, rare snow leopards, have won the zoo recognition from the International Union for the Conservation of Nature. The Granby pair are on loan from Chicago's Lincoln Park Zoo and New York's Bronx Zoo and are expected to produce a family by spring 1990. Don't miss out on this rare opportunity to see and support the revival of one of nature's most elegant species. The complex includes amusement park rides and souvenir shops as well as playground and picnic area. *347 rue Bourget, tel. 514/372-9113. Admission: $8 adults, $5.50 senior citizens, $4.75 children 5-17, $2 children 1-4. Open May-Oct. daily 10-5.*

Granby is also gaining repute as the townships' gastronomic capital. Each October, the month-long Festival Gastronomique attracts more than 10,000 *gastronomes* who use the festival's "gastronomic passport" to sample the cuisines at several dining rooms. To reserve a passport, write: *Festival gastronomique de Granby et région, Box 882, Granby PO J2G 8W9, tel. 514/372-7272.*

The **Yamaska** recreation center on the outskirts of town features sailboarding, swimming, and picnicking all summer, and cross-country skiing and snowshoeing in winter.

In the past two decades, l'Estrie has developed into a scenic and increasingly popular ski center. Although it is still less crowded and commercialized than the Laurentians, it boasts ski hills on four mountains that dwarf anything the Laurentians have to offer, with the exception of lofty Mont Tremblant. And, compared with Vermont, ski pass rates are still a bargain.

The larger downhill slopes include **Mont Brome** in Bromont (site of the 1986 World Cup) with 26 trails, **Mont Orford** with 33, **Owl's Head** with 21, and **Mont Sutton** with 38. The steepest drop, one of 2,800 feet (853 meters), is at Orford. All four resorts feature interchangeable lift tickets so skiers can test out all the major runs in the area. Call Ski East, tel. 819/564-8989.

141

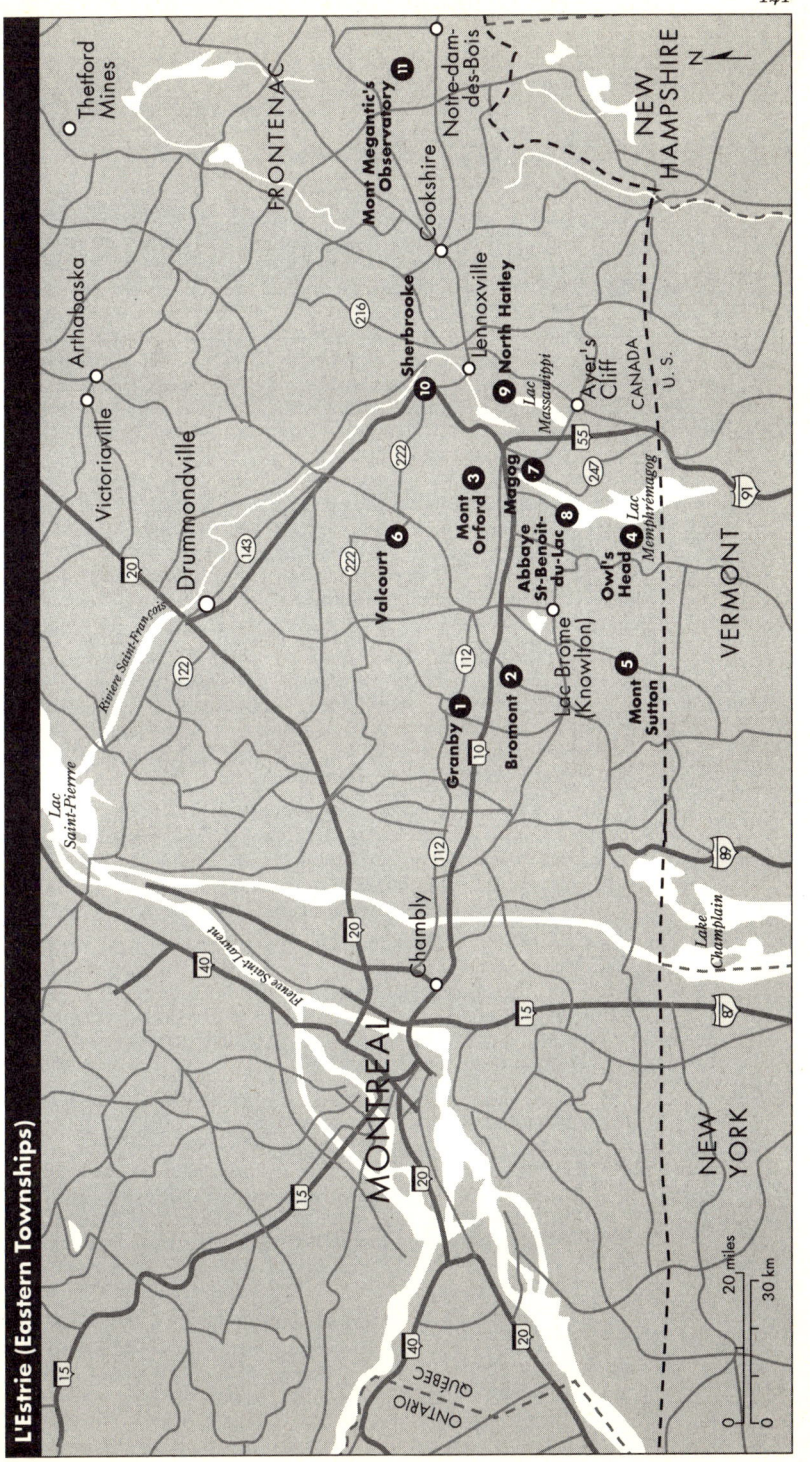

The area's 26 cross-country trails are peaceful getaways. Trails at Bromont criss-cross the site of the 1976 Olympic equestrian center. Three inns—Le Manoir Hovey, Auberge Hatley, and the Ripplecove Inn—offer the **Skiwippi**, a week-long package of cross-country treks from one inn to another. The network covers some 20 miles (32 kilometers) of l'Estrie (*see* Dining and Lodging, below).

Bromont, closest to Montreal, is as lively at night as during the day. It offers the only night skiing in l'Estrie and a slope-side disco, **Le Debarque,** where the action continues into the night après-ski. **Mont Orford,** located at the center of a provincial park, offers plenty of challenges for alpine and cross-country skiers, from novices to veterans. **Owl's Head** has become a mecca for skiers looking for fewer crowds on the hills. It also boasts a 4-kilometer intermediate run, the longest in l'Estrie. Aside from superb skiing, Owl's Head offers tremendous scenery. From the trails you can see nearby Vermont and Lac Mephremagog. (You might even see the lake's legendary sea dragon, said to have been sighted some 90 times since 1816.) As it has for decades, **Mont Sutton** attracts the same die-hard crowd of mostly Anglophone skiers from Quebec. It's also one of the area's largest resorts, with trails that plunge and wander through pine, maple, and birch trees slope-side. **Sutton** itself is a well-established community with craft shops, cozy eateries, and bars (La Paimpolaise is a favorite among skiers).

Bromont, Orford, and Sutton are active all summer as well. Bromont and Orford are *stations touristiques* (tourist centers), meaning that they offer a wide range of activities in all seasons —boating, camping, golf, horseback riding, swimming, tennis, water parks, trail biking, canoeing, fishing, hiking, cross-country and downhill skiing, snowshoeing, etc.

As the former Olympic equestrian site, Bromont is horse country, and every mid-July it holds a riding festival (tel. 514/534–3255). A water-slide park (tel. 514/534–2200)—take exit 78 off Autoroute 10—and a large flea market (weekends from May to mid-November) offer pleasant additions to horseback riding.

Cycling is at its best in the Sutton area, with **Velotour de l'Estrie** (tel. 514/538–2361), a cycling tour company, based in town. The company offers two- and three-day weekend excursion packages for bicycling throughout l'Estrie. The tours begin and end in Sutton, with overnight stops at the area's inns (breakfast and dinners included).

Valcourt is the birthplace of the inventor of the snowmobile, so it follows that this is a world center for the sport, with 1,000-plus miles of paths cutting through the woods and meadows. The **Musée Joseph-Armand Bombardier** displays this innovator's many inventions year-round (tel. 514/532–2258). Every February, Valcourt holds a snowmobile festival with races and demonstrations, including the **Grand Prix Labatt snowmobile race** (tel. 514/372–7272). Maps outlining scenic routes are available through L'Estrie tourist associations (tel. 819/566–7404).

South of Mont Orford at the northern tip of Lac Memphremagog, a large body of water reaching into northern Vermont, lies the bustling resort town of **Magog,** which celebrated its centenary in 1988. A once sleepy village, the town has grown into a four-season resort destination. Two sandy beaches, great bed-and-breakfasts, hotels and restaurants, boating, ferry rides, bird-watching, sailboarding, aerobics, horseback riding, and snowmobiling are just some of the activities offered.

Stroll along Magog's **rue Principale** for a look at boutiques, art galleries, and craft shops with local artisans' work. Other shops are spread throughout the town's downtown, where the streets are lined with century-old homes and churches, some of which have been converted into storefronts, galleries, and theaters.

Night owls will also find Magog's nightlife lively, with a variety of bars, cafés, bistros, and great restaurants to suit every taste and pocketbook. **La Brise discotheque** (tel. 819/847-0313) is a popular hangout. The more sedentary may find **La Source's** (tel. 819/843-0319) array of cheeses, pâtés, and Swiss chocolates irresistible.

❽ Near Magog is the **Abbaye St-Benoit-du-Luc.** To reach St-Benoit from Magog, take the road to Austin and then follow the signs for the side road to the abbey. This abbey's slender bell tower juts up above the trees like a Disneyland castle. Built on a wooded peninsula in 1912 by the Benedictines, the abbey is home to some 60 monks, who sell apples and apple cider from their orchards as well as distinctive cheeses: Ermite, St-Benoit, and ricotta. Gregorian masses are held daily. Check for those open to the public (tel. 819/473-7278). The abbey is also known as a favorite retreat for some of Quebec's best-known politicians; they abandon the thrust-and-cut of their secular concerns for spiritual rejuvenation.

❾ One of the pastimes of **North Hatley** crosses language barriers easily. The town on the tip of Lac Massawippi is home to **The Pilsen,** Quebec's earliest micro-brewery, which gives group tours by reservation (tel. 819/842-4259). If you prefer to sample the local brew in a more social setting, head for **The Pilsen Pub** (tel. 819/842-2971), which has great pub food, loads of atmosphere, and a convivial crowd year-round.

❿ The region's unofficial capital and largest city is **Sherbrooke,** named in 1818 for Canadian Governor-General Sir John Coape Sherbrooke. Founded by Loyalists in the 1790s, and located along the St-François River, it boasts a number of art galleries, the **Musée des Beaux-Arts de Sherbrooke** (1300 blvd. Portland; admission free; open Sun.–Fri. 1–5 PM), and the historic **Domaine Howard,** headquarters of the Townships' historic society, which conducts city tours from this site weekdays from June to September.

⓫ For a more cosmic experience, continue from Sherbrooke along Route 212 to **Mont Megantic's Observatory.** Both amateur stargazers and serious astronomists are drawn to this site, located in a beautifully wild and mountainous part of l'Estrie. The observatory is at the summit of l'Estrie's second highest mountain (1,098 meters), whose northern face records annual snowfalls rivaling any in North America. The observatory is a joint venture by l'Université de Montréal and l'Université Laval. Its powerful telescope allows resident scientists to observe celestial bodies 10 million times smaller than the human eye can detect. There's a welcome center on the mountain's base, where amateur stargazers can get information about the evening celestial sweep sessions, Thursdays through Saturdays. *Notre-Dame-Des-Bois, tel. 819/888-2822. Open daily late June–Labor Day, 10–6.*

Dining and Lodging

Granby and its environs is one of Quebec's foremost regions for traditional Québécois cuisine, here called *la fine cuisine estrienne*. Specialties include mixed game meat pies like *cipaille* and sweet, salty dishes like ham and maple syrup. Actually, maple syrup—on everything and in all its forms—is a mainstay of Québécois dishes. L'Estrie is one of Quebec's main sugaring regions.

Sugar Huts Every March the combination of sunny days and cold nights causes the sap to run in the maple trees. Sugar huts (*cabanes à sucre*) go into operation boiling the sap collected from the trees in buckets (now, at some places, complicated tubing and vats do the job). The many commercial shacks scattered over the area host "sugaring offs" and tours of the operation, including the tapping of maple trees, boiling vats, etc. and *tire sur la neige*, when hot syrup is poured over cold snow to give it a taffy consistency just right for "pulling" and eating. A number of cabanes offer hearty meals of ham, baked beans, and pancakes, all drowned in maple syrup. It's best to call before visiting any of these cabanes.

Ayer's Cliff **Erabliere Robert Lauzier,** chemin Audet, tel. 819/838-4433.

Cookshire **Bolducs:** on Route 253, tel. 819/875-3167; and 525 chemin Lower, tel. 819/875-3022.

In addition to maple sugar, cloves, nutmeg, cinnamon, and pepper—the same spices used by the first settlers—have never gone out of fashion here, and local restaurants make good use of them in their distinctive dishes. The full country experience of l'Estrie includes warm hospitality at lodges and inns in the area as well.

Ayer's Cliff **The Ripplecove Inn.** This inn vies with the Hatley and Hovey
Dining and Lodging inns for best in the region. Its dining, accommodations, and service are consistently excellent. Ripplecove's dining room is an award winner. Its English-pub style dining offers a combination of classical and nouvelle cuisine with such dishes as confit de canard Lac Brome followed by *rable de lapin* (rabbit served with honey sauce), topped off by a sublime dessert such as au chocolat arabica (a mousse laced with coffee flavor). Rooms have an antique feel. Family cottages are also available. *700 chemin Ripplecove, Box 246, Ayer's Cliff, Quebec, J0B 1C0, tel. 819/838-4296. 26 rooms. Facilities: winter skating rink, groomed cross-country ski trails, wet-bar boat that cruises Massawippi. Reserve 1 day in advance for restaurant. Closed 2 weeks in November. AE, MC, V. Very Expensive.*

Bromont **Le Château Bromont Resort Spa.** This is a brand-new Euro-
Dining and Lodging pean-style resort spa. Here you can receive therapeutic massages, algotherapy, electropuncture, algae wraps, facials, and aroma therapy. The Atrium houses an indoor pool, hot tubs, and a sauna. There are also outdoor hot tubs, squash, racquetball, tennis courts, and a Nautilus-equipped gym. After your workout, head for the Château's dining room, Les Quatres Canards, where "cuisine sauvage" is created by chef Norman Rivard. (There is also a special spa menu offered. Its L'Equestre Bar, named for Bromont's equestrian interests, features a cocktail hour and live entertainment. *90 rue*

L'Estrie

Stanstead, Bromont, Quebec, J0E 1L0, tel. 514/534-3433. 154 rooms. Facility: restaurant. AE, MC, V. Expensive.

Eastman Dining and Lodging

Centre de Sante Eastman. This four-season resort offers respite to the bone-weary and bruised skier. Holistic spa treatments include massage (Swedish and Shiatsu) and gentle gymnastic workouts. *712 chemin Diligence, Eastman, Quebec, J0E 1P0, tel. 514/297-3009. 16 rooms. Facility: dining room. MC, V. Moderate. Packages include 3 meals.*

Lennoxville Lodging

Bishop's University. If you're on a budget this is a great place to stay. The prices can't be beat—$17.50–$22.50 per person for a single room, $15 per person for a double—and the location near Sherbrooke is good for touring. The university's grounds are lovely, with a river cutting through the campus and its golf course. Much of the architecture is reminiscent of stately New England campuses. Visit the university's 132-year-old chapel and also look for the butternut tree, an endangered species in l'Estrie. *College St., Lennoxville, Quebec, J1M 1Z7, tel. 819/ 822-9651. Facilities: sports complex with Olympic-size indoor pool, outdoor tennis courts. Open mid-May–Labor Day. Inexpensive.*

Magog Dining

Auberge de l'Etoile. This popular restaurant in Magog serves three meals a day in casual surroundings. (The restaurant is part of a motel with 26 units facing the lake. A double room costs $80–$95.) *1133 rue Principale O, tel. 819/843-6521. Reservations recommended. AE, MC, V. Open daily. Moderate.*

Lodging

Club Azur. This is a Club Med–type condo facility that is perfect for family ski trips. There are activities for children, as well as tennis courts and indoor and outdoor pools. For the summertime it is a convenient two-minute walk from the beach. *81 Desjardins, Magog, Quebec, J1X 3W9, tel. 819/847-2131 or 800/567-3535. 190 rooms. Facilities: saunas, tennis, recreation complex, bistro, restaurant, convenience store, day-care center. AE, MC, V. Expensive.*

O'Berge du Village. Half of this condo complex is on a timeshare basis, while the other condos are run like a hotel. There is a casual outdoor restaurant. At press time an indoor pool and a more elaborate restaurant were under construction. *262 rue Merry S, Magog, Quebec, J1X 3L2, tel. 819/843-6566 or 800/ 567-6089. 113 rooms. AE, MC, V. Moderate.*

North Hatley Dining and Lodging

Auberge Hatley. Gourmet cuisine is the main attraction at this country inn. Its dining room was named the top restaurant in Quebec in the third annual Ordre du Merite de la restauration awards in 1988. A member of the Relais & Chateaux, it is home to award-winning chef Guy Bohec. After eating one of his fine meals, guests sleep it off in one of the 21 charmingly decorated rooms in this 1903 country manor. *Box 330, North Hatley, Quebec, J0B 2C0, tel. 819/842-2451. 24 rooms, some with Jacuzzi and fireplace. Facilities: 4-star restaurant. AE, MC, V. Closed last 2 weeks in November. Expensive–Very Expensive.*

Le Manoir Hovey. This inn is acclaimed for its gastronomic delights as well as for its accommodations. It is a former private estate dating to 1899. Do reserve ahead for the dining room. Expect such dishes as scallop mousseline with essence of clam and tarragon, or lamb trilogy—three cuts of lamb braised with a light sauce of *morilles* (morels). Its rooms are elegantly furnished, some featuring four-poster beds and fireplaces. *Box 60,*

North Hatley, Quebec, J0B 2C0, tel. 819/842-2421. 35 rooms. AE, MC, V. Very Expensive.

Notre-Dame-des-Bois **Aux Berges de l'Aurore.** This tiny bed-and-breakfast is situated
Dining and Lodging at the foot of Mont Megantic. It has been attractively furnished by its owners, Michel Martin and Daniel Pepin. The draw here is the inn's cuisine. The four-star restaurant features a five-course meal with ingredients supplied from the inn's huge fruit, vegetable, and herb garden, as well as wild game from the surrounding area: boar, fish, hare, and quail. The inn does a thriving business in winter, much of it owing to its close proximity to Sugar Loaf Mountain in Vermont. *Chemin de l'Observatoire, Notre-Dame-des-Bois, Quebec, J0B 2E0. 4 rooms. Inexpensive. Restaurant: reservations suggested; open daily in summer; autumn closed Mon.–Tues.; winter open Fri.–Sun. MC, V. Moderate.*

Orford **Auberge Estrimont.** An exclusive complex of rooms, condos,
Lodging and villas, these lodgings each have a foyer, balcony, a coffee maker and a hair dryer. *44 ave. de l'Auberge, Box 96, Orford-Magog, Quebec, J1X 3W7, tel. 819/843-1616 or 800/567-7320. 84 rooms. Facilities: indoor/outdoor pools, tennis, health-care center, downhill and cross-country ski trails. AE, MC, V. Very Expensive.*

Sherbrooke **Restaurant Au P'tit Sabot.** This restaurant recently won an
Dining award for the best local-style eatery in the region. *1410 King St. W, tel. 819/563-0262. Open year-round. Expensive.*

Sutton **Auberge La Paimpolaise.** This auberge is located right on Mont
Lodging Sutton, 50 feet from the ski trails. *615 Maple St., Sutton, Quebec, J0E 2K0, tel. 514/538-3213. 29 rooms with 2 double beds and color TV. AE, MC, V. Moderate.*
Auberge Le Refuge. In contrast to the area's many resorts, this small inn has only 12 rooms and operates as a B&B during the winter season. *33 Maple St., Sutton, Quebec, J0E 2K0, tel. 514/538-3802. Open summer Thurs.–Sun; daily in winter. AE, MC, V. Inexpensive.*
Auberge Schweizer. This lodge operates year-round. They have their own farm, and guests feast on home-cooked meals with vegetables straight from the farm. The lodge is surrounded by a lake and a pond for swimming as well as some hiking trails. Ski trails are nearby in winter. The lodge has four rooms with two shared baths, but there are also three chalets on the property that can be rented. *357 Schweizer Rd., Sutton, Quebec, J0E 2K0, tel. 514/538-2129. V. Moderate.*

The Arts

Lac Brome **The Lac Brome Theatre** (tel. 514/243-0361 or 800/363-7079) is an English summer theater troupe that presents a three-play season of classic Broadway and West End hits. So successful has founding artistic director and British expatriate Emma Stevens been in galvanizing local community support and summer resident attendance that the company moved into a newly built, 200-seat, $250,000, air-conditioned theater last year. Located behind Knowlton's popular pub of the same name, the theater was a gift from Knowlton Pub owner Gerry Wood. Discounted theater tickets are available if visitors book the special B&B packages offered at local inns. Inquire when making reservations in Lac Brome.

Lac Massawippi	**L'Association du Festival du Lac Massawippi** presents an annual antiques and folk-art show (tel. 819/842–4380) each July. The association also sponsors concerts, exhibitions, and poetry readings at various venues throughout the town year-round.
Lennoxville	Lennoxville's **Centennial Theatre and Consolidated-Bathurst Theatre** at Bishop's University (tel. 819/563–4966) presents a roster of international, Canadian, and Québécois jazz, classical, and rock concerts, as well as dance, mime, and children's theater. Jazz greats Gary Burton, Carla Bley and Larry Coryell have appeared here, as have classical artists like the Amsterdam Guitar Trio and the Allegri String Quartet.
Magog	**Theatre Le Vieux Clocher** (64 rue Merry N, tel. 819/847–0470) presents summer pop and rock concerts, as well as French plays.
North Hatley	**The Piggery** reigns supreme in l'Estrie cultural life. Housed in a former pig barn in North Hatley on the shores of Lac Massawippi, the Piggery is renowned for its risk taking, often presenting new plays by Canadian playwrights and even experimenting with bilingual productions. An attractive on-site restaurant serves country suppers and picnic fare indoors and out before the 8 PM curtain. *P.O. 390 North Hatley, Quebec J0B 2C0, tel. 819/842-2191 or 842-2431. Reservations required. Season runs June–Aug.*
Orford	Orford's regional park is the site of an annual arts festival highlighting classical music, pops as well as chamber orchestra concerts. For the past 38 summers, some 300 students have come to the **Orford Arts Center** to study and perform classical music. Canada's internationally celebrated Orford String Quartet originated here. Lately, Festival Orford has expanded to include jazz and folk music. Budding musicians rub shoulders and trade notes at master classes and in public performances with big name artists such as jazz pianist Oliver Jones and the inimitable folksinging duo, Kate and Anna McGarrigle. The Center also welcomes artisans during its summer art exhibitions. Musicians give concerts in the gracefully designed concert hall or in the park, where they often practice while seated among the outdoor sculptures. *Orford Arts Center, Box 280, Magog, Quebec, J1X 3W8, tel. 819/843-3981 or in Canada from May to Aug. 800/567-6155.*
Sutton	Sutton is also home to the visual and performing arts. **Arts Sutton** (7 Academy, tel. 514/538–2563) is a long-established mecca for the visual arts. Aside from exhibitions of work by renowned Quebec artists, the center also runs summer workshop sessions in many media, with many of the seasonal instructors drawn from the Saidye Bronfman Centre's faculty members.
	Arts and Music Sutton (tel. 514/596–1729) also offers intensive workshops in dance, music, and theater, which culminate in public performances.

5 Quebec City

Introduction

by Alice H. Oshins

A New York–based freelance writer, Alice H. Oshins has written extensively on French Canada.

An excursion to French-speaking Canada is incomplete without a visit to Quebec City, located in one of the most beautiful natural settings in North America. Don't be fooled by the fact that the area called la Vieille Ville (Old City) is only 1 square mile; it actually has a lot of ground to cover. This well-preserved part of town is a small and dense place, steeped in four centuries of history and French tradition. Once you begin to explore first hand the 17th- and 18th-century buildings, the ramparts that once protected the city, and the numerous parks and monuments, you will soon realize how much there is to see.

The oldest municipality in Quebec province, Quebec City was the first settlement of French explorers, fur trappers, and missionaries in the 17th century, who came here to establish the colony of New France. Today it still resembles a French provincial town in many ways, with its family-oriented residents with strong ties to their pasts. More than 95% of its metropolitan population of 500,000 are French-speaking. It is also a fortified city, the only one in North America, an attribute that led UNESCO to declare it a world heritage treasure.

Quebec City is huddled on a cliff above the St. Lawrence River, at a point where the body of water narrows; this strategic location has forged its historic destiny as a military stronghold. When Winston Churchill visited Quebec City in the early 1940s, he named it "Gibraltar of North America" because of its position at the gateway to the continent. The city's military prominence paved the way for its leading political role, first as the French colony's administrative center and eventually as the capital of Quebec province.

In 1535, French explorer Jacques Cartier first came upon what the Algonquin Indians called "Kebec," meaning "where the river narrows." New France, however, was not actually founded in the area of what is now Quebec City until 1608, when another French explorer, Samuel de Champlain, recognized the military advantages of the location and set up a fort. Along the banks of the St. Lawrence, on the spot now called Place Royale, this fort developed into an economic center for fur trade and shipbuilding. Twelve years later, de Champlain realized the French colony's vulnerability to attacks from above and expanded its boundaries to the top of the cliff, where he built the fort Château St.-Louis on the site of the present-day Château Frontenac.

During the early days of New France, the French and British fought for the control of the area. In 1690, when an expedition led by Admiral Sir William Phipps arrived from England, Comte de Frontenac, New France's most illustrious governor, issued his famous statement, "Tell your lord that I will reply with the mouth of my cannons."

England was determined to conquer New France. The French constructed walls and other military structures and had the advantage of the defensive position on top of the cliff, but they still had to contend with Britain's naval supremacy. On September 13, 1759, the British army led by General James Wolfe scaled the colony's cliff and took the French troops led by Général Louis-Joseph Montcalm by surprise. The British de-

Metropolitan Quebec City

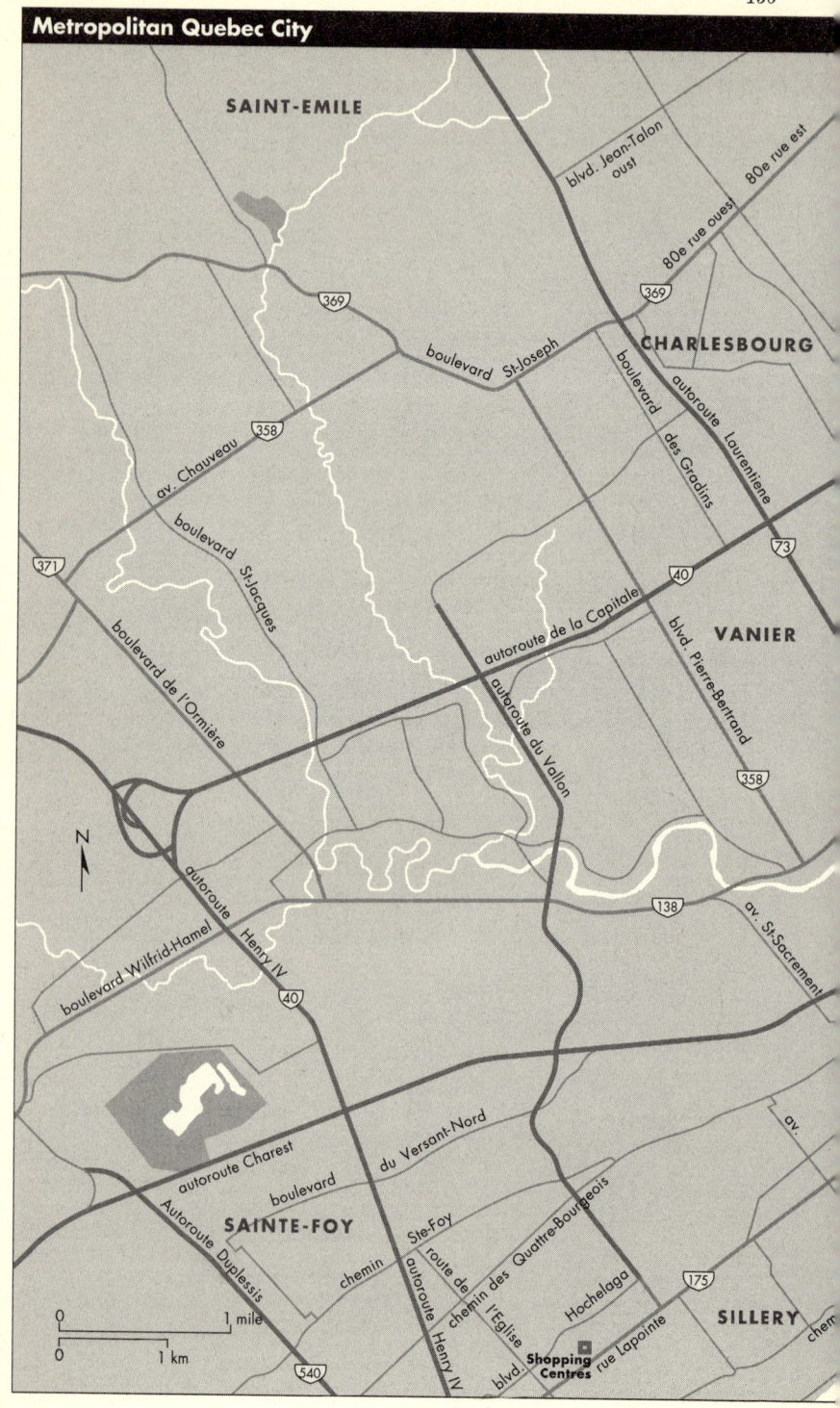

150

151

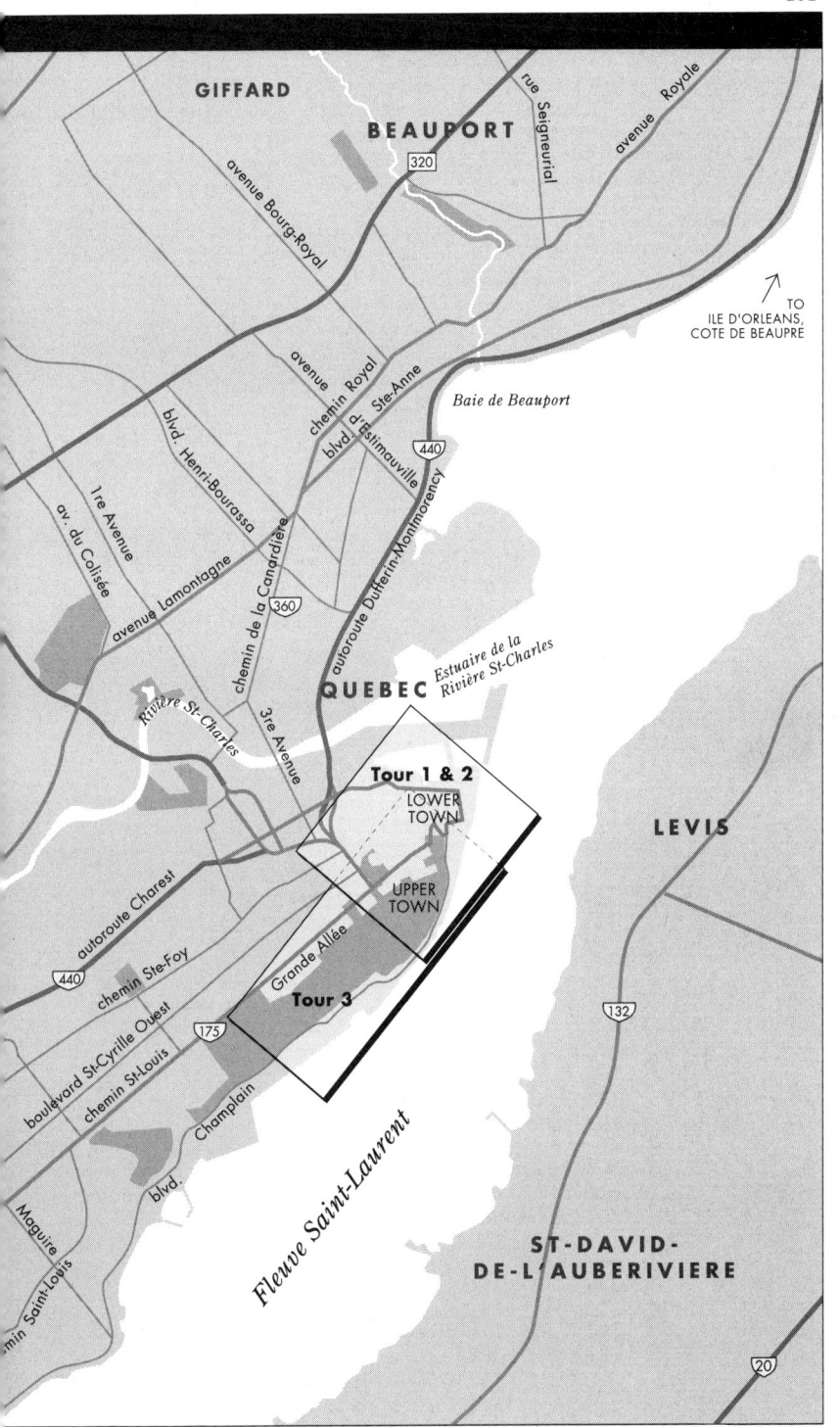

feated the French in a 20-minute battle on the Plains of Abraham, and New France came under English rule.

The British brought their mastery of trade to the region. In the 18th century, Quebec City's economy prospered because of the success of the fishing, fur trading, shipbuilding, and timber industries. In order to further protect the city from invasion, the British continued to expand upon the fortifications left by the French. Defensive structures that were built included a wall encircling the city and a star-shaped citadel, both of which still enhance the city's urban landscape. The city remained under British rule until 1867, when the Act of Confederation united several Canadian provinces (Quebec, Ontario, New Brunswick, and Nova Scotia) and designated Quebec City the capital of the province of Quebec.

During the mid-19th century, the economic center of Eastern Canada shifted west from Quebec City to Montreal and Toronto. Today government is Quebec City's main business: More than 30,000 civil employees work and live in the area. Like most other North American communities, the city has recently experienced a boom in the financial-services industry. Office complexes continue to appear outside the older portion of town; modern malls, convention centers, and imposing hotels now cater to an established business clientele.

Despite the period of British rule, Quebec City has remained a center of French-Canadian culture. It is home to Université Laval (Laval University), a large Catholic institution that grew out of Séminaire de Québec (Quebec Seminary) founded in 1663 by French bishop François de Montmorency Laval; today Laval has a sprawling campus in the suburb of Sainte-Foy. Quebec City also has several theaters, including the Grand Théâtre de Québec, where local artists perform plays that deal directly with French-Canadian culture. The Quebec government has completely restored many of the centuries-old buildings of Place Royale, one of the oldest districts on the continent. The city's ancient stone churches and homes, as well as its cultural institutions, such as Musée de Québec and Musée de la Civilisation, are firmly rooted in French-Canadian society.

Quebec City is a wonderful place in which to wander on foot. Its natural beauty is world renowned. You're bound to enjoy the view from Parc Montmorency (Montmorency Park), where the Laurentian Mountains jut majestically over the St. Lawrence River. Even more impressive vistas may be gazed upon if you walk along the walls or climb to the city's highest point, Cap Diamant (Cape Diamond). Several blissful days may be spent investigating the narrow cobblestone streets of the historic Old City; browsing for local arts and crafts in the boutiques of quartier Petit-Champlain; or strolling the Terrasse Dufferin promenade along the river. When you've worked up an appetite, you can stop to indulge in one of the many reliable cafés and restaurants, with a choice of French, Québécois, and international fare. If you've had enough of the past, another vibrant, modern part of town beckons beyond the city gates. And if you're tired of walking you can always board a *calèche* (horse-drawn carriage) near the city gates or hop on the ferry across the St. Lawrence River to Lévis for a thrilling view of the Quebec City skyline. What follows will help you uncover some of the secrets of this exuberant, romantic place.

Arriving and Departing

By Plane

Airports/Airlines Quebec City has one airport, **Quebec City International Airport,** located in the suburb of Sainte-Foy, approximately 12 miles (19 kilometers) from downtown. Few U.S. airlines fly directly to Quebec City. You usually have to stop in Montreal or Toronto and take one of the regional and commuter airlines such as Air Canada's **Air Alliance** tel. 418/692–0770) or **Intair,** tel. 418/692–1031).

Between the Airport and Quebec City The ride from the airport into town should be no longer than 30 minutes. Most hotels do not have an airport shuttle, but they will make a reservation for you with a bus company. If you're not in a rush, a shuttle bus offered by Maple Leaf Tours (*see* below) is convenient and only half the price of a taxi.

By Bus **Maple Leaf Tours** (575 Aragoe, tel. 418/687–9226) has a shuttle bus that runs from the airport to hotels and costs $6.75 one-way, $12 round-trip. The shuttle makes about seven trips to and from the airport every day except Saturday, when it makes only two trips each way. Stops include the major hotels in town, and any other hotel upon request. Reservations are recommended.

By Taxi Taxis are always available immediately outside the airport exit near the baggage claim area. Some local taxi companies are **Taxi Québec** (975 8 ième Ave., tel. 418/522–2001) and **Taxi Coop de Québec** (496 2ième Ave., tel. 418/525–5191), the largest company in the city. A ride into the city will cost approximately $20.

By Limousine Private limo service is expensive, starting at $40 for the ride from the airport into Quebec City. Try **Service de Limousines** (250 Des Lilas O, tel. 418/626–5269). Some of the local tour companies offer car service to the airport or act as a referral service. **Maple Leaf Tours** (575 Arago O, tel. 418/687–9226) has a private car service for about $44. **Visite Touristique de Québec** (1572 du Parc, Sainte-Foy, tel. 418/653–9722) offers car service for about $80.

By Car If you're driving from the airport, take Route 540 to Route 175 (boulevard Laurier), which becomes Grande Allée and leads right to the Old City. The ride is about 30 minutes and may be only slightly longer (45 minutes or so) during rush hours (7:30 AM–8:30 AM into town, and 4 PM–5:30 PM leaving town).

By Car, Train, and Bus

By Car Montreal and Quebec City are connected by Autoroute 20 on the south shore of the St. Lawrence River and by Autoroute 40 on the north shore. On both highways, the ride between the two cities is about 150 miles (240 kilometers) and takes approximately three hours. U.S. I–87 in New York, U.S. I–89 in Vermont, and U.S. I–91 in New Hampshire connect with Autoroute 20. Highway 401 from Toronto also connects with Autoroute 20.

Driving northeast from Montreal on Autoroute 20, follow signs for Pont Pierre-Laporte (Pierre-Laporte Bridge) as you approach Quebec City. After you've crossed the bridge, turn right onto boulevard Laurier (Route 175), which becomes the Grande Allée leading into Quebec City.

It is only necessary to have a car if you are planning to visit outlying areas. The narrow streets of the Old City leave few two-hour metered parking spaces available. However, there are several parking garages at central locations in town, with rates running approximately $6 to $9 a day. Main garages are located at City Hall, Place d'Youville, Complex G, Place Québec, Château Frontenac, Québec Seminary, rue St-Paul and the Old Port.

Rental Cars See Renting Cars in Chapter 1.

By Train **VIA Rail,** Canada's passenger rail service, travels three times daily (morning, afternoon, and evening) from Montreal to Quebec City along the south shore of the St. Lawrence River. The trip takes about three hours. The train makes a stop in Sainte-Foy and has first-class service available. Tickets must be purchased in advance at any VIA Rail office or travel agent. The basic price is $30 each way; first-class service is an additional $19 each way. *Tel. 418/692-3940 or 800/361-5390 in Quebec City; in Sainte-Foy, tel. 418/524-6452; in Quebec province, tel. 800/362-5390.*

The train arrives in Quebec City at the 19th-century **Gare du Palais** (450 rue St-Paul, tel. 418/524-6452), in the heart of the Old City. Take a taxi to your hotel or walk, depending on how much luggage you have and on where your hotel is located.

By Bus **Voyageur Inc.** provides regular service from Montreal to Quebec City daily, departing hourly 6 AM-9 PM and again at 11 PM and 1 AM. The cost for the three-hour ride is $26.20 one-way and $52.40 round-trip. The only way to buy tickets is at the terminal; tickets are not sold on the bus.

Bus Terminals **Montreal:** Voyageur Terminal (505 blvd. de Maisonneuve E, tel. 514/842-2281).

Quebec: Downtown Terminal (225 blvd. Charest E, tel. 418/524-4692).

Sainte-Foy: 2700 blvd. Laurier, tel. 418/651-7015.

Staying in Quebec City

Getting Around

Walking is the best way to explore Quebec City. The Old City measures only 1 square mile, so most historic sites, hotels, and restaurants are located within the walls or a short distance outside. City maps are available at tourist information offices.

By Bus The public transportation system in Quebec City is dependable, and buses run frequently. You can get to anywhere in Quebec City and the outlying areas although you may be required to transfer. The city's transit system, **Commission de Transport de la Communauté Urbaine de Québec (CTCUQ)** (tel. 418/627-2511) runs buses approximately every 15 or 20 minutes that stop at major points around town. The cost is $1.30 for adults, 75¢ for children; you'll need exact change. All buses stop in Lower Town at Place Jacques-Cartier or outside St-Jean

Staying in Quebec City 155

Gate at Place d'Youville in Upper Town. Transportation maps are available at tourist information offices.

By Taxi Taxis are stationed in front of major hotels, including the Château Frontenac, Hilton International, Loews Le Concorde, and Hôtel des Gouverneurs, as well as in front of Hôtel de Ville (City Hall) along rue des Jardins and Place d'Youville outside St-Jean Gate. For radio dispatched cars, try **Ligue de Taxis de Québec** (tel. 418/648-9199), **Taxi Québec** (tel. 418/522-2001), and **Taxi Québec-Metro** (tel. 418/529-0003). Passengers are charged an initial $2, plus 75¢ for each kilometer.

By Limousine **Sec-Pro** (812 Marguerite-Bourgeois, tel. 418/687-3311) and **Service de Limousines Québec** (250 Deslelas O, tel. 418/626-5269) have 24-hour service.

Important Addresses and Numbers

Tourist Information **Quebec City Region Tourism and Convention Bureau** has two tourist information centers:

Quebec City: 60 rue d'Auteuil, tel. 418/692-2471. Open Nov.-Mar., weekdays 8:30-5; Apr.-May and Sept.-Oct., open weekdays 8:30-5:30; June-Labor Day, open daily 8:30 AM-8:30 PM.

Sainte-Foy: 3005 blvd. Laurier (near the Québec and Pierre-Laporte bridges), tel. 418/651-2882. Open Sept.-May, daily 8:30-6; June-Aug., daily 8:30-8.

Quebec Government Tourism Department: 12 rue Ste-Anne (Place d'Armes), tel. 418/643-2280 or 800/443-7000. Open 9-5; summer open 8:30-7:30.

U.S. Consulate The consulate (2 Place Terrasse Dufferin, tel. 418/692-2095) faces the Governors Park near the Château Frontenac.

Emergencies **Police** and **fire,** tel. 418/691-6911; **Provincial police,** tel. 418/632-6262).

Hospitals **Hôtel-Dieu Hospital** (11 côte du Palais, tel. 418/694-5042) is the main hospital inside the Old City; **Jeffrey Hale Hospital** (1250 chemin Sainte-Foy, tel. 418/683-4471) is opposite St. Sacrament Church.

24-hour Medical Service (tel. 418/687-9915).

24-hour Health Information (tel. 418/648-2626).

Distress Center (tel. 418/683-2153).

24-hour Poison Center (tel. 418/656-8090).

Dental Service 1175 rue Lavigerie, Room 100, Sainte-Foy, tel. 418/653-5412. Open weekdays 8 AM-9 PM; weekends, tel. 418/656-6060.

Pharmacy **Pharmacie Lippens** (Les Galeries Charlesbourg, 4266 1ène Ave., north of Quebec City in Charlesbourg, tel. 418/623-1571) is open daily 8 AM-2 AM.

Road Conditions Tel. 418/643-6830.

Weather Tel. 418/648-7293.

English-Language Bookstore **Librairie Garneau** (47-49 rue Buade, tel. 418/692-4262) has a large selection of books in English.

Travel Agencies **American Express Inter-Voyage** (1155 rue Claire-Fontaine, tel. 418/524-1414), located on the first floor of the Édifice La

Quebec City

Laurentienne (Laurentian Building) behind the Parliament, is open weekdays 9–5.

Opening and Closing Times

Most banks are open Monday through Wednesday 10–3, Thursday and Friday 10–9. **Bank of Montreal** (Place Laurier, 2700 blvd. Laurier, Sainte-Foy, tel. 418/525–3786) is open on Saturday. For currency exchange, **Banque d'Amérique** (24 côte de la Fabrique, tel. 418/694–1937) is open weekdays 9–5:30, weekends 9–5. **Deak International** (615 Grande Allée E, tel. 418/529–1155) is open daily 9–5, during summer months 10–9.

Museum hours are typically 10–6, with longer evening hours during summer months. Most are closed on Monday.

Shopping hours are Monday through Wednesday 9:30–5:30, Thursday and Friday 9:30–9, and Saturday 9:30–5. Stores tend to stay open later during summer months.

During the winter, many attractions and shops change their hours; visitors are advised to call ahead.

Guided Tours

Orientation Tours
By Bus
The three major touring companies—Gray Line, Maple Leaf, and Visite Touristique de Québec—offer similar full- and half-day tours in English in a guided motorbus. Tours cover such sights as Quebec City, Montmorency Falls, and Sainte-Anne-de-Beaupré; combination city and harbor cruise tours are also available. Quebec City tours operate year-round; other excursions to outlying areas may operate only in the summer.

Gray Line offers guided bus tours. Tickets can be purchased at most major hotels or at the kiosk at Terrasse Dufferin at Place d'Armes. Prices range $10–$30; half price for children. *720 rue des Rocailles, tel. 418/622–7420. City tours year-round; others May–Oct. or June–Labor Day.*

Maple Leaf Sightseeing Tours (575 Arago O, tel. 418/687–9226) offers guided tours in a minibus. Call for a reservation, and the company will pick you up at your hotel. Prices range $16–$55; children are charged 6% of the adult price.

Visite Touristique de Québec (C.P. 174, Sillery, tel. 418/653–9722) gives tours in a panoramic bus, costing $16–$55.

Smaller companies offering tours include **La Tournée du Québec Inc.** (tel. 418/831–1385), **Fleur de Lys** (418/831–0188), and Group **Voyages Québec Inc.** (tel. 418/525–4585).

By Ferry
The Québec-Lévis ferry offers a 15-minute crossing of the St. Lawrence River to the town of Lévis. It leaves daily from the pier at rue Dalhousie across from Place Royale every half hour from 7:30 AM until 6:30 PM, then hourly until 2:30 AM. *Tel. 418/692–0550. Cost: $1 adults, 50¢ children and senior citizens.*

By Horse-drawn Carriage
Hire a *calèche* (horse-drawn carriage) on rue d'Auteuil between the St-Louis and Kent gates from **André Beaurivage** (tel. 418/687–9797). The cost is about $40 for a 45-minute tour of the Old City.

Special-Interest Tours
Boat Trips
Beau Temps, Mauvais Temps (911 rue Prévost, Île d'Orléans, tel. 418/828–2275) has a river cruise that stops to tour neighboring islands. The boat departs from the pier at Saint-

François, on Île d'Orléans at 9:30–6 and 2–10 pm. The cost is $43 for adults, $28 for children, including meal, tax, and service.

Excursions AML Inc. (Chouinard Pier, 10 rue Dalhousie, tel. 418/692–1159) runs cruises on the St. Lawrence River aboard the *M/V Louis-Jolliet*. One- to three-hour cruises from June through September cost $12–$18 for adults, half price for children.

Île d'Orléans **Beau Temps, Mauvais Temps** (911 rue Prévost, Île d'Orléans, 418/828–2275) has guided tours of Île d'Orléans by bus, walking tours of the island's historic manors and churches, and trips to a maple-sugar hut (*see* Chapter 6).

Walking Tours **Baillairgé Cultural Tours, Inc.** (2216 chemin du Foulon, Sillery, tel. 418/658–4799), has a 2½-hour walking tour, "Quebec on Foot," from July 1 through October 15 at 9:30 AM and 2 PM daily. The tour begins at the Musée du Fort and includes sights in both the Upper and Lower towns.

Exploring Quebec City

Quebec City's split-level landscape is notable for having one part on the cape (Upper Town) and the other along the shores of the St. Lawrence (Lower Town). If you look out from the Terrasse Dufferin boardwalk in Upper Town, you will see the rooftops of Lower Town buildings directly below. Separating these two sections of the city is steep and precipitous rock, against which were built the city's more than 25 *escaliers* (staircases). Today you can also take the *funiculaire* (funicular), a cable car that climbs and descends the cliff between Terrasse Dufferin and the Maison Jolliet in Lower Town.

With the exception of some of the outlying suburbs, most of Quebec City's historic area will interest tourists. The first two tours offered here remain primarily in the oldest sections of town, while the third tour strays off the beaten path to provide a glimpse of the modern part of the city.

Tour 1: Upper Town

Numbers in the margin correspond with points of interest on the Tours 1 and 2: Upper and Lower Towns map.

This tour takes you to the most prominent buildings of its earliest inhabitants, who came from Europe in the 17th century to set up political, educational, and religious institutions. Upper Town became the political capital of the colony of New France and, later, of British North America. It was also the place where the religious orders first set down their roots: The Jesuits founded the first school for priests in 1635; the Ursuline nuns, a school for girls in 1639; and the Augustine nuns, the first hospital in 1639. Historic buildings, with thick stone walls, large wooden doors, glimmering copper roofs, and majestic steeples, comprise the heart of the city.

❶ Begin this tour where rue St-Louis meets rue du Fort at Upper Town's most central location, **Place d'Armes**. For centuries, this square seated on a cliff has been a meeting place for parades and military events. It is bordered by government buildings; at its west side, the majestic **Ancien Palais de Justice** (Old Court-

Tours 1 and 2: Upper and Lower Towns

Antiques District, **26**
Basilique Notre-Dame-de-Québec, **11**
Cavalier du Moulin, **5**
Château Frontenac, **2**
Couvent des Ursulines, **6**
Édifice Price, **9**
Église Notre-Dame-des-Victoires, **20**
Holy Trinity Anglican Cathedral, **7**
Hôtel Clarendon, **8**
Jardin des Gouverneurs, **4**
Lévis-Québec Ferry, **23**
Maison Chevalier, **18**
Maison des Vins, **21**
Maison Louis-Jolliet, **16**
Maison Montcalm, **27**
Monastère des Augustines, **12**
Musée de la Civilisation, **24**
Musée du Fort, **15**
Parc de l'Artillerie, **28**
Parc Montmorency, **14**
Place d'Armes, **1**
Place de Paris, **22**
Place Royale, **19**
Rue du Trésor, **10**
Rue du Petit-Champlain, **17**
Séminaire de Québec, **13**
Terrasse Dufferin, **3**
Vieux-Port de Québec, **25**

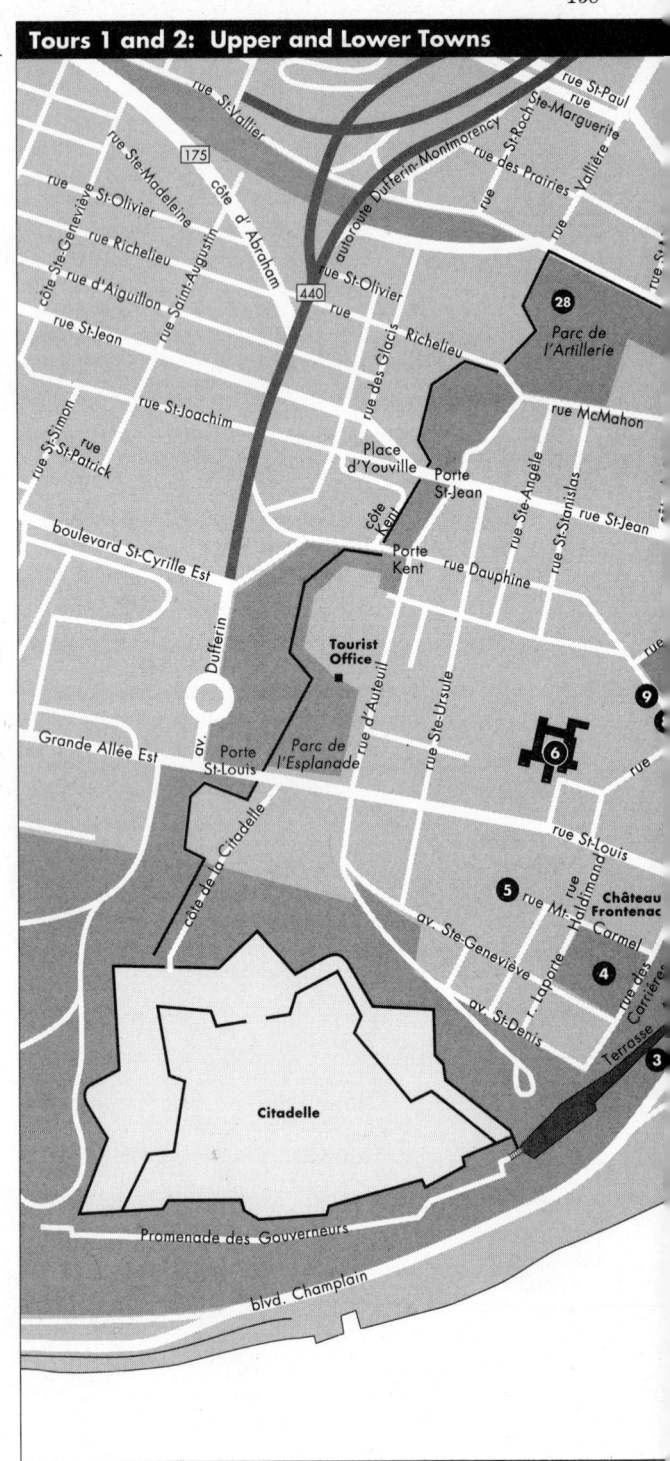

Québec

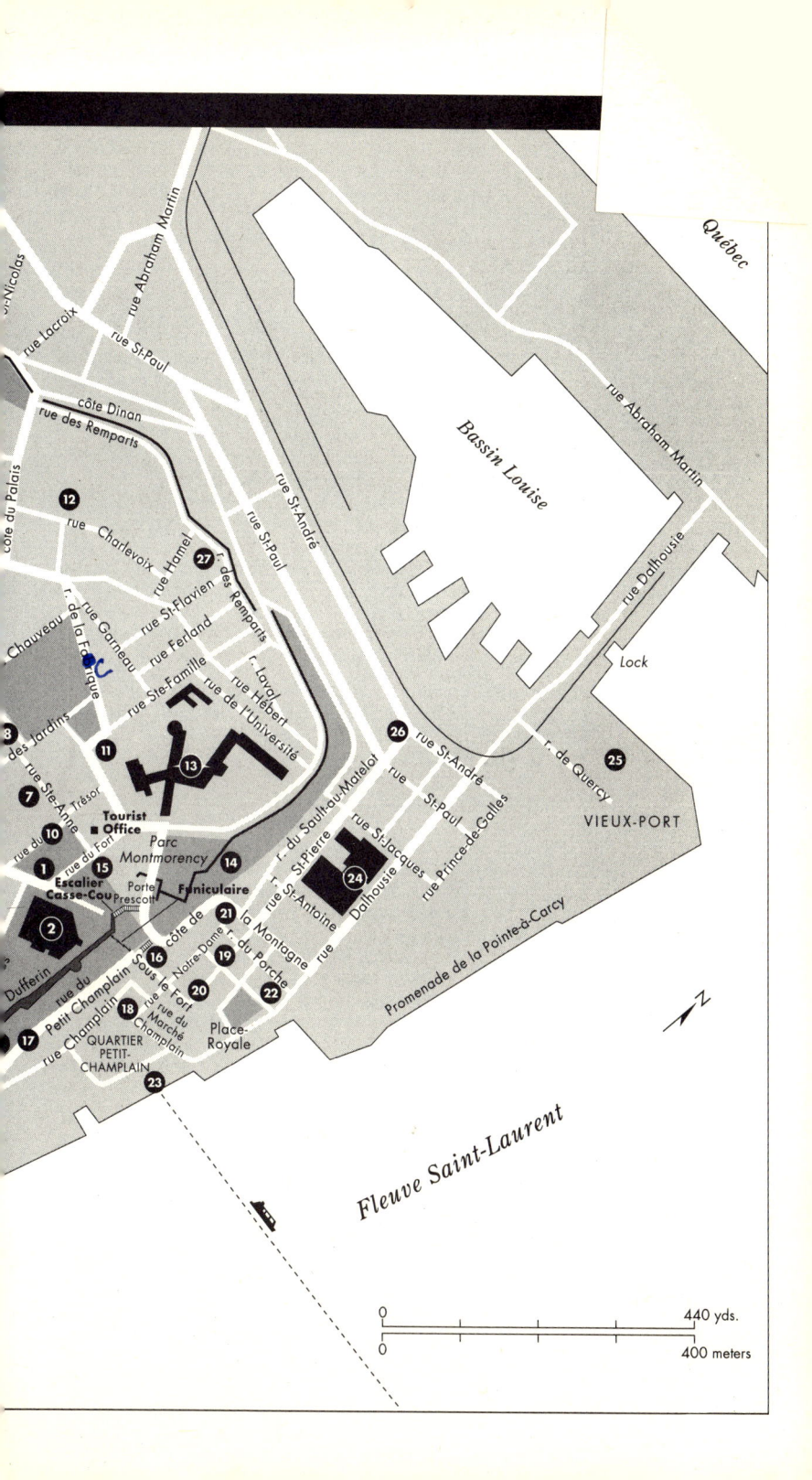

Bassin Louise

rue Abraham Martin
rue Lacroix
rue St-Paul
côte Dinan
rue des Remparts
côte du Palais
rue Charlevoix
rue St-Flavien
rue Hamel
rue des Remparts
rue St-André
rue St-Paul
rue Abraham Martin
rue Dalhousie
Lock
r. de Quercy

Chauveau
r. de la Fabrique
rue Garneau
rue Ferland
rue Ste-Famille
rue Hébert
rue Laval
rue de l'Université

des Jardins
rue du Trésor
rue Ste-Anne
rue du Fort
Parc Montmorency
Tourist Office
Funiculaire
Escalier Casse-Cou
Porte Prescott
Dufferin
rue du Petit Champlain
Sous le Fort
côte de la Montagne
rue Notre-Dame
rue du Porche
rue St-Pierre
rue St-Antoine
rue St-Jacques
rue Prince-de-Galles
r. du Sault-au-Matelot
rue St-Paul
rue St-André
Place-Royale
rue du Marché Champlain
QUARTIER PETIT-CHAMPLAIN

VIEUX-PORT

Promenade de la Pointe-à-Carcy

Fleuve Saint-Laurent

N

0 — 440 yds.
0 — 400 meters

house), a Renaissance building from 1887, replaced the original 1650 courthouse, which was smaller and situated farther away from the square. The present courthouse stands on land that was occupied by a church and convent of the Recollet missionaries (Franciscan monks), who in 1615 were the first order of priests to arrive in New France. The Gothic fountain at the center of Place d'Armes pays tribute to their arrival.

The colony's former treasury building, **Maison Maillou,** at the south end at 17 rue St-Louis, possesses architectural traits typical of New France: a sharply slanted roof, dormer windows, concrete chimneys, shutters with iron hinges, and limestone walls. Built between 1736 and 1753, it marks the end of rue du Trésor, the road colonists took on their way to pay rent to the king's officials. Maison Maillou is not open to tourists and is now used as the location for the Quebec City Chamber of Commerce offices.

❷ You are now within a few steps east of Quebec City's most celebrated landmark, **Château Frontenac** (1 rue des Carrières, tel. 418/692–3861), once the administrative and military headquarters of New France. The imposing green-turreted castle with its slanting copper roof owes its name to the Comte de Frontenac, the governor of the French colony between 1672 and 1698. Looking at the magnificence of the château, you can see why Frontenac said, "For me, there is no site more beautiful nor more grandiose than that of Quebec City."

Samuel de Champlain, who founded Quebec City in 1608, was responsible for Château St-Louis, the first structure to appear on the site of the Frontenac; it was built between 1620 and 1624 as a residence for colonial governors. In 1784, Château Haldimand was constructed here, but it was demolished in 1892 to make way for Château Frontenac. The latter was built as a hotel in 1893, and it was considered to be remarkably luxurious at that time; guest rooms contained fireplaces, private bathrooms, marble fixtures, and a special commissioner traveled to England and France in search of antiques for the establishment. The hotel was designed by New York architect Bruce Price, who also worked on Quebec City's **Gare du Palais** (Rail Station) and other Canadian landmarks such as Montreal's Windsor Station. The Frontenac was completed in 1925 with the addition of a 20-story central tower. Owned by Canadian Pacific Hotels, it has accumulated a star-studded guest roster including Queen Elizabeth, Madame Chiang Kai-shek, Ronald Reagan, and French President François Mitterrand, as well as Franklin Roosevelt and British Prime Minister Winston Churchill, who convened here in 1943 and 1944 for two wartime conferences.

As you head to the boardwalk behind the Frontenac, notice the glorious bronze statue of Samuel de Champlain, situated where he built his residence. The statue's steps are made of des Vosges granite, and the pedestal consists of Chateau-Landon stone, the same material used for the Arc de Triomphe in Paris. A few yards from the Champlain figure is the smaller bronze, granite, and glass monument that commemorates UNESCO's designation of Quebec City as a world heritage treasure, the first North American city to be so honored.

❸ Walk south along the boardwalk called the **Terrasse Dufferin** for a panoramic view of the St. Lawrence River, the town of Lévis on the opposite shore, Île d'Orléans, and the Laurentian Mountains. The wide boardwalk, with an intricate wrought-iron guardrail, was named after Lord Dufferin, who was governor of Canada between 1872 and 1878 and who had this walkway constructed in 1878. At its western tip begins the **Promenade des Gouverneurs,** which skirts along the cliff and leads up to Quebec's highest point, Cap Diamant (Cape Diamond), and also to the Citadel.

❹ As you pass to the southern side of the Frontenac, you will come to a small park called **Jardin des Gouverneurs** (Governors Park), which is bordered by three streets of old manors. During the French regime, the public area served as a garden for the governors who resided in Château St-Louis. The park's Wolfe-Montcalm Monument, a 50-foot obelisk, is unique in that it pays tribute to both a winning (English) and a losing (French) general. The monument recalls the 1759 battle on the Plains of Abraham, which ended French rule of New France. British General James Wolfe lived only long enough to hear of his victory; French Général Louis-Joseph Montcalm died shortly after Wolfe with the knowledge that the city was lost. *Admission free. Open daily.*

On the southeast corner of the park is the **U.S. Consulate** (2 Place Terrasse Dufferin). On the south side of the park is **avenue Ste-Geneviève,** lined with well-preserved Victorian homes dating from 1850 to 1900 that have been converted to quaint old-fashioned inns.

Once you've stopped admiring the view from the park, make your way to the north side and follow rue Mont Carmel until you come to another small park landscaped with footpaths and ❺ flower beds, **Cavalier du Moulin.** The park's stone windmill, one of the few remnants of the French fortifications, was considered during the 17th century to be located on the outskirts of town because most of the city was situated below the cliff. The windmill was strategically placed so that its cannons could destroy the Cap-Diamant Redoubt (situated near Promenade des Gouverneurs) and the St-Louis Bastion (near St-Louis Gate) in the event that New France was captured by the British. *Admission free. Open daily May–Nov., 7 AM–9 PM.*

Retrace your steps down rue Mont Carmel, turn left on rue Haldimand and left again on rue St-Louis; then make a right on rue du Parloir until it intersects with a tiny street called rue ❻ Donnacona. At 12 rue Donnacona, you'll find the **Couvent des Ursulines** (Ursuline Convent), the site of North America's oldest teaching institution for girls, which is still a private school. Founded in 1639 by two French nuns, the convent has many of its original walls still intact.

Within the convent walls, the **Musée des Ursulines** (Ursuline Museum) is housed in the former residence of one of the founders, Madame de la Peltrie. The museum offers an informative perspective on 120 years of the Ursulines' life under the French regime, from 1639 to 1759. Exhibits tell of the early days of New France. For instance, you'll discover that because the Ursulines were without heat in winter, their heavy clothing sometimes weighed as much as 20 pounds. You'll also see why it took an Ursuline nun nine years of training to attain the level of a professional embroiderer; the museum contains magnificent pieces of ornate embroidery, such as altar frontals having gold and silver threads intertwined with precious jewels. *12 rue Donnacona, tel. 418/694-0694. Admission: $2 adults, 75¢ students and senior citizens, $4.25 families. Open Jan. 6–Nov., Tues.–Sat. 9:30–noon and 1:30–5, Sun. 12:30–5:30.*

At the same address is the **Chapelle des Ursulines** (Ursuline Chapel), where French Général Montcalm was buried after he died in the 1759 battle. The chapel's exterior was rebuilt in 1902, but the interior contains the original chapel, which is the work of sculptor Pierre-Noël Levasseur, accomplished between 1726 and 1736. The votive lamp here was lit in 1717 and has never been extinguished. *12 rue Donnacona. Admission free. Open May–Oct., same hours as Ursuline Museum.*

Next to the museum at the **Centre Marie-de-l'Incarnation** is a bookstore and an exhibit on the life of the Ursulines' first superior, who came from France and co-founded the convent. *10 rue Donnacona, tel. 418/692-1569. Admission free. Open Tues.–Sat. 10–11:30 and 2–5, Sun. 2–5.*

Time Out The neon-lit **Café Taste-Vin**, on the corner of rue des Jardins and rue St-Louis, shares a kitchen with the gourmet restaurant next door. The two eateries also share chefs when it comes to salads, pastries, and desserts, making the café an ideal stop for the weary tourist. *32 rue St-Louis, tel. 418/692-4191. AE, DC, MC, V. Open 8 AM–11 PM.*

❼ From rue Donnacona, walk north to rue des Jardins. Within a few yards you'll see the **Holy Trinity Anglican Cathedral.** This stone church dates back to 1804 and is the first Anglican cathedral outside the British Isles. Its simple and dignified facade is reminiscent of London's St. Martin-in-the-Fields. The cathedral's land was originally given to the Recollet fathers (Franciscan monks from France) in 1681 by the king of France for a church and monastery. When Quebec came under British rule, the Recollets made the church available to the Anglicans for services. Later, King George III of England ordered construction of the present cathedral, the requirement being that an area be set aside for members of the royal family. A portion of the north balcony still remains exclusively for the use of the reigning sovereign or her representative. The church houses precious objects donated by George III. The oak benches were imported from the Royal Forest at Windsor. The cathedral's impressive rear organ has more than 2,500 pipes. *31 rue des Jardins, tel. 418/692-2193. Admission free. Open June–Sept., daily 10–5; Oct.–May, Tues.–Sat. 1–3.*

❽ The building on the corner of rue des Jardins and rue Ste-Anne is one of Quebec City's finest Art Deco structures. Geometric patterns of stone and wrought iron decorate the interior of the **Hôtel Clarendon** (57 rue Ste-Anne, tel. 418/692-2480). Although the Claredon dates back to 1866, it was reconstructed with its current Art Deco decor in 1930 (*see* Lodging, below).

❾ More Art Deco design can be found next door at 65 rue Ste-Anne, the 15-story **Édifice Price** (Price Building). The city's first skyscraper was built in 1929 and served as the headquarters of the Price Brothers Company, the lumber company founded in Canada by Sir William Price. Today it is owned by the provincial government and houses the offices of Quebec City's mayor. Don't miss the interior: Exquisite copper plaques depict scenes of the company's early pulp and paper activities,

Exploring Quebec City 163

while the two artfully carved maple-wood elevators are '30s classics.

Head back on rue Ste-Anne past the Holy Trinity Anglican Cathedral, continue straight, and turn left into a narrow alley
❿ called **rue du Trésor,** where hundreds of colorful prints, paintings, and other art works are on display. You won't necessarily find masterpieces here, but this walkway is a good stop for a souvenir sketch or two. During the French regime people came to this street to pay rent to the crown; the royal treasury stood at the end of the street, at Maison Maillou.

At the bottom of rue du Trésor, turn left on rue Buade. When you reach the corner of côte de la Fabrique, you'll see the
⓫ **Basilique Notre-Dame-de-Québec** (Our Lady of Quebec Basilica), with the oldest parish in North America, dating back to 1647. The basilica has been rebuilt on three separate occasions: in the early 1700s, when François de Montmorency Laval was the first bishop; in 1759, when cannons at Lévis aimed fire at it during the siege of Quebec, and in 1922, after a fire. This basilica has a somber ambience despite its ornate interior, which includes a canopy dais over the episcopal throne, a ceiling of clouds decorated with gold leaf, richly colored stained-glass windows, and a chancel lamp that was a gift of Louis XIV. Perhaps the solemn mood here may be attributed to the basilica's large and famous crypt, which was Quebec City's first cemetery; more than 900 people are interred here, including 20 bishops and four governors of New France (de Champlain, de Frontenac, de Callières, and de la Jonquière). *16 rue Buade, tel. 418/692-2533. Admission free. Open daily 7 AM–8 PM.*

The basilica marks the beginning of Quebec City's Latin Quarter, which extends to the streets northwest of Quebec Seminary (rue Buade, rue des Remparts, côte de la Fabrique, and côte du Palais) as far as rue St-Jean. This district was deemed the Latin Quarter because Latin was once a required language course at the seminary and was spoken among the students. Although Latin is no longer compulsory and Quebec Seminary–Laval University has moved out to a larger campus in Sainte-Foy, students still cling to this neighborhood.

Head down côte de la Fabrique and turn right when it meets rue Collins. The cluster of old stone buildings sequestered at
⓬ the end of the street is the **Monastère des Augustines de l'Hôtel-Dieu de Québec** (Augustine Monastery). Augustine nuns arrived from Dieppe, France, in 1639 with a mission to care for the sick in the new colony, and they established the first hospital north of Mexico, the **Hôtel-Dieu Hospital,** which is the large building west of the monastery. The **Musée des Augustines** (Augustine Museum) is housed in hospitallike quarters with large sterile corridors leading into a ward that features a small exhibit of antique medical instruments used by the Augustines, such as an 1850 microscope and a pill-making device from the 17th century.

Upon request, the Augustines also offer guided tours of the chapel (1800) and the cellars used by the nuns as a hiding place beginning in 1659, during bombardments from the British. *32 rue Charlevoix, tel. 418/692-2492. Admission free. Open Tues.–Sat 9:30–11:30 and 1:30–5, Sun. 1:30–5.*

Time Out For a crusty white or whole-wheat croissant, try **Croissant Plus,** 50 rue Garneau, tel. 418/692–4215).

Retrace your steps on Collins Street and côte de la Fabrique. When you reach rue Ste-Famille on the left, you will find the wrought-iron entrance gates of the **Séminaire de Québec** (Quebec Seminary). Behind these gates lies a tranquil courtyard surrounded by austere stone buildings with rising steeples; these structures have housed classrooms and student residences since 1663. The seminary was founded by François de Montmorency Laval, the first bishop of New France, to train priests of the new colony. In 1852 the seminary became Université Laval (Laval University), the first Catholic university in North America. The university eventually outgrew these cramped quarters; in 1946, Laval moved to a larger modern campus in the suburb of Sainte-Foy. *1 côte de la Fabrique, tel. 418/692–3981. Admission free. Open Mon.–Sat. 9:30–5:30, Sun. noon–5:30.*

At this entrance (the seminary's west entrance) you'll find the small Roman-style **Chapelle Extérieure** (Outer Chapel) built in 1888, after the fire destroyed the first chapel, built in 1750. In 1950 a memorial crypt, in which Laval is now buried, was added here. *Admission free. Open mid-June–Aug., Mon.–Sat 9:30–5:30, Sun. noon–5:30.*

Head north across the courtyard to the **Musée du Séminaire** (Seminary Museum). Housed in a former student residence, the museum focuses on the three centuries of the seminary's existence, until 1940. It emphasizes European secular and religious works of art; there are more than 400 landscape and still-life paintings dating as far back as the 15th century. The museum also houses a showcase of scientific instruments that were acquired through the centuries for the purposes of research and teaching. A former chapel has been renovated and now holds an exhibit of elegant religious and secular antique silver. The museum also has a rare collection of Canadian money that was used in colonial times. *9 rue de l'Université, tel. 418/692–2843. Admission: $2 adults, $1 students and senior citizens, 50¢ children. Open June–Sept., Tues.–Sun. 11–6; Oct.–May, Tues.–Sun. 11–5. Closed Mon. year-round.*

Now exit the seminary from the east at rue de l'Université and head south to côte de la Montagne, where **Parc Montmorency** (Montmorency Park) straddles the hill between Upper Town and Lower Town. This park marks the spot where Canada's first wheat was grown in 1618 and where the nation's first legislation was passed in 1694. A monument stands in tribute to Louis Herbert, a former apothecary and the first Canadian farmer, who cleared and tilled this area's land.

In 1688, Monseigneur de Saint-Vallier, the second bishop of New France, had his residence, the first episcopal palace, built here. In 1792 the palace's chapel became the seat of the first parliament of Lower Canada. The chapel was demolished in 1833, and a new legislative building was constructed that served as Quebec's parliament until 1883, when it was destroyed by fire. A park monument commemorates Georges-Étienne Cartier, a French-Canadian political leader and a father of the 1867 Confederation.

Exploring Quebec City 165

On the south side of the park, walk across an arched bridge called Porte Prescott (Prescott Gate), which the British added to the three gates built by the French. However, in 1871 Prescott Gate was demolished because it was considered a hindrance to traffic; it was rebuilt in 1983.

Take the **Escalier Frontenac** (Frontenac Stairway) up to the north end of the Terrasse Dufferin. You may be out of breath, but the climb is worth it for the 30-minute recap on the six sieges of Quebec City at the **Musée du Fort** (Fort Museum). This museum's sole exhibit is a sound-and-light show with a model of 18th-century Quebec that reenacts the region's most important battles, including the Battle of the Plains of Abraham and the 1775 attack by American generals Arnold and Montgomery. *10 rue Ste-Anne, tel. 418/692-2175. Admission: $3 adults, $1.75 students and senior citizens. Open summer, daily 10-6; spring and fall, Mon.-Sat. 10-5, Sun. 1-5; winter, weekdays 11-5, Sat. 10-5, Sun. 1-5. Closed Dec. 1-20.*

As you exit from the museum, head southeast to the funicular booth along Terrasse Dufferin. Ride the funicular (75¢) to Lower Town to begin Tour 2.

Tour 2: Lower Town

New France began to flourish in the streets of Lower Town along the banks of the St. Lawrence River. These streets became the colony's economic crossroads, where furs were traded, ships came in, and merchants established their residences.

Despite the status of Lower Town as the oldest neighborhood in North America, its narrow and time-worn thoroughfares have a new and polished look. In the '60s, after a century of decay as the commercial boom moved west and left Lower Town an abandoned district, the Quebec government committed millions of dollars to restore the area to the way it had been during the days of New France. Today modern boutiques, restaurants, galleries, and shops catering to tourists occupy the former warehouses and residences.

Begin this tour on the northern tip of rue du Petit-Champlain at **Maison Louis-Jolliet** (16 rue du Petit-Champlain, tel. 418/692-2613), which houses the lower station of the funicular and a souvenir shop. Built in 1683, this home was used by the first settlers of New France as a base for further westward explorations. The first Canadian born in Quebec to make history, Louis Jolliet discovered the Mississippi River in 1672. A monument that commemorates this discovery stands in the park next to the house.

At the north side of the house is **Escalier Casse-cou** (Breakneck Steps), the city's first iron stairway. You can easily see from its steepness how it got its name. Its ambitious 1893 design was by Charles Baillairgé, a city architect and engineer, and it was built on the site of the original 17th-century stairway that linked the Upper and Lower towns during the French regime. Today tourist shops, quaint boutiques, and restaurants are situated at various levels.

Heading south on **rue du Petit-Champlain,** the city's oldest street, you'll notice the cliff on the right that borders this narrow thoroughfare, with Upper Town situated on the heights above. Rue du Petit-Champlain retains its size from when it was the main street of a harbor village, replete with trading posts and the homes of rich merchants. In 1977 artists, craftsmen, and private investors decided to initiate a revival of the street; today it consists of pleasant boutiques and cafés. The best buys here are found in the ceramics, wood carvings, and jewelry done by local artists. Natural-fiber weaving, Eskimo carvings, hand-painted silks, and enameled copper crafts are some of the local specialties for sale.

When rue du Petit-Champlain intersects with boulevard Champlain, make a U-turn to head back north. One block farther, at the corner of rue du Marché-Champlain, you'll find **Maison Chevalier,** an annex of the ethnographic Civilization Museum. This old stone house was built in 1752 for shipowner Jean-Baptiste Chevalier. When it was restored in 1959, Maison Chevalier was combined with two other buildings, Maison Chenaye de la Garonne, built in 1695, and Maison Frérot, dating from 1675. Inside the buildings, you can see the original wooden beams and stone fireplaces, and period artifacts are also on display. *60 rue du Marché-Champlain, tel. 418/643-9689. Admission free. Open Tues.–Sun. 10–5. Closed Mon.*

East of Maison Chevalier, take rue Notre-Dame, which leads directly to **Place Royale,** formerly the heart of New France. This cobblestone square is encircled by buildings with steep Normandy-style roofs, dormer windows, and several chimneys. These were once the homes of wealthy merchants. Until 1686 the area was called Place du Marché, but its name was changed when a bust of Louis XIV, *le Roi Soleil* (the Sun King), was erected at its center.

In the late 1600s and early 1700s, when Place Royale was continually under threat of attacks from the British, the colonists progressively moved to higher and safer quarters atop the cliff in Upper Town. Yet after the French colony fell to British rule in 1759, Place Royale flourished again with shipbuilding, logging, fishing, and fur trading.

The small stone church at the south side of the Place Royale is the **Église Notre-Dame-des-Victoires** (Notre-Dame-des-Victoires Church), the oldest church in Quebec, dating back to 1688. It was built on the site of Samuel de Champlain's first residence, which also served as a fort and trading post. However, the church had to be completely restored on two occasions: after a fire in 1759, and more recently in 1969. It got its name from two French victories against the British, one in 1690 against Admiral William Phipps and another in 1711 against Sir Hovendon Walker. The interior contains copies of European masters such as Van Dyck, Rubens, and Boyermans; its altar resembles the shape of a fort. A scale model suspended from the ceiling represents Le Brezé, the boat that transported French soldiers to New France in 1664. The side chapel is dedicated to Sainte-Geneviève, the guardian saint of Paris. Mass is offered on Sunday mornings at 8, 10, and noon. *Place Royale, tel. 418/692-1650. Admission free. Open May–Oct. 15, Mon.–Sat. 9–4:30, Sun. 7:30–4:30; Oct. 16–Apr., Tues.–Sat. 9–noon, Sun. 7:30–1.*

Turn to the northwest corner of the square to the cool, dark, and musty cellars of the **Maison des Vins,** a former warehouse dating back to 1689; here the Québec Société des Alcools sells more than 1,000 kinds of rare and vintage wines, which range in price from $7 to $1,000. *1 Place Royale, tel. 418/643-1214. Admission free. Open mid-June–Labor Day, Mon.–Wed. 9:30–6, Thurs. and Fri. 9–9, Sat. 9:30–5. Rest of the year, closed Mon.; closed Sun. year-round.*

㉒ On the east side of Place Royale, take rue de la Place, which leads to an open square, **Place de Paris,** a newcomer to these historic quarters. Looming at its center is a black-and-white geometric sculpture, *Dialogue Avec l'Histoire (Dialogue with History),* a gift from France positioned on the site where the first French settlers landed. Paris Mayor Jacques Chirac inaugurated the square in August 1987 with Quebec City's Mayor Jean Pelletier. Its French counterpart is the Place du Québec inaugurated in 1984 at St-Germain-des-Prés in Paris.

㉓ At this point of the tour you may conveniently catch the 15-minute **ferry to Lévis** on the opposite shore of the St. Lawrence River. The boat docks a block south on rue Dalhousie; we recommend you take the ferry for the opportunity of an unprecedented view of Quebec City's skyline, with the Château Frontenac and the Quebec Seminary high above the cliff. *Ferry departs every half hour 7:30–6:30, then every hour until 2:30 AM. Cost: $1 adults, 50¢ children and senior citizens.*

Time Out | **Café Loft,** located in a converted garage on rue Dalhousie between Place de Paris and the Civilization Museum, offers delectable desserts, such as a pyramid-shape chocolate cake. Grab an inviting *baguette* sandwich and equally scrumptious quiches and salads. *49 rue Dalhousie, tel. 418/692-4864. AE, DC, MC, V. Open 9 AM–midnight.*

㉔ Continue north on the rue Dalhousie until you come to the **Musée de la Civilisation** (Civilization Museum). Wedged into the foot of the cliff, this spacious museum, with its striking limestone and glass facade, has been artfully designed to blend into the city landscape. Architect Moshie Safdie skillfully incorporated three historic buildings into the museum's modern structure: the house Estèbe, the site of the First Bank of Quebec, and the Maison Pagé-Quercy. Many of the materials that were used to construct the newer portions of the museum are native to Quebec province. The building's campanile echoes the shape of church steeples throughout the city.

The museum, which opened officially in 1988, houses innovative, entertaining, and sometimes playful exhibits devoted to aspects of Quebec's culture and civilization. Several of the shows, with their imaginative use of art work, video screens, computers, and sound, will appeal to both adults and children. In the entrance hall, the sculpture *La Débâcle,* with its large concrete slabs immersed in water, symbolizes the breaking of ice on the St. Lawrence River in the spring, an event the Québécois refer to as "the debacle." The sculpture contains stones that are remnants of the colony's old wharf. If you look close enough, you can see the original rings used to harbor boats.

The museum features several temporary shows a year; its excellent permanent exhibition, "Memoires" ("Memories") considers both Quebec's history and French-Canadian society today. This comprehensive display evokes domestic life in the early days of the cold northern frontier by means of historic artifacts and music. Other sections of the exhibit touch upon key political events, local inventions, regional celebrations, and the opinions of Québécois on contemporary issues.

The museum also offers dance, music, and theater performances and a good boutique for quality souvenirs. Guides are available in the exhibition rooms. *85 rue Dalhousie, tel. 418/ 643–2158. Admission: $4 adults, $3 senior citizens. Open June 15–Sept. 15, daily 10–8; Sept. 15–June 15, Tues.–Sun. 10–5; closed Mon.*

㉕ From rue Dalhousie, head east towards the river to the **Vieux-Port de Québec** (Old Port of Quebec). The breezes here from the St. Lawrence provide a cool reprieve on a hot summer's day. The old harbor dates back to the 17th century when ships first arrived from Europe bringing supplies and settlers to the new colony. At one time this port was among the busiest on the continent: Between 1797 and 1897, Quebec shipyards turned out more than 2,500 ships, many of which passed the thousand-ton mark. Yet Quebec City's port saw a rapid decline after steel replaced wood and the channel to Montreal was deepened to allow larger boats to reach a good port upstream.

In 1984 the 72-acre port was restored with a $100 million grant from the federal government; today it encompasses several parks and the **Agora,** the city's largest open-air theater. You can stroll along the riverside promenade where merchant and cruise ships are docked. At its northern end, where the St. Charles meets the St. Lawrence, a lock protects the marina in the Louise basin from the generous tides of the St. Lawrence. Because Quebec City is close to the Atlantic Ocean, it is susceptible to tides, which can range between nine and 16 feet. At the northwest area of the port, an exhibition center, **Port de Québec in the 19th Century,** presents the history of the port in relation to the lumber trade shipbuilding. *112 rue Dalhousie, tel. 418/692–0043. Information center, tel. 418/692–0100.*

The port's northwestern tip features the **Marché du Vieux-Port** (Farmers' Market), where farmers come from the countryside to sell their fresh produce. *Admission free. Open May–Nov., daily 8–8.*

㉖ You are now in the ideal spot to explore Quebec City's **antiques district.** One block south from rue St-André, antiques boutiques cluster along the rue St-Pierre and rue St-Paul (*see* Shopping, below). St-Paul was formerly part of a business district where warehouses, stores, and businesses once abounded. After World War I, when shipping and commercial activities plummeted, the street mainly consisted of empty warehouses and offices. In 1964 the low rent and commercial nature of the area attracted several antiques dealers, who set up shops along St-Paul. Today numerous cafés, restaurants, and art galleries have turned this area into one of the town's more fashionable sectors.

Walk west along rue St-Paul and turn left onto a steep brick incline called côte Dambourges; when you reach côte de la Canoterie, take the stairs back on the cliff to rue des Remparts. Continue approximately a block west along rue des Remparts until you come to the last building in a row of purple houses.

㉗ **Maison Montcalm** was the home of French Général Louis-Joseph Montcalm from 1758 until the capitulation of New

France. A plaque dedicated to the general is situated on right side of the house.

Continue west on rue des Remparts and turn left on rue de l'Arsenal, which brings you to the **Parc de l'Artillerie** (Artillery Park). This National Historic Park is a complex of 20 military, industrial, and civilian buildings, situated to guard the St. Charles River and the Old Port. Its earliest buildings served as headquarters for the French garrison and were taken over in 1759 by the British Royal Artillery soldiers. The defense complex was used as a fortress, barracks, and cartridge factory during the American siege of Quebec in 1775 and 1776. The area was converted to an industrial complex providing ammunition for the Canadian army from 1879 until 1964, when it became an historic park.

One of the three buildings you may visit is a former **powder house,** which in 1903 became a shell foundry. The building houses a detailed model of Quebec City in 1808, rendered by two surveyors in the office of the Royal Engineers Corps, Jean-Baptiste Duberger of Quebec and John By of England. Carved from wood, the model was intended to show British officials the strategic importance of Quebec (it was sent to England in 1813) so that more money would be provided to expand the city's fortifications. The model offers the most accurate picture of the city during the early 19th century, detailing its houses, buildings, streets, and military structures.

The **Dauphine Redoubt** (*dauphine* in French means "heir apparent") was named after the son of Louis XIV and was constructed from 1712 to 1748. It served as a barracks for the French garrison until 1760, when it became an officers' mess for the Royal Artillery Regiment. When the British called their soldiers back to England in 1871, it became a residence for the Canadian Arsenal superintendent.

The **Officers' Quarters** building, a dwelling for Royal Artillery officers until 1871 when the British army departed, is now a museum for children, with shows on military life during the British regime. *2 rue d'Auteil, tel. 418/648-4205. Admission free. Open Feb.–Mar., weekdays 9–noon and 1–5; Apr.–May 6 and Nov., weekdays 10–noon and 1–5; May 9–Oct., Mon. 1–5, Tues.–Sun. 10–5. Closed Dec. and Jan.*

Tour 3: Outside the City Walls

Numbers in the margin correspond with points of interest on the Tour 3: Outside the City Walls map.

In the 20th century, Quebec City grew into a modern metropolis outside the city walls and its historic confines. In this tour, you will see a glimpse of modern-day Quebec City and explore neighborhoods typically left off the tourist track.

Start close to St-Louis Gate at **Parc de l'Esplanade** (Esplanade Park), the site of a former military drill and parade ground. In the 19th century, this area was a clear and uncluttered space surrounded by a picket fence and poplar trees. Today you'll find the completely renovated **Poudrière de l'Esplanade** (Powder Magazine), which the British constructed in 1820; it houses a model depicting the evolution of the wall surrounding the Old City. *100 rue St-Louis, tel. 418/648-7016. Admission free.*

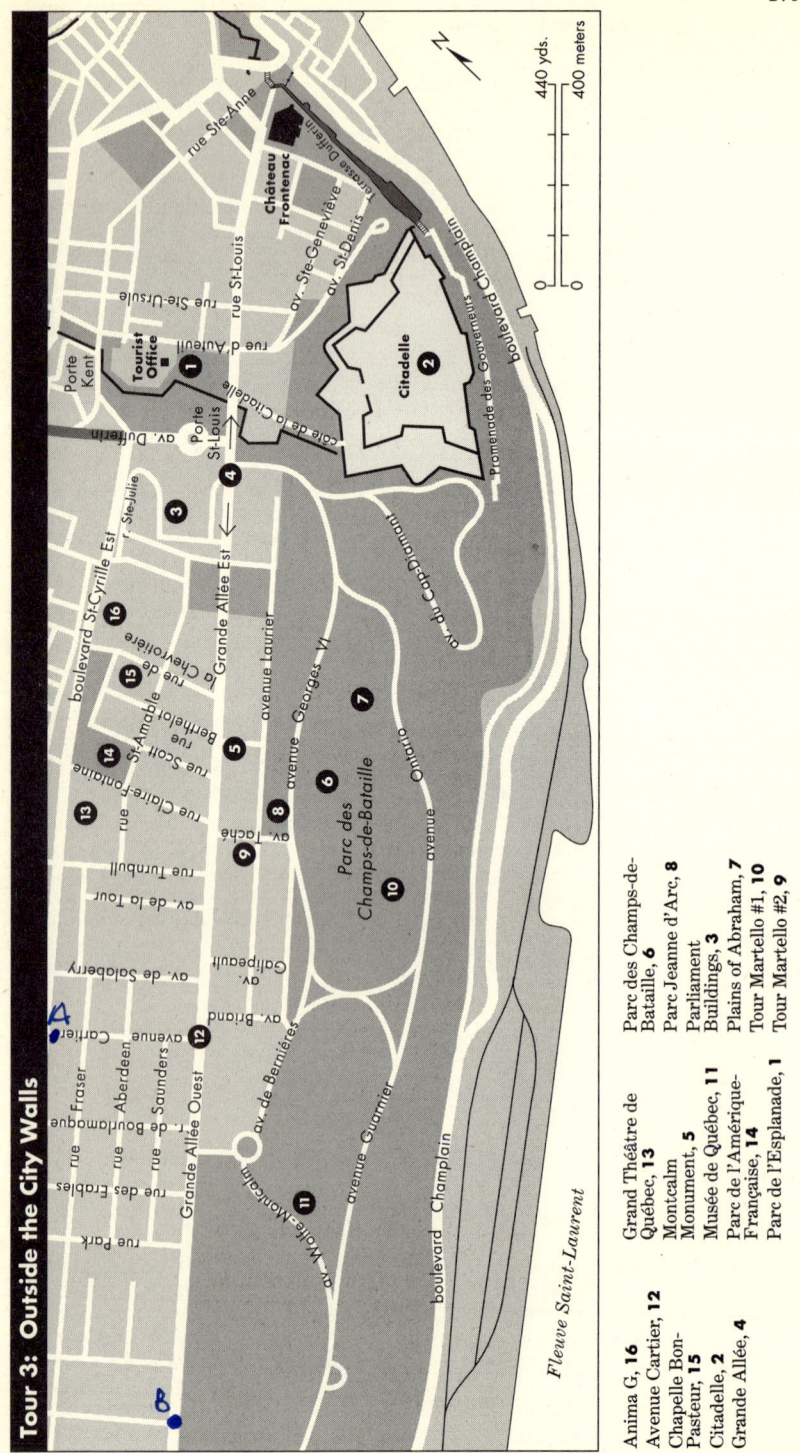

Tour 3: Outside the City Walls

Anima G, **16**
Avenue Cartier, **12**
Chapelle Bon-Pasteur, **15**
Citadelle, **2**
Grande Allée, **4**
Grand Théâtre de Québec, **13**
Montcalm Monument, **5**
Musée de Québec, **11**
Parc de l'Amérique-Française, **14**
Parc de l'Esplanade, **1**
Parc des Champs-de-Bataille, **6**
Parc Jeanne d'Arc, **8**
Parliament Buildings, **3**
Plains of Abraham, **7**
Tour Martello #1, **10**
Tour Martello #2, **9**

170

Exploring Quebec City 171

Open mid-May–June, weekdays 10–5; July–Labor Day, daily 10–5; Sept.–mid-Oct., Wed.–Sun. 9–5.

Esplanade Park is also the starting point to walk the city's 3 miles (4.6 kilometers) of walls; in the summer, guided tours begin here. The French began building ramparts along the city's natural cliff as early as 1690 to protect themselves from British invaders. But by 1759, when the British gained control of New France, the walls were still incomplete; the British took a century to finish them.

❷ From the Powder Magazine, head south on côte de la Citadelle, which leads directly to the **Citadelle** (Citadel). Built at the city's highest point, the Citadel is the largest fortified base in North America still occupied by troops. The 25-building fortress was intended to protect the port, prevent the enemy from taking up a position on the Plains of Abraham, and provide a last refuge in case of an attack. The French had constructed previous structures on this site based on plans of Quebec engineer Gaspard Chaussegros de Léry, who came to the region in 1716.

Having inherited incomplete fortifications, the British sought to complete the Citadel to protect themselves against retaliations from the French. As fate would have it, by the time the Citadel was completed in 1832, the invasions and attacks against Quebec City had ended.

The Citadel's star-shaped plan is characteristic of the classical fortification plan used in Europe by the military engineer under Louis XIV, Sébastien Le Prestre de Vauban (1633–1707). The facility includes the governor-general's residence, the officers' mess, five heavily fortified bastions, and the Cap-Diamant Redoubt (Cape Diamond Redoubt), which dates from 1693 and is one of the very first defensive structures built under French rule.

Since 1920 the Citadel has served as a base for the Royal 22nd Regiment. A collection of firearms, uniforms, and decorations from the 17th century are housed in **The Royal 22nd Regiment Museum,** located in the former powder house, built in 1750. If weather permits, you may witness the Changing of the Guard, an elaborate ceremony in which the troops parade before the Citadel in the customary red coats and black fur hats. *1 côte de la Citadelle, tel. 418/648-5363 and 418/648-5234. Guided tours only. Admission: $3 adults, $1 students. Free for children under 7 and handicapped persons. Open Mar.–Apr. and Oct., weekdays 9–4; May–mid-June and Sept., daily 9–5; mid-June–Labor Day, daily 9–7; Nov., weekdays 9–noon. Dec.–Feb., reservations are necessary. Changing of the Guard, mid-June–Labor Day, daily at 10. Tattoo, July–Aug., Tues., Thurs., Sat., and Sun. at 7 PM. Cannon fire from the Prince-de-Galles Bastion (Prince of Wales Bastion), daily noon and 9:30 PM.*

❸ Retrace your steps back down côte de la Citadelle to Grande Allée. Continue west until you come to the Renaissance-style **Parliament Buildings,** which mark the area known as **Parliament Hill,** the headquarters of the provincial government. The constitution of 1791 designated Quebec City the capital of Lower Canada until the 1840 Act of Union that united both Upper and Lower Canada and made Montreal the capital. In 1867, the Act of Confederation, uniting Quebec, Ontario, New Brunswick, and Nova Scotia, made Quebec City the capital of Quebec province. Today the government is the biggest employer in

Quebec City, with more than 30,000 civil servants working and living in the area.

The Parliament Buildings, erected between 1877 and 1884, is the seat of **L'Assemblée Nationale** (The National Assembly) of 125 provincial representatives. Quebec architect Eugène-Étienne Taché designed the classic and stately buildings in the late 17th-century Renaissance style of Louis XIV, with four wings set in a square around an interior court. In front of the Parliament, statues pay tribute to important figures of Quebec history: Cartier, de Champlain, de Frontenac, Wolfe, and Montcalm. Also notice the words "Je me souviens" over the Parliament's front door, a phrase that can also be found on Quebec's automobile license plates. The motto represents the collective remembrance of the Québécois' French heritage.

The Parliament offers a 30-minute tour (in English or French) of the President's Gallery, the National Assembly Chamber, and the Legislative Council Chamber. The chamber of the 125-member National Assembly is decorated in green, white, and gold, colors that correspond to the House of Commons in both London and in Ottawa. *Corner of ave. Dufferin and Grande Allée E, door 3, tel. 418/643-7239. Admission free. Guided tours Sept.–Nov. and Jan.–May, weekdays 9–4:30; June 24–Aug., daily 10–5:30. Closed Dec. and June 1–23.*

Across from the Parliament on the south side of Grande Allée is the **Manège Militaire,** a turreted granite armory built in 1888, four years after the Parliament Buildings. It was also designed by Taché. It is still a drill hall for the 22nd Regiment.

❹ Continue along **Grande Allée,** Quebec City's version of the Champs Élysées with its array of trendy cafés, clubs, and restaurants. One of the oldest streets, Grande Allée was the route people took from outlying areas to sell their furs in Quebec City. The street actually has four names: in the old city, it is rue St-Louis; outside the walls, Grande Allée; farther west, chemin St-Louis; and farther still, boulevard Laurier.

One block after the armory, on your left (the south side of Grande Allée) you'll come to Place Montcalm. If you turn left, ❺ you'll be facing the **Montcalm Monument.** France and Canada joined together to erect this monument honoring Louis-Joseph Montcalm, who claimed his fame by winning four major battles in North America, but his most famous battle was the one he lost, when the British conquered New France on September 13, 1759. Montcalm was north of Quebec City at Beauport when he learned that the British attack was imminent. He quickly assembled his troops to meet the enemy and was wounded in battle in the leg and stomach. Montcalm was carried into the walled city, where he died the next morning.

Continue south on Place Montcalm to one of North America's ❻ largest and most scenic parks, **Parc des Champs-de-Bataille** (Battlefields Park). This 250-acre area of gently rolling slopes offers unparalleled views of the St. Lawrence River. West of ❼ the citadel are the **Plains of Abraham,** the site of the famous 1759 battle that decided the fate of New France. The Plains of Abraham were named after the river pilot Abraham Martin, who arrived in 1620 and owned several acres here. *A free 25-min guided bus of the Plains of Abraham area is available, with 13 stops, including an exhibition center and the Martello towers. The bus leaves from the Visitors Reception and Inter-*

Exploring Quebec City *173*

pretation Center *(390 ave. de Bernières, tel. 418/648-4071) June–Sept. 11–2 and 2:30–6.*

Take avenue Laurier, which runs parallel to Battlefields Park, a block west until you come to a neatly tended garden called
❽ **Parc Jeanne d'Arc** (Joan of Arc Park); it is abundant with colorful flowers and is centered on an equestrian statue of Jeanne d'Arc. A symbol of courage, this statue stands in tribute to the heroes of 1759 near the place where New France was lost to the British. The park also commemorates the Canadian national anthem "Oh Canada"; it was played here for the first time on June 24, 1880.

If you continue west on avenue Laurier, you'll see a stone oval
❾ defense tower, **Tour Martello #2** (Martello Tower), on the north corner of avenue Taché and avenue Laurier. This is the second of four Martello towers built in the early 19th century around Quebec City to slow the enemy's approach to the city. Towers One and Two are the only Martellos open to the public. At the
❿ left, toward the south end of the park, stands **Tour Martello #1,** which was built between 1802 and 1810. *Admission free. Open June–Sept., Mon. noon–5:30, Tues.–Sun. 9:30–5.*

Out of the 16 Martello towers in all of Canada, four were built in Quebec City because the British government feared an invasion after the American Revolution. Tower Three was located near Jeffery Hale Hospital in order to guard westward entry to the city, but it was demolished in 1904. Tower Four, located on rue Lavigueur overlooking rivière St-Charles (St. Charles River), is closed.

Continue a block west on rue de Bernières and then follow avenue George V along the outskirts of Battlefields Park until it intersects with avenue Wolfe-Montcalm. You'll come to the tall **Wolfe Monument,** which marks the spot where the British general died. Wolfe landed his troops less than 2 miles from the city's walls; the 4,500 English soldiers scaled the cliff and opened fire on the Plains of Abraham. Wolfe was mortally wounded in battle and was carried behind the lines to this spot.

Turn left on avenue Wolfe-Montcalm for a leisurely stroll
⓫ through the **Musée de Québec** (Quebec Museum). This neoclassical beaux-arts showcase houses the finest collection of Quebec art. With one of the largest acquisition budgets of Canada's museums, it possesses more than 12,000 traditional and contemporary pieces. The portraits done by artists well known in the area, such as Ozias Leduc (1864–1955) and Horatio Walker (1858–1938), are particularly notable; some locals find paintings of their relatives on the walls here.

The museum's very formal and dignified building in Battlefields Park was designed by Wilfrid Lacroix and erected in 1933 to commemorate the tricentennial anniversary of the founding of Quebec. By 1991, however, the museum will have doubled its exhibition space by incorporating the space of a neighboring former prison, which dates from 1867. *1 ave. Wolfe-Montcalm, tel. 418/643-2150. Admission free. Open June 15–Sept. 14, daily 10–9; Sept. 15–June 14, Tues.–Sun. 10–6, Wed. until 10 PM. Closed Mon.*

From the museum, head north on avenue Wolfe-Montcalm and turn right on Grande Allée a block until you reach avenue Cartier. At 115 Grande Allée Ouest is the **Kreighoff House.** This typical Quebec home with its bell-shaped roof and dormer windows is closed to tourists, but it's worth noting for its former owner, Cornelius Krieghoff, who lived there from 1858 to 1860. One of Canada's most famous landscape painters, Kreighoff was among the first to depict Quebec scenery. Born in Amsterdam in 1815, he served in the American army, married a French Canadian in 1839, and settled in Quebec in 1852.

12 Head north on **avenue Cartier** to indulge in the pleasures offered by the many good restaurants, clubs, and cafés lining the block. On the east side, stroll through the food mall, **Alimentation Petit-Cartier** (1191 avenue Cartier, tel. 418/524–3682). Here you'll find a supermarket and shops that sell French delicacies—cheeses, pastries, breads, and candies. Some of the better stores are: **Boulangerie La Mère-Michele,** for breads and pastries such as petit-fours; **Deco-Ustentile,** with state-of-the-art kitchenware; and **Le Vrac du Quartier,** where you can buy just about anything from spices to cookies in amounts you measure yourself. The mall also houses three restaurants: Chez Maxie, L'Entrepain, and Le Graffiti (*see* Dining, below).

Time Out On the east side of avenue Cartier is **Café Krieghoff,** named after the 19th-century painter who lived nearby. Grab a newspaper, play a game of chess, drink some of the best coffee in town, and complement it with a quiche, a croissant, or a dessert. *1089 avenue Cartier, tel. 418/522–3711. No credit cards. Open 7–3.*

If you continue north along avenue Cartier, the first major intersection is boulevard St-Cyrille Est. Turn right and walk two
13 blocks to the concrete modern building of the **Grand Théâtre de Québec,** a center for the city's performing arts and home to the music school, La Conservatoire de Musique de Québec. Opened in 1971, the theater incorporates two main halls, both named after 19th-century Canadian poets. The "Grande Salle" of Louis-Frechette, named after the first Quebec poet and writer to be honored by the French Academy, holds 1,800 seats and is used for concerts, opera, and theater. The "Petite Salle" of Octave-Crémazie, used for experimental theater and variety shows, derives its name from the poet who stirred the rise of Quebec nationalism in the mid-19th century.

As the complex was being constructed, Montreal architect Victor Prus commissioned Jordi Bonet, a Quebec sculptor, to work simultaneously on a three-wall mural. The themes depicted in three sections are death, life, and liberty. Bonet wrote "La Liberté" on one wall to symbolize the Québécois' struggle for freedom and cultural distinction. The theater has a full repertoire in the winter, but no shows in the summer. *269 blvd. St-Cyrille E, tel. 418/643–4975. Open daily 9–4.*

High-waving flags east of the Grand Théâtre are displayed in
14 the **Parc de L'Amérique-Française,** dedicated to places in North America with a French-speaking population. Quebec's own Fleur de Lys leads the way. The colors of blue and white, an emblem of Sun King Louis XIV, is a reminder of Quebec's French origins, culture, and language. Inaugurated in 1985 by Quebec Prime Minister Réne Lévesque, the park also has flags from Acadia, British Columbia, Manitoba, Saskatchewan, Louisiana, and Ontario.

Exploring Quebec City

Take rue Claire Fountaine a block south, turn left on rue St-Amable, and then left again on rue de la Chevrotière. On the west side of the street you'll see the **Chapelle Bon-Pasteur** (Bon-Pasteur Chapel), which is surrounded by modern office complexes. This slender church with a steep sloping roof was designed by Charles Baillargé in 1868. Its ornate interior in a baroque style has wooden carved designs painted elaborately in gold leaf. The chapel houses 32 religious paintings done by the Sisters of the community from 1868 to 1910. *1080 rue de la Chevrotière, tel. 418/641-1069. Admission free. Open weekdays 8:30-noon and 1-4:30; musical artists' Mass Sun. at noon.*

Across rue de la Chevrotière is the entrance of a large, gray concrete modern office tower called **Anima G** (Complex G), Quebec's tallest office building. The structure, 31 stories high, has by far the best view of the city and the environs. An express elevator ascends to the observation gallery on top. *1037 rue de la Chevrotière, tel. 418/644-9841. Admission free. Open Apr.-May and Sept.-Nov., weekdays 10-5, Sun. 1-5; June-Aug., weekdays 10-8, weekends 1-5; Dec.-Mar., weekdays 10-4, Sun. 1-5.*

Quebec City for Free

Anima G (Complex G), *see* Tour 3, above.

Basilique Notre-Dame-de-Québec (Our Lady of Quebec Basilica), *see* Tour 1, above.

Cavalier du Moulin, *see* Tour 1, above.

Chapelle Bon-Pasteur (Bon-Pasteur Chapel), *see* Tour 3, above.

Édifice Price (Price Building), *see* Tour 1, above.

Église Notre-Dame-des-Victoires (Notre-Dame-des-Victoires Church), *see* Tour 2, above.

Grand Théâtre de Québec, *see* Tour 3, above.

Holy Trinity Anglican Cathedral, *see* Tour 1, above.

Maison Chevalier, *see* Tour 2, above.

Maison Louis-Jolliet, *see* Tour 2, above.

Musée des Augustines (Augustine Museum), *see* Tour 1.

Parc de l'Artillerie (Artillery Park), *see* Tour 2, above.

Parc des Champs-de-Bataille (Battlefields Park), *see* Tour 3, above.

Parliament Buildings, *see* Tour 3, above.

Poudrière de l'Esplanade (Powder Magazine), *see* Tour 3, above.

Skating on St. Charles River, *see* Sports, below.

Tours Martello (Martello Towers), *see* Tour 3, above.

Vieux-Port (Old Port), *see* Tour 2, above.

What to See and Do with Children

Aquarium du Québec (Quebec Aquarium). Situated above the St. Lawrence River, the aquarium houses more than 300 species of marine life, including reptiles, exotic fish, and seals from the lower St. Lawrence River. A wooded picnic area makes this spot ideal for a family outing. The Quebec City transit system, **Commission de Transport de la Communauté Urbaine de Quebec (CTCUQ)** (tel. 418/627–2511) runs buses here. *1675 ave. du Parc, Sainte-Foy, tel. 418/659–5266. Admission: $3 adults, $1.50 children and senior citizens; Nov.–Apr. half price. Open daily 9–5.*

Jardin Zoologique du Québec (Quebec Zoological Gardens). Children usually enjoy going to zoos, but this one is especially scenic because of the DuBerger River, which traverses the grounds. About 250 animal species reside here, including bears, wildcats, primates, and birds of prey. Kids will enjoy the farm and the horse-drawn carriage rides. The zoo is situated 7 miles west of Quebec City on Route 73. If you don't have a car, Quebec Urban Community Transit (tel. 418/627–2511) runs buses here. *8191 ave. du Zoo, Charlesbourg, tel. 418/622–0312. Admission: $5 adults, $2 children and senior citizens; Nov.–Apr.: admission free weekdays, half price weekends. Open May–Oct., daily 9:30–6; Nov.–Apr., daily 9:30–5.*

Parc Cartier-Brébeuf. Stretched along the north bank of the St. Charles River, this national historic park commemorates the area where French explorer Jacques Cartier spent his first winter in Canada (1535–36); it also pays tribute to Father Jean de Brébeuf, founder of the Jesuit Order in New France. A replica of the *Grande Hermine*, the ship Cartier used on his second expedition to America, is stationed here. Playgrounds and 5½ miles (9 kilometers) of walking paths are available. *175 rue de l'Espinay, tel. 418/648–4038. Admission free. Open May 9–Aug. 28, Mon. 1–5, Tues.–Sun. 9–5; Apr. 1–22, Aug. 29–Dec. 2, and Jan. 30–Mar. 31, Mon. and weekends 1–4, Tues-Fri. 10–noon and 1–4. Closed Apr. 23–May 8 and Dec. 3–Jan. 29.*

Parc de l'Artillerie (Artillery Park). This 20-building complex near St-Jean Gate has for centuries played an important part in the city's defense structures. The Officers' Quarters, barracks for Royal Artillery officers until 1871, has a special program for children designed to show how the military lived when Quebec was a British colony, from 1759 to 1867. Children's toys and educational games are also available. *2 rue d'Auteil, tel. 418/648–4205. Admission free. Open Feb.–Mar., weekdays 9–noon and 1–5; Apr.–May 6 and Nov., weekdays 10–noon and 1–5; May 9–Oct., Mon. 1–5, Tues.–Sun. 10–5. Closed Dec.–Jan.*

Parc du Porche. This playground has ladders and swings in a historic setting just outside Place Royale (between rue du Porche and rue de l'Union). *Admission free. Open daily.*

Shopping

Shopping is European-style along the fashionable streets of Quebec City. The boutiques and specialty shops clustered along narrow streets (such as rue du Petit-Champlain, or rue Buade and rue St-Jean in the Latin Quarter) are located within one of the most striking historic settings on the continent.

Prices in Quebec City tend to be on a par for the most part with those in Montreal and other North American cities, so you won't have much luck hunting bargains. When sales occur, they are usually listed in the French daily newspaper, *Le Soleil*.

Shopping

Stores are generally open Monday through Wednesday 9:30 to 5:30; Thursday and Friday until 9; and Saturday until 5. During the summer, shops may be open seven days a week and most have later evening hours.

Shopping Centers

The mall situated closest to the Old City is **Place Québec** (5 Place Québec, tel. 418/529-0551), near the National Assembly. This multilevel shopping complex and convention center with 75 stores is connected to the Hilton International. **Alimentation Petit-Cartier,** (1191 avenue Cartier, tel. 418/524-3682), located off Grande Allée and a 15-minute walk from St-Louis Gate, is a food mall for gourmets, with everything from utensils to petits fours.

Other shopping centers are approximately a 15-minute drive west along Grande Allée. **Place Sainte-Foy** (2452 blvd. Laurier, Sainte-Foy, tel. 418/653-4184) has 115 specialty stores. Next door is the massive **Place Laurier** (2700 blvd. Laurier, Sainte-Foy, tel. 418/653-9318), with more than 350 stores.

Quartier Petit-Champlain in Lower Town is a pedestrian mall with some 50 boutiques, local businesses, and restaurants. This popular district is the best area to find native Quebec arts and crafts, such as wood sculptures, weaving, ceramics, and jewelry. Recommended stores in the area are **Pot-en-Ciel** (27 rue du Petit-Champlain, tel. 418/692-1743) for ceramics; **Pauline Pelletier** (46 rue du Petit-Champlain, tel. 418/692-4871) for porcelain; and **Soirita** (83 rue du Petit-Champlain, tel. 418/692-0931) for silk paintings.

Department Stores

Large department stores can be found in the malls of the suburb of Sainte-Foy, but most of them have outlets inside Quebec City's walls.

Holt & Renfrew & Co., Ltd. (35 rue Buade, tel. 418/692-3680), one of the city's more exclusive stores, carries furs, perfume, and tailored designer collections for men and women.
La Baie (Place Laurier, Sainte-Foy, tel. 418/627-5959) is Quebec's version of the Canadian Hudson Bay Company conglomerate, founded in 1670 by Montreal trappers Pierre Radisson and Medard de Groseillers; the company established the first network of stores in the Canadian frontier. Today, La Baie carries both men's and women's clothing and household wares.
Simons (20 côte de la Fabrique, tel. 418/692-3630), one of Quebec City's oldest family stores, used to be the city's only source for fine British woolens and tweeds, and now the store has added a large selection of designer clothing, linens, and other household items.

Food and Flea Markets

Marché du Vieux-Port enables farmers from the Quebec countryside to sell their fresh produce in the Old Port near rue St-André, from May through November, 8 AM–8 PM.
Rue du Trésor offers a flea market near the Place d'Armes that features sketches, paintings, and etchings by local artists. Fine portraits of the Quebec City landscape and region are plentiful.

Good inexpensive souvenirs also may be purchased here (*see* Exploring, Tour 1, above).

Specialty Stores

Antiques   Quebec City's antiques district is located in the area of rue St-Paul and rue St-Pierre, across from the Old Port. French-Canadian, Victorian, and Art Deco furniture, along with clocks, silverware, and porcelain, are some of the rare collectibles that can be found here. Authentic Quebec pine furniture, characterized by simple forms and lines, is becoming increasingly rare and costly.

L'Héritage Antiquités (109 rue St-Paul, tel. 418/692–1681) specializes in precious Québéçois furniture from the 18th century.
Louis Zaor (112 rue St-Paul, tel. 418/692–0581), the oldest store on rue St-Paul, is still the best place in the area to find excellent English, French, and Canadian antiques. The floor upstairs houses a fine collection of Quebec wood furniture.

Art   **Aux Multiples Collections** (69 rue Ste-Anne, tel. 418/692–1230; 70 rue Dalhousie, tel. 418/692–4434) features a good selection of Inuit art done by Canada's native people, as well as antique furniture and accessories such as sculpted wood ducks.
Galerie Christin (113 rue St-Paul, tel. 418/692–4471), one of Quebec's finest galleries, displays work by new and better-known local artists.
Galerie du Musée du Québec (24 blvd. Champlain, tel. 418/694–7975), operated by the Quebec Museum, sells works by Quebec's most talented contemporary artists.
Galerie Madeleine Lacerte (1 côte Dinan, tel. 418/692–1566), situated in Lower Town, features contemporary art and sculpture for sale.

Books   English-language books are difficult to find in Quebec. One of the city's first bookstores, **Librarie Garneau** (47–49 rue Buade, tel. 418/692–4262), is centrally located near City Hall and carries mostly volumes in French, with the best selection of English-language titles in the area. Other popular bookstores in the city include **La Maison Anglaise** (33 blvd. St. Cyrille O, tel. 418/ 649–0339) and **Classic Bookshop** (Place Laurier, blvd. Laurier, tel. 418/653–8683).

Clothing   **Boutique Amelia** (47 rue Sous Le Fort, tel. 418/692–2875) sells fashionable clothes and accessories at reasonable prices. The staff is helpful and willing to assist you in putting together an outfit or two.
François and Hélène Cote (18½ Cul de Sac, tel. 418/692–3395) is a chic boutique with fashions for men and women.
La Maison Darlington (7 rue Buade, tel. 418/692–2268) carries well-made woolens, dresses, and suits for women by fine names in couture.
Louis Laflamme (2 côte de la Fabrique, tel. 418/692–3774), wedged between Notre-Dame Basilica and the Quebec Seminary, has a large selection of stylish men's clothes.

Crafts   **L'Herbier de Jouvence** (88½ rue du Petit-Champlain, tel. 418/692–4451) specializes in aromatic teas, jams, soaps, and skin products made in Quebec.

Fur   Fur trade has been an important industry for centuries in the area. Quebec City is a good place to purchase quality furs at fairly reasonable prices. Since 1894, one of the best furriers in town has been **Jos Robitaille** (700 rue Richelieu, tel. 418/522-3288). The department store **J.B. Laliberté** (Mail Centre-Ville, tel. 418/525-4841) also carries furs.

Gifts **Collection Lazuli** (774 rue St-Jean, tel. 418/525-6528) features a tasteful selection of unusual art objects, gifts, and jewelry from around the world.

Jewelry **Blanc d'Ivoire** (48 rue du Petit-Champlain, tel. 418/692-4425) specializes in ivory, with all pieces made at the store. Exclusive jewelry can also be found at **Zimmermann** (1115 rue St-Jean, 418/692-2672).

Sports and Fitness

Two parks are central to Quebec City: the 250-acre Battlefields Park with its panoramic views of the St. Lawrence River, and Cartier-Brébeuf Park, which runs along the St. Charles River. Both are favorite spots for outdoor sports such as jogging, biking, and cross-country skiing. Scenic rivers and mountains close by (no more than 30 minutes by car) make this city ideal for the sporting life. For information about sports and fitness, contact **Quebec City Region and Convention Bureau** (60 rue d'Auteuil, Quebec G1R 4C4, tel. 418/692-2471) or **Quebec City Bureau of Parks and Recreation** (1595 Monseigneur-Plessis, Quebec G1M 1A2, tel. 418/691-6017).

Participant Sports

Bicycling Short bike paths with rolling hills are found in Battlefields Park, located at the south side of the city. The best bet for a longer ride over flat terrain is the path north of the city skirting the St. Charles River; this route can be reached from Third Avenue near the Marie de l'Incarnation Bridge. Paths along the côte de Beaupré, beginning at the union of the St. Charles and St. Lawrence rivers, are especially scenic. They begin northeast of the city at rue de la Verandrye and boulevard Montmorency and continue 6 miles (10 kilometers) along the coast to Montmorency Falls.

Bicycles can be rented at **Location Petit Champlain** (92 rue du Petit-Champlain, tel. 418/692-4178) or **Le Harfang** (599 10th St., tel. 418/848-0464).

Boating Lakes around the Quebec City area have facilities for boating and canoeing. Take Route 73 north of the city to Saint-Dunstan de Lac Beauport, then take exit 157, boulevard du Lac, to **Lac Beauport** (tel. 418/849-2821), one of the best nearby resorts. Boats and boards can be rented at **Campex** (7 de l'Orrée chemin, Lac Beauport, tel. 418/849-2236) for canoeing, kayaking, and windsurfing. You can also rent boats in **Lac St-Joseph**, 25 miles (40 kilometers) northwest of Quebec City, at **Lavigie** (tel. 418/875-1884).

Fishing Permits are needed for hunting and fishing in Quebec. They are available from the **Ministry of Recreation, Hunting, and Fishing** (Place de la Capitale, 150 blvd. St-Cyrille E, tel. 418/643-3127). The ministry also publishes a pamphlet on fishing regulations that is available at tourist information offices. Most sporting goods stores provide permits. One of them is **Sport Expert** (915 rue Vallier E, tel. 418/694-9213).

Réserve Faunique des Laurentides (tel. 418/848–2422) is a wildlife reserve with good lakes for fishing approximately 30 miles (48 kilometers) north of Quebec City via Route 73. Stocked trout may be fished year-round in special fish ponds, one of which is on the Île d'Orléans off Chemin Royal (the main road) in Sainte-Famille.

Golf The Quebec City region has 18 golf courses, and several are open to the public. Reservations during summer months are essential. **Club de Golf Métropolitain** (4135 ave. Chauveau, tel. 418/872–9292) in Sainte-Foy, with nine holes, is one of the closest courses to Quebec City. **Club de Golf de Beauport** (3233 rue Clemenceau, tel. 418/663–1578), a nine-hole course, is 20 minutes by car via Route 73 N. **Parc du Mont Sainte-Anne** (Rte. 360, C.P. 400 Beaupré, GOA 1EO, tel. 418/827–2229), a half-hour drive north of Quebec, has one of the best 18-hole courses in the region.

Health and Fitness Clubs One of the city's most popular health clubs is **Club Entrain** (Place Belle Cour, 2600 blvd. Laurier, tel. 418/658–7771). Facilities include a weights room with Nautilus, a sauna, a whirlpool, aerobics classes, racquetball, and squash.

Nonguests at **Hôtel des Gouverneurs** (690 blvd. St-Cyrille E, tel. 418/647–1717) can use the health club facilities, which includes Nautilus equipment, a sauna, a whirlpool, and an outdoor heated pool, for a $20 fee.

Hilton International Québec (3 Place Québec, tel. 418/647–2411) has a smaller health club with weights, a sauna, and an outdoor pool available to nonguests for a $10 fee.

Pool facilities cost $1.50 at the **YMCA** (855 ave. Holland, tel. 414/683–2155).

Hiking/Jogging The Parc Cartier-Brébeuf north of the Old City, along the banks of the St. Charles River, has about 8 miles (13 kilometers) of hiking trails. For more mountainous terrain, head 12 miles (19 kilometers) north via Route 73 to Lac Beauport. **Villages des Sports** (860 blvd. Valcartier, Val Cartier, tel. 418/844–3725), a man-made sports complex 15 miles (24 kilometers) from downtown on Route 371, has 10 miles (16 kilometers) of trails. For jogging, Battlefields Park and Parc Cartier-Brébeuf are the most popular places in the area.

Rafting Jacques Cartier River, about 30 miles (48 kilometers) northwest of Quebec City, provides good rafting; the waterway flows south from Laurentian Park 35 miles (56 kilometers) from Quebec City into the St. Lawrence River.

Jacques Cartier Excursions (878 ave. Jacques Cartier, Tewkesbury, tel. 418/848–7238) offers half-day ($45) or full-day ($58) rafting trips on the Jacques Cartier River. Tours originate from Tewkesbury, a half-hour drive from Quebec City, from May through September.
Nouveau Monde, Expeditions en rivière (2360 chemin Ste-Foy, tel. 418/658–3862) has half-day and full-day excursions mid-May through September to the Jacques Cartier River. *Half-day: weekdays $39, weekends $45. Full-day: weekdays $49, weekends $59.*

Skating The skating season runs December through March. There is a 2.4-mile (3.8-kilometer) stretch for skating along the St. Charles River, between the Samson and Marie de l'Incarnation bridges,

January through March, depending on the ice. Rentals and changing rooms are nearby. *Skating hours: weekdays noon–10, weekends 10–10.*

Place d'Youville, just outside St-Jean Gate, has an outdoor skating rink that has been recently renovated, with heated facilities from November to April. Nighttime skating can be done at **Villages des Sports** (1860 blvd. Valcartier, Val Cartier, tel. 418/844–3725).

Skiing
Cross-country Numerous trails exist for cross-country skiing enthusiasts. Battlefields Park on Quebec City's south side, which you can access on Place Montcalm, has scenic marked trails (for information, call **Quebec City Bureau of Parks and Recreation**, tel. 418/691–6017). Lac Beauport, 12 miles (19 kilometers) north of the city, has more than 50 marked trails (155 miles; 250 kilometers). Contact **Centre l'Éperon** (506 Tour du Lac, tel. 418/849–2778) or **Le Saisonnier** (78 chemin du Brûlé, tel. 418/849–2821). **Parc du Mont Sainte-Anne** (Rte. 360, C.P. 400 Beaupré, GOA 1EO, tel. 418/827–4561), which is 25 miles (40 kilometers) northeast of Quebec City, has 109 miles (174 kilometers) of cross-country trails. Contact **Rang Saint-Julien** (tel. 418/826–2323).

Downhill Four alpine ski resorts, all with night skiing, are located within a 30-minute drive from Quebec City. **Parc du Mont Sainte-Anne** (Rte. 360, C.P. 400 Beaupré, GOA 1EO, tel. 418/827–4561) is the largest resort in eastern Canada, with more than 40 downhill trails, 14 lifts, and a gondola. **Stoneham** (1420 ave. Hibou, Stoneham, Quebec, GOA 4PO, tel. 418/848–2411) is known for its long, easy slopes with 24 downhill runs and 10 lifts. Two smaller alpine centers can be found at Lac Beauport: 14 trails at **Mont St-Castin** (82 chemin du Tour du Lac, Lac Beauport, Quebec, GOA 2CO, tel. 418/849–6776), and 15 trails at **Le Relais** (1084 blvd. du Lac, Lac Beauport, Quebec, GOA 2CO, tel. 418/849–3037).

A municipal bus service, **Skibus** (tel. 418/627–2511), leaves from major hotels in downtown Quebec and Sainte-Foy daily between 7:30 AM and 8:30 AM to Mont Sainte-Anne and returns once a day at 4:30 PM. For Lac Beauport ski areas and Stoneham, the bus runs weekdays for night skiing only, departing at 6 PM and returning at 10 PM; weekends it departs at 8 AM and returns at 4 PM. The cost is $10.

Tennis At **Montcalm Tennis Club** (901 blvd. Champlain, tel. 418/687–1250), south of Quebec City in Sillery, four indoor and seven outdoor courts are open daily from 7 AM to 11 PM. Six indoor courts are also available at **Tennisport** (4230 blvd. Hammel, Ancienne Lorette, tel. 418/872–0111).

Spectator Sports

Tickets for sporting events can be purchased at **Colisée de Québec** (Quebec Coliseum; 2205 ave. du Colisée, tel. 418/523–3333 or 800/463–3333) or through Billetech, whose main outlet is located at the **Grand Théâtre de Québec** (269 blvd. St-Cyrille E, tel. 418/643–8182). Other outlets are situated at Bibliothèque Gabrielle-Roy, Palais Montcalm, La Baie department store (Place Laurier, Sainte-Foy, tel. 418/627–5959), and Provigo Supermarkets. The outlet hours vary depending on the location.

Harness Racing Horse racing is on view at the racetrack **Hippodrome de Québec.** *C.P. 2053, Parc de L'Exposition G1K 7M9, tel. 418/524-5283. Admission: $2 adults, $1 children and senior citizens. Open summer only.*

Hockey A National Hockey League team, the Québec Nordiques, plays at the **Colisée de Québec** (Quebec Coliseum). *2205 ave. du Colisée, Parc de l'Exposition, tel. 418/523-3333 or 800/463-3333. Open mid-Sept.–Apr.*

Dining

Quebec City reveals its French heritage most obviously in its cuisine. You'll discover a French touch in the city's numerous cafés and brasseries and in the artful presentation of dishes at local restaurants. Most dining establishments usually have a selection of dishes à la carte, but you'll usually find more creative specialties by opting for the *table d'hôte,* a two- to four-course meal chosen daily by the chef. At dinner, most restaurants will offer a *menu de dégustation,* a tastefully crafted five- to seven-course dinner of the chef's finest creations.

Although most visitors will find a gourmet meal in their price range, budget-conscious diners may want to try out the more expensive establishments during lunchtime. Lunch usually costs about 30% less than dinner, and many of the same dishes are available. Lunch is usually served 11:30 AM through 2:30 PM; dinner, 6:30 until about 11 PM. You should tip about 15% of the bill.

Quebec City is the best place in the province to sample French-Canadian cuisine, composed of robust, uncomplicated dishes that make use of the region's bounty of foods, including fowl and wild game (caribou, quail, venison), maple syrup, and various berries and nuts. Because Quebec has a cold climate for a good portion of the year, it has a traditionally heavy cuisine with such specialties as *cretons* (pâtés), *tourtière* (a meat pie) and *tarte au sucre* (maple-syrup pie).

Highly recommended restaurants in each price category are indicated by a star ★.

Category	Cost*
Very Expensive	over $30
Expensive	$20–$30
Moderate	$10–$20
Inexpensive	under $10

*per person, excluding drinks, service, and 9% sales tax for meals over $3.25

Very Expensive

★ **À la Table de Serge Bruyère.** This restaurant has put Quebec on the map of great gastronomic cities. The city's most famous culinary institution serves classic French cuisine presented with plenty of crystal, silver, and fresh flowers, and with relentless attention to detail. Only one sitting is offered each night. Chef Serge Bruyère came to Quebec City from Lyons, France, and worked at various restaurants until he opened his own in 1980. The menu de dégustation costs approximately $45; an extensive and pricey wine list starts at $30 and goes up to $900. Specialties include scampi in puff pastry with fresh tomatoes, scallop stew with watercress, and duckling supreme with blueberry sauce. (In 1984, Bruyère expanded inside the restaurant's old 1843 Livernois building and created a minimall with a European-style tearoom, a contemporary piano bar, and a gourmet food store—all serving gourmet treats from his celebrated kitchen. If À la Table de Serge Bruyère is out of your price range, **À la Petit Table** in the food mall is less formal and expensive, with such dishes as seafood terrine and pork with estragon sauce.) *1200 rue St-Jean, tel. 418/694-0618. Reservations required. Jacket required. AE, DC, MC, V. No lunch weekends.*

Café de la Paix. An evening spent at this local favorite takes you back to a dining experience in Paris circa 1930. The tables could not get closer nor the lights dimmer amid the art deco extravagance of lamps in Venetian glass, wood sculpted in geometric patterns, and stained-glass windows. The food is on a par with other fine restaurants in the city, but there are hints that the chefs are relying on their reputations (the restaurant dates back from 1952). The table d'hôte includes such tasty dishes as pheasant with peaches. Salmon comes with four sauces: raspberry vinegar, hollandaise, tarragon, or mustard. The meat entrées, including filet mignon and leg of lamb, are also recommended. You choose your dessert from a cart; try the fresh fruit and the chocolate truffle cake. The service is prompt and attentive. Private dining rooms are available on the second floor. *44 rue des Jardins, tel. 418/692-1430. Reservations advised. Jacket required. AE, DC, MC, V. No lunch Sun.*

★ **Gambrinus.** This comfortable restaurant offers excellent Continental cuisine in two elegant, mahogany-panelled dining rooms with green plants and windows facing the street. Its reliable menu features a range of meat, fish, and pasta entrées, with such specialties as pheasant supreme with fruit, seafood in puff pastry with saffron, and rack of lamb with basil. The table d'hôte is a good bet and provides generous portions and delectable desserts. Service here is unrushed and thoroughly professional. A talented singer-guitarist may accompany your meal; don't be surprised if one of the waiters also bursts into song. Gambrinus is conveniently located near rue du Trésor and the Château Frontenac. *15 rue du Fort, tel. 418/692-5144. Reservations advised. Dress: casual but neat. AE, DC, MC, V. No lunch weekends.*

Le Marie Clarisse. Wood-beam ceilings, stone walls, sea-blue decor, and a lit fireplace make this dining spot one of the coziest in town. Housed in an ancient building on the bottom of the Breakneck Steps near Place Royale, Le Marie Clarisse is well-known for its unique seafood dishes such as halibut with nuts and honey and scallops with port and paprika. Occasionally, the menu includes a good game dish such as caribou with curry. The *menu du jour* has about seven entrées to choose from; dinner includes soup, salad, dessert, and coffee. Wines are served from the restaurant's cellar downstairs. *12 rue du Petit-Champlain, tel. 418/692-0857. Reservations required. Dress: casual but neat. AE, DC, MC, V. Closed lunch Sat. and all day Sun.*

★ **Le Saint-Amour.** This restaurant has all the makings of a true haute-cuisine establishment without having a pretentious at-

Quebec City Dining and Lodging

Dining
À la Table de Serge Bruyère, **18**
Aux Anciens Canadiens, **23**
Café de la Paix, **22**
Chez Temporel, **19**
Casse-Crepe Breton, **15**
Chalet Suisse, **20**
Gambrinus, **33**
L'Apsara, **10**
L'Astral, **4**
Le Café Canadien, **29**
L'Échaudée, **34**
Le Cochon Dingue, **31**
Le Graffiti, **3**
Le Marie Clarisse, **32**
Le Paris Brest, **6**
Le Saint-Amour, **11**
Pizzeria d'Youville, **14**
Restaurant au Parmesan, **24**

Lodging
Château Bonne Entente, **1**
Château de la Terrasse, **28**
Château Frontenac, **30**
Hilton International Québec, **9**
Hôtel Château Laurier, **7**
Hôtel Clarendon, **21**
Hôtel des Gouverneurs, **8**
Hôtel Loews Le Concorde, **5**
Hôtel Maison Sainte-Ursule, **12**
L'Auberge du Quartier, **2**
L'Auberge Saint-Louis, **25**
Le Château de Pierre, **26**
L'Hôtel du Vieux Québec, **17**
Manoir d'Auteuil, **13**
Manoir des Remparts, **35**
Manoir Sainte-Geneviève, **27**
Manoir Victoria, **16**

185

Map of Vieux-Québec

Streets and landmarks labeled:

- rue St-Vallier
- rue St-Paul
- rue Sous-le-Cap
- r. des Remparts
- rue St-Pierre
- rue Dalhousie
- côte du Palais
- rue McMahon
- rue Charlevoix
- rue Collins
- rue Couillard
- rue Garneau
- rue Hébert
- rue Ste-Famille
- rue de la Fabrique
- côte de la Montagne
- rue St-Jean
- rue Dauphine
- rue Ste-Anne
- rue Ste-Ursule
- rue d'Auteuil
- rue des Jardins
- rue du Trésor
- Escalier Casse-Cou
- Château Frontenac
- rue St-Louis
- rue Haldimand
- rue des Carrières
- rue du Fort
- rue Laporte
- terrasse Dufferin
- Place Terrasse-Dufferin
- rue du Petit-Champlain
- Funiculaire
- Porte St-Jean
- Porte Kent
- Porte St-Louis
- avenue Dufferin
- avenue Ste-Geneviève
- avenue St-Denis
- Grande Allée Est
- côte de la Citadelle
- Citadelle
- Promenade des Gouverneurs
- boulevard Champlain
- rue Champlain
- avenue Ontario
- rue Dalhousie
- Fleuve Saint-Laurent

Numbered points: 9, 10, 11, 12, 13, 14, 15, 16, 17, 18, 19, 20, 21, 22, 23, 24, 25, 26, 27, 28, 29, 30, 31, 32, 33, 34, 35

N ↓

0 — 440 yds.
0 — 400 meters

mosphere. A light and airy atrium, with a retractable roof used for outdoor dining in summer, creates a relaxed dining ambience. Chef Jean-Luc Boulay continues to educate himself by taking various courses in France; his studies pay off in the creation of such specialties as stuffed quails in port sauce and salmon with light chive mousse. Sauces here are light, with no flour or butter. The menu de dégustation has seven courses with a scrumptious house apple sherbet to cleanse the palate. Wines can be ordered by the glass to complement courses. The chef's true expertise shines when it comes to his diverse dessert menu. Try the nougat ice cream with fresh figs or the three-chocolate cake. Better yet, order the Saint-Amour assortment of desserts. *48 rue Ste-Ursule, tel. 418/694-0667. Reservations advised. Dress: casual but neat. AE, DC, MC, V.*

Expensive

★ **Aux Anciens Canadiens.** This establishment is named after a book by Philippe-Aubert de Gaspé, who once resided in the house. The prices have recently gone up, but the place is worth trying for the experience of tasting authentic French-Canadian cooking. The house dates back to 1675 and has four dining rooms with different themes. The recently decorated *vaisselier* (dish room) is bright and cheerful with colorful antique dishes, a fireplace, and an antique stove. Another room displays guns from the French regime. The hearty specialties include duck in maple glaze or lamb with blueberry wine sauce. The restaurant also serves the best caribou drink in town. (Caribou is a local beverage made with sweet red wine and whiskey; it is known for its kick.) *34 rue St-Louis, tel. 418/692-1627. Reservations advised. Dress: casual. AE, CB, DC, MC, V.*

L'Astral. This circular restaurant on the 29th floor of the Hôtel Loews Le Concorde revolves high above Battlefields Park and the Old City. The food, while showing signs of improvement, is not the best in town, but the views are excellent. The modern and uninspired decor does not detract from the view, either; there's no room for anything besides the dining tables next to large windows and the vast buffet of salads, meat, and poultry dishes. Sunday brunch offers more than 45 items for $18.75. *1225 Place Montcalm, tel. 418/747-2222. Reservations advised. Dress: casual but neat. AE, DC, MC, V.*

Le Graffiti. A good alternative to Old City dining, this restaurant housed in a modern gourmet food mall serves the cuisine of Provence. Pink tablecloths contrast with dark mahogany-paneled walls to contribute to the romantic setting, while large bay windows look out onto the passersby along avenue Cartier. The distinctive menu typically includes a choice of chicken, beef, and seafood dishes such as scampi spiced with basil and red pepper, and chicken liver mousse with pistachios. The reasonably priced table d'hôte comes with soup, appetizer, entrée, dessert, and coffee. Desserts are made fresh each day. *1191 avenue Cartier, tel. 418/529-4949. Reservations advised. Dress: casual but neat. AE, DC, MC, V.*

★ **Le Paris Brest.** This busy restaurant on Grande Allée serves a gregarious crowd attracted to its tastefully presented French dishes. Art deco lamps, a sculpted mahogany bar at the center, frosted mirrors, and wine bottles shelved in the walls create an atmosphere reminiscent of early 20th-century France. Traditional fare such as *escargots au Pernod* (snails with Pernod) and steak tartare are offered with special touches such as a tomato carved in the shape of a rose. Popular dishes served here include lamb with herbs from Provence and beef Wellington. À la carte and main-course dishes come accompanied with a generous side platter of vegetables. Wine prices range from $18 to $180. *590 Grande Allée E, tel. 418/529-2243. Reservations advised. Dress: casual but neat. AE, DC, MC, V.*

Restaurant au Parmesan. From the red-and-white checkered tablecloths to its standard pasta offerings, this restaurant has everything you expect in an Italian establishment and then some. Thousands of bottles with unusual shapes line the walls, and an accordion player will serenade you over typical dishes such as *gnocchi* (potato dumplings) with tomato sauce and tortellini with cream sauce. The service can be slow and inattentive, but with the jovial, boisterous crowd, you might not mind the wait. *38 rue St-Louis, tel. 418/692-0341. Reservations advised. Dress: casual. AE, DC, MC, V.*

Moderate

Chalet Suisse. This large chalet close to the Place d'Armes serves Swiss cuisine. Fondues are a mainstay, and there are 14 different ones to choose from, with the Gruyère and the chocolate fondues being two of the tastiest house specialties. Another popular dish is *raclette*, a Swiss dish with melted cheese, served with bread and potatoes as well as diverse flavorings such as onions, pickles, and ham. The spacious chalet looms three stories high with clichéd murals of alpine scenes. In the summer, there are umbrella-shaded café tables outside. *32 rue Ste-Anne, tel. 418/694-1320. Reservations accepted. Dress: informal. AE, CB, DC, MC, V.*

L'Apsara. Near St-Louis Gate, this restaurant serves innovative dishes from Vietnam, Thailand, and Cambodia. The Cambodian family who owns the restaurant excels at using both subtle and tangy spices to create unique flavors that are ideal for those seeking a reprieve from French fare. The decor combines Western and Eastern motifs, with flowered wallpaper, Oriental art, and small fountains. Good starters are *fleur de pailin* (a rice paste roll filled with fresh vegetables, meat, and shrimp) or *mou sati* (pork kebabs with peanut sauce and coconut milk). The assorted miniature Cambodian pastries are delicious when served from a little elephant container. *71 rue d'Auteuil, tel. 418/694-0232. Reservations accepted. Dress: casual. AE, MC, V.*

Le Café Canadien. This restaurant housed in the landmark Château Frontenac does not share the hotel's opulence, but it does offer a view along Terrasse Dufferin and the St. Lawrence River. You can try the businessman's breakfast buffet of fruits, omelets, and croissants and an à la carte lunch menu of salads and sandwiches. Standard, but dependable, Continental dishes are served during the lunch and dinner buffets. *Château Frontenac, 1 rue Carrières, tel. 418/692-3861. Reservations accepted. Dress: casual but neat. AE, DC, MC, V.*

★ **L'Échaudée** (Whitewash). This chic black-and-white bistro attracts a mix of business and tourist clientele because of its location between the financial and antiques district in Lower Town. The modern decor features a stark dining area with menus written on a mirrored wall and a stainless-steel bar where you dine on high stools. Lunch offerings include *cuisse de carnard confit* (duck confit) with french fries and fresh seafood salad. The five-course brunch for Sunday antiques shoppers includes giant croissants and a tantalizing array of desserts. *73 Sault-au-Matelot, tel. 418/692-1299. Weekend reservations advised. Dress: casual. AE, DC, MC, V. Closed Sun. night.*

Inexpensive

Casse-Crêpe Breton. Crepes in generous compact proportions are served in this small, square, diner-style restaurant on rue St-Jean. From a menu of 20 ingredients, pick your own chocolate or fruit combinations, or design a larger meal with cheese, ham, and vegetables. The tables surround three round hot plates at which you watch your creations being made. Crepes made with two to five ingredients cost under $5. *1136 rue St-Jean. tel. 418/692-0438. No reservations. No credit cards. Open 8 AM–2 AM.*

★ **Chez Temporel.** Tucked behind rue St-Jean and côte de la Fabrique, this homey café is an experience *très Français*. The aroma of fresh coffee fills the air. The rustic decor incorporates wooden tables, chairs, and benches, while a tiny staircase winds to an upper level. Croissants are made in-house; the staff will fill them with Gruyère and ham or anything else you want. Try the equally delicious croque-monsieur and quiche lorraine. *25 rue Couillard, tel. 418/694-1813. No reservations. No credit cards. Open 7:30 AM–1:30 AM.*

Le Cochon Dingue (The Crazy Pig). Across the street from the ferry in Lower Town, this cheerful café with sidewalk tables and indoor dining rooms has artfully blended the chic and the antique. Black-and-white checkerboard floors contrast with ancient stone walls that are typical of the oldest sections of town. Café fare includes dependably tasty homemade quiches (spinach, broccoli, seafood), thick soups, and desserts such as fresh raspberry tarte and maple sugar pie. *46 blvd. Champlain, tel. 418/692-2013. No reservations. Dress: informal. AE, DC, MC, V. Open 7:30 AM–midnight.*

Pizzeria d'Youville. This restaurant located in the Latin Quarter has a pizza for everyone, with more than 30 combinations. Tasty pies are cooked in a wood oven and then heated by fire at your table. You can go beyond tomato sauce and cheese here, and try the Hawaiian pizza, with ham, cheese, and pineapple, or L' Amalfitana, which combines tomato sauce, cheese, shrimp, and garlic. Meat dishes, pasta, and salads are also offered on the menu. Its Latin Quarter location is one of Quebec City's liveliest neighborhoods, perfect for an after-dinner stroll. *1014 St-Jean, tel. 418/694-0299. Reservations accepted. Dress: informal. AE, DC, MC, V.*

Lodging

With more than 35 hotels within its 1-square-mile radius, Quebec City has a range of lodging options. Landmark hotels stand as prominent as the city's most historic sites. Modern high rises outside the ramparts offer spectacular views of the Old City. Or visitors can immerse themselves in the city's historic charm by staying in one of the many old-fashioned inns where no two rooms are alike.

Whichever kind of accommodations you choose, be sure to make a reservation during peak season, from May through September. If you are planning to visit during the summer or at the

Lodging 189

time of the Winter Carnival in February, you may have trouble finding a room without one. During busy times, hotel rates are usually 30% above prices at other times of the year. From November through April, many of the city's lodging places offer discount weekend packages and other promotions.

Highly recommended properties in each price category are indicated by a star ★.

Category	Cost*
Very Expensive	over $140
Expensive	$85–$140
Moderate	$50–$85
Inexpensive	under $50

All prices are for a standard double room, excluding an optional service charge.

Very Expensive

Château Bonne Entente. If you have a car, you may want to stay at this sprawling resort located 10 minutes from the airport and 20 minutes from the walled city. The hotel is more commonly called "The Other Château," in country-style juxtaposition to the urban Frontenac. It was a private mansion until 1940, when it became a hotel; after a $7 million renovation last year, this establishment has become a popular spot for the well-heeled. Rooms have been decorated in contemporary furnishings with fine wood, plush carpeting, and all the modern amenities. The property encompasses 11 acres of land with a main complex as well as separate cottage rooms in back. *3400 chemin Ste-Foy, Sainte Foy, G1X 1S6, tel. 418/653–5221 or 800/463–4390. 170 rooms. Facilities: bar, 2 restaurants, outdoor pool, tennis court, trout fishing in back pond, full day care. AE, DC, MC, V.*

★ **Château Frontenac.** Towering above the St. Lawrence River, the Château Frontenac is indisputably Quebec City's most renowned landmark. As a modern hotel, it can no longer claim to be the city's top-rated place to stay; nevertheless the mystique of staying at "the château" is an enduring tradition. Its public rooms, from the intimate piano bar to its 700-seat ballroom, which is reminiscent of the Versailles Hall of Mirrors, have all the opulence of years gone by, while almost all the guest rooms offer excellent views. You must make a reservation in advance, as the average booking rate is 80% a year. Last year, Canadian Pacific Hotels committed $50 million to modernize its rooms and facilities, keeping in mind the hotel's refined French Renaissance decor. The Frontenac has one of the finer restaurants in town, Le Champlain, where classic French cuisine is served by waiters dressed in traditional French costumes. The ground floor has several luxury shops and a restaurant, Le Café Canadien *(see Dining, above). 1 rue des Carrières, G1R 4P5, tel. 418/692–3861 or 800/268–9420. 525 rooms. Facilities: 2 restaurants. AE, CB, DC, MC, V.*

★ **Hilton International Québec.** Just outside St-Jean Gate, the Hilton rises from the shadow of Parliament Hill as the city's finest luxury hotel. It has such spacious facilities and efficient services that it could easily cater exclusively to the convention crowd. Instead, it has adapted its renowned comfort and dependable service to tourists. The sprawling atrium lobby is flanked with a bar and an open-air restaurant, and it offers the added convenience of being connected with the mall, Place Québec, with 75 shops and boutiques. Ultramodern rooms with pine furniture feature tall windows so that rooms on upper floors afford fine views of the Old City. *3 Place Québec, G1K 7M9, tel. 418/647-2411 or 800/268-9275. 563 rooms, 36 suites. Facilities: outdoor pool, health club, sauna, whirlpool, 2 restaurants. AE, CB, DC, MC, V.*

Hôtel des Gouverneurs. Opposite the Parliament Buildings, this large full-service establishment is part of a Quebec chain with 14 hotels in the province. Formerly called Auberge des Gouverneurs when it opened in 1975, the hotel has upgraded its light and spacious rooms by furnishing them with luminous pastel decor, wood furniture, and marble bathrooms. The recently added VIP floors were designed to lure the business traveler, but there is also plenty of room for tourists. Although it is part of a tall office complex, the hotel occupies only the first six floors, so views of the Old City are limited. The hotel does boast, however, the city's best health club and a year-round outdoor swimming pool, perfect for use even when the weather is most frigid. *690 blvd. St-Cyrille E, G1R 5A8, tel. 418/647-1717 or 800/463-2820. 378 rooms with private bath. Facilities: health club, heated outdoor pool, sauna, whirlpool, piano bar, restaurant. AE, DC, MC, V.*

★ **Hôtel Loews Le Concorde.** When Le Concorde was built in 1974, the shockingly tall concrete structure went up with controversy because it was taking the place of 19th-century Victorian homes. Yet of all the modern hotels outside the city gates, tourists will probably find that Le Concorde occupies one of the most convenient locations for city touring and nightlife. Inside the hotel there's almost as much going on as at the cafés and restaurants along the nearby Grande Allée; Le Concorde offers the revolving restaurant L'Astral, a sidewalk café, a bar, and a disco. Rooms have good views of Battlefields Park and nearly all have been redone in modern decor combined with traditional furnishings. Amenities for business travelers have expanded; one of the new VIP floors is reserved for female executives. *1225 Place Montcalm, G1R 4W6, tel. 418/647-2222 or 800/223-0888. 422 rooms. Facilities: indoor and outdoor pools, sauna, whirlpool, health club, bar, disco, 2 restaurants (L'Astral on the 28th floor, and a sidewalk café). AE, CB, DC, MC, V.*

Expensive

Hôtel Clarendon. The experience of staying at the Clarendon resembles that of residing at the Château Frontenac, but on a smaller scale. You can immerse yourself in history by staying in a landmark, while you'll also be in the center of the Old City. The Clarendon is Quebec City's oldest hotel, established in 1870. Since then, it has experienced only one major renovation, in 1930. This gave it its present stunning Art Deco design, influencing every aspect of the building—the lamps, banisters, doors, and reception area. The spacious rooms are decorated in blue and red hues. The Clarendon is known for its famous jazz bar, the city's oldest and still its finest. Its Victorian-style restaurant, Le Charles Baillargé, has live music six days a week. *57 rue Ste-Anne, G1R 3X4, tel. 418/692-2480. 89 rooms with private bath. Facilities: restaurant, bar. AE, DC, MC, V.*

Lodging

Le Château de Pierre. Built in 1853 and converted from a private residence in 1960, this tidy Victorian manor on a picturesque street has kept its English origins alive. The high-ceilinged halls have ornate chandeliers. The rooms are imaginatively decorated with floral themes, and each usually has some special added feature—a balcony, fireplace, or vanity room—to lend some extra charm. Rooms in the front face imposing old stone buildings across the way that date from the English regime. *17 ave. Ste-Geneviève, G1R 4A8, tel. 418/694-0429. 15 rooms with private bath and air-conditioning. V.*

L'Hôtel du Vieux Québec. Located on a secluded street in the Latin Quarter, this hotel has a brick exterior that gets lost amid the more striking historic structures around it. The establishment was once an apartment building and has the long-term visitor in mind. The interior design is also nondescript, featuring sparsely decorated but comfortable rooms done in earth tones. Most rooms have a full kitchenette with a stove, cabinets, a sink, and a refrigerator; all have cable TV. *8 rue Collins, G1R 1S6, tel. 418/692-1850. 28 units with private bath. AE, MC, V.*

★ **Manoir d'Auteuil.** Originally a private home, this lodging is one of the more lavish manors in town, artfully revamped at great taste and expense. An ornate sculpted iron banister wraps around four floors. Guest rooms feature lavish trimmings in mahogany and marble and blend modern design with precious Art Deco antiques. Each room differs in terms of shape and design; one room was formerly the residence's chapel, while another has become a duplex with a luxurious marble bathroom on the second floor. Some rooms look out to the wall between the St-Louis and St-Jean gates. *49 rue d'Auteuil, G1R 4C2, tel. 418/694-1173. 16 rooms with private bath. AE, MC, V.*

Manoir Sainte-Geneviève. This quaint and elaborately decorated hotel dating from 1880 stands near the Château Frontenac, on the southwest corner of the Jardin des Governeurs. A plush Victorian ambience is created with fanciful wallpaper and rooms decorated with precious stately English manor furnishings, such as marble lamps, large wooden bedposts, and velvet upholstery; you'll feel as if you are staying in a secluded country inn. A hidden porch facing the Citadel is perfect for relaxing and soaking in the atmosphere of Upper Town. Service here is personal and genteel. One suite on the ground floor has a private entrance. *13 ave. Ste-Geneviève, G1R 4A7, tel. 418/694-1666. 9 rooms with private bath; some rooms have air-conditioning and color TV. No credit cards.*

Moderate

Château de la Terrasse. While this four-story inn may not have the same charm as others in the city, it does have something that the others are lacking: This is the sole inn within the area that has a view of the St. Lawrence River. However, only half of the rooms face the river; others in the rear look out onto the backs of buildings. While the interior hints at having once possessed a refined and elegant decor because of its high ceilings and stained glass lining the large bay windows, the furnishings these days are plain and unremarkable. *6 Place Terrasse Dufferin, G1R 4N5, tel. 418/694-9472. 18 rooms with private bath. AE, DC, MC, V.*

Hôtel Château Laurier. This medium-size hotel closely resembles a dormitory, which may explain why it attracts a youthful clientele. Located at one of the louder intersections in town, it has front doors that open up to the nightlife on Grande Allée. The lobby consists of couches clustered around a central television. Guest rooms are spacious, but some of the no-frills furnishings appear worn. Some rooms look out onto Parliament Hill, while the others, facing Grande Allée, may be noisy at night. *695 Grande Allée E, tel. 418/522-8108. 55 rooms with private bath. Free parking. AE, DC, MC, V.*

★ **L'Auberge du Quartier.** This small, amiable inn, situated in a house dating from 1852, will please those seeking moderately-priced lodging with a personal touch. Proprietors Lise Provost and Pierre Couture are highly attentive to their guests' needs. The cheerful rooms, without phones or televisions, are modestly furnished but well-maintained; two of them have fireplaces. Rooms 5 and 8 are recommended to couples. A suite of rooms on the third floor can accommodate a family at a reasonable cost. This is one of the few inns in the area that offers a tasty Continental breakfast of warm croissants, homemade banana bread and preserves, strong coffee, and fresh fruits. A 20-minute walk west from the Old City, L'Auberge du Quartier is convenient to avenue Cartier and Grande Allée nightlife; joggers can use Battlefields Park across the street. *170 Grande Allée, G1R 2G9, tel. 418/525-9726. 13 rooms: 11 with private bath, 2 rooms share bathroom. Free parking. AE, MC, V.*

L'Auberge Saint-Louis. This hotel is perfect for the traveler with convenience in mind; its central location on the main street of the city can't be beat. The inn features small rooms, tall staircases, and a lobby resembling a European pension. The newly decorated guest rooms contain comfortable but bare-bones furniture. The ultrabudget room on the fourth floor is just big enough for a bed. The service here is friendly and hospitable. Most guest rooms share floor bathrooms or have a semi-bathroom. *48 rue St-Louis., G1R 3Z3, tel. 418/692-2424. 22 rooms, 9 with private bath. MC, V.*

★ **Manoir Victoria.** In the heart of the bohemian quarter off St-Jean street stands this conservative-looking hotel. By design, it appears more suitable for the business traveler, but because of its price and location it attracts a youthful crowd. The lobby with Greco-Roman pillars is furnished with white couches and blue carpeting. Formerly known as the Hotel Victoria, this 90-year-old building was recently transformed into a modern-day manor. The brightly decorated rooms have all the modern conveniences. *44 côte du Palais, tel. 418/692-1030. 84 rooms with private bath. Facilities: free parking, color TV, air-conditioning, hair salon. AE, DC, MC, V.*

Inexpensive

★ **Hôtel Maison Sainte-Ursule.** Situated on a tiny street west of the Ursuline Convent, this well-kept hotel is a boon for the sophisticated yet economical traveler, with historic charm and reasonable prices all in one. The building, constructed in 1780, is typical of the architecture of New France, with dormer windows, small doors, and a slanting roof. Immaculate accommodations contain the old-fashioned basics, with sturdy and simple wood furniture; some rooms even have the original pint-size doors. Seven rooms are located in an annex in a private rear courtyard that becomes a garden in the summer. The amiable staff is eager to see that you are comfortable. *40 rue Ste-*

Ursule, G1R 4E2, tel. 418/694-9794. 15 rooms, 12 with private bath. AE, DC, MC, V. Closed in Jan.
Manoir des Remparts. There's nothing fancy about this hotel, which is on a residential street bordering the north side of Quebec City's natural cliff. But this manor offers just enough to attract the budget-conscious traveler: spacious and clean rooms with back-to-basics old-time furnishings. The halls are well-lighted and considered large for a residence in the Old City. Guest rooms have private bath or share a bath on the floor, but none has telephones or televisions. *3½ rue des Remparts, G1R 3R4, tel. 418/692-2056. AE, MC, V.*

Quebec City has a large number of bed-and-breakfast and hostel accommodations. To guarantee a room during peak season, be sure to reserve in advance. **Quebec City Tourist Information** (60 rue d'Auteuil, G1R 4C4, tel. 418/651-2882) has B&B listings.

Bed-and-Breakfasts

Bed and Breakfast-Bonjour Québec (3765 blvd. Monaco, G1P 3J3, tel. 418/527-1465). This agency has several B&Bs to choose from in or close to the Old City. Reserve in advance in the summer. Prices range from $30 for a single room to $50 for a double.
Bed and Breakfast in Old Quebec (35 rue des Remparts, G1K 4J2, tel. 418/525-9826). This upscale, deluxe B&B is located in a 250-year-old home in the Old City. Single rooms start at $45, and doubles range between $60 and $100.

Hostels

Centre International de Séjour (19 rue Ste-Ursule, G1R 4E1, tel. 418/694-0755). In the Old City, the center has 250 beds in rooms accommodating four to 16 beds. Cost is $11–$13 for one person. All meals are available in the cafeteria.
Service des résidences de l'Université Laval (Pavillon Parent, Local 1643, Université Laval, Sainte-Foy, Quebec G1K 7P4, tel. 418/656-2921). From May through August, rooms are available in the dormitories of the Laval University campus, located west of the Old City in suburban Sainte-Foy. Prices are $20 for a single; $25 for a double. Reserve at least two days in advance. Meals are served in the cafeteria.
YWCA (855 ave. Holland, G1S 3S5, tel. 418/683-2155). Near Jeffrey-Hale Hospital, this women's organization offers 59 singles at $25 a night, and 23 doubles at $34. Rooms are open to men during the summer only. Reservations are suggested. Meals are available in the cafeteria.

The Arts and Nightlife

For a place its size, Quebec City boasts a wide variety of cultural events, from the reputable Quebec Symphony Orchestra to several small theater companies. The arts scene changes significantly depending on the season. From September to May, a steady repertoire of concerts, plays, and performances is presented in theaters and halls around town. In summer, indoor theaters close to make room for several outdoor stages.

For arts and entertainment listings in English, consult the *Québec Chronicle-Telegraph*, published on Wednesdays. Each day in the French-language daily newspaper, *Le Soleil*, listings appear on a page called "Où Aller à Québec" ("Where to Go in Quebec"). *Voilà Québec* and *Hospitalité Québec* are bilingual quarterly entertainment guides distributed free in tourist information areas.

Tickets for most shows can be purchased through **Billetech**, whose main outlet is the Grand Théâtre de Québec (269 blvd. St-Cyrille E, tel. 418/643-8131). Other outlets are located at Bibliothèque Gabrielle-Roy, Colisée, Implanthéâtre, Palais Montcalm, Salle Albert-Rousseau, La Baie department store (Place Laurier, tel. 418/627-5959), and Provigo supermarkets. Outlet hours vary, depending on the location.

The Arts

Dance **Grand Théâtre de Québec** (269 blvd. St-Cyrille E, tel. 418/643-8131) presents a dance series with both Canadian and international companies. Dancers also appear at Bibliothèque Gabrielle-Roy, Salle Albert-Rousseau, and the Palais Montcalm (*see* Theater, below, for more information).

Film Most theaters present French films and American films dubbed into French. Two popular theaters are **Cinéma de Paris** (966 rue St-Jean, tel. 418/694-0891) and **Cinéma Place Charest** (500 du Pont, tel. 418/529-9745). **Cinéma Place Québec** (5 Place Québec, tel. 418/525-4524) almost always features films in English.

Music **L'Orchestre Symphonique de Québec** (Quebec Symphony Orchestra) is Canada's oldest. It performs at Louis-Frechette Hall in **Grand Théâtre de Québec** (269 blvd. St-Cyrille E, tel. 418/643-8131).
Bibliothèque Gabrielle-Roy (350 rue St-Joseph, tel. 418/529-0924). Classical concerts are offered at the Auditorium Joseph Lavergne. During winter months, a special Sunday-morning series is presented called "Concerts-Croissants." Tickets must be purchased in advance at the library.
Colisée de Québec (2205 ave. du Colisée, parc de l'Exposition, tel. 418/691-7211). Popular music concerts are often booked here.

Theater All theater productions are in French. The following theaters schedule shows from September through May:

Grand Théâtre de Québec (269 blvd. St-Cyrille E, tel. 418/643-8131). Classic and contemporary plays are staged by the leading local theater company, le Théâtre du Trident (tel. 418/643-5873).
Implanthéâtre (2 rue Crémazie E, tel. 418/648-9989). This multipurpose, experimental theater offers about 200 presentations a year, including performances for children.
Palais Montcalm (995 Place d'Youville, tel. 418/670-9011). This municipal theater outside St-Jean Gate features a broad range of productions.
Salle Albert-Rousseau (2410 chemin Ste-Foy, Sainte-Foy, tel. 418/659-6710). A diverse repertoire, from classical to comedy, is offered here.
Théâtre de la Bordée (1143 rue St-Jean, tel. 418/694-9631). This local company presents small-scale productions.

The Arts and Nightlife

Théâtre du Petit-Champlain (68 rue du Petit-Champlain, tel. 418/692–0100). On Quebec City's smallest and oldest street, this theater's performances are staged in a café atmosphere.

Summer Theater **Agora** (Édifice du Havre, 160 rue Dalhousie, tel. 418/692–0100). The largest open-air amphitheater in the Old Port between the river and the customs building features variety shows, plays, and classical and contemporary music concerts.

Place d'Youville (tel. 418/670–9011). In the summer, open-air concerts are presented here, just outside St-Jean Gate. Recent renovations have made this spot quite enjoyable.

Théâtre du Bois du Coulonge (office: 81 rue St-Pierre, tel. 418/692–3064). One of the most delightful theater settings in town is situated in Battlefields Park near the Quebec Museum.

Nightlife

Nightlife in Quebec City is centered on the clubs and cafés of rue St-Jean, avenue Cartier, and Grande Allée. In the winter, evening activity is livelier toward the end of the week beginning on Wednesday. But as the warmer temperatures set in, the café-terrace crowd emerges, and bars stay open seven days a week. Most bars and clubs stay open until 3 AM.

Bars and Lounges **Le Central** (1200 rue St-Jean, tel. 418/694–0618). At this stylish piano bar at Serge Bruyère's restaurant's complex, you can order from the restaurant's sophisticated haute-cuisine menu.

Le Pub Saint-Alexandre (1987 rue St-Jean, tel. 418/694–0015). This popular English-style pub, formerly a men-only tavern, is a good place to look for your favorite brand of beer.

Le St-O (570 Grand Allée E, tel. 418/529–0211). A chic, distinguished crowd frequents this club with an outdoor café along Grande Allée.

Vogue and **Sherlock Holmes** (1170 d'Artigny, tel. 418/529–9973). You'll find mainly Yuppies at these two bars stacked one on top of the other. Sherlock Holmes is a pub-restaurant downstairs; for dancing, try Vogue upstairs.

Disco **Chez Dagobert** (600 Grande Allée E, tel. 418/522–0393). You'll find a little bit of everything—live rock bands to loud disco—at this large and popular club.

Le Dancing (1225 Place Montcalm, tel. 414/647–2222). Music videos and a loud stereo blare from this night spot on the lower level of the Hôtel Loews Le Concorde.

Le Tube Hi-Fi (139 rue St-Pierre, tel. 418/692–0257). A majestic old bank building in Lower Town now houses a glitzy disco with giant Greco-Roman columns, lasers, a dance floor, billiard tables, and video games.

Merlin (1175 avenue Cartier, tel. 418/529–0211). This one-room pub-style disco is a favorite Québécois hangout.

Folk, Jazz, **Chez Son Père** (24 St-Stanislas, tel. 418/692–2124). French-
and Blues Canadian folk songs fill this smoke-filled pub on the second floor of an old building in the Latin Quarter. Singers perform every night of the week.

Le d'Auteuil (35 rue d'Auteuil, tel. 418/692–2263). Rhythm and blues, jazz, and blues emanate from this converted church across from Kent Gate.

L'Emprise at Hôtel Clarendon (57 rue Ste-Anne, tel. 418/692–2480). The first jazz bar in Quebec City is the preferred spot for enthusiasts. The Art Deco decor sets the mood for the Jazz Age rhythms.

Le Foyer (1044 rue St-Jean, tel. 418/692-0708). Folk and rock shows at this club in the student quarter attract an early-20s crowd.

Le Pape Georges (8 Cul de Sac, tel. 418/692-1320). This miniature, cozy wine bar offers live Québécois folk singing on a tiny dead-end street near Place Royale.

Soirée de Danse Moderne et Canadienne (155 blvd. Charest E, tel. 418/647-5858). An orchestra always plays here on Saturdays.

6 Excursions from Quebec City

Côte de Beaupré

by Alice H. Oshins

As legend tells it, when explorer Jacques Cartier first gained sight of the north shore of the St. Lawrence River in 1535, he exclaimed, *"Quel beau pré!"* ("What a lovely meadow!"), because the area was the first inviting piece of land he had spotted since leaving France. Today this fertile meadow, first settled by French farmers, is known as Côte de Beaupré (Beaupré coast), stretching 25 miles (40 kilometers) from Quebec City to the famous pilgrimage site of Sainte-Anne-de-Beaupré. The impressive Montmorency Falls are located midway between these two points.

Getting Around

By Car To reach Montmorency Falls, take Route 440 (Dufferin-Montmorency Autoroute) northeast from Quebec City. Approximately 6 miles (9.6 kilometers) east of the city is the exit for Montmorency Falls. To drive directly to Sainte-Anne-de Beaupré, continue northeast on Route 440 for approximately 18 miles (29 kilometers) and exit at Sainte-Anne-de-Beaupré.

An alternative way to reach Sainte-Anne-de-Beaupré is to take Route 360 or avenue Royale. Take Route 440 from Quebec City, turn left at d'Estimauville, and right on boulevard des Chutes until it intersects with Route 360. Also called "le chemin du Roi," (the King's Road), this panoramic route is one of the oldest in North America, winding 18.8 miles (30 kilometers) along the steep ridge of the Beaupré coast. The road borders 17th- and 18th-century farmhouses, historic churches, and Normandy-style homes with half-buried root cellars. Route 360 goes past the Sainte-Anne-de-Beaupré Basilica.

Tourist Information

Beaupré Coast Interpretation Center, housed in the old mill Petit-Pré, built in 1695, features displays on the history and development of the region. *7007 ave. Royale, Château-Richer, tel. 418/824-3677. Admission free. Open June-Oct., daily 9-noon and 1-5.*

The offices of **Quebec City Region Tourism and Convention Bureau** (418/522-3511) can provide information on tours of the Beaupré coast (*see* Staying in Quebec City, Chapter 5).

Guided Tours

Quebec City touring companies, such as **Gray Line** (tel. 418/622-7420) and **Maple Leaf Sightseeing Tours** (tel. 418/653-9722), offer day excursions along the Beaupré coast, with stops at Montmorency Falls and the Sainte-Anne-de-Beaupré Basilica from April through November.

Montmorency Falls

Begin this excursion with a visit to **Montmorency Falls.** The Montmorency River, named after Charles de Montmorency, who was a governor of New France, cascades over a coastal cliff and offers one of the most beautiful sites in the province. The falls, which are actually 50% higher than the wider Niagara

Falls, measure 274 feet (83 meters) in height. During very cold weather conditions, the falls' heavy spray freezes and forms a giant loaf-shaped ice cone known to Québécois as the Pain du Sucre (Sugarloaf); this phenomenon attracts sledders and sliders from Quebec City. In the warmer months, a park in the river's gorge leads to an observation terrace that is continuously sprayed by a fine drizzle from water pounding onto the cliff rocks. The top of the falls can be observed from avenue Royale. *Admission free. Open daily.*

Time Out **Restaurant Baker** (8790 ave. Royale, Château-Richer, tel. 418/824-4878), on the way to Sainte-Anne-de Beaupré on Route 360, is a good, old-fashioned rustic restaurant that serves hearty, traditional French-Canadian dishes such as meat pie, pea soup, pâtés, and maple-sugar pie.

Basilique Sainte-Anne-de-Beaupré

The monumental and inspiring **Basilique Sainte-Anne-de-Beaupré** (Sainte-Anne-de-Beaupré Basilica) is located in a small town with the same name. The basilica has become a popular attraction as well as an important shrine: more than half a million people visit the site each year.

The French brought their devotion to Saint Anne with them when they sailed across the Atlantic to New France. In 1650, Breton sailors caught in a storm vowed to erect a chapel in honor of this patron saint at the exact spot where they would land. The present-day neo-Roman basilica constructed in 1923 was the fifth to be built on the site where the sailors first touched ground.

According to local legend, Saint Anne was responsible over the years for saving voyagers from shipwrecks in the harsh waters of the St. Lawrence. Tributes to her miraculous powers can be seen in the shrine's various mosaics, murals, altars, and church ceilings. A bas-relief at the entrance depicts Saint Anne welcoming her pilgrims, while ceiling mosaics represent details from her life. Numerous crutches and braces posted on the back pillars have been left by those who have felt the healing powers of Saint Anne.

The basilica, which is in the shape of a Latin cross, has two granite steeples jutting from its gigantic structure. Its interior has 22 chapels and 18 altars, as well as round arches and numerous ornaments in the Romanesque style. The 214 stained-glass windows by Frenchmen Auguste Labouret and Pierre Chaudière, finished in 1949, tell a story of salvation through personages who were believed to be instruments of God over the centuries. Other features of the shrine include intricately carved wooden pews decorated with various animals and several smaller altars (behind the main altar) that are dedicated to different saints.

The original wooden chapel built in the village of Sainte-Anne-de-Beaupré in the 17th century was situated too close to the St. Lawrence and was swept away by flooding of the river. In 1676, the chapel was replaced by a stone church that was visited by pilgrims for more than a century, but this structure was also demolished in 1872. The first basilica, which replaced the stone church, was destroyed by a fire in 1922. The following year architects Maxime Rosin from Paris and Louis-N. Audet from Quebec province designed the basilica that now stands. *10-018 ave. Royale, Sainte-Anne-de-Beaupré, tel. 418/827-3781. Admission free. Open year-round. Reception booth open daily May–mid-Sept., 8:30–5. Tours daily in summer at 1 PM start at the information booth (open mid-Apr.–mid-Oct.) at the southwest corner of the courtyard outside the basilica.*

Across the street from the basilica on avenue Royale is the **Commemorative Chapel** built in 1878 and designed by Claude Bailiff. The memorial chapel was constructed on the location of the transept of a stone church built in 1676 and contains the old building's foundations. Among the remnants housed here are the old church's bell, dating from 1696; an early 18th-century altar designed by Vezina; a crucifix sculpted by François-Noël Levaseur in 1775; and a pulpit designed by François Baillargé in 1807.

Northeast of the basilica stands the small **Scala Santa** (Chapel of the Holy Stairs). Erected in 1891, it features a replica of the stairs that Christ mounted before appearing before Pontius Pilate. *Both chapels: ave. Royale, tel. 418/827-3781. Admission free. Open May–Oct., daily 8–5.*

West of the Scala Santa is the **Chemin de la Croix** (Way of the Cross). The path crosses a hill and is lined with 14 life-size, cast-iron figures installed between 1913 and 1946. *ave. Royale. Open all day.*

Ile d'Orléans

Île d'Orléans, an island slightly downstream in a northeasterly direction from Quebec City, exemplifies the historic charm of rural Quebec province with its quiet, traditional lifestyle. A drive around the island will take you past stone churches that are among the oldest in the region and centuries-old houses amid acres of lush orchards and cultivated farmland. Horse-drawn carriages are still a means of transport. Île d'Orléans is also an important market place that provides fresh produce daily for Quebec City; roadside stands on the island sell a variety of local products, such as crocheted blankets, woven articles, maple syrup, homemade bread and jams, and fruits and vegetables.

The island was discovered at approximately the same time as Quebec City in 1535. Explorer Jacques Cartier noticed an abundance of vines on the island and called it the "Island of Bacchus," after the Greek god of wine. In 1536, Cartier renamed the island in honor of the duke of Orléans, son of the king of France, François I. Long considered part of the domain of Beaupré coast, the island was not given its seignorial autonomy until 1636, when it was bought by La Compagne des Cents Associés, a group formed by Louis XIII to promote settlement in New France.

The island, about 5 miles (9 kilometers) wide and 21 miles (34 kilometers) long, is now composed of six small villages. These villages have sought over the years to remain relatively private residential and agricultural communities; the island's bridge to the mainland was built only in 1935.

Ile d'Orléans

Getting Around

By Car Île d'Orléans has no public transportation; cars are the only way to get to and around the island, unless you take a guided tour (*see* Guided Tours, below). Parking on the island is never a problem; you can always stop and explore certain villages on foot. The main road, chemin Royal (Route 368), extends 40 miles (67 kilometers) through all the island's six villages; street numbers along chemin Royal begin at No. 1 for each municipality.

From Quebec City, take Route 440 (Dufferin-Montmorency Autoroute) northeast. After a drive of approximately 7 miles (10 kilometers) take the bridge, Pont de l'Île d'Orléans, to reach the island. Before you get to the island's only traffic light, turn right heading west on chemin Royal to begin the exploring tour below.

Important Addresses and Numbers

Tourist Information **Beau Temps, Mauvais Temps** has a tourist office located in Saint-Pierre (991 rte. Prévost, tel. 418/828–2275). *Open Mon. 8–5:30, Tues–Sat. 8:30–7, and Sun. 11–3.*

The island's Chamber of Commerce operates a tourist information kiosk situated at the west corner of côte du Pont and chemin Royal. *490 côte du Pont, Saint-Pierre, tel. 418/828–9411. Open June–Sept., daily 8:30–7:30.*

Medical Clinic **Centre Medical** (1015 rte. Prévost, Saint-Pierre, tel. 418/828–2213) is the only medical clinic on the island.

Escorted Tours

Beau Temps, Mauvais Temps (991 rte. Prévost, Saint-Pierre, Île d'Orléans, tel. 418/828–2275) offers guided tours of all six villages and river excursions that depart from Saint-François, May–November. The company is also a referral service for lodging.

The Quebec City touring companies **Maple Leaf Sightseeing Tours** (tel. 418/687–9226), **Gray Line** (tel. 418/622–7420), and **Visite Touristiques de Québec** (tel. 418/653–9722) offer full- and half-day bus tours of the western tip of the island combined with sightseeing along the Beaupré coast, May–October 15.

Any of the offices of **Quebec City Region Tourism and Convention Bureau** can also provide information on tours and accommodations on the island (*see* Staying in Quebec City, Chapter 5).

Exploring Île d'Orléans

Numbers in the margin correspond with points of interest on the Île d'Orléans map.

Because the general pace of Île d'Orléans is slow, we advise allowing yourself plenty of time to bask in the island's tranquil scenery. You'll want to stroll along the country roads and take time to observe the traditional French and English architecture of the homes. You may also wish to sample homemade preserves or a just-picked apple from a roadside stand.

This tour explores all six of the island's villages. You'll soon notice how each of the small communities recalls a rich, nearly four-century-long history. For instance, the north side of the island is mainly agricultural, because the first farmers settled there on its higher ground, while sailors and river pilots built homes in the island's southern villages near the St. Lawrence River. Also included in this tour are the historic churches of Saint-Jean, Sainte-Famille, and Saint-Pierre—three of the eight oldest in the province.

Start heading west on chemin Royal to **Sainte-Pétronille,** the first village to be settled on the island. Founded in 1648, the community was chosen in 1759 by British General James Wolfe for his headquarters. With 40,000 soldiers and a hundred ships, the English bombarded French-occupied Quebec City and Côte de Beaupré.

During the late-19th century, the English population of Quebec developed Sainte-Pétronille into a resort village. This section is considered by many to be the island's most beautiful area, not only because of the spectacular views it offers of Montmorency Falls and Quebec City, but also for the stylish English villas and exquisitely tended gardens that can be seen from the roadside.

On the left at 20 chemin Royal is the **Plante family farm,** where you can stop to pick apples (in season) or buy some of the island's fresh fruits and vegetables.

❶ Farther along on the right is the **Maison Gourdeau de Beaulieu House** (137 chemin Royal), the island's first home, built in 1648 for Jacques Gourdeau de Beaulieu, who was the first seigneur of Sainte-Pétronille. Today this white building with blue shutters is still owned by his descendants. Over the years, the house has been remodeled so that it incorporates both French and Québécois styles. Its thick walls and dormer windows are characteristic of Brittany architecture, but its sloping bell-shaped roof, designed to protect buildings from large amounts of snow, is typically Québécois.

After you descend an incline, turn right beside the river on the ❷ tiny street called **rue Horatio-Walker,** named after the 19th-century painter known for his landscapes of the island. Walker lived on this street from 1904 until his death in 1938. Around the corner are his home and studio, where exhibits of his paintings are held in the summer. *13 rue Horatio-Walker. Open only upon reservation late-May–Oct. with Beau Temps, Mauvais Temps (tel. 418/828–2275).*

Rue Horatio-Walker was also the place where people crossed the St. Lawrence by an ice path in the winter to go from the island to the mainland before the bridge was built in 1935.

Farther along chemin Royal, at the border of Sainte-Pétronille and Saint-Laurent, look for a large boulder situated in the middle of nowhere. The **roche à Maranda,** named after the owner of the property where the rock was discovered in the 19th century, is one of the oldest rock formations in the world. When the glaciers melted in 9000 BC, the land at the foot of the Laurentian mountains (today the Beaupré coast) was flooded and formed the Sea of Champlain. As the waters receded, the island detached itself from the land, and rocks such as this one were found after

Ile d'Orléans

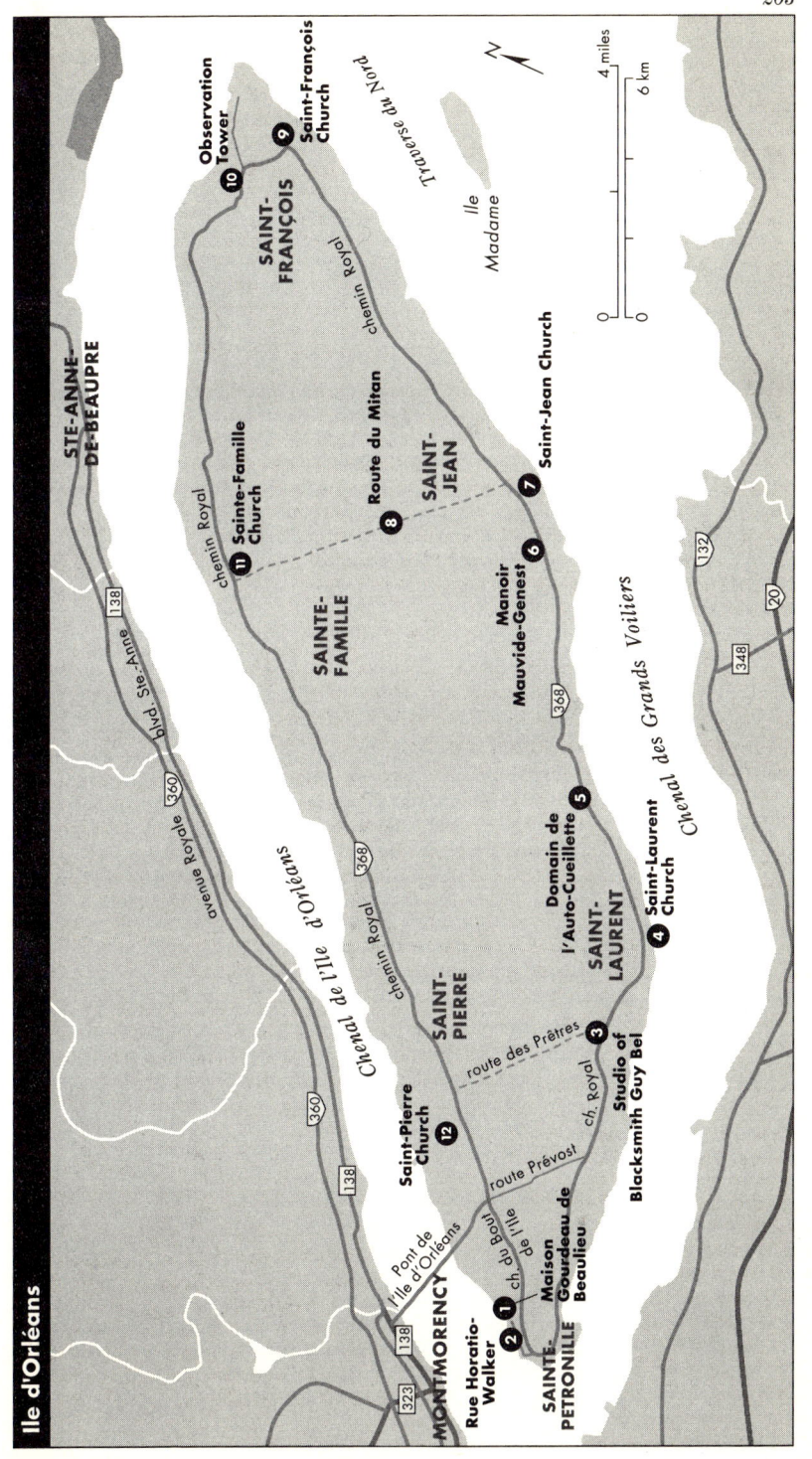

203

they had rolled down with glacial water from the Laurentians onto lower land.

❸ As you approach the village of Saint-Laurent, you'll find the **studio of blacksmith Guy Bel** (2200 chemin Royal, tel. 418/828–9300), a talented and well-known local craftsman who has done the ironwork restoration for Quebec City. Born in Lyons, France, he studied there at the École des Beaux Arts. You can watch him hard at work; his stylish candlesticks, mantels, and other ironworks are for sale.

Saint-Laurent, founded in 1679, is one of the island's maritime villages. Until as late as 1935, residents here used boats as their main means of transportation. Next to the village's marina stands the tall, inspiring **Saint-Laurent Church.** Built in 1860, it was erected on the site of an 18th-century church, which, because of its poor construction, had to be torn down. One of the church's procession chapels is a miniature stone replica of the church; the other wooden chapel houses a gallery where artists display their work in the summer. *1532 chemin Royal. Admission free. Open daily in summer only.*

Generally speaking, crops that grow close to the earth tend to be among the island's best. You won't find better strawberries anywhere else in the province. There are about two dozen spots
❺ where you can pick your own. One of the larger fields, **Domaine de l'Auto-Cueillette** (211 chemin Royal), is located in Saint-Laurent. You can buy an empty basket here for 25¢; a full basket of strawberries will cost about $4.

Time Out **Moulin de Saint-Laurent** is an old stone early-18th-century mill. Dine here in the herb and flower garden out back. Scrumptious snacks such as quiches, bagels, and salads are available at the café-terrace. *754 chemin Royal, tel. 418/829–3888. AE, MC, V. Open May–Oct. 15 for lunch and dinner.*

If you continue on chemin Royal, you'll come to the southern side of the island, **Saint-Jean,** a village whose inhabitants were once river pilots and navigators. Most of its small, homogeneous row homes were built close to the river between 1840 and 1860. Being at sea most of the time, the sailors did not need large homes and plots of land as did the farmers. The island's sudden drop in elevation is most noticeable in Saint-Jean.

❻ Saint-Jean's beautiful Normandy-style manor, **Manoir Mauvide-Genest,** was built in 1734 for Jean Mauvide, surgeon to Louis XV, and his wife, Marie-Anne Genest. Most notable about this house, which still has its original thick walls, ceiling beams, and fireplaces, is the degree to which it has held up over the years, in spite of its being targeted by English guns during the 1759 siege of Quebec City. The home is a pleasure to roam; all rooms are furnished with original antiques from the 18th and 19th centuries. It also offers an exhibit on French architecture and a downstairs restaurant that serves French cuisine. *1451 chemin Royal, tel. 418/829–2630. Open summer only 10–5.*

North of the manor stands **Théâtre Paul-Hébert,** an indoor summer theater founded four years ago by an actor who lives on the island.

❼ At the opposite end of the village, you'll see **Saint-Jean Church,** a massive granite structure with large red doors and a tower-

Ile d'Orléans

ing steeple built in 1749. The church bears a remarkable resemblance to a ship; it is big and round and appears to be sitting right on the St. Lawrence River. Paintings of the patron saints of seamen line the interior walls. The church's cemetery is also intriguing, especially if you can read French. Back in the 18th century, piloting the St. Lawrence was a dangerous profession; the boats could not easily handle the rough currents. The cemetery tombstones recall the tragedies of lost life in these harsh waters. *Admission free. Open daily.*

❽ As you leave Saint-Jean, chemin Royal mounts the incline and crosses **route du Mitan**. In old French, *mitan* means "halfway." This road, dividing the island in half, is the most direct route from north to south. It is also the most beautiful on the island, with acres of tended farmland, apple orchards, and maple groves. If you're running out of time and want to end the tour here, take route du Mitan, which brings you to Saint-Pierre and the bridge to the mainland.

When you come to 17th-century farmhouses separated by sprawling open fields, you know you've reached the island's least-toured and most rustic village, **Saint-François**. At the eastern tip of the island, this community is the one situated farthest from the St. Lawrence River and was originally settled mainly by farmers. Saint-François is also the perfect place to visit one of the island's *cabanes à sucre* (maple-sugaring huts) found along chemin Royal. Stop at a hut for a tasting tour; syrup is gathered from the maple groves and boiled down so that, when poured on ice, it tastes like a delicious toffee. The maple season is late March through April, but these huts stay open year-round.

In Saint-François, the rue du Quai intersects with chemin Royal and leads to the quay where boats depart for excursions around the Île d'Orléans and neighboring islands (*see* Escorted Tours, above).

❾ Straight on chemin Royal is **Saint-François Church,** built in 1734 and one of eight provincial churches dating from the French regime. At the time the English seized Quebec in 1759, General Wolfe knew Saint-François to be among the better strategic points along the St. Lawrence. Consequently, he stationed the British troops here and used the church as a military hospital. In May 1988, a fatal car crash set the church on fire. While it is in the process of being rebuilt, most of the interior treasures were lost.

The **1870 schoolhouse** next to the church is also worth seeing; here you can buy crafts and woven articles by artists living on the island. About a mile down the road is a picnic area with a
❿ wooden **observation tower** situated for perfect viewing of the majestic St. Lawrence at its widest point, 10 times as wide as it is near Quebec City. During the spring and autumn months, you can observe wild Canada geese here.

Heading north on chemin Royal, you'll come to one of the island's earliest villages, Sainte-Famille, which was founded in 1661. The scenery is exquisite here; there are abundant apple orchards and strawberry fields with a view of the Beaupré coast and Mont Sainte-Anne in the distance. But the village also has plenty of man-made historic charm; it has the area's highest concentration of stone houses dating from the French regime.

⑪ Take a quick look at **Sainte-Famille Church,** which, dating back to 1749, was constructed later than some of the others on the island. This impressive structure is the oldest church in the province, and the only one to have three bell towers at the front. Its ceiling was redone in the mid-19th century with elaborate designs in wood and gold. The church also holds a famous painting, *L'Enfant Jésus Voyant La Croix*, done in 1670 by Frère Luc (Father Luc), who was sent from France to decorate churches in the area. *Admission free. Open daily.*

The next village situated on the north side of the island, **Saint-Pierre,** was established a bit later than Sainte-Famille, in 1679. Its church dates back to 1717 and is officially the oldest on the ⑫ island. **Saint-Pierre Church** is no longer open for worship, but it was restored in the 1960s and is open to tourists. Many of its original components are still intact, such as benches with compartments below, where hot bricks and stones were placed to keep people warm during winter services. *1243 chemin Royal. Admission free. Open daily.*

Because Saint-Pierre is situated on a plateau with the island's most fertile land, the village has long been the center of traditional farming industries. The best products grown here are potatoes, asparagus, and corn, and the many dairy farms have given the village a renowned reputation for butter and other dairy products. At 2370 chemin Royal is the former home of Felix Leclerc, one of the many artists that have made the island their home. Leclerc, the father of Québécois folksinging, lived here until he died in August 1988.

If you continue west on chemin Royal, just up ahead is the bridge back to the mainland and Route 440.

Dining and Lodging

For price categories, *see* Quebec City Dining and Lodging in Chapter 5.

Dining **La Goéliche.** Although this rustic inn has a romantic dining
Very Expensive room with windows overlooking the St. Lawrence River and a view of Quebec City, the main reason to dine here is the good food. The first rule of the kitchen is that only the freshest ingredients from the island's farms can be used. The menu is classic French and depends upon the fruits and vegetables in season. Lunch is a more moderately priced à la carte selection of salads, quiches, and omelets. The evening's *menu de dégustation* feature specialties such as quail with red vermouth and chicken with pistachio mousseline. The desserts, such as maple syrup mousse with strawberry syrup, have a regional flavor. *22 rue du Quai, Sainte-Pétronille, tel. 418/828–2248. Reservations advised. Dress: casual but neat. AE, DC, MC, V. Open lunch and dinner; in winter, dinner only.*

Expensive **L'Atre.** After you park your car, you take a horse-drawn carriage to a 17th-century Normandy-style house furnished with Québécois pine antiques. True to the establishment's name, which means "hearth," all the traditional dishes are cooked and served from a fireplace. The menu emphasizes hearty fare, such as beef Bourguignon and *tourtière* (a meat pie) and maple-sugar pie for dessert. *4403 chemin Royal, Sainte-Famille, tel. 418/829–2474. Reservations required. Dress: casual but neat. AE, MC, V. Closed Oct.–mid-May.*

Manoir Mauvide-Genest. The dining room in one of the island's most beautiful and well-maintained homes (*see* Exploring, above) serves both elegant and home-style French cuisine. Specialties include such dishes as snails in Armagnac; the chef here excels at both traditional fowl dishes such as *confit de canard* (duck confit) and more exotic creations such as quail with a sweet white wine sauce. *1451 chemin Royal, Saint-Jean, tel. 418/829-2630. Reservations advised. Dress: casual but neat. MC, V. Open mid-May–Oct.*

Lodging **Auberge le Chaumonot.** This medium-size hotel in rural Saint-
Moderate François is right near the St. Lawrence River at its widest point. The inn's large bay windows capitalize on the view of the river and neighboring islands, but otherwise the decor is uninspired, with simple wood furniture of the island. The service here is efficient and friendly. The restaurant serves Continental cuisine, with *table d'hôte* and à la carte menus. *425 chemin Royal, Saint-François, G0A 4C0, 418/829-2735. 8 rooms with private bath. Facility: outdoor swimming pool. Restaurant. MC, V. Open summer only.*

La Goéliche. This 1890 Victorian country inn stands just steps away from the St. Lawrence River in the village of Sainte-Pétronille. Québécois antiques decorate light and spacious rooms with their original wood floors. Rooms are on the second and third floors, and half of them look out across the river to Quebec City. The rooms have no television, but they do have phones. *22 rue du Quai, Sainte-Pétronille, G0A 4C0, tel. 418/828-2248. 18 rooms with private bath. Facilities: 2 restaurants. AE, DC, MC, V.*

You can get to know the island by staying at one of its 30 bed-and-breakfasts. Reservations are necessary. Price for a room, double occupancy, runs about $45. **Beau Temps, Mauvais Temps** (tel. 418/828-2275) is a referral service for these accommodations.

French Vocabulary

Words and Phrases

	English	*French*	*Pronunciation*
Basics	Yes/no	Oui/non	wee/no
	Please	S'il vous plait	seel voo play
	Thank you (very much)	Merci (beaucoup)	mare-**see** (boh-**koo**)
	You're welcome	De rien	deh ree-**en**
	That's all right	Il n'y a pas de quoi	eel nee ah pah deh kwah
	Excuse me, sorry	Pardon	pahr-**doan**
	Sorry!	Désolé(e)	day-zoh-**lay**
	Good morning/afternoon	Bonjour	bone-**joor**
	Good evening	Bonsoir	Bone-**swar**
	Goodbye	Au revoir	o ruh-**vwar**
	Mr.(Sir)/Mrs.(Ma'am)/ Miss	Monsieur/madame/ mademoiselle	meh-see-**ur**/mah-**dahm** / mad-mwah-**zel**
	Pleased to meet you	Enchanté(e)	on-shahn-**tay**
	How are you?	Comment allez-vous?	ko-men-tahl-ay-**voo**
	Very well, thanks	Très bien, merci	tray bee-**en**, mare-**see**
	And you?	Et vous?	ay voo?
Numbers	one	un	un
	two	deux	dew
	three	trois	twa
	four	quatre	**cat**-ruh
	five	cinq	sank
	six	six	seess
	seven	sept	set
	eight	huit	wheat
	nine	neuf	nuf
	ten	dix	deess
	eleven	onze	owns
	twelve	douze	dues
	thirteen	treize	trays
	fourteen	quatorze	ka-torz
	fifteen	quinze	cans
	sixteen	seize	sez
	seventeen	dix-sept	deess-**set**
	eighteen	dix-huit	deess-**wheat**
	nineteen	dix-neuf	deess-**nuf**
	twenty	vingt	vant
	twenty-one	vingt-et-un	vant-ay-**un**
	thirty	trente	trahnt
	forty	quarante	ka-**rahnt**
	fifty	cinquante	sang-**kahnt**
	sixty	soixante	swa-**sahnt**
	seventy	soixante-dix	swa-sahnt-**deess**
	eighty	quatre-vingts	cat-ruh-**vant**

French Vocabulary

	ninety	quatre-vingt-dix	cat-ruh-vant-**deess**
	one hundred	cent	sahnt
	one thousand	mille	meel

Colors			
	black	noir	nwar
	blue	bleu	blu
	brown	brun	brun
	green	vert	vair
	orange	orange	o-**ranj**
	pink	rose	rose
	red	rouge	rouge
	violet	violette	vee-o-**let**
	white	blanc	blahnk
	yellow	jaune	jone

Days of the Week			
	Sunday	dimanche	dee-**mahnsh**
	Monday	lundi	lewn-**dee**
	Tuesday	mardi	mar-**dee**
	Wednesday	mercredi	mare-kruh-**dee**
	Thursday	jeudi	juh-**dee**
	Friday	vendredi	van-dra-**dee**
	Saturday	samedi	sam-**dee**

Months			
	January	janvier	jan-**vyay**
	February	février	feh-vree-**ay**
	March	mars	mars
	April	avril	a-**vreel**
	May	mai	may
	June	juin	jwan
	July	juillet	jwee-**ay**
	August	août	oot
	September	septembre	sep-**tahm**-bruh
	October	octobre	oak-**toe**-bruh
	November	novembre	no-**vahm**-bruh
	December	décembre	day-**sahm**-bruh

Useful Phrases			
	Do you speak English?	Parlez-vous anglais?	par-lay vooz ahng-**glay**
	I don't speak French	Je ne parle pas français	jeh nuh parl pah fraun-**say**
	I don't understand	Je ne comprends pas	jeh nuh kohm-prahn **pah**
	I understand	Je comprends	jeh kohm-**prahn**
	I don't know	Je ne sais pas	jeh nuh say **pah**
	I'm American/British	Je suis américain/anglais	jeh sweez a-may-ree-**can**/ahng-**glay**
	What's your name?	Comment vous appelez-vous?	ko-mahn voo za-pel-ay-**voo**
	My name is . . .	Je m'appelle . . .	jeh muh-**pel** . . .
	What time is it?	Quelle heure est-il?	kel ur et-**il**
	How?	Comment?	ko-**mahn**

	When?	Quand?	kahnd
	How much is it?	C'est combien?	say comb-bee-**en**
	It's expensive/cheap	C'est cher/pas cher	say sher/pa sher
	A little/a lot	Un peu/beaucoup	un puh/bo-**koo**
	More/less	Plus/moins	ploo/mwa
	Enough/too (much)	Assez/trop	a-**say**/tro
	I am ill/sick	Je suis malade	jeh swee ma-**lahd**
	Please call a doctor	Appelez un docteur	a-pe-lay un dohk-**tore**
	Help!	Au secours!	o say-**koor**
	Stop!	Arrêtez!	a-ruh-**tay**
	Fire!	Au feu!	o fuw
	Caution!/Look out!	Attention!	a-tahn-see-**own**
Dining Out	A bottle of . . .	une bouteille de . . .	ewn boo-**tay** deh
	A cup of . . .	une tasse de . . .	ewn tass deh
	A glass of . . .	un verre de . . .	un vair deh
	Ashtray	un cendrier	un sahn-dree-**ay**
	Bill/check	l'addition	la-dee-see-**own**
	Bread	du pain	due pan
	Breakfast	le petit déjeuner	leh pet-**ee** day-zhu-**nay**
	Butter	du beurre	due bur
	Cheers!	A votre santé!	ah vo-truh sahn-**tay**
	Cocktail/aperitif	un apéritif	un ah-pay-ree-**teef**
	Dinner	le dîner	leh dee-**nay**
	Dish of the day	le plat du jour	leh pla do **zhoor**
	Enjoy!	Bon appétit!	bone a-pay-**tee**
	Fixed-price menu	le menu	leh may-**new**
	Fork	une fourchette	ewn four-**shet**
	I am diabetic	Je suis diabétique	jeh swee-dee-ah-**bay-teek**
	I am on a diet	Je suis au régime	jeh sweez o ray-**jeem**
	I am vegetarian	Je suis végétarien (ne)	jeh swee vay-jay-ta-ree-**en**
	I cannot eat . . .	Je ne peux pas manger de . . .	jeh nuh puh pah mahn-**jay** deh
	I'd like to order	Je voudrais commander	jeh voo-**dray** ko-mahn-**day**

French Vocabulary

I'd like . . .	Je voudrais . . .	jeh voo-**dray**
I'm hungry/thirsty	J'ai faim/soif	jay fam/swahf
Is service/the tip included?	Est-ce que le service est compris?	ess keh leh sair-veess ay comb-**pree**
It's good/bad	C'est bon/mauvais	say bon/mo-**vay**
It's hot/cold	C'est chaud/froid	say sho/frwah
Knife	un couteau	un koo-**toe**
Lunch	le déjeuner	leh day-juh-**nay**
Menu	la carte	la cart
Napkin	une serviette	ewn sair-vee-**et**
Pepper	du poivre	due **pwah**-vruh
Plate	une assiette	ewn a-see-**et**
Please give me . . .	Donnez-moi . . .	doe-nay-**mwah**
Salt	du sel	dew sell
Spoon	une cuillère	ewn kwee-**air**
Sugar	du sucre	due **sook**-ruh
Waiter!/Waitress!	Monsieur!/Mademoiselle!	meh-see-**ur**/mad-mwah-**zel**
Wine list	la carte des vins	la cart day **van**

Index

Abbaye cistercienne d'Oka (abbey), *128*
Abbaye St-Benoit-du-Luc (abbey), *143*
Abercrombie and Fitch (shop), *79*
Agora (theater), *168*, *195*
Agora Dance Theatre, *117*
Air du Temps, L' (jazz club), *56*, *118–119*
Airports, *42*, *153*
Air Show, *7*
Air travel, *12–13*, *17–18*, *20*, *42–43*, *153*
Alain Giroux (boutique), *79*
À la Petit Table (restaurant), *183*
À la Table de Serge Bruyère (restaurant), *182–183*
Aldred Building, *54*
Alexander (shop), *75*
Alfred Sung (shop), *78*
Alimentation Petit-Cartier (food mall), *174*, *177*
Alpine Inn, *134*
Ancien Palais de Justice, *157*, *160*
André, Brother, *72–73*
André Antiques, *82*
Anima G (office complex), *175*
Antiques shops, *83*, *168*, *178*. See also specific antiques shops
Antiquités Ambiance & Discernement, *83*
Antiquités Je Me Souviens, *84*
Antiquités Marielle Moquin and Michelle Parent, *83*
Après L'Eden (shop), *84*
Après-Vous Pub, *131*

Apsara, L' (restaurant), *187*
Aquarium de Montréal, *71*, *73*
Aquarium du Québec, *175–176*
Aquascutum of London (shop), *78*, *79*
Aquatic Center, *70*
Aquatic Park, *131*
Artes (art gallery), *85*
Art galleries, *178*. See also specific art galleries
Arthur's Café Baroque, *111*, *118*
Artisans du Meuble Québecois, Les (shop), *82*
Arts, the, *116–118*, *146–147*, *193–195*
Arts and Music Sutton, *147*
Art Select (art gallery), *84*
Arts Sutton, *147*
Assemblée Nationale, L', *172*
Association du Festival du Lac Massawippi, L', *147*
Astor, John Jacob, *38*
Astral, L' (restaurant), *186*, *190*
Atelier Bernard Chaudron, Inc. (shop), *135*
Atout Fringues (shop), *85*
Atre, L' (restaurant), *206*
Auberge de Jeunesse Internationale de Montréal (hostel), *115*
Auberge de l'Etoile (restaurant), *145*
Auberge du Coq de Montagne (inn), *138*
Auberge du Lac des Sables (inn), *136*

Auberge du Quartier, L' (inn), *192*
Auberge Estrimont (hotel), *146*
Auberge Hatley (inn and restaurant), *139*, *142*, *145*
Auberge La Paimpolaise (inn), *146*
Auberge Le Château (inn), *136–137*
Auberge le Chaumonot (hotel), *207*
Auberge Le Refuge (inn), *146*
Auberge le Vieux St. Gabriel (restaurant), *96*
Auberge Mont Gabriel (resort), *134*
Auberge Saint-Denis (inn and restaurant), *130–131*
Auberge Saint-Louis, L' (hotel), *192*
Auberge Schweizer (lodge), *146*
Auberge Swiss Inn, *132*
Auberge Villa Bellevue (inn), *137*
Au Coton (shop), *79*
Audet, Louis-N., *200*
Auteuil, Le d' (blues and jazz bar), *195*
Automatic teller machines (ATMs), *9–10*
Aux Anciens Canadiens (restaurant), *186*
Aux Berges de l'Aurore (bed-and-breakfast), *146*
Aux Multiples Collections (art gallery), *178*
Avenue Books (bookstore), *86*
Avenue Cartier, *174*
Avenue du Parc, *68*
Avenue Laurier, *68*

Avenue Ste-Geneviève, *161*
Ayer's Cliff (town), *144*

Baby-sitters, *21*
Baccarat Comfort Inn, Le, *113–114*
Bagatelle (restaurant), *102*
Bagel Factory, *104*
Bagel Place, *104*
Bagels, *68–69*, *104*
Bagel Shop, *69*, *104*
Baie, La (department store, Montreal), *58*, *75*, *80*
Baie, La (department store, Quebec City), *177*
Bailiff, Claude, *200*
Baillargé, Charles, *165*, *175*
Baillargé, François, *200*
Ballets Classiques de Montréal, *117*
Ballets Eddy Toussaint, Les, *117*
Ballets Jazz de Montréal, Les, *117*
Bally (shop), *78*, *80*
Banking hours, *46*, *156*
Bank of Montreal, *52*
Bars, *195*. See also specific bars
Baseball, *88*
Basilières (antiques shop), *83*
Basilique Notre-Dame-de-Québec (church), *163*
Basilique Sainte-Anne-de-Beaupré (church), *199–200*
Basses Laurentides, Les (mountain range), *126*, *128–129*. See also Laurentides, Les
Battlefields Park, *179*, *180*, *181*
Beaulieu, Jacques Gourdeau de, *202*

212

Index

Beau Rivage, Le (restaurant), *114*
Beauty's (restaurant), *68*
Beaver Club (restaurant), *60, 94, 111*
Bed and breakfast à Montréal, *115*
Bed and Breakfast-Bonjour Québec, *193*
Bed and Breakfast in Old Quebec, *193*
Bed-and-breakfasts, *106, 115–116, 193, 207.* See also specific bed-and-breakfasts
Bel, Guy, *204*
Bens (restaurant), *61, 91*
Benson & Hedges International Fireworks Competition, *5*
Bernard Primeau's Trio, *119*
Bernhardt, Sarah, *65, 119*
Berri-UQAM metro stop, *65*
Bibliothèque Gabrielle-Roy (library), *194*
Bibliothèque nationale du Québec (library), *65*
Bicycling, *86, 88, 142, 179*
Biddle, Charles, *119*
Biddle's (jazz club), *119*
Bijou, Le (jazz club), *119*
Bijouterie (shop), *81*
Bikini Village (shop), *79*
Binerie Mont-Royal, La (restaurant), *101*
Birger Christensen at Holt Renfrew (furrier), *75, 81*
Birks Jewellers, *75*
Bishop Street, *61*
Bishop's University, *145*
Blacksmiths, *204*
Blanc d'Ivoire (shop), *179*
Blues (music), *195*

Boating, *179.* See also Boat trips; Ferries; Sailing
Boat trips, *47, 156–157.* See also Boating; Ferries; Sailing
Bocca d'Oro (restaurant), *99*
Bolducs (sugar hut), *144*
Bombardier, Joseph-Armand, *139*
Bonaventure (hotel), *106, 107*
Bonet, Jordi, *105, 174*
Books about Montreal, *23*
Books about Quebec City, *24*
Bookstores, *46, 155, 178.* See also specific bookstores
Botanical Garden, *70*
Boulangerie La Mère-Michele (shop), *174*
Boulevard René Lévesque, *40*
Boulevard St-Laurent, *67*
Bouquet, Le (restaurant), *112*
Bourassa, Robert, *50*
Bourgeau, Victor, *52, 60*
Bourgeoys, Marguerite de, *55*
Boutique Amelia, *178*
Boutique Confort, *85*
Boutiques. See specific boutiques
Brasserie des Fortifications (restaurant), *56*
Breakfast Room (restaurant), *114*
Brébeuf, Jean de, *176*
Brin d'Elle, Un (boutique), *84*
Brioche Lyonnaise, La (restaurant), *104*
Brise discotheque, La, *143*
Briskets (restaurant), *91*
Brisson & Brisson (shop), *81*
British travelers, tips for, *12–13*

Broadway Theatre, *118*
Bromont (town), *142, 144*
Brossard, Georges, *70*
Brown's (shop), *79*
Bruestle (shop), *81*
Bujold, Michel, *67*
Bulau, Horst, *137*
Burne-Jones, Edward, *62*
Burns, Robert, *61*
Business, Le (disco), *119*
Bus tours, *156*
Bus travel, *43, 44–45, 124, 139, 153, 154–155*
By, John, *169*
By American (shop), *79*
By George (shop), *85*

Cabs, *45, 153, 155*
Cacharel (shop), *85*
Cache-Cache (shop), *85*
Cactus (shop), *79*
Café Canadien, Le, *187, 189*
Café Conc, Le, *118*
Café de la Paix, *183*
Café de Paris, Le, *63, 94–95, 112*
Café du Musée, *62*
Café Fleuri, Le, *110*
Café Krieghoff, *174*
Café Loft, *167*
Café Taste-Vin, *162*
Cage aux Sports, La (singles bar), *119–120*
Calèches (horse-drawn carriages), *47, 52, 72, 152, 156*
Callières, Louis-Hector de, *163*
Cambodian restaurants, *187.* See also specific restaurants
Canadian Guild of Crafts, *82*
Caplan Duval (shop), *75*
Caroline B. (shop), *79*
Car racing, *138*

Car rentals, *18*
Carré St.-Louis (square), *41*
Carriage House (inn), *132*
Cartier (shop), *81–82*
Cartier, George-Étienne, *37, 55, 164, 172*
Cartier, Jacques, *38, 149, 176, 198, 200*
Cartier-Brébeuf Park, *179, 180*
Car travel, *43, 124, 139, 153–154, 198, 201*
Casavant family, *52*
Cash machines, *9–10*
Casse-Crêpe Breton (restaurant), *188*
Castillon, Le (restaurant), *107*
Cathay Restaurant, *90–91*
Cavalier du Moulin (park), *161*
Cemi (shop), *79*
Centaur Theatre, *51, 117*
Centennial Theatre and Consolidated-Bathurst Theatre, *147*
Central, Le (bar), *195*
Centre Canadien d'Architecture, Le, *61–62, 73*
Centre de Ceramique de Bonsecours, *82*
Centre de Sante Eastman (resort), *145*
Centre d'exposition du Vieux-Palais, *129*
Centre d'interprétation historique de Terrebonne Museum, *126*
Centre Eaton (shopping complex), *79*
Centre International de Séjour (hostel), *193*
Centre Marie-de-l'Incarnation, *162*
Centre Sheraton, Le (restaurant), *107, 110*

Index

Chacok (shop), *85*
Chalet Suisse (restaurant), *187*
Champlain, Le (restaurant), *189*
Champlain, Samuel de, *38, 149, 160, 163, 166, 172*
Champs de Mars (former military parade ground), *54*
Chantecler, Le (hotel), *132*
Chapelle Bon-Pasteur (chapel), *175*
Chapelle des Ursulines (chapel), *162*
Chapelle Extérieure (chapel), *164*
Charles Baillargé, Le (restaurant), *190*
Chartreuse, La (restaurant), *103*
Château, Le (boutique), *80, 84–85*
Château Bonne Entente (resort), *189*
Château Bromont Resort Spa, Le, *144–145*
Château de la Terrasse (hotel), *191*
Château de Pierre, Le (hotel), *191*
Château Frontenac (hotel), *160, 187, 189*
Château Hélène de Champlain (restaurant), *70*
Château Ramezay (museum), *55*
Château Versailles (restaurant), *106, 114*
Chatel Vienna (restaurant), *136*
Chaudière, Pierre, *199*
Chemin de la Croix (way of the cross), *200*
Chemin du Roi, Le (panoramic route), *198*
Chénier, Jean-Olivier, *128*
Chevalier, Jean-Baptiste, *166*
Chez Antoine (restaurant), *113*
Chez Dagobert (disco), *195*
Chez Delmo (restaurant), *102–103*
Chez Girard (restaurant), *136*
Chez Son Père (folk music bar), *195*
Chez Temporel (restaurant), *188*
Children, traveling with, *20–21, 73–74, 132, 175–176*
Chinatown, *64*
Chinese restaurants, *90–91, 112*. See also specific restaurants
Chirac, Jacques, *167*
Chocolate shops, *104*
Chocolat Heyez (restaurant), *104*
Chomedey, Paul de, *38, 52, 56*
Christ Church Cathedral, *58*
Churches, *72–73*. See also specific churches
Churchill, Winston, *149*
Church of St. Andrew and St. Paul, *62*
Cinéma de Paris, *118, 194*
Cinéma Place Charest, *194*
Cinéma Place Québec, *194*
Cinémathèque Québécoise, *65, 118*
Cinq Saisons (shop), *86*
Citadelle (citadel), *171*
Citadelle, La (hotel), *107*
City of Québec Day, *7*
City walls, outside the (neighborhood), *169–175*
map of, *170*
Classic Bookshop, *178*
Classique Cycliste de Montréal, La (competition), *5, 88*
Clef des Champs, La (restaurant), *134*
Climate, *3–4*
Clothing for the trip, *7*
Clothing stores, *178*. See also specific clothing stores
Club Azur (condo complex), *145*
Club de Chasse and Pêche du Lac Beauregard (inn), *125*
Club des Guides (inn), *125*
Club Jazz 2080, *119*
Club Monaco (boutique), *78*
Club Soda (rock club), *119*
Coach House Antiques, *86*
Cochon Dingue, Le (restaurant), *188*
Colborne, John, *128*
Colisée de Québec, *182, 194*
Collection Lazuli (shop), *179*
Commemorative Chapel, *200*
Complexe Desjardins (hotel, mall, office, and shopping complex), *41, 64, 80*
Complexe Guy-Favreau (office complex), *64*
Concerts. See Music
Connaisseur Antiques, *86*
Consulates, *46, 155, 161*
Continental restaurants, *183*. See also specific restaurants
Cormier, Ernest, *50*
Costs of trip, *10*
Côte de Beaupré (meadow), *198–200*
Cours Mont-Royal, Les (shopping complex), *61, 78*
Couvent des Ursulines (convent), *161*
Craft shops, *178*. See also specific craft shops
Créateurs associés, Les (art gallery and boutique), *135*
Credit cards, *8, 9, 10, 24*
Crescent Street, *61, 89*
Cricca, La (boutique), *78*
Crisma Toys, *86*
Croissanterie, La (restaurant), *131*
Croissant Plus (restaurant), *164*
Cuisine, *14–15*. See also Restaurants; specific restaurants
Curling, *86*
Customs, *11, 12, 75, 78*
Cuttle's Tremblant Club (condo complex and hotel), *137–138*

Dack (shop), *80*
Dalmy's (shop), *79*
Dance, *117–118, 194*
Dancing, Le (disco), *195*
Danielle J. Malynowsky Inc. (antiques shop), *83*
Daulier, André, *126*
Dauphine Redoubt (former barracks), *169*
David M. Stewart Museum, *71, 72*
David S. Brown Antique, *81*
Debarque, Le (disco), *142*
Deco-Ustentile (shop), *174*
Défi sur Neige (festival), *133*
Déjà Vu (rock club), *119*
De La Muse (restaurant), *114*
Delicatessens, *67–68, 91, 94, 131*. See also specific delicatessens
Delta Montreal (hotel), *112*
Deltaplaning, *125–126*
Delta St-Sauveur (hotel), *131*

Index

Dentists, 46, 155
Department stores, 80–82, 177. See also specific department stores
Desmarais & Robitaille (shop), 82
Desserte, La (restaurant), 103–104
Deuxièmement (antiques shop), 83
Diaghilev (shop), 85
Diamond Club (disco), 119
Diligence, La (dinner theater), 118
Dinner theaters, 118. See also Theaters; specific dinner theaters
Disabled travelers, 21–22
Discos, 119, 195. See also specific discos
Dixversions (shop), 84
Doctors, 15, 46, 201
Domaine de l'Auto-Cueillette (strawberry field), 204
Domaine Howard (historic society), 143
Dominion Gallery, 81
Dominion Square. See Dorchester Square
Dominion Square Building, 40
Dorchester Boulevard. See Boulevard René Lévesque
Dorchester Square, 40, 60–61
Doré, Jean, 37
Dorval International Airport, 42
Double Hook (bookstore), 86
Double Vé (shop), 85
Downtown B & B Network, 115–116
Downtown Montreal, 50, 57–64, 78–82
map of, 59
Dow Planetarium, 73
Drapeau, Jean, 37, 70
Drivers' licenses, 18

Drugs, prescription, 15
Drugstores, 46, 155
Drummondville World Folklore Festival, 5
Duberger, Jean-Baptiste, 169
Du Côté de Chez Swann (singles bar), 120
Duluth Street, 68
Dunn's Famous Smoked Meat Shoppes and Delis, 131
Duties. See Customs
Dutoit, Charles, 41, 63, 116
Duty-free, 11. See also Customs
Dynastie de Ming (restaurant), 112

Eastern Townships. See Estrie, L'
Eastman (town), 145
Eaton (department store), 58, 80
Eaton le 9e (restaurant), 58
Eau à la Bouche, L' (hotel and restaurant), 133
Échaudée, L' (restaurant), 187–188
Edifice Price (building), 162–163
Église Notre-Dame-des-Victoires (church), 166
1870 schoolhouse, 205
Elca London Gallery, 81
Electric current, 7, 13
Elena Lee-Verre d'Art (art gallery), 81
Emergencies, 46, 155, 201
Emprise at Hôtel Clarendon, L' (jazz bar), 195
Equestre Bar, L', 144
Erabliere Robert Lauzier (sugar hut), 144
Erskine and American United Church, 62
Escalier Casse-cou (stairway), 165
Escalier Frontenac (stairway), 165
Estérel (town), 135
Estrie, L' (Eastern Townships), 122, 138–147
map of, 141
Étang des Moulins, L' (restaurant), 104–105
Excursions, 122–147, 198–207
Expo-Québec, 7
Expotec (exhibition), 5, 55, 73
Express, L' (restaurant), 96–97

Fairmount Avenue, 68
Fairmount Bagel Factory, 68–69
Fall Fest, 7
Faubourg Ste-Catherine (shopping complex), 78
Ferme avicole d'Oka (poultry farm), 128
Ferre (shop), 78
Ferries, 156, 167. See also Boating; Boat trips; Sailing
Ferroni (antiques shop), 82
Festin du Gouverneur, Le (dinner theater), 72, 118
Festival de Montgolfière du Haut-Richelieu Hot Air Balloon Festival and North American Championships, 6
Festival Gastronomique, 140
Festival Internationale de Nouvelle Danse, 6, 117–118
Festival of Colours, 7
Festivals and seasonal events, 4–7. See also specific festivals and seasonal events
Fête des Neiges, La (festival), 4
Fête National des Québécois, La (festival), 5
Filles du Roy, Les (restaurant), 55, 100–101
Film, traveling with, 13
Films, 4, 6, 7, 41, 118, 194. See also specific festivals and theaters
Fishing, 87, 125, 179–180
Fitness centers. See Health clubs
Flea markets, 83, 177–178. See also specific flea markets
Folk music, 195, 196
Food, 14–15. See also Restaurants; specific restaurants
Food markets, 177
Foolhouse Theatre Company, 118
Formula 2000 "Jim Russell Championships," 138
Foufounes Electriques (rock club), 119
Fox, Terry, 6
Foyer, Le (folk and rock club), 196
France-Martin (art gallery), 80
François and Hélène Cote (boutique), 178
François Villon (shop), 79
Franklin Silverstone (art gallery), 81
Free activities, 73, 175
French-Canadian restaurants, 100–101, 105, 144, 186, 199, 206. See also specific restaurants
French restaurants, 56, 94–97, 104, 114, 133–134, 182–183, 186–187, 189, 206,

Index

French restaurants (continued) 207. *See also specific restaurants*
Friday's (singles bar), *119*
Frontenac, Governor, *126, 149, 160, 163*
Fuller, Buckminster, *72*
Funicular, *70*
Furriers, *75, 178–179. See also specific furriers*

Galerie Barbara Silverberg, *82*
Galerie Christin, *178*
Galerie Daniel, *82*
Galerie D'Art Eskimau, *81*
Galerie du Musée du Québec, *178*
Galerie Esperanza, *82*
Galerie Madeleine Lacerte, *178*
Galerie St-Paul, *82*
Galerie Samuel Lallouz, *81*
Galleries 2001 (office and shopping complex), *58*
Gambrinus (restaurant), *183*
Gamineries, Les (shop), *81*
Gardens, *70. See also specific gardens*
Gare Centrale (railway station), *60*
Gare du Palais (railway station), *160*
Gaspé, Philippe-Aubert de, *186*
Gazebo (shop), *79*
Genest, Marie-Anne, *204*
George-Étienne Cartier Museum, *55*
George III (king of England), *162*
Gibbys (restaurant), *56*
Gift shops, *179. See also specific gift shops*
Gigi (shop), *78*

Gillis, Margie, *117*
Giorgio Armani (boutique), *81*
Gisela's (antiques shop), *83*
Goéliche, La (inn and restaurant), *206, 207*
Golden Square Mile (neighborhood), *39, 62*
Golf, *86, 132, 180*
Graffiti, Le (restaurant), *186*
Graham, Laurie, *137*
Granby (town), *140*
Grand Café, Le (jazz club), *119*
Grande Allée (street), *172*
Grande Hermine (ship), *176*
Grand Hôtel, Le, *112–113*
Grand Prix Bar, *120*
Grand Prix Cyclistes, Le, *6, 88*
Grand Prix Labatt snowmobile race, *142*
Grands Ballets Canadiens, Les, *41, 117*
Grand Théâtre de Québec, *152, 174, 194*
Gray Rocks Inn, *122–123, 136–137*
Greek restaurants, *68, 97. See also specific restaurants*
Greene Avenue, *85–86*
Greenwich, Sonny, *119*
Griffe (shop), *85*
Grosvenor (shop), *75*
Gucci (boutique), *81*
Guided tours, *47, 86, 156–157, 198, 201*
Guilde Graphique, La (art gallery), *82*
Guy Laroche (shop), *85*

Halles, Les (restaurant), *95*
Hamburger restaurants, *98*
Handicapped travelers, *21–22*

Harness racing, *89, 182*
Hautes Laurentides, Les (mountain range), *129–138. See also Laurentides, Les*
Health clubs, *86–87, 180, 190. See also specific health clubs*
Herbert, Louis, *164*
Herbier de Jouvence, L' (shop), *178*
Héritage Antiquités, L', *178*
Heritage House (shop), *79*
Hiking, *180*
Hilton International Québec, *180, 189–190*
Hippodrome de Québec, *182*
History of Montreal, *37–40, 51, 52, 56, 65*
History of Quebec City, *149, 152, 157, 160*
"Hiver en Nord, L'" (festival), *136*
HMV Canada (shop), *79*
Hockey, *6, 89, 182*
Holiday Inn Crowne Plaza, *113*
Holiday Inn Le Richelieu, *113*
Holt Renfrew (department store, Montreal), *62, 79, 80–81*
Holt Renfrew (department store, Quebec City), *177*
Holy Trinity Anglican Cathedral, *162*
Home exchanges, *20*
Horseback riding, *87*
Horse-drawn carriages. *See Calèches*
Horse racing, *89, 182*
Hospitals, *155*
Hostels, *106, 115, 193. See also specific hostels*
Hôtel and Restaurant de l'Institut, *65, 113*
Hôtel Château

Champlain, *40, 60, 110*
Hôtel Château Laurier, *191–192*
Hôtel Clarendon, *162, 190*
Hotel Courtyard (restaurant), *112*
Hôtel de la Montagne, *61, 106, 110*
Hôtel des Gouverneurs, *180, 190*
Hôtel de Ville (city hall), *54*
Hôtel-Dieu Hospital, *163*
Hôtel du Vieux Québec, L', *191*
Hôtel la Sapinière, *135*
Hotel Loews Le Concorde, *186, 190*
Hôtel Maison Sainte-Ursule, *192–193*
Hôtel Maritime, *114*
Hôtel Quatre Saisons, *63*
Hotels, *106–115, 144–146, 188–193. See also specific hotels* maps of, *108–109, 184–185*
Hunting, *87, 125, 179*

Ice-skating, *87, 180–181*
Île d'Orléans (island), *200–206* map of, *203*
Île Notre-Dame (island), *72*
Île Ste-Hélène (park), *70*
Il était une fois (restaurant), *98*
Images du Futur (exhibition), *5, 55, 73*
IMAX Super Cinema, *55, 73*
Implanthéâtre, *194*
Impromptu, L' (bar), *118*
Indian restaurants, *98. See also specific restaurants*

Index

Inns, *124–125. See also specific inns*
Inoculations, *15*
Insectarium, *70, 73*
Insurance, *12, 15–17*
International Children's Folklore Festival, *6–7*
International Festival of Films on Art, *4*
International Festival of Young Cinema, *4*
International Jazz Festival (Montreal), *5, 41*
International Jazz Festival (Quebec City), *6*
Italian restaurants, *98–99, 187, 188. See also specific restaurants*

J. B. Laliberté (department store), *179*
Jacnel (shop), *79*
Jacob (shop), *79*
Jaeger (boutique), *75*
Japanese Garden, *70*
Japanese restaurants, *99–100. See also specific restaurants*
Jardin des Gouverneurs, *161*
Jardin Zoologique de Granby, *140*
Jardin Zoologique du Québec, *176*
Jazz, *5, 6, 41, 118–119, 195*
Jewelry stores, *179. See also specific jewelry stores*
Jogging, *87, 180*
Johannsen, "Jackrabbit" Herman Smith, *123*
Jolliet, Louis, *165*
Jones, Oliver, *119*
Jonquière, Governor, *163*
Jos Robitaille (furrier), *179*
Just For Laughs Festival, *5*

Katsura (restaurant), *99–100*
Keg, Le (singles bar), *120*
Kosher restaurants, *68. See also specific restaurants*
Krieghoff, Cornelius, *174*
Krieghoff House, *173–174*

Labelle, Antoine, *129*
Labouret, Auguste, *199*
Lac Beauport (lake), *179, 181*
Lac Brome (town), *146*
Lac Brome Theatre, *146*
Lachine Canal, *86*
Lachine Rapids, *51*
Lac Massawippi (town), *147*
Lacoste (shop), *79*
Lacroix, Wilfrid, *173*
Lac St-Joseph (lake), *179*
Lac Tremblant (lake), *137*
Lafontaine (park), *69*
LaLaLa Human Steps (dance company), *117*
Lalla Fucci (shop), *79*
Lambert, Phyllis, *61, 74*
Lanaudiere Summer Festival, *5*
Lancia Uomo (shop), *78*
Language, *13–14*
LaRonde Amusement Park, *70–71, 73*
Latin Quarter (neighborhood, Montreal), *40, 64, 65*
Latin Quarter (neighborhood, Quebec City), *163, 188*
Laura Ashley (shop), *82*
Laura Secord (candy shop), *79*
Laurentians. *See* Laurentides, Les
Laurentides, Les (mountain range), *122–138*
map of, *127*

Laurier BBQ (restaurant), *101*
Laurier Ouest (neighborhood), *85*
Laval, François de Montmorency, *152, 163, 164*
Leclerc, Felix, *206*
Leduc, Ozias, *173*
Lennoxville (town), *145, 147*
Lenôtre Paris (restaurant), *68, 104*
Léonidas (restaurant), *104*
Léry, Gaspard Chaussegros de, *171*
Levaseur, François-Noël, *200*
Levasseur, Pierre-Noël, *162*
Lévesque, René, *174*
Librairie Delteil (bookstore), *84*
Librairie Flammarion Scorpion (bookstore), *84*
Librairie Garneau (bookstore), *178*
Librairie Kebuk (bookstore), *84*
Librairie Lettre Son (bookstore), *85*
Libraries, *65, 194*
Lily Simon (shop), *79, 81, 85*
Limousines, *153, 155*
Lola's Paradise (singles bar), *120*
Lord Berri (hotel), *114*
Lotus Blanc, Le (shop), *85*
Louis Laflamme (shop), *178*
Louis Zaor (antiques shop), *178*
Lower Laurentians. *See* Basses Laurentides, Les
Lower Town (neighborhood), *165–169*
map of, *158–159*
Luggage, *7–8*
Luna (shop), *85*
Lutetia (restaurant), *61, 95, 106, 110*

Lux (bar-restaurant-tobacconist-newsstand), *69*

M.A.D. objets de collection (shop), *85*
McComber (shop), *75*
McCord, David Ross, *63*
McCord Museum, *63*
MacDonald, John A., *60*
McGill, James, *63*
McGill Chamber Orchestra, *117*
McGill Ghetto, *63*
McGill Student Apartments, *115*
McGill University, *63*
Magog (town), *142–143, 145, 147*
Mail service, *23*
Maison Anglaise, La (bookstore), *178*
Maison Chevalier (museum annex), *166*
Maison Darlington, La (shop), *178*
Maison de la Sauvegarde, *54*
Maison des Cooperants, La (office complex), *37, 58*
Maison des Vins (wine shop), *166–167*
Maison du Calvet (shop), *55*
Maison du Patriote (candy shop), *82*
Maison Gourdeau de Beaulieu House, *202*
Maison Louis-Jolliet, *165*
Maison Maillou (former treasury building), *160*
Maison Montcalm, *168–169*
Ma Maison (shop), *78*
Man and His World (Expo pavilions), *72*
Manège Militaire (armory), *172*
Manoir d'Auteuil (hotel), *191*
Manoir des Remparts (hotel), *193*
Manoir d'Ivry (hotel), *136*

Manoir Globenski, 129
Manoir Hovey, Le (inn and restaurant), 139, 142, 145–146
Manoir Mauvide-Genest (manor and restaurant), 204, 207
Manoir Rouville Campbell (restaurant), 105
Manoir Sainte-Geneviève (hotel), 191
Manoir Victoria (hotel), 192
Map of Montreal, 48–49
Map of Quebec City, 150–151
Marathons, 6, 89
Marché aux puces (flea market), 83
Marché Bonsecours (former street market), 56
Marché du Vieux-Port (street market), 168, 177
Marie-Claire (shop), 79
Marie Clarisse, Le (restaurant), 183
Marks & Spencer (department store), 78–79
Martin, Abraham, 172
Martin Antiques, 83
Mary Queen of the World Cathedral, 40, 60
Masson, Joseph, 126
Maurice Richard Arena, 70
Mauvide, Jean, 204
Mayfair (shop), 79
Medical services, 15, 46, 201
Mehta, Zubin, 41
Meridien, Le (hotel), 110–111
Merlin (disco), 195
Metro (subway), 41, 44–45, 63
map of, 45
Metropolis (disco), 119
Michael Montanaro Dance Company, 117
Michel Tétrault (art gallery), 84
Midget Palace, 74–75
Mignardises, Les (restaurant), 65, 95–96
Milos (restaurant), 68, 97
Mirabel International Airport, 42
Mitoyen, Le (restaurant), 104
Moe Willensky's Light Lunch, 69
Moishe's Steakhouse, 68, 103
Molson Grand Prix du Canada, 5, 72, 88
Monastère des Augustines de l'Hôtel-Dieu de Québec, 163
Money, 8–10
Mont Brome (ski area), 140
Montcalm, Louis-Joseph, 149, 161, 162, 168–169, 172
Montcalm Monument, 172
Mont Megantic's Observatory, 143
Montmorency, Charles de, 198
Montmorency Falls, 198–199
Mont Orford (ski area), 140, 142
Montreal Canadiens, 89
Montréal Danse, 117
Montreal Expos, 88
Montreal Forum, 117
Montreal History Center, 56–57
Montreal International Festival of Films and Videos by Women, 4
Montreal International Festival of New Cinema and Video, 6
Montreal International Jazz Festival, 5, 41
Montreal International Marathon, 6, 89
Montreal International Music Competitions, 5
Montreal International Music Festival, 6
Montreal International Rock Festival, 5
Montreal World Film Festival, 6, 41, 118
Mont-Rolland (town), 134
Mont Royal (hill), 50
Mont Royal (neighborhood), 50, 83–84
Mont Royal (park). See Parc Mont Royal
Mont Royal Belvedere (lookout), 50
Mont Sutton (ski area), 140, 142
Morency (art gallery), 84
Morin Heights (town), 131–132
Morris, William, 62
Moulin de Saint-Laurent (restaurant), 204
Moulin Legaré (water mill), 129
Mountain-climbing, 136
Movies. See Films
Musée d'art contemporain de Montreal, 73, 74
Musée de la Civilisation, 152, 167–168
Musée de Québec, 152, 173
Musée des Augustines, 163
Musée des Beaux-Arts de Montréal, 62
Musée des Beaux-Arts de Sherbrooke, 143
Musée des Ursulines, 161–162
Musée du Fort, 165
Musée du Séminaire, 164
Musée Joseph-Armand Bombardier, 142
Musée Marc-Aurèle Fortin, 57
Museum hours, 46, 156. See also specific museums
Music, 116–117, 118–119, 194. See also specific festivals and types of music
Musique Archambault (shop), 84

Nicol, Phillipe, 74
Nightlife, 116, 118–120, 195–196
"Nord en fête, Le" (festival), 136
North Hatley (town), 143, 145–146, 147
Notre-Dame Basilica, 51, 52, 54
Notre-Dame-de-Bonsecours Chapel, 55
Notre-Dame-des-Bois (town), 146
Notre-Dame Ouest (neighborhood), 83
Nouvel Hôtel, Le, 114
Nuits Magiques (rock club), 119

O'Berge du Village (condo complex), 145
Observation tower, 205
Officers' Quarters, 169
Ogilvy (department store), 61, 80, 81
Oka Calvary (chapels), 128
Old Courthouse, 54
Old Customs House, 56
Older travelers, 22–23
Old Fort, 71
Old Stock Exchange, 56
Olmstead, Frederick Law, 72
Olympic Park, 69–70
map of, 71

Index

Olympic Stadium, *42, 69–70, 117*
100 Days of Contemporary Art (festival), *6*
Opéra de Montréal, L', *41, 117*
Orchestre Metropolitain de Montreal, *41, 117*
Orchestre Symphonique de Montréal, *41, 116–117*
Orchestre Symphonique de Québec, L', *194*
Orford (town), *142, 146, 147*
Orford Arts Center, *147*
Orphee (boutique), *85*
Ouimetoscope (revival cinema), *118*
Outfitters (innkeepers), *124–125*
Owl's Head (ski area), *140, 142*

Package deals, *3*
Paimpolaise, La (bar), *142*
Palais de Congrès de Montréal Convention Center, *64*
Palais de Justice, *54*
Palais Montcalm (theater), *194*
Pape Georges, Le (folk music bar), *196*
Parachute (boutique), *78, 79, 84*
Parc Cartier-Brébeuf, *176*
Parc de la Fontaine, *73*
Parc de L'Amérique-Française, *174*
Parc de l'Artillerie, *169, 176*
Parc de l'Esplanade, *169, 171*
Parc des Champs-de-Bataille, *172*
Parc du Mont Sainte-Anne, *181*
Parc du Porche, *176*
Parc Jeanne d'Arc, *173*
Parc Jeanne-Mance, *68*
Parc Montmorency, *164*
Parc Mont Royal, *37, 38, 68, 72, 73*
Parc Mont Tremblant, *138*
Parc régional de la Rivière-du-Nord, *129*
Paris, Le (restaurant), *97*
Paris, Texas (boutique), *84*
Paris Brest, Le (restaurant), *186–187*
Parks, *69–72*. See also specific parks
Par le trou de la Serrure (shop), *85*
Parliament Buildings, *171–172*
Parliament Hill, *171–172*
Paryse, La (restaurant), *98*
Passports, *10–11, 12*
Pâtisserie Grande-Cote (bakery and pastry shop), *129*
Pauline Pelletier (shop), *177*
Pee-Wee Hockey Tournament, *6*
Pegabo (shop), *80*
Pelletier, Jean, *167*
Pension Ste-Adèle en Haut Bed and Breakfast, *132*
Pepsi Celebrity Ski Invitational, *130*
Petite Ardoise, La (restaurant), *68*
Petit Musée (antiques shop), *81*
P'tit Train du Nord, *122, 129*
Pets, *11*
Pharmacies, *46, 155*
Phipps, William, *149, 166*
Piggery, The (theater), *147*
Pilsen (brewery), *143*
Pilsen Pub, *143*
Pizzaiole (restaurant), *99*
Pizzeria d'Youville, *188*
Place Bonaventure (hotel, office, and shopping complex), *60, 79–80*
Place d'Armes (square, Montreal), *52*
Place d'Armes (square, Quebec City), *157*
Place de Paris (square), *167*
Place des Arts, *41, 63–64*
Place du Canada (park), *60*
Place du Canada (shopping complex), *40*
Place d'Youville (square), *195*
Place Jacques Cartier (square), *51, 54*
Place Laurier (shopping complex), *177*
Place Montreal Trust (shopping complex), *61, 78–79*
Place Québec (convention center and shopping complex), *177*
Place Royale (district), *152*
Place Royale (square, Montreal), *56*
Place Royale (square, Quebec City), *166*
Place Sainte-Foy (shopping complex), *177*
Place Vauquelin, *54*
Place Ville Marie (mall, office, and shopping complex), *40, 58, 60, 79*
Plains of Abraham (battle site), *172–173*
Plante family farm, *202*
Plateau (neighborhood), *83–84*
Player's Challenge Tennis Championships, *6, 89*
Pointe-à-Callières (park), *56*
Polish restaurants, *100*. See also specific restaurants
Polo Ralph Lauren (boutique), *81*
Port de Québec in the 19th Century, *168*
Portes & Vitraux Anciens du Grand Montreal (antiques shop), *83*
Port of Montreal Exhibition Ground, *55*
Pot-en-Ciel (shop), *177*
Poudrière de l'Esplanade (powder magazine), *169, 171*
Pourvoirie des 100 Lacs Nords (inn), *125*
Powder house, *169*
Prego (restaurant), *69, 98–99*
Prescription drugs, *15*
Presse, La (building), *52*
Price, Bruce, *160*
Prince Arthur (neighborhood), *67–69*
map of, *66*
Prince Arthur Street (mall), *40–41*
Promenade (boardwalk), *129*
Promenade des Gouverneurs, *161*
Promenades de la Cathédrale, Les (shopping complex), *79*
Pronuptia (shop), *79*
Prus, Victor, *174*
Pub Saint-Alexandre, Le, *195*
Puces Libres (antiques shop), *84*
Puzzle's Jazz Bar, *118*

Index

Quartier Petit-Champlain (mall), *177*
Quatre Saisons, Le (hotel), *106, 111*
Quatres Canards, Les (restaurant), *144*
Quebec City International Airport, *153*
Québec International Book Fair, *6*
Québec International Film Festival, *7*
Quebec International Summer Festival, *7*
Québec Nordiques, *182*
Québécois restaurants. *See* French-Canadian restaurants
Québec Winter Carnival, *6*

Rafting. *See* River rafting
Ramada Renaissance du Parc (hotel), *111*
Ramezay, Claude de, *55*
Reine Elizabeth, La (hotel), *60, 106, 111–112*
Reitman's (shop), *79*
René Derhy (shop), *79*
Réserve Faunique des Laurentides (wildlife reserve), *180*
Restaurant, Le, *96, 111*
Restaurant au Parmesan, *187*
Restaurant Au P'tit Sabot, *146*
Restaurant Baker, *199*
Restaurant Les Cent-Ciels, *133–134*
Restaurants, *89–105, 144–146, 182–188*. *See also specific restaurants*
maps of, *92–93, 184–185*
Revenge (boutique), *84, 85*
Rialto Cinema, *118*
Riding, *87*
Rioux, Huguette, *74*

Ripplecove Inn, *142, 144*
Ritz-Carlton (hotel), *63, 106, 112*
River rafting, *87–88, 125, 180*
Rivière Rouge (river), *125*
Robert Krief (shop), *84*
Roche à Maranda (boulder), *202, 204*
Rock music, *119, 196*
Rodier of Paris (shop), *78, 80*
Rose, Peter, *62*
Rosin, Maxime, *200*
Rothmans-Porsche Turbo Cup, *138*
Rouet Métiers d'Art, Le (shop), *79, 82*
Route du Mitan, *205*
Route 360, *198*
Royal Roussillon, Le (hotel), *114*
Royal 22nd Regiment Museum, *171*
Rue de la Montagne (street), *61*
Rue du Petit-Champlain (street), *165–166*
Rue du Trésor (street), *163, 177–178*
Rue Horatio-Walker (street), *202*
Rue Principale (street), *143*
Rue St-Amable (street), *55*
Rue St-Denis (street), *65*
Rue St-Paul (street), *51–52, 56*
Rue St-Sulpice (street), *54*
Russian restaurants, *101–102*. *See also specific restaurants*

Safdie, Moshe, *167*
Saidye Bronfman Centre, *73, 74, 117*
Sailing, *88.* See also Boating; Boat trips; Ferries
St-Amable, Le (restaurant), *54*
Saint-Amour, Le

(restaurant), *183, 186*
Saint Anne's Day Celebrations, *7*
St-Denis (neighborhood), *40, 41, 65, 67, 83–84*
map of, *66*
Sainte-Adèle (town), *133*
Sainte-Agathe-des-Monts (town), *135–136*
Sainte-Famille (village), *205–206*
Sainte-Famille Church, *206*
Sainte-Marguerite-du-Lac-Masson (town), *134*
Sainte-Pétronille (village), *202, 204*
Saint-Eustache (town), *128–129*
Saint Francis of the Birds (church), *130*
Saint-François (village), *205*
Saint-François Church, *205*
Saint-Jean (village), *204–205*
Saint-Jean-Baptiste Day, *7*
Saint-Jean Church, *204–205*
Saint-Jérôme (town), *129*
St. Joseph's Oratory (church), *72–73*
Saint-Laurent (village), *204*
Saint-Laurent Church, *204*
St-Louis (neighborhood), *40, 50*
St-O, Le (bar), *195*
Saint-Pierre (village), *206*
Saint-Pierre Church, *206*
Saint-Sauveur Church, *130*
Saint-Sauveur-des-Monts (town), *130*
Saint-Vallier, Monseigneur de, *164*
Salle Albert-Rousseau (theater), *194*

Santa Claus Village, *135*
Sarosi (shop), *80*
Scala Santa (chapel), *200*
Schwartz's Delicatessen, *67–68, 91, 94*
Seafood restaurants, *102–103*. *See also specific restaurants*
Seasonal events. *See* Festivals and seasonal events
Secrets (rock club), *119*
Seigneurie de Terrebonne, La, *126*
Seigneurie du Lac-des-Deux-Montagnes, La, *126, 128*
Séminaire de Québec, *164*
Service des résidences de l'Université Laval (hostel), *193*
Shangrila, Le (hotel), *112*
Sherbrooke (city), *143, 146*
Sherbrooke (street), *39–40*
Sherbrooke, John Coape, *143*
Sherlock Holmes (bar), *195*
Shopping, *75–86, 176–179.* See also *specific boutiques, department stores, and shops*
map of, *76–77*
store hours, *46–47, 75, 156, 177*
Shopping complexes, *177.* See also Shopping; *specific shopping complexes*
Shots, *15*
Shuchat (shop), *75*
Sieur Duluth chapeaux, bijoux et accessoires, Le (shop), *84*
Simons (department store), *177*
Singles bars, *119–120.* See also *specific singles bars*

Index

Sir Winston Churchill Pub, *119*
Skating, *87, 180–181*
Skiing, *88, 122, 123, 124, 130, 132, 134, 137, 140, 142, 181*
Ski Morin Heights, *131–132*
Skin-diving, *136*
Skiwippi (cross-country treks), *142*
Snowboarding, *131*
Société d'alcools du Québec (wine shop), *78, 79*
Soirée de Danse Moderne et Canadienne, *196*
Soirita (shop), *177*
Source, La (shop), *143*
Specialty stores, *178–179. See also specific specialty stores*
Spectrum (concert hall), *117*
Sports, *86, 87–89, 179, 180–182. See also specific sports*
Square St-Louis, *65, 67*
Squash, *88*
Stash's (restaurant), *100*
Station Mont Tremblant Lodge, *137*
Station 10 (rock club), *119*
Steakhouses, *68, 103. See also specific steakhouses*
Stewart, Jackie, *138*
Student and youth travel, *19–20*
Sucrerie de la Montagne, La (restaurant), *105*
Sugar huts, *144. See also specific sugar huts*
Sulpician Seminary, *54*
Sun Life Building, *40, 60*
Super glissades de glace, *133*
SuperMotocross Laurentide (competition), *4*
Super Splash (water slides), *133*
Sutton (town), *142, 146, 147*
Swimming, *88*
Swiss restaurants, *187. See also specific restaurants*
Symposium (restaurant), *68*

Taché, Eugène-Étienne, *172*
Taillibert, Roger, *42*
Taj, Le (restaurant), *98*
Tangente (dance company), *117*
Taxis, *45, 153, 155*
Tearooms, *103–104*
Telephones, *23*
Tennis, *88, 89, 181*
Terrasse Dufferin (boardwalk), *160–161*
Terrasses, Les (shopping complex), *58*
Thai restaurants, *187. See also specific restaurants*
Thalie (boutique), *84*
Theaters, *117, 194–195. See also Dinner theaters; specific theaters*
Théâtre de la Bordée, *194*
Théâtre de Mont-Rolland, *134*
Théâtre Denise Pelletier, *117*
Théâtre de Quat-Sous, *117*
Théâtre du Bois du Coulonge, *195*
Théâtre du Nouveau Monde, *117*
Théâtre du Petit-Champlain, *195*
Théâtre du Rideau Vert, *117*
Theatre Festival of the Americas, *4*
Théâtre Le Vieux Clocher, *147*
Théâtre Morin Heights, *132*
Théâtre Paul-Hébert, *204*
Théâtre St-Denis, *65, 117*
Thirsty's (singles bar), *119*
Thunder Dome (disco), *119*
Thursday's (dance club and singles bar), *61, 110, 119*
Tilted Tower, *70*
Tipping, *23*
Toman Pastry Shop, *104*
Tour de L'Île de Montréal, Le (competition), *5, 88*
Tour de Ville (restaurant), *113, 118*
Tour groups, *2–3, 12*
Tourist information and offices, *2, 12, 45–46, 54, 58, 124, 140, 155, 193, 198, 201*
Tour Martello #1 (tower), *173*
Tour Martello #2 (tower), *173*
Toy Box (shop), *85*
Train travel, *18, 43, 154*
Travel agencies, *46, 155–156*
Traveler's checks, *8, 10*
Tricots d'Ariane, Les (shop, Montreal), *85*
Tricots d'Ariane, Les (shop, Saint-Sauveur-des-Monts), *131*
Tripp Distribution & Importation, *82*
Trois & Un (shop), *85*
Tube Hi-Fi, Le (disco), *195*
2020 University (office and shopping complex), *58*

Underground City, *41, 57, 58, 60*
Ungaro (shop), *81*
Université de Montréal Residence, *115*
Université du Québec à Montréal, *65*
Université Laval, *152*
Upper Laurentians. *See Hautes Laurentides, Les*
Upper St-Laurent (neighborhood), *84–85*
Upper Town (neighborhood), *157–165*
map of, *158–159*

Valcourt (town), *142*
Val David (town), *135*
Vauban, Sébastien Le Prestre de, *171*
Velodrome, *70*
Victoire Paris (shop), *85*
Vieille Ville (old city, Quebec City), *149*
Vietnamese restaurants, *103, 187. See also specific restaurants*
Vieux-Montréal (old city, Montreal), *50, 51–57, 82–83*
map of, *53*
Vieux-Port de Québec, *168*
Village de Seraphin, *134*
Village du Mont-Castor, *136*
Villages des Sports, *180, 181*
Villa rentals, *20*
Ville d'Estérel (resort), *135*
Visas, *10–11, 12*
Vogue (bar), *195*
Vol de Nuit (singles bar), *120*
Voute Boutique, La, *131*
Vrac du Quartier, Le (shop), *174*

W. H. Smith (bookstore), *79*
Waddington & Gorce (art gallery), *81*
Waldman's Fish Market, *67, 84*
Walker, Horatio, *173, 202*

Walker, Hovendon, *166*
Walking tours, *47, 51–69, 157–175*
maps of, *158–159, 170*
Walter Klinkhoff (art gallery), *81*
Warshaw's Supermarket, *67*
Watchtower, *72*
Westmount Square (mall), *85*
Wheeler, Lucile, *123*
Wilensky's Light Lunch, *94*
Windsor Hotel, *40*
Windsor Station, *60*
Windsurfing, *88*
Winston Churchill Pub, *61*
Wolfe, James, *149, 161, 172, 173, 202, 205*
Wolfe Monument, *173*
World Film Festival, *41*
Xuan (restaurant), *103*
Yamaska (recreation center), *140*
Yiddish Theatre Group, *74*
YMCA (Montreal), *114–115*
YMCA (Quebec City), *180*
Youth and student travel, *19–20*
Youth hostels. *See* Hostels
Youville Stables, *56*
Yü (shop), *79*
YWCA (Montreal), *115*
YWCA (Quebec City), *193*
Zhivago (restaurant), *101–102*
Zimmermann (shop), *179*
Zone (shop), *84*

Personal Itinerary

Departure *Date*

Time

Transportation

Arrival *Date* *Time*

Departure *Date* *Time*

Transportation

Accommodations

Arrival *Date* *Time*

Departure *Date* *Time*

Transportation

Accommodations

Arrival *Date* *Time*

Departure *Date* *Time*

Transportation

Accommodations

Personal Itinerary

Arrival *Date*   *Time*

Departure *Date*   *Time*

Transportation

Accommodations

Arrival *Date*   *Time*

Departure *Date*   *Time*

Transportation

Accommodations

Arrival *Date*   *Time*

Departure *Date*   *Time*

Transportation

Accommodations

Arrival *Date*   *Time*

Departure *Date*   *Time*

Transportation

Accommodations

Personal Itinerary

Arrival *Date* *Time*

Departure *Date* *Time*

Transportation

Accommodations

Arrival *Date* *Time*

Departure *Date* *Time*

Transportation

Accommodations

Arrival *Date* *Time*

Departure *Date* *Time*

Transportation

Accommodations

Arrival *Date* *Time*

Departure *Date* *Time*

Transportation

Accommodations

Addresses

Name	*Name*
Address	*Address*
Telephone	*Telephone*
Name	*Name*
Address	*Address*
Telephone	*Telephone*
Name	*Name*
Address	*Address*
Telephone	*Telephone*
Name	*Name*
Address	*Address*
Telephone	*Telephone*
Name	*Name*
Address	*Address*
Telephone	*Telephone*
Name	*Name*
Address	*Address*
Telephone	*Telephone*
Name	*Name*
Address	*Address*
Telephone	*Telephone*
Name	*Name*
Address	*Address*
Telephone	*Telephone*

Addresses

Name	*Name*
Address	*Address*
Telephone	*Telephone*
Name	*Name*
Address	*Address*
Telephone	*Telephone*
Name	*Name*
Address	*Address*
Telephone	*Telephone*
Name	*Name*
Address	*Address*
Telephone	*Telephone*
Name	*Name*
Address	*Address*
Telephone	*Telephone*
Name	*Name*
Address	*Address*
Telephone	*Telephone*
Name	*Name*
Address	*Address*
Telephone	*Telephone*
Name	*Name*
Address	*Address*
Telephone	*Telephone*

Fodor's Travel Guides

U.S. Guides

- Alaska
- Arizona
- Atlantic City & the New Jersey Shore
- Boston
- California
- Cape Cod
- Carolinas & the Georgia Coast
- The Chesapeake Region
- Chicago
- Colorado
- Disney World & the Orlando Area
- Florida
- Hawaii
- Las Vegas
- Los Angeles, Orange County, Palm Springs
- Maui
- Miami, Fort Lauderdale, Palm Beach
- Michigan, Wisconsin, Minnesota
- New England
- New Mexico
- New Orleans
- New Orleans (Pocket Guide)
- New York City
- New York City (Pocket Guide)
- New York State
- Pacific North Coast
- Philadelphia
- The Rockies
- San Diego
- San Francisco
- San Francisco (Pocket Guide)
- The South
- Texas
- USA
- Virgin Islands
- Virginia
- Waikiki
- Washington, DC

Foreign Guides

- Acapulco
- Amsterdam
- Australia, New Zealand, The South Pacific
- Austria
- Bahamas
- Bahamas (Pocket Guide)
- Baja & the Pacific Coast Resorts
- Barbados
- Beijing, Guangzhou & Shanghai
- Belgium & Luxembourg
- Bermuda
- Brazil
- Britain (Great Travel Values)
- Budget Europe
- Canada
- Canada (Great Travel Values)
- Canada's Atlantic Provinces
- Cancun, Cozumel, Yucatan Peninsula
- Caribbean
- Caribbean (Great Travel Values)
- Central America
- Eastern Europe
- Egypt
- Europe
- Europe's Great Cities
- France
- France (Great Travel Values)
- Germany
- Germany (Great Travel Values)
- Great Britain
- Greece
- The Himalayan Countries
- Holland
- Hong Kong
- Hungary
- India, including Nepal
- Ireland
- Israel
- Italy
- Italy (Great Travel Values)
- Jamaica
- Japan
- Japan (Great Travel Values)
- Kenya, Tanzania, the Seychelles
- Korea
- Lisbon
- Loire Valley
- London
- London (Great Travel Values)
- London (Pocket Guide)
- Madrid & Barcelona
- Mexico
- Mexico City
- Montreal & Quebec City
- Munich
- New Zealand
- North Africa
- Paris
- Paris (Pocket Guide)
- People's Republic of China
- Portugal
- Rio de Janeiro
- The Riviera (Fun on)
- Rome
- Saint Martin & Sint Maarten
- Scandinavia
- Scandinavian Cities
- Scotland
- Singapore
- South America
- South Pacific
- Southeast Asia
- Soviet Union
- Spain
- Spain (Great Travel Values)
- Sweden
- Switzerland
- Sydney
- Tokyo
- Toronto
- Turkey
- Vienna
- Yugoslavia

Special-Interest Guides

- Health & Fitness Vacations
- Royalty Watching
- Selected Hotels of Europe
- Selected Resorts and Hotels of the U.S.
- Shopping in Europe
- Skiing in North America
- Sunday in New York